Islam in Process—Historical and Civilizational Perspectives
Yearbook of the Sociology of Islam
Volume 7

YEARBOOK OF THE SOCIOLOGY OF ISLAM
Edited by Georg Stauth and Armando Salvatore

The *Yearbook of the Sociology of Islam* investigates the making of Islam into an important component of modern society and cultural globalization.

Sociology is, by common consent, the most ambitious advocate of modern society. In other words, it undertakes to develop an understanding of modern existence in terms of breakthroughs from ancient cosmological cultures to ordered and plural civic life based on the gradual subsiding of communal life. Thus, within this undertaking, the sociological project of modernity figures as the cultural machine that dislodges the rationale of social being from local, communal, hierarchic contexts into the logic of individualism and social differentiation.

The conventional wisdom of sociology has been challenged by post-modern debate, abolishing this dichotomous evolutionism while embracing a more heterogeneous view of coexistence and exchange between local cultures and modern institutions.

Islam, however, is often described as a different cultural machine for the holistic reproduction of pre-modern religion, and Muslims are seen as community-bound social actors embodying a powerful potential for the rejection of and opposition to Western modernity.

Sociologists insist on looking for social differentiation and cultural differences. However, their concepts remain evolutionist and inherently tied to the cultural machine of modernity.

The *Yearbook of the Sociology of Islam* takes these antinomies and contradictions as a challenge. It aims at no less than an understanding of the ambiguous positioning of Islam in the global construction of society, and thus attempts to combine original research on Islam with conceptual debates in social theory and cultural studies.

SCIENTIFIC ADVISORY BOARD

Stefano Allievi, University of Padua
Fanny Colonna, University of Marseille
Eberhard Kienle, IREMAM, Aix-en-Provence
Mark LeVine, University of California, Irvine
Khalid M. Masud, ISIM, Leiden
Cynthia Nelson, American University of Cairo, †
Sami Zubaida, Birkbeck College, University of London

JOHANN P. ARNASON, ARMANDO SALVATORE, GEORG STAUTH (EDS.)
ISLAM IN PROCESS—
HISTORICAL AND CIVILIZATIONAL PERSPECTIVES

Yearbook of the Sociology of Islam
Volume 7

[transcript]

This volume was prepared with support by *Kulturwissenschaftliches Institut NRW, Essen*, and *Sonderforschungsbereich der Deutschen Forschungsgemeinschaft 295 »Kulturelle und sprachliche Kontakte«* an der *Johannes Gutenberg-Universität Mainz*.

All rights reserved. No part of this book may be reprinted or reproduced or utilized in any form or by any electronic, mechanical, or other means, now known or hereafter invented, inlcuding photocopying and recording, or in any information storage or retrieval system, without permission in writing from the publisher.

© 2006 transcript Verlag, Bielefeld
Coverlayout: Kordula Röckenhaus, Bielefeld
Typeset by: Jörg Burkhard, Bielefeld
Printed and bound in Great Britain by Marston Book Services Ltd, Oxfordshire
ISBN 3-89942-491-3

Table of Contents

Editor's Note · 7

Introduction · 8
JOHANN P. ARNASON, ARMANDO SALVATORE,
AND GEORG STAUTH

Crystallizations

Chapter 1
Marshall Hodgson's Civilizational Analysis of Islam:
Theoretical and Comparative Perspectives · 23
JOHANN P. ARNASON

Chapter 2
The Middle Period: Islamic Axiality in the Age of
Afro-Eurasian Transcultural Hybridity · 48
BABAK RAHIMI

Chapter 3
Identity Formation in World Religions:
A Comparative Analysis of Christianity and Islam · 68
ARPAD SZAKOLCZAI

Chapter 4
The Emergence of Islam as a Case of Cultural Crystallization:
Historical and Comparative Reflections · 95
JOHANN P. ARNASON

Crossroads and Turning Points

Chapter 5
Revolution in Early Islam: The Rise of Islam as a
Constitutive Revolution · 125
SAÏD AMIR ARJOMAND

Chapter 6
'Abdallah b. Salam: Egypt, Late Antiquity and
Islamic Sainthood   158
GEORG STAUTH

Chapter 7
Story, Wisdom and Spirituality: Yemen as the Hub
between the Persian, Arabic and Biblical Traditions   190
RAIF GEORGES KHOURY

Chapter 8
Islam and the Axial Age   220
JOSEF VAN ESS

Cultural and Institutional Dynamics

Chapter 9
Islam and the Path to Modernity: Institutions of
Higher Learning and Secular and Political Culture   241
SAÏD AMIR ARJOMAND

Chapter 10
Global Ages, Ecumenic Empires and Prophetic Religions   258
ARPAD SZAKOLCZAI

Chapter 11
Reflexivity, Praxis, and "Spirituality":
Western Islam and Beyond   279
ARMANDO SALVATORE

Chapter 12
Public Spheres and Political Dynamics in
Historical and Modern Muslim Societies   306
SHMUEL N. EISENSTADT

Abstracts   319

Contributors   327

Editors' Note

Contributors to this volume come from very different disciplines including classical oriental studies, history and sociology. This diversity in disciplinary approach was from the start reflected in terminology and attitude towards sources and texts. We thought it valuable to maintain this diversity, and specifically we have not engaged in homogenising difference in transliteration and forms of quotation – in some cases resembling different traditions to write Arabic in Latin letters and to give reference to sources and material. The individual texts, as they stand, reflect the homogeneous attitudes of the authors and we do believe that this contributes to flavour the dialogue which we pursue with this book.

Sigrid Noekel – as so often – has taken the considerable task of coordinating and participating in editing this volume at various stages of its growth and we would like to express our very special thanks.

Professor Jörn Rüsen, President of the KWI (Kulturwissenschaftliches Institut) in Essen, Germany, and Professor Walter Bisang, Speaker of the "Sonderforschungsbereich 295: Kulturelle und sprachliche Kontakte," Univerity of Mainz, Germany, with their support have made the preparation of this volume possible, again we convey our gratitude.

Frankfurt am Main, September 2006.
G.S.

Introduction

JOHANN P. ARNASON, ARMANDO SALVATORE, AND GEORG STAUTH

The papers included in this issue of the *Yearbook of the Sociology of Islam* come from two workshops held at the Kulturwissenschaftliches Institut (Institute for Advanced Study in the Humanities), Essen, in April 2004 and April 2005. The program of the first one linked the comparative analysis of Islam to ongoing debates on Axial Age theory as related to the formation of major civilizational complexes. The second workshop was primarily concerned with the historical sources and constellations involved in the formation of Islam as a religion and a civilization. Since the two stages of the project were closely related, it seems appropriate to publish the results in one place and allow for multiple foci.

The origins of the axial hypothesis

It has been observed that Max Weber's sociology of religion and in particular some passages from an article on Hinduism and Buddhism published in 1916 in the *Archiv für Sozialwissenschaft und Sozialpolitik* prefigures the core hypothesis of Axial Age theory (Arnason 2005: 22)[1]. This theory is based on a comprehensive hypothesis concerning the nature of the radical transformations that made possible a momentous breakthrough in the complexification of community life and the differentiation of social fields out of archaic communities regulated by cyclical and mythical views of the cosmological order. The Axial approach facilitates examining on a comparative basis the basically simultaneous discovery of "transcendence" across various civilizations.

Historical and civilizational analysis is oriented here to Axial Age theory intended as a research program for locating and explaining, in historical-comparative and sociological terms, the type of breakthrough that allowed, through the shaping of notions of transcendence, for the emergence of a type of human reflexivity conventionally identified as the passage from the narrativity of *mythos* to the rationality of *logos* (Jaspers 1953 [1949]). As maintained by Björn Wittrock, transcendence is not to be interpreted in strictly theological terms, but as the emergence of a form of reflexivity that transcends those activities tied to the

---

1 Arnason, Johan P. (2005) "The Axial Age and its Interpreters: Reopening a Debate." In: Johann P. Arnason/Shmuel N. Eisenstadt/Björn Wittrock (eds.) Axial Civilizations and World History, Leiden: Brill, pp. 19-49.

daily necessities of human beings, as also reflected in elaborate mythologies of cosmological shape or in what we might call the ritual integration of community (Wittrock 2005: 62)².

More than any other particular line of inquiry, new historical and sociological approaches to the Axial Age revived the idea of comparative civilizational analysis and channeled it into more specific projects. A closer look at the problematic place of Islam in this context will help to clarify questions about the axial version of civilizational theory as well as related issues in Islamic studies. For pre-sociological interpretations of the Axial Age, exemplified by Jaspers's well-known essay on *The Origin and Goal of History* (Jaspers 1953 [1949]), Islam was at best of marginal interest. The phase of intellectual and/or religious breakthroughs, occurring in major civilizational centers, was – roughly speaking – dated from the eighth to the third century BC; this strictly chronological demarcation excluded the much later rise of Islam. Further reflection should, however, have highlighted precisely the Islamic case as a problem for the chronological model. The Islamic vision of a new order based on transcendent imperatives was at least as close to the ideal type of an axial breakthrough as any other example. Islam defined itself as a perfected and definitive version of an axial innovation, namely monotheism; and it translated its claim into civilizational patterns on a larger scale than any earlier culture or religion of the axial type had done.

Another potentially critical point was the historical role of Islam as a synthesizer and transmitter of Hellenic and Judaic legacies. Comparison with this other successor civilization, on which the Western Christian rediscovery of classical sources had at first been dependent, might have cast doubt on the tacitly Eurocentric presuppositions of early axial theory. The failure to pursue these problems is obviously linked to a longer history of European relations with and perceptions of the Islamic world, and to concomitant trends in civilizational studies. Seen from Western Europe, Islam had for a long time represented a more advanced civilization whose achievements could to some extent be borrowed across religious barriers. In the early modern era, it was still perceived as a dangerous adversary: until late in the seventeenth century, the strongest Islamic power – the Ottoman Empire – could threaten the heartland of Western Christendom, whereas Christian advances against the Islamic world were confined to more peripheral areas.

During the 18th century, as the West gained the upper hand against Islam, it also began to come into closer contact with the Indian and Chinese worlds, and these new encounters posed more complex hermeneutical problems than the interaction with Islam had ever done – because of the greater cultural distance and

---

2   Arnason, Johan P. (2005) "The Axial Age and its Interpreters: Reopening a Debate." In: Johann P. Arnason/Shmuel N. Eisenstadt/Björn Wittrock (eds.) Axial Civilizations and World History, Leiden: Brill, pp. 19-49.

as a result of changes to Western self-interpretations. Reflections on civilizational pluralism and its world-historical meaning (never more than an intermittent tradition in Western thought) tended then to focus on the eminently Oriental Indian and Chinese cases, whereas Islam became a more marginal theme.

The crux of Islam within comparative civilizational analysis

Two outstandingly seminal visions of universal history, developed in an early and a late phase of global European ascendancy, may be cited to illustrate this trend. In Hegel's philosophy of history, China and India appear as distinctive and necessary stages on the road to a full realization of reason in history, while Islam looks more like an anomalous sideshow: since it exists, it must be fitted into the model, but this cannot occur on the same conceptual level as for China or India. Max Weber's comparative studies of Eurasian civilizations deal with multiple contrasts between China, India and Western Europe; although a planned study of Islam was never written, enough is known about Weber's views on this subject to conclude that conceptual obstacles counted for something in this failure.

The career of the axial model after Jaspers reflects this traditional neglect of Islam, with some qualifications and corrective trends. Marshall Hodgson's work (which will be discussed at some length in this volume) is a crucially important exception to the pattern described above. Hodgson responded to Jaspers's formulation of the axial model, at a time when it went otherwise unnoticed among comparative historians, and revised it in ways more conducive to an adequate understanding and appraisal of Islamicate civilization or "Islamdom" (a term of his coin). But Hodgson was in many respects ahead of his time, and a sustained discussion of his work is only beginning; his influence on Islamic studies was limited, and there is no evidence of a significant impact of his work on axial theory.

When S.N. Eisenstadt shifted the methodological terrain of analysis from philosophical interpretation to a historical sociology of axial civilizations, he did not – at first – alter the chronological framework. On this view, the rise of Islam was the result of much later developments and took place in a very different historical milieu; but since the new, historical-sociological model was explicitly designed to explain long-term historical trends, it had to go beyond Jaspers's account and accommodate Islam within a broader perspective. Eisenstadt's initial solution to this problem was the concept of a "secondary breakthrough," applicable to Islam as well as Christianity and some less radical innovations in other civilizational settings (such as Neo-Confucianism in East Asia). According to Eisenstadt, breakthroughs of this kind were characterized by comprehensive reinterpretations of axial traditions and strong aspirations to establish a new institutional order.

The concept was later abandoned, on the compelling grounds that it implied an a priori denial of the originality of post-axial transformations, and Eisenstadt moved towards a major revision of the axial model. He argued that a typological frame of reference would be more useful than the chronological one: axiality could thus be redefined as a set of characteristics that enhance the transformative potential of culture, and do so in specific ways linked to visions of transcendent reality. Changes along such lines may have been particularly widespread and intensive during the Axial Age, but that is not a valid reason for defining them in chronological terms. Axial transformations can occur and axial patterns can crystallize in other historical situations; it is the structural aspect that matters, rather than the genetic one.

From this point of view, Islam appears as a key case to be included in the typological core. Eisenstadt has unequivocally accepted this conclusion, with the result that questions relating to Islamic societies and their historical dynamics have become more important in his most recent work.

Yet the typological turn is only one of the new trends emerging in debates around the axial framework of inquiry, and it poses a whole set of new problems. If axiality is to be understood as a mode of transformation, it can easily shrink to a stage in a rather uniform progression towards higher levels of reflexivity and enlarged horizons of human action. On the other hand, the general category of "axial civilizations" (supposed to replace "Axial Age civilizations") seems to involve quite strong and debatable assumptions about cultural orientations embodied in and constitutive of whole civilizational complexes. A more limited conception of axial patterns, centered on the relationships between intellectual and political elites and their role in historical transformations, would have to allow for contextual determinants that vary from case to case.

More generally speaking, the axial model is now being transformed through discussions that continue to produce arguments for and against contending views. It would be vastly premature to try to close the debate, and misguided to bypass it. The divergent approaches have more or less direct implications for Islamic Studies and for the sociology of Islam. As will be seen, contributors to this volume differ in their opinions on these issues; for introductory purposes, it may be useful to outline a cautiously defined common ground, limited to a heuristic use of the axial model finalized to highlight significant features of Islam as a religion and a civilizational formation. Some basic considerations in that vein will help to sketch in a background to more disputed questions. We can, without making any strong assumptions about the scope or status of axial theory, examine the *axial dimensions* of Islam from a comparative viewpoint. This applies, first and foremost, to the Islamic vision of transcendence: more precisely, to its version of monotheist transcendence.

The Islamic message defined itself as a purifying, radicalizing and restorative twist to preexisting monotheisms; at the same time, it was from the outset much more directly intertwined with political strategies and processes. The prophet Muhammad and his first following were very soon drawn into a state-building project, and the codification of the new religious teaching soon overlapped with a process of empire-building on a vast scale.

Yet a comparative approach must also take into account the spatial and temporal distance from established models. Islam emerged outside the central domain of axial transformations, and long after they had matured into cultural and institutional paradigms. The same cannot be said of Christianity: most historians would now agree that the original "Jesus movement" was part of an ongoing reformist current within Judaism, and that the mutation into a separate universal religion was a complex process, decisively affected by the catastrophic defeat of the Jewish rebellion against Rome in the 1st century CE.

Because of the different historical context, Islam related to *axial sources* on a different basis and in varying ways. With regard to major axial traditions, the emphasis was sometimes on religious and sometimes on broader civilizational aspects. Judaism was of crucial importance as a religious source, whereas interaction with the persisting diasporic Jewish civilization was very limited; the occasional episodes of more intensive contact were – possibly with the exceptions to which the papers of Stauth (chapter 6) and Khoury (chapter 7) point in this volume – more productive on the Jewish side; Persian sources were primarily put to use on the civilizational level; the Hellenic legacy was essential to the flowering of Islam as a civilization during its classical period, but it also played a significant role in attempts to rationalize the religious foundations of Islamic identity and make them more compatible with philosophical modes of thought.

Apart from these central connections, recent scholarship has taken note of inputs from more marginal or interstitial sources. South Arabian traditions, including a monotheist turn that does not seem to have been a simple reproduction of the Judaic model, are now widely seen as a distinctive and important part of the background. The issue of Islamic links to the Judaeo-Christian sects that had tried to bridge the gap between two increasingly alienated communities remains more controversial.

If a comparative history of Islamic civilization has to deal with axial sources, it is by the same token tempting to interpret Islam as an *axial synthesis*. But this suggestion calls for some qualifications. It seems clear that Manichaeism had aspired to synthesize several axial traditions (including Buddhism). This was, however, a precedent the prophet Muhammad and his followers were thoroughly unwilling to recognize. Manichaeism was never included among the religions of the book, and when Manichean communities came under Islamic rule, they were massively persecuted. On the religious level, the original Islamic vision did not aim at a synthesis, but at the final and unadorned grasp of fundamentals that had previously been obscured by adaptation to specific contexts and perverted through further assimilation.

Nonetheless, as new civilizational patterns crystallized around the imperial power structures built under the banner of a new religion, the radically monotheistic and universalistic world-view became a framework for the fusion of different civilizational legacies. But if the cultural traditions of conquered regions were brought together in a synthesis, there was no uniform pattern of integration. A vigorous but selective appropriation was, as noted above, crucial to the creativity and radiating power of Islam during its classical age. Peter Brown has suggested that Islamic civilization retained closer links to the Greek ideal of *paideia* than did other heirs to the classical legacy of antiquity. The assimilation of Persian traditions was a more long-drawn-out-process, and they became a more enduring component of political culture.

A new pattern of interaction emerged as a result of the Islamic expansion into a third major civilizational area. Whether the idea of a civilizational synthesis can be applicable to the Indo-Islamic world will depend on more substantive interpretations of this very particular case: was it a civilizational formation encompassing two very different religions, or a regional complex made up of two civilizations? The question will not be discussed in this volume, but it should at least be noted that the Indian part of the Islamic experience was – for both comparative historians as well as students of Islam – long overshadowed by the more familiar record of the Middle East and the Mediterranean.

The long-term *axial dynamics* of Islam are a further theme for comparative analysis, going beyond and building on those mentioned above. The civilizations most directly associated with the axial model are, as has often been stressed, characterized by a dialectics of traditionalism and renewal. Reinterpretations of core traditions provide frameworks for socio-cultural transformations, while at the same time maintaining a recognizable civilizational pattern across historical divides. This combination of change and revival is a recurrent and well-known feature of Islamic civilization. So is another closely related phenomenon, particularly prominent in analysis of axial traditions: the interplay of orthodoxy and heterodoxy.

Constellations of that kind were central to all phases and branches of Islamic history, even if it seems clear that the tension between the two poles never reached the level of a civilizational schism comparable to the 16th century rupture within Western Christendom. Finally, axial theorists have noted the need for more detailed study of the connections between cultural traditions – more specifically religious ones – and imperial formations, but this is still a relatively underdeveloped domain of comparative analysis. The history of imperial power in the Islamic world took a distinctive course that suggests several lines of comparison with other traditions. The formative and classical phases (until the later 9th century) were characterized by uniquely close links between the growth of imperial power and the crystallization of a new civilizational pattern. During the following five to six centuries (the "middle periods" according to Hodgson's scheme), political fragmentation went hand in hand with the consolidation of cultural unity on a more global scale than any other civilization achieved in premodern times.

This is not the only case of marked divergences between the dynamics of cultural and political integration, but the contrast became exceptionally stark in the Islamic case, all the more so through the cultural assimilation of the disunited heirs to foreign conquest: the Mongol successor states. But the islamization of Inner Asian conquerors also became the starting-point for the three imperial projects of the early modern era: the Ottoman, the Safavid, and the Mughal (Hodgson's "gunpowder empires"). In all three cases, imperial expansion within the Islamic civilizational domain was combined with conquest across its borders. The plurality of imperial centers within one civilizational formation bear some resemblance to the modern constellation in Western Europe, but because of the very different spatial dimensions, contacts between the empires were of a limited kind, and these empires never embarked on the distinctively European enterprise of overseas conquest.

The last question to be considered in this context has to do with *axial closure*. This theme has not been in the foreground of the debate, but it merits more discussion. Although the axial model stresses new openings of multiple kinds, conducive to higher levels of diversity and conflict, efforts to reintegrates such trends into definitive and comprehensive frameworks are also typical of the traditions in question. Axial transformations give rise to new forms of change as well as new ways of containing it. Both ideological and institutional modes of closure reflect their specific civilizational contexts. Western perceptions of Islam, shaped by very asymmetrical encounters, have tended to exaggerate its resistance to change, whether generated from within or induced from without. Scholarly analysis has modified this view, but not disposed of the problem.

The distinctively Islamic dynamics and strategies of closure are still important topics for comparative analysis. To conclude this part of the discussion, three key historical signposts should be noted. The first centuries of the second millennium CE are no longer seen as a phase of transition to long-term stagnation or even regression; a much more complex image of this period is emerging from current scholarship, so that the specific achievements of Islam's later centuries are now more adequately understood. Yet from a comparative perspective, the available evidence and the most plausible accounts of it nevertheless suggest that the Islamic world did not experience anything comparable to the innovative developments that took place in Western Europe and East Asia between the 11th and the 13th century.[3]

When it comes to more recent transformations, especially those interconnected with the global rise of Western power, there is no denying that the Islamic world did not match the most salient non-Western responses to or reinventions of Western models. There is no Islamic parallel to the East Asian reinvention of

---

3 This refers to arguments developed in the two books coming out of Firenze Uppsala workshops: Axial Civilizations and World History & Eurasian Transformations, 1000-1300: Crystallizations, Divergences, Renaissances.

both modern capitalism and the project that began as an alternative but became a detour towards the same goal, and nothing comparable to the Indian experience of democracy. Nationalism in the Islamic world has – notwithstanding crucial differences between Arab and non-Arab parts of this world – a long history of problematic and unsettled relations with Islam.

At the beginning of the 21st century, the redefinition of the inherited relationship between religion and politics is posing more complex problems in Islamic societies than anywhere else. "Fundamentalism" may be a misleading term, and the most insightful analyses of the phenomenon in question have rightly underlined its modern features, but this does not alter the fact that it reflects an unfinished and particularly conflict-ridden process of transposing a religious and civilizational legacy into a modern context.

All these aspects of the Islamic trajectory call for integration into a more systematic historical analysis, which would in turn lay the foundations for more precisely targeted comparative studies. But at the present moment, combinations of historical and comparative approaches to the study of Islam tend to focus on particular aspects or episodes, rather than on problems of civilizational identity and difference. Marshall Hodgson's work remains the most ambitious and original attempt to reconstruct the long-term dynamics of the Islamic world as a civilizational complex. This is not to deny its shortcomings, some of them obvious from the outset and others more apparent in retrospect.

Hodgson's *The Venture of Islam* is an unfinished work, and some parts more visibly so than others, especially the sections dealing with early modern Islam and with Islamic responses to the global impact of what he called "the great Western transmutation." More recent work has thrown new light on various issues and raised questions about established views that Hodgson took for granted. To take the most spectacular example, ongoing controversies between traditionalists, revisionists and post-revisionists have changed the whole framework of research on Islamic origins (see chapters 4 and 5 by Arnason and Arjomand in the present volume). Together with other developments, increased knowledge of the Ismaili tradition has enriched and modified the received picture of the late classical and early middle periods (Hodgson was one of the pioneering scholars in the field of Ismaili studies, but further progress was made after his death).

Finally, the revival of civilizational theory during the last quarter of a century has made it easier to identify and criticize Hodgson's theoretical premises. However, allowing for all these critical considerations, it must be added that no comparable project has so far emerged, and that *The Venture of Islam* set standards for future efforts, even if an enterprise of that caliber can now only be imagined as an *ipso facto* unlikely fusion of multiple specialized perspectives.

Islam in the historical process: civilizational and comparative perspectives

Although only a few of the papers in this volume engage explicitly with Hodgson's ideas, they share with his work an interest in the historical dynamics of Islam as a civilization, in a comparative perspective with other cases of similar dimensions. The chapters are grouped into three sections which are systematically, not chronologically ordered.

The first section embraces the dimension of "crystallization" of the civilizational analysis of Islam and is therefore closest to Hodgson's own approach, albeit with sensible alterations. In chapter 1 Johann P. Arnason discusses the conceptual and historical foundations of Hodgson's program for civilizational studies, with particular reference to the role of the intellectual and religious traditions that constituted the core of city-centered high cultures.

Hodgson's variations on axial themes are discussed in relation to his distinctive interpretation of Islam. The second part of the chapter deals with the classical period in *The Venture of Islam*, reconstructs its main lines of argument, and confronts it with more recent scholarship in key areas. Hodgson's concept of absolutism as a political pattern typical of agrarianate societies is compared to the Weberian model of patrimonialism and taken as a starting-point for a more nuanced approach to the processes of state formation.

Chapter 2, by Babak Rahimi, focuses on the "middle period" of Islamic civilization, as demarcated in Hodgson's scheme, and links this chronological category to the more theoretical questions raised in an essay on the historical interrelations of societies, where Hodgson argued for a more polycentric conception of world history. Rahimi then develops these combined themes in ways partly aligned with more widespread views on the early second millennium CE as a time of innovative developments on an Afro-Eurasian scale, by laying a particularly strong emphasis on intercivilizational encounters and transcultural formations both within and on the margins of major civilizational areas. Against this background, he finally analyzes the emergence of Turkish and Persianate regional and civilizational variants within the Islamic world or, as he terms it, "Islamic axiality."

Chapter 3, by Arpad Szakolczai, examines contrasts and parallels between Islam and Christianity as prophetic religions, particularly ways of identifying prophetic founders and the implications of different solutions to this problem for the self-images of religious communities and their modes of relating to unbelievers. Moving away from macro-civilizational analysis, Szakolczai argues that identity formation in world religions is best analyzed in terms of the dynamics of experience and recognition; building-blocks for such a theoretical framework can be found in the works of Max Weber, Alessandro Pizzorno, Victor Turner and René Girard.

Johann P. Arnason provides in chapter 4 a theoretical elaboration of the concept of socio-cultural crystallization to the development of Islamic civilization which began with religious and political innovations on a local scale and culminated in new imperial and civilizational structures. Several aspects as well as phases of this process can be distinguished. It resulted in the imperial unification of a region that had not been controlled by one political centre since the collapse of the Persian empire and its ephemeral Macedonian successor; more importantly, civilizational unity was for the first time imposed on that same region and consolidated in a form that proved capable of further expansion. This chapter concludes with a brief discussion of the Ismaili movement as a schismatic current within this civilizational pattern.

The second section probes into specific "crossroads and turning points" which are particularly significant for the civilizational analysis of different momentums of Islamic history, beginning with the rise of Islam. This process has occasionally been described as a revolution, without however providing further reflection on the implications of that label. Said Amir Arjomand's chapter 5 is the first systematic attempt to situate early Islam within the framework of a typology of revolutions, and at the same time to draw on this crucial case to advance our understanding of types less familiar to modern western interpreters of revolutionary phenomena. A constitutive revolution is, according to Arjomand, one that establishes a new political order by imposing a central authority on a previously segmented society. The emergence of Islam exemplifies this general pattern, but some unique features set it apart from other cases: in particular, this was the only constitutive revolution that coincided with and depended on the promulgation of a new monotheism, and this factor affected both the initial project and its later metamorphoses in multiple ways. Comparative and theoretical perspectives can thus be brought to bear on disputes that have mostly developed in isolation from broader contexts.

Two contributions deal with specific countries and their roles in the historical formation of Islamic traditions. Egypt constitutes a markedly different case which does not fit easily into typologies linking radical socio-political transformations and axial crystallizations. The civilization of the Nile had been central to religious and intellectual cross-currents of Late Antiquity, but became more marginal to the schisms and crystallizations of early Islam. Georg Stauth's chapter 6 argues that despite the recent interest in Egypt in the context of Late Antiquity, the axial framework of analysis, by focusing on monotheism and revelation, has largely sidelined Egypt as a residual cultural heritage within patterns of cultural reconstruction culminating in Christianity and Islam. This chapter attempts to show some of the antagonisms which relate to the synchronic coexistence of the civilizational heritage of Pharaonic religion-*cum*-politics and the reasserted and radicalized, monotheistic visions of rising Islam. Such antagonisms have shaped the vitality of a lived religion, specifically in local contexts – as viewed here – in the Eastern Nile Delta. Taking a view on the role of ʿAbdallah b. Salam – the first Jewish witness of Muhammad's monotheistic revelations in the prophetic tradition, and at the same time a locally venerated Islamic saint in that region – it becomes evident that the 'denial' of the civilizational heritage of the Nile is as much a source of orthodox monotheist reconstruction in Islam (as it was in Christianity), as it bears a great part of the symbolic, legendary and mythological legacy which played an important role in orthodox theology and in popular imaginary from the early Islamic period onwards. Paradoxically, the Islamic negations of Pharaonic civilization and its wonders still occupy a great role within orthodox practice and modern reflection of Islam. This negation at the same time preserves and incorporates the archaism which it wishes to suppress. This is a possible qualification and a point of critique of the axial framework.

Yemen was, as historians are now coming to recognize, not only an important cultural centre in its own right and a prominent part of the civilizational background to Islam, but also – as Raif G. Khoury argues in chapter 7 – a meeting ground of multiple traditions. The Yemeni share in political, cultural and religious life during Islam's early centuries was highly significant, but it has proved difficult to trace – not least because it was later obscured by dominant traditions – and is still a controversial theme. Khoury shows how important Yemeni connections and crossroads were for conceptual, historiographical and literary developments that took place during the first phase of the classical period of Islamic civilization.

A concluding paper in this section, chapter 8 by Josef van Ess, critically reassesses the core idea of breakthrough or radical transformation that underlies the axial framework of analysis in its successive adaptations and revisions. Van Ess digs deeply into the reasons of why the axial idea of Jaspers was itself at odds with Islam for being at the service of a distinctive idea of the "modern subject" that needs, by definition, a convenient other, a civilization resistant to those radical transformations that are supposedly rooted in the "self." Indeed, Islamic civilization is characterized by innovation and reformation within a stronger line of continuity with Late Antiquity. Van Ess suggests that the notion of "turning points" in a longer term perspective of civilizational developments and cross-civilizational influences seems to be more suitable to the analysis of Islam than the original axial idea of "breakthroughs."

The third and last section includes contributions summarizing "cultural and institutional dynamics" of Islamic civilization, partly in a comparative perspective referring to other world religions and their civilizational ramifications. Here again the reframing of the axial problematic becomes more explicit.

Said Amir Arjomand's chapter 9 considers the divergent paths of Western Christendom and the Islamic world from a specific angle, concerning the institutions of higher learning and their relationship to political culture. This approach differs from the line taken by those who consider the role of universities only in relation to the genesis of modern science; it gives due weight to the interplay of structural and contingent factors; and it stresses different ways of appropriating older traditions. According to Arjomand, the failure to translate Aristotle's *Poli-*

tics conditioned the development of political thought in medieval Islam. Yet the significance of his intellectual blockage can only be understood in connection with larger patterns of Islamic history before and after the Mongol invasions.

Arpad Szakolczai's chapter 10 links these issues to even broader historical horizons. Szakolczai does not deny that the idea of the Axial Age has helped to open up comparative perspectives. He insists, however, that it has also obscured other important themes for comparative analysis: in particular the question of similarities and differences between prophetic religions. Only some of the innovations commonly ascribed to the Axial Age were associated with prophetic figures; on the other hand, the prophetic religions that had the most massive impact on world history emerged long after the end of the Axial Age. A different historical frame of reference is therefore needed. Moreover, a closer analysis of prophetic religions will draw attention to another topic that has often been noted by axial theorists, but never fully integrated into their problematic: the ecumenic empires, with which the religions in question interacted in very different ways.

In chapter 11 Armando Salvatore questions both the typological conception of axiality and the interpretation that subsumes axial breakthroughs under a more general and much too abstract category of reflexivity. Drawing on Voegelin's descriptions of the "metastatic," i.e. exponentially and uncontrollably transformative character of axial discourse, especially in its prophetic variant, he stresses the sustained and divergent but sometimes interconnected dynamics of traditions that grew out of axial beginnings, as well as the need for an adequate concept of tradition that could provide the key to a comparative understanding of varying cases. An informed definition of axiality can only emerge out of such historical and comparative studies. In that context, Salvatore argues that Islam and Christianity are best seen as interrelated parts of a Western complex of axial traditions and that much more work remains to be done on Islamic sources of European thought.

The section and the volume conclude with S.N. Eisenstadt's reflections on public spheres and political dynamics in Islamic societies in chapter 12. Growing interest in the political aspects of modernity has brought the varying types of public spheres and civil societies to the forefront of comparative analysis; and since the prospects of political modernity in the Islamic world have seemed particularly troubled, this has led to distorted views of Islamic political traditions. The widespread notion of despotic rule as an enduring characteristic of Islamic societies is incompatible with the historical record. But as Eisenstadt argues, the Islamic experience is also particularly instructive with regard to the distinction between public sphere and civil society. Public spheres exist in widely varying forms in different civilizational settings, but the development of civil society depends on more specific conditions for individual and collective access to the political domain. Vigorous public spheres, centered on a set of distinctive institutions, were characteristic of Islamic societies, but other components of the institutional framework blocked or minimized access to political centers.

Crystallizations

Chapter 1

Marshall Hodgson's Civilizational Analysis of Islam: Theoretical and Comparative Perspectives

JOHANN P. ARNASON

Civilizational perspectives, of a more or less consistent kind, are often implicit in area studies; but it is very rare for area specialists to engage in sustained reflection on this background, and to develop their own variations on key themes of civilizational analysis. Marshall Hodgson is perhaps the most outstanding example. His historical analysis of 'Islamdom' and 'Islamicate civilization,' to use his own neologisms, is grounded in a very explicit and sophisticated version of civilizational theory, and the connection works both ways: the civilizational approach throws new light on Islam as a historical phenomenon, and at the same time, it is developed along specific lines that reflect the distinctive features of the case in question.[1] The result is, as far as I can judge, the most ambitious and theoretically articulate Western attempt to understand the Islamic world. If we want to bring Islamic studies and the comparative analysis of civilizations into closer mutual contact, this would seem to be the most promising starting-point. But it has, so far, attracted much less attention than it would merit. There has been no extensive discussion of Hodgson's assumptions and arguments; the current ideological controversies about 'Orientalism' (an overstretched notion if ever there was one) tend to bypass his work, perhaps because it demands a level of historical sensitivity that has now become unfashionable.

The following discussion – a brief and tentative sketch which I hope to develop into a more systematic interpretation – will begin with a glance at Hodgson's conception of civilizations as 'primary units of reference' for large-scale comparative history, and then move on to his analysis of Islam. Within the limits of this paper, I can only deal with a few parts of a vast field. Hodgson's interpre-

1   'Islamdom' is obviously coined by analogy with 'Christendom,' more precisely with the use of the latter term to describe a civilization rather than a religion which is only a part of it – admittedly a defining part, but not to be equated with the whole. Similarly, to describe a civilizational formation as 'Islamicate,' rather than 'Islamic,' is to stress the general point that a civilization is never educible to its religious premises, as well as the more specific ones that this civilization integrated important elements of other traditions, subordinating them to Islamic principles without dissolving their distinctive contents, and that its history was more discontinuous than a straightforward Islamic identity would allow for.

tation of the formative period will be examined at some length; I will then conclude with some reflections on the broader interrelated questions of unity and diversity as well as continuity and discontinuity in the historical destinies of Islamicate civilization.

Defining and demarcating civilizations

In the "general prologue" to the first volume of *The Venture of Islam*, Hodgson describes his project in the following terms (Hodgson 1974, 1: 90-91):

In this work, we shall speak more of masterpieces of art and dynastic policies, of religious geniuses, and scientific discoveries, than of everyday life on the farm and in the kitchen. Hence we will include in our scope those peoples among whom a few privileged men shared such masterpieces and discoveries, however much those peoples differed among themselves, in farmwork or in homemaking. This may seem like arbitrary preference for the spectacular. I believe it answers to a legitimate human need to understand ourselves. In any case, we must be clear as to what we are doing, and its consequences.

A strong interest in 'high culture,' or rather a rejection of the various attempts to debunk or discount it, is no doubt a defining characteristic of the civilizational approach; it is not to be mistaken for a claim that this is where the ultimate meaning or the fundamental determinants of human history will be found. The point is, rather, that in specific contexts this level of analysis is crucial to the understanding of the social-historical world; there is no suggestion that we should neglect the interaction of civilizational patterns, visible at the level of high culture, with local or popular forms of socio-cultural life. But the shared focus on high culture ('the arbitrary preference for the spectacular,' to quote Hodgson's anticipation of a likely critical response) does not necessarily reflect the same line of reasoning – or the same choice of context – in every single version of civilizational analysis. We must therefore take a closer look at Hodgson's specific reasons for adopting this view.

To begin with, let us note the most general historical co-ordinates of civilization studies, as defined by Hodgson. Writing in the mid-1960s, he argued (and he would probably take the same view today) that the analysis of 'pre-modern citied societies' – another of his neologisms – had lagged behind the study of non-citied societies on the one hand and modern technical societies on the other. Anthropologists and sociologists had moved ahead, whereas the world-historical framework required for the study of "the periods and areas between – that is, from Sumer to the French Revolution" (ibid., 1: 31) had proved more difficult to develop. One of the most striking features of this long historical period was the constitution of cultural units of a new kind, capable of encompassing a broad variety of local cultures with a more limited reach. These superimposed cultural formations, more self-reflexive and as a result both more clearly demarcated and more dynamic than the subordinate ones, are the civilizations that Hodgson wants to place at the centre of comparative history. Sociologically speaking, they depend on urban centres, literate elites and cumulative traditions. As for the defining contents, they are "constituted by standards of cultural evaluation, basic expectations, and norms of legitimation" (ibid., 1: 93). A civilization is, in other words, an "expression of formative ideals" (ibid., 1: 90) – this is perhaps the best condensed formulation of Hodgson's approach.

Among formative ideals, religious ones stand out in virtue of their strong and comprehensive claims: "A religious commitment, by its nature, tends to be more total than any other" (ibid., 1: 94). Here it is necessary to say a few words about Hodgson's definition of religion, which is crucial to his understanding of Islam, and it seems best to begin with a quotation: "Properly, we use the term "religious" for an ultimate orientation (rather than 'philosophical' or 'ideological'), so far as the orientation is personally committing and is meaningful in terms of a cosmos, without further precision of what this may come to" (ibid., 1: 88). As Hodgson notes in passing, this emphasis on a person's "ultimate cosmic orientation and commitments and the ways in which he pays attention to them" (ibid., 1: 88) leads to the inclusion of Buddhism among religions (atheism is not an obstacle), whereas Marxism does not qualify ("the relation person-cosmos plays a relatively slight role there"). The cosmic orientation can turn towards a sense of cosmic transcendence and human dependence; this is, of course, particularly pronounced in Islam (although Hodgson does not quote Becker's description of Islam as the 'most Schleiermacherian' of all religions, it seems clear that he agreed with it).

There is thus a close affinity, but not an invariant relationship between religious and civilizational orientations. Religious commitments tend to figure prominently among the formative ideals that constitute a civilizational pattern, but some religions are more civilizational than others, and some civilizations are more religion-centred than others. At this point we may note some distinctive features of the Islamic case, as seen by Hodgson. First and foremost, Islam has – more than any other religion – tended to make the 'kind of total demand on life' that is potentially inherent in a religious commitment as such. A comparison with the other monotheistic world religion underscores the point: "The reader will find that Islam, rather more than Christianity, tended to call forth a total social pattern in the name of religion itself" (ibid., 1: 89). The internal totalizing logic translates into external unity. Hodgson speaks of an 'Islamicate civilization,' almost coextensive with the spread of Islam as a religion (although he notes the existence of Muslims – e.g. in China – whose religion does not entail much participation in a broader civilizational pattern). He does not think that there is a comparable pan-Christian civilization: the mutual isolation of Ethiopia and Western Christendom is cited as a case in point. He also rejects – without further discussion – the idea of a Buddhist civilization. In short, Islam stands out as the only world religion associated with – indeed embodied in – a single civilization.

On the other hand, "even Islam could not be total" (ibid., 1: 89). The religious vision could more easily put its stamp on some cultural spheres than others; "in many other spheres, such as trade or poetry" (ibid.), it had to grant significant autonomy to extra-religious values and meanings. Moreover, "Islam is unique among the religious traditions for the diversity of the peoples that have embraced it" (ibid., 1: 85). Civilizational unity was superimposed on this diversity, and that could not happen without complex adaptive and transformative processes. Hodgson concludes: "When we look at Islam historically, the integral unity of life it seemed to display when we looked at it as a working out of the act of *isl?m* almost vanishes" (ibid., 1: 85). Almost, but not quite. For one thing, the aspiration to integral unity remained alive in pious minds and was intermittently activated in more practical ways. The question of unity and diversity is thus posed in very stark terms. It will be reconsidered below.

But first we need to take another look at Hodgson's case for the civilizational approach. He is keenly aware of the limits to its validity and utility: as he stresses, it is sometimes – depending on the context of inquiry – more appropriate to analyze history in terms of regional boundaries and continuities. We can thus think of the Near East (or the lands from Nile to Oxus, to use Hodgson's preferred term) or of India as regions with a history of their own, before and after the emergence or intrusion of Islam; and in some contexts, a European region (in a broad sense that includes Anatolia) may be a more meaningful unit of reference than the civilization of Western Christendom. Some specific cases will always prove difficult to fit into a civilizational framework; Hodgson refers to the Georgians and the Armenians as peoples that cannot be subsumed under one civilization. (It is tempting to elaborate a bit further on these two cases: in the first instance, Hodgson is obviously thinking of their borderline position between the Eastern Christian and Iranian worlds, but it might be added that they responded to this situation by developing particularly distinctive and resilient collective identities – somewhat resembling civilizational patterns in miniature, but the restricted scale and scope set limits to the analogy).

Notwithstanding such qualifications, Hodgson insists on the centrality of the civilizational approach to the study of world history 'from Sumer to the French Revolution,' and we must now try to clarify his reasons. This will entail some reconstruction: *The Venture of Islam* is an unfinished work, and basic assumptions are not always stated as clearly as they might have been if the author had lived long enough to put the finishing touches to the text. It seems to me that five main points can be distinguished.

The first has to do with Hodgson's conception of traditions and their role in history. His reflections on this topic read like a radical critique of the impoverished concept of tradition that had prevailed in the orbit of modernization theory (the University of Chicago was obviously a place where direct contact with this intellectual current was unavoidable). For Hodgson, growth, change and development are essential to a cultural tradition: "the more so, the broader its scope" (ibid., 1: 79). As we shall see, the reference to a broad scope is important for his civilizational perspective. But before going on to consider that point, the dynamics of cultural traditions should be defined in more specific terms. Hodgson's key statement on this subject is worth quoting at length: as he sees it (ibid., 1: 80),

we may describe the process of cultural tradition as a movement composed of three moments: a creative action, an occasion of inventive or revelatory, even charismatic encounter: for instance, the discovery of a new aesthetic value; the launching of a new technique of craftsmanship; a rise to a new level of social expectation, one man of another; the assertion of a new ruling stock or even the working out of new patterns of governing; or, in the case of religion, an occasion of fresh awareness of something ultimate in the relation between ourselves and the cosmos – that is, an occasion of spiritual revelation, bringing a new vision.

Hodgson goes on to mention the Quran and its challenge as a prime example of creative foundation.

The group commitment and the interaction within the group are inseparable from a conflict of interpretations and a "continuing cumulative dialogue" (ibid., 1: 81). As Hodgson notes, this pattern is not limited to religious, ideological or scientific fields; the same applies to the forms of economic and political life, where the conflictual dynamic of interests and interpretations is at work. In all these regards, the civilizational frame of reference is crucial: the interpretive conflicts and the cumulative dialogues unfold on that scale, and we must adopt a correspondingly broad view if we want to put them in proper perspective. The widely shared and articulated high cultural traditions are the most representative examples of the broader pattern that Hodgson calls the 'process of cultural tradition.' In that sense, the civilizational perspective is needed to do justice to the general problematic of tradition. We may add a point that fits into Hodgson's scheme, even if he did not elaborate on it. There is a reflexive side to the creative moment which he lists as the first part of his model: Cultural traditions construct retrospective images of their foundational episodes and figures, often in the form of a more or less explicitly sacred history, and the most important of such constructions have crystallized and operated on a civilizational scale. The Islamicate civilization is, in that regard, as good an example as any other.

To conclude this discussion of traditions and their civilizational dimension, one more aspect should be noted. After criticizing one-sided comparisons of East and West (including some arguments put forward by Max Weber), Hodgson draws a very far-reaching conclusion that is best quoted in full (ibid., 1: 37):

The difference between major traditions lies not so much in the particular elements present within them, but in the relative weighting of them and the structuring of their interplay within the total context. If this structuring remains relatively constant (in the very nature of tradition, it cannot remain absolutely so), it will be because the predisposing conditions remain relatively constant, and because they are further reinforced by the institutionalizing of attitudes appropriate to them.

Different traditions are, in other words, characterized not by the presence or absence of specific themes, ideas or orientations, but by different combinations of shared components. This view is best treated as a working hypothesis that will still need extensive testing; but it would seem to be in line with current trends of comparative studies (one case that comes to mind is the question of the idea of creation in the Chinese tradition: it is now widely accepted that it was not simply absent, as earlier historians of ideas tended to think; rather, its contextual meaning differed from the Western Eurasian traditions). And the civilizational perspective is at least a plausible corollary of the hypothesis: it takes a civilizational scale for the available components and the possible combinations to become fully visible.

2. The second point can be stated relatively briefly, since it has already been touched upon in the preceding discussion. Civilizations are, in Hodgson's view, expressions of formative ideals, and there are two sides to the formative potential. On the one hand, the high cultural traditions that constitute the core of a civilization can be diffused beyond their original social context and affect the patterns of local and popular cultures in more or less decisive ways. This is an obvious implication of the conception of civilizations as superimposed cultures. On the other hand, the formative ideals can be reaffirmed and reinterpreted by concerned minorities, aiming at a reordering of social life. Once again, the historical dimensions of such projects can only be grasped if they are studied on a civilizational scale, and the record of Islamic revivalist movements is as good an example as any other.

3. The third point is linked to a vision of world history and a controversy about the proper way of writing it. I mean the – real or potential – debate between Hodgson and William McNeill, about which we know less than we would like to. They were colleagues at the University of Chicago, working on their main projects at roughly the same time, but it is unclear whether there was an ongoing exchange of views. But the only published part of the debate (apart from arguments implicit in *The Venture of Islam* is a long excerpt from Hodgson's letter to John O. Voll, dated 1966 and included in a posthumous collection of essays (Hodgson 1993: 91-94). Here Hodgson begins with a brief criticism of three defunct visions of history: the Christian, the Marxist and the Westernist, and then moves on to discuss an emerging alternative which he calls the "four region pattern." As he sees it, the new paradigm reached its "first fulfilment" in McNeill's *Rise of the West* (which Hodgson describes as the "first genuine world history ever written"); but on close examination, this work appears as an uneasy compromise between the four region model (with the Chinese, Indian, Near Eastern

and European worlds as the main units of reference) and an underlying Westernist one. Hodgson even suggests that McNeill's version of world history might not be immune to a Westernist takeover, and he links this to a complaint about the "unphilosophical structure" of the work: an absence of critical reflection on philosophical presuppositions inherited from Western traditions, and an insensitivity to the contexts of meaning that determine the nature and limits of diffusion.

To Hodgson, the four-region pattern was obviously a step in the right direction, but it did not go far enough. As other texts show, he was developing a more elaborate model of regional differentiation. More importantly (in the present context), he insisted on the distinction as well as the connection between regions and civilizations. To counter the persistent influence of Westernism, world history had to be reconstructed in both regional and civilizational terms. Hodgson's discussion of this task did not get beyond rough outlines, but we can reconstruct the basic orientations, and it seems appropriate to begin with the references to the Axial Age: although Hodgson's views on that subject differ markedly from the most influential approaches, his case confirms that the axial connection is essential to a full-fledged model of civilizational analysis. When discussing Hodgson's specific version of it, we should bear in mind that he engages directly with Jaspers's philosophical interpretation of the Axial Age; the later historical-sociological approaches had not yet taken shape.

For Hodgson, the Axial Age was less unique than Jaspers had suggested. 'Citied agrarianate societies,' as he called the social formations that succeeded each other from Sumer to the French Revolution, were on the whole resistant to radical innovation. Technological conditions set limits to the accumulation and investment of surplus, and in a more elusive general sense, cultural patterns privileged continuity: "there was an inherent tendency in style which militated against radical innovation" (ibid., 1: 236-37). There were, nevertheless, a few strikingly creative periods of "cultural florescence," as Hodgson called it, and the Axial Age was one of them (other, more localized examples included India in the early centuries CE, China under the Tang and Song dynasties, and the Western European Renaissance – but in this last case, florescence was followed by something much more unprecedented: the 'Great Western Transmutation'). As for the specific achievements of the Axial Age, Hodgson seems to have drawn from Jaspers's reflections the sceptical conclusion that interpretations in terms of a shared intellectual or spiritual direction were premature. He refers in very general terms to a new interest in transcendence (this is perhaps comparable to Benjamin Schwartz's loose definition of that concept as a way of "standing back and looking beyond" – cf. Schwartz 1975), and to a widespread concern with the individual, but all things considered, he thinks it makes more sense to define the Axial Age in terms of its long-term consequences than its initial aspirations or self-understandings. The innovations of the Axial Age laid the foundations for civilizational traditions that divided the main cultural zones of Eurasia between themselves during the following two millennia of premodern history. Greek, Sanskritic (or Indic) and Chinese (or Sinic) traditions go back to these parallel but not common beginnings. In all cases, the civilizational patterns have a regional identity: Hodgson would no doubt have agreed with Braudel's statement that civilizations can in principle be located on a map. But the abovementioned distinction between regions and civilizations is also relevant: the traditions in question are characterized by a capacity – unequally developed and channelled in different directions – to spread beyond their original regional settings.

There is, of course, a major and obvious exception to this generalization about the Axial Age. In the Nile-to-Oxus region, the birthplace of the most important archaic civilizations, no new unifying pattern emerged from the innovations of the middle centuries of the last millennium BCE. Hodgson refers to monotheistic tendencies in the Iranian and Semitic traditions (he thought that Zoroastrian 'dualism' was best understood as a version of or a step in the direction of monotheism); but these developments did not crystallize into a pattern of regional unity and trans-regional diffusion, comparable to those of the previously less developed regions. We should perhaps note in passing that although Hodgson mentions only Iranian and Semitic forms of monotheism, his general argument does not exclude the possibility of analogous trends in earlier phases and other places: both the abortive monotheistic revolution in Egypt (Akhenaten) and the peripheral monotheistic turn in South Arabia could be fitted into the picture.

This incomplete axial transformation of the Nile-to-Oxus region is the background to Hodgson's interpretation of Islam. It was Islamicate civilization that for the first time achieved the cultural unification of this part of the world, and it did so through a new elaboration of the monotheistic themes inherited from Iranian and Semitic sources. But the civilizational pattern that served to integrate the region also manifested a trans-regional expansive and integrative dynamic that has no parallel in premodern history. The formative classical period of Islamicate civilization (Hodgson dates it from 692 to 945, i.e. from the definitive crystallization of the Marwanid caliphate to the irreversible decline of the Abbasid one) thus stands apart as a very specific phase of cultural florescence, different from the more dispersed innovations of the Axial Age as well as from the more localized ones of the other periods mentioned above.

4. The fourth point has to do with responses of non-Western civilizations in general and the Islamicate one in particular – to the 'Great Western Transmutation.' This latter formulation sums up one of the most interesting but least developed parts of Hodgson's argument. Here it must suffice to say that he was adumbrating a very distinctive (but in a very general sense Weberian) analysis of early European modernity, centred on the 17th century and on interconnections between the absolutist state, the scientific revolution and the developments that later economic historians have described as 'industrious' or 'proto-industrial' revolutions. But in the present context, our main concern is with repercussions and responses on the non-Western side, and although Hodgson's reflections on this are not always easy to follow, there seem to be two main thematic foci.

On the one hand, he suggests that reactions to the abrupt global empowerment of the West – as a result of the transmutation – must be interpreted in civilizational terms. The legacies of the respective high cultural traditions and their 'cumulative dialogues' were in all cases reflected in the ideological and practical responses to the Western challenge. But in the light of more recent experience, it is tempting to go beyond Hodgson's explicit statements and argue that the significance of civilizational legacies manifests itself most clearly in the failure of attempts to neutralize them. The ascendancy of political Islam – on the ruins of various nationalisms and socialisms – is obviously the most spectacular case in point. But the politicization of Hinduism in post-Congress India and the ideological development of post-Communist China would seem to support the same conclusion.

On the other hand, Hodgson finishes his third volume with reflections on the crisis of modernity and the possible significance of premodern traditions in that regard. The thrust of these reflections is best described as aporetic: Hodgson argues that the dynamic of modernity generates a whole series of problems – from the atomization of social life to the destruction of the environment – that call for a 'new vision.' But such a vision cannot be built on the utilitarian-technicalistic premises that have come to dominate modern culture. It is tempting to turn to the surviving premodern traditions. But "we cannot say that the religious heritages are in fact able to offer such vision: it may be that they are too drastically handicapped by the element of wishful thinking that has been so rooted in their whole history" (ibid., 3: 436). We can only find out through closer study; and the work that Hodgson put into the study of Islamic traditions suggests that he was prepared to give them the benefit of doubt.

5. The fifth and final point will only be briefly mentioned here. It has to do with the ultimate presuppositions of Hodgson's work, and with a philosophical anthropology which he was rather reluctant to spell out. But he said enough to make it clear that he saw a comparative analysis of civilizations as essential to the understanding of the human condition and its potentialities, and that he liked to think of the major civilizations as 'human heritages,' some of which surpassed others in the exploration and articulation of specific dimensions of human being-in-the-world. As for the most distinctive achievements of Islamicate civilization, seen from that angle, I will only quote a few remarks from the last passages of the 'general prologue' in the first volume of *The Venture of Islam*. On the aesthetic level, Hodgson described Islamicate visual arts as "the greatest ever known in which the elements of sheer visual design could be given priority over all other considerations." More provocatively, he suggests that Islamicate literatures are "perhaps unparalleled in – among other things – their mastery of the esoteric as a dimension of human experience," here he was obviously thinking of the Sufi tradition, to which he felt strongly attracted. But he goes on to note that "the Islamicate society represents, in part, one of the most thoroughgoing attempts in history to build a world-wide human community as if from scratch on the basis of an ex-

plicitly worked out ideal" (ibid., 1: 98). The implications of that point for comparative study of human societies and their histories can hardly be overstated.

Islamic religion and Islamicate civilization

Civilizational patterns are, in principle, irreducible to religious visions; but religious orientations are, by definition, likely to play a central role among the formative ideals that characterize a civilization, and some sets of religious orientations are more translatable into a civilizational logic than others. As we have seen, the Islamic vision was – compared to other world religions – more totalizing and more explicitly oriented towards an all-round ordering of human life, from it most natural foundations to its most demanding moral dimensions. But even so, it had to fall short of a total impact. The religious vision had to adapt to other trends and forces already at work in the region which it took over and from which embarked on the path of global expansion; as it unfolded on an ever larger geopolitical and geocultural scale, it also released forces and triggered transformative processes which it had to accommodate but could not absorb.

To clarify this relationship between religious vision and civilization, we must first go back to the beginnings. Islamicate civilization – as Hodgson calls it – took shape during the formative period from 692 to 945. It was not simply imposed on the Nile-to-Oxus region by conquerors coming in from the periphery; rather, it was the outcome of complex developments and innovations, separate at first but finally brought together in a new synthesis. The region was a configuration of heterogeneous cultures with a long history of interaction and conflict, but aspects of the new pattern had been in the making long before the Islamic conquest. According to Hodgson, they included monotheistic traditions – in different Semitic and Iranian forms – as well as the growing strength of mercantile classes, and the egalitarian social ethics (sometimes spiralling into movements) that drew support from both of these trends. But this is not to suggest that the Islamic input *sensu stricto* was of minor importance. The 'Islamic infusion,' as Hodgson calls it, was the catalyst that brought about a creative fusion of the other components.

However, when it comes to the concrete history of the events in question, Hodgson's approach seems more conventional than his understanding of classical Islamicate civilization as a synthesis of multi-traditional sources. To put it another way, there is a tension between the theoretical framework and the narrative. As is well known, there is now a flourishing current of revisionist historiography on early Islam. The historical validity of the traditional account of the conquest and the early caliphs is being called into question. It would be more than misleading to lump all the revisionists together: for example, the line taken by John Wansbrough (1977; 1978) is a good deal more extreme than the view of Christian Décobert (1991). One can even observe major shifts within the work of individual authors (Crone and Cook 1977 is much more extreme and less convincing than Crone 1987). But a search for concrete anticipations of revisionism in Hodgson's work would not be very rewarding. The first part of the first volume includes a chapter called "Muhammad's challenge," here Hodgson notes that "we know far less about Muhammad than was once supposed" (ibid., 1: 160). This does not go beyond the critical stance of classical Western scholarship on Islam, as represented e.g. by Goldziher. And Hodgson goes on to state that we nevertheless know a good deal more about Muhammad than about Jesus. As for the sources of this superior knowledge, he seems to have no doubt that "we can rely on the Quran as direct evidence" (ibid., 1: 160). Today's revisionists would take strong exception to this statement. Here I cannot pursue the question further. But I would like to suggest that Hodgson's interpretive model, i.e. his analysis of the emergence of Islam as a synthesis of multiple sources on a regional scale – is perfectly compatible with a moderate version of the revisionist view; indeed, it positively calls for that kind of approach. If the 'infusion' of a somewhat inchoate but also incipiently rationalizing monotheism from the periphery was a crucial factor in the formation of a new civilization, it seems a plausible hypothesis that this aspect of the process was retrospectively stylized into a sacred history, and that the record transmitted to later generations must be seen in that light.

These considerations apply to other questions raised by the revisionists. In particular, Hodgson had next to nothing to say about the Yemeni connection (no surprise, given the then very limited knowledge of the whole South Arabian background), but I think it can be easily fitted into his model – it is one more component of the synthesis. There is, however, another recent line of thought about classical Islam that may pose more serious problems. The traditional idea of a 'decline and fall of the Roman Empire' has now been replaced by an alternative model best summed up in terms of a 'transformation of the Roman world' (this was, among other things, the title of a vast interdisciplinary project launched under the auspices of the European Science Foundation [for one of the best discussions of the whole problematic, cf. Fowden 1993]). This should probably be seen as one of the major historical paradigm shifts of the last decades. It involves a new perspective on Islam as one of the three successor civilizations into which the Roman world mutated, and each of which transformed the legacy of late antiquity in its specific way. It can hardly be said that Hodgson anticipated this turn. He was obviously aware of the presence of the Roman Empire in the region that was to be transformed by Islam, but he did not do much to place this transformation in a broader context involving the whole Roman world. He made a valid point when he noted that the experience of the Maghreb showed how much more alien to the Roman past Islam was than the two other successors; but that is not the whole story.

Let us now return to Hodgson's more specific conception of the formative period. The most striking aspect of his periodization is the choice of precise dates – 692 and 945 – for the beginning and the end of the 'classical civilization of the High Caliphate.' The late beginning implies a long prehistory that includes both

Arabic origins and the early expansion. Hodgson's main reasons for separating this long-drawn-out prelude from the classical phase have to do with the relationship between religion and politics. He is reluctant to treat the militant Islamic community of the first decades as a stage within an ongoing process of state formation. Muhammad's regime in Medina was a "new and total moral order" (ibid., 1: 197), a "new social order" (ibid., 1: 187); but although a subtitle refers to a "new polity" (ibid., 1: 176), and Muhammad is – in passing credited with building a state (ibid., 1: 193), a later note (ibid., 1: 321 n.) refers to Medina as having neither state nor church. The principles and problems of statehood seem to have been overshadowed by the total fusion of prophecy and government, the total union of the believers' community, and the vision of prophet and community as vehicles of divine command. The situation changed when the community turned to sustained expansion, but the first solutions to new problems were improvised and unstable. According to Hodgson, the caliphate began as an emergency arrangement (there was no preconceived substitute for prophetic rule, and no consensus on ways to regulate succession), and continued as a central authority for the community at war. The crisis began with the transition from Umar to Uthman and was not overcome until the second *fitna* ended with Abd-al-Malik's victory over his rivals in 692.

On this view, the "early Muslim state" mentioned in the title of the last chapter of Hodgson's "book one" (ibid., 1: 187) was at best a proto-state, and in some key respects an anti-state. As will be argued in another contribution to this volume(on the emergence of Islam), there are – especially in light of more recent scholarship – reasons to propose a more nuanced model, and to link a longer phase of crystallization to a more continuous dynamic of state formation. Hodgson's interpretation would thus seem too dependent on classical Islamic images of Muhammad's Medina and the early caliphate. However, this does not mean that his analysis of formative processes during the period he defined as classical should be discarded: it still seems more systematic, more theoretically articulate and more attuned to civilizational perspectives than any other available work of its kind. Here I will try to reconstruct its essentials in terms somewhat closer to the 'state of the art' in civilizational analysis, and therefore not always in close alignment with Hodgson's own conceptual framework. More work will be needed to integrate his problematic into current debates among civilizational theorists.

In contrast to the first *fitna,* where religious and communitarian concerns had affected the course of events, the second one was fought through to the end, and settled by superior military force. The primacy of power was symbolically underscored by the fact that a claimant based in conquered territory (Syria) defeated a rival in control of Islam's original centres. As a result, the new empire was for the first time brought under unified central rule. The imperial Islamic state now had to be consolidated on a huge scale, and throughout a region particularly rich in diverse traditions of political organization, culture and imagery. Hodgson sees the development of the Marwanid state after 692 (he prefers this term to the more conventional notion of a continuous Umayyad dynasty) against this background. His analytical frame of reference merits closer attention: although definitions of basic concepts leave much to be desired, and there is no mention of Max Weber, it does not seem far-fetched to speak of an implicit alternative to Weber's sociology of domination. The key category is a generalized concept of absolutism, which Hodgson explicitly applies to Eurasian societies from Western Europe to China, and which may be seen as a less reductionistic answer to the Weberian model of patrimonialism. As Hodgson argues, a legitimizing social rationale for strong monarchic rule is common to agrarianate societies, or at least to those that go beyond minimal size: an unchallenged supreme ruler appears as a necessary check on privileged minorities seeking to maximize wealth and power. In a state consistently based on this principle, the monarch's authority must be absolute, "one before which the rich and the well-born were as vulnerable as the little man" (ibid., 1: 282). It is this claim to unconditional primacy over all other centres of social power that constitutes the defining feature of the absolutist model. It is obviously not realized everywhere to the same degree; the regimes most familiarly associated with the label should not be mistaken for the most perfect examples; and to add a qualifying point which Hodgson does not discuss, specific circumstances could transform the oligarchic adversaries of absolutism into pioneers of broader political transformations.

The absolutist model is by nature prone to opposite deviations: a weak ruler can become an instrument of the forces he is supposed to control, but a more assertive one is easily tempted into arbitrary and oppressive uses of power. Some safeguards – or at least mitigating devices – against both dangers are built into symbolic and institutional frameworks of monarchic rule. Such patterns develop within all political traditions, with significant variations from one civilizational context to another. The recurrent core structures include models of court culture and society, designed to enhance the authority and prestige of the power centre, but also capable of channelling it in certain directions; more or less developed bureaucratic apparatuses that translate the monarchic principle into practical control; and the highly diverse paradigms of sacral rulership (divine kingship in the literal sense was only an archaic variant). When the victors of the second *fitna* set about consolidating their imperial domain, they faced a situation where the absolutist model was inescapably operative on a grand scale, and at the same time they fell heirs to its multiple traditional versions. As Hodgson stresses, prior progress towards cultural unity of the 'Irano-Semitic area' made empire-building easier, but different cultural traditions were still firmly entrenched. On the other hand, the conquerors had brought with them not so much a new model as a whole new problematic of sacral rulership. The close connection between religion and imperial expansion made it obligatory to define and legitimize political power with reference to the revealed message and its bearer; but there could be no simple continuation of the exceptional authority vested in the prophet. Although historians of early Islam seem to agree that the image of Muhammad as the last prophet was not as definitive as it later became, his specific status had to be enshrined, and when new models of leadership or rulership seemed to transgress that rule, they were vulnerable to accusations of heresy (sectarian traditions also faced this problem, but their terms of reference differed from those of the mainstream). In short, the imperative need to derive legitimacy from prophetic origins went together with the unsettled problem of defining the precise nature of the connection. Different models of sacral rulership could be envisaged, within limits that were in turn disputed by the more militantly heterodox currents. This distinctive but still in many ways undetermined framework for ordering the relationship between religion and power was a key part of what Hodgson calls the 'Islamic infusion': it shaped the Islamic forms of absolutism.

Another part was, however, a "tradition of faith" that "developed most actively in an atmosphere of political opposition to the ruling forms" (ibid., 1: 241). At its most explicit, it became a "programme of the piety-minded" (ibid., 1: 252) that challenged an existing political order. But this political challenge was grounded in a broader religious vision. The triumphant faith had a transformative logic of its own that could and had to compromise with imperial absolutism, but did not lend itself to complete instrumentalization. Universalistic claims, inherent in the self-understanding of purified monotheism, had already transcended the Arab context, and they found a much more effective outlet at the imperial level. The original equality of believers, although never untempered by internal ranking, could be invoked to justify protests against the new power structures. These autonomous religious factors were reinforced by the circumstances of early Islamic history. Here it may be useful to link Hodgson's analysis to later work by Fred M. Donner (1998). Donner's interpretation of historical consciousness and historical writing in early Islam stresses the importance as well as the multiple modes of legitimation. He uses the latter concept in a very broad sense, perhaps best understood as synonymous with self-definition and orientation in the context of the divergences and struggles that followed the first conquests. His four types of legitimation can then be equated with fundamental but to some extent alternative ways of articulating the relationships between ethnic, religious and imperial aspects of a new formation. Theocratic legitimation, in the loose sense of those in power ruling by God's will, and legitimation through piety – a particularly militant, all-embracing and at first apocalyptic style of piety – represented different and easily polarized positions. Historicizing legitimation, based on narratives about the past and especially about the beginnings of Islam, could be aligned with both sides; but in Donner's opinion, it changed the basically ahistorical outlook of earliest Islam and was in due course refined into a rich historiographical tradition. The religious content evident in all these forms of legitimation was also associated with the fourth one: genealogical legitimation had a long pre-Islamic history, but in this specific case it had to do with genealogical demarcation of the Arabic community, in its capacity as a privileged recipient of the revelation, as well as with dissensions and rivalries within its ranks, and problems arising in the latter respect converged with those of historicizing legitimation.

In regard to Hodgson's line of argument, this analysis lends weight to the emphasis on religion as an autonomous factor. The various legitimizing or self-defining uses of a religious tradition in the making led to increased demand for specialized and authoritative knowledge in that field; an emerging religious elite of a new kind, with its own agenda, thus became an active participant in the conflicts that shaped the course of Islamic history for a long time to come. The result was, as Hodgson sees it, that an "Islamic religion in the full sense, as a comprehensive aspect of human culture, began to take form" (ibid., 1: 249). The Islamic opposition contains the germs of later differentiation, but it would be misleading to describe its beginnings in sectarian terms. In an earlier publication, Hodgson (1955) had argued – and it now seems to be generally accepted – that the sectarian turn of the Shia took place later than historians had tended to assume. The succession to Muhammad was disputed, and conflicts over that issue were transfigured into symbolic beginnings of later sectarian divisions, but such concerns were not yet paramount for the 7th-century protagonists. Only the Kharijis, who according to the traditional chronology broke with Ali in 657, can be seen as an early case of ideological opposition: they maintained the "uncompromising claims for egalitarian justice" (Hodgson 1974, 1: 216) that were much less important to the main contenders for the succession. At later stages, their militantly dissident stance – with minimal doctrinal elaboration – often merged with tribal resistance to state formation; they remained marginal to the history of Islamicate civilization. As for the struggle between Ali and his victorious Umayyad rivals, it became much more central to conflicting identities and interpretations within the Islamic universe of discourse, but Hodgson's view is that there were two trends at work. On the one hand, Ali was retrospectively de-marginalized and integrated into the idealized picture of early Islamic leadership that was adopted by the mainstream; on the other hand, he and his descendants were re-imagined by the sectarian Shia – in increasingly divergent ways – and canonized as embodiments of ideas of later origin.

The 'Islamic opposition' that – as Hodgson sees it – emerged in tandem with caliphal absolutism was still at the very beginning of a long history of conflicts and compromises between orthodoxies and heterodoxies. But it already signalled a new twist to the relationship between religion and politics, and more precisely between religious authority and imperial power. There was no clear-cut division of spheres: the aspirants to absolutist rule could no more dispense with the legitimizing resources of a triumphant religion than the interpreters of a totalizing religious vision could ignore the problems of political life. The new constellation was, in other words, marked by more problematic relations between mutually dependent forces. This view of the transition to the classical phase is central to Hodgson's understanding of Islamicate civilization, and some key implications should therefore be noted. Most obviously, Hodgson's argument runs counter to the entrenched idea – convincingly criticized by many scholars, but still not quite disposed of – that Islam as such excludes the differentiation of religion and politics that could more easily develop in some other cultural environments. His analysis also shows that differentiation was not only a matter of adapting to the conditions and legacies of older states conquered during the initial phase of rapid expansion. It is true that imperial administration of conquered territories with old traditions of statehood brought political imperatives and priorities to the fore in a particularly massive way; but the new situation exposed and exacerbated the tensions between religious and political goal-orientations that had remained latent during the brief episode of charismatic-prophetic rule over a small territory. At the same time, idealized memories of the earliest stage served to reinvigorate visions of a total unity of the two spheres. The outcome thus reflected a complex interaction between internal and external factors. Hodgson's account of it seems more adequate than G.E. Grunebaum's thesis, first formulated in a lecture on Islam and the medieval world delivered in 1945. Although this text deserves notice as one of the first cases of comparative reflection on the three civilizations succeeding the Roman Empire, there are good reasons to doubt the claim that the relation between temporal and spiritual power "was least troublesome in Islam, where the spiritual power was never formally organized, while the temporal remained satisfied with the role of a *defensor fidei* without arrogating the right of developing or even interpreting the body of religious doctrine" (Grunebaum 1969 [1946]: 2). Neither the recurrent sectarian challenges, nor the new problems posed as the dynamics of state formation and religious expansion diverged ever more markedly, are easy to fit into this picture.

The problematic relationship between the religious and political spheres was also crucial for further contacts with other civilizations. That aspect of Islamic history has often been explained in terms of a generalized cosmopolitan attitude. S.D. Goitein (1966: 64) stressed "the general receptivity of Islam which was due to its originally universalistic and eclectic character." This inherent openness is supposed to have facilitated extensive borrowing from other traditions and successful integration of their cultural products, and most notably the Islamic appropriation of the Greek heritage. The long-accepted image of Mecca as a cosmopolitan trading centre made such perspectives more plausible, but it has now been demolished, and as Goitein noted in more detailed comments, the 'general receptivity' was in practice very selective. Following Hodgson, it may be suggested that the problematic of interrelated but mutually unassimilable religious and political spheres determined the specific direction and limits of intercivilizational borrowing. Efforts to develop a more elaborate doctrinal framework for the prophetic message led to active interest in the intellectual resources of older traditions, and during the classical period this resulted in extensive appropriation of Greek philosophy, up to a point wher the most ambitious philosophical projects could aspire to alternative versions of basic religious premises. A later backlash imposed a much more restrictive pattern of relations between religion and philosophy, but considering the trajectory of Islamic thought as a whole, it now seems misleading to speak (as Grunebaum did) of an elimination of the Hellenic heritage: its later destinies are better described in terms of mutation and relocation. Henry Corbin's reconstruction of the continuing and active Neo-Platonic strain in later Iranian thought has done much to accredit the latter view.

On the political side, Fred M. Donner suggests in a recent paper that the Byzantine imperial vision, asserted with incomparable vigour by Justinian in the 6th century and reaffirmed through Heraclius's early 7th-century counteroffensive against Persia, should perhaps figure more prominently in the genealogy of Islam than has mostly been the case. "The idea of a distinctive religious message underpinning a God-guided kingdom that would – or should – embrace all mankind, and that was particularly hostile to paganism, was thus another part of the intellectual environment in which Muhammad and his Believers worked and acted" (Donner 2005: 517). But if there was a historical connection with the final Christian-imperial form of Greco-Roman civilization, it did not translate into historical interest in the background: Muslim notions of Greco-Roman history were notoriously vague, and the most distinctive aspects of Greco-Roman political experience were wholly ignored. On the other hand, the demands of court culture obviously counted for something in the work undertaken to preserve and continue Greek philosophy and science. The 9th – and 10th-century translation movement, sponsored by the caliphal authorities in Baghdad, may be seen as the most productive result of converging political and intellectual interests. In the long run, however, both statecraft and court culture were much more decisively shaped by reactivated Persian traditions (the legacy of an empire that had been taken over *in toto)* in the first phase of expansion), and in contrast to the Greek case, this long-drawn-out encounter with a conquered civilization led to the acceptance of Persian as another pre-eminent cultural language, albeit without the religious status reserved for Arabic.

Hodgson's account of the early classical constellation may also help to clarify another issue that remains central to debates on Islam's place in history: the question of cultural memory and the specific form it took in relation to Islamic origins. Western students of Islamicate civilization seem to have had trouble in reconciling the emphasis on cultural openness during the golden age with the closure and discontinuity evident in the internal view of Islamic origins. Goitein's statements on all-round receptivity, quoted above, sum up the background to his description of Islam between 850 and 1250 CE as an "intermediate civilization" (Goitein 1966: 54-70).[2] As we have seen, Hodgson also stressed the civilizational

---

2 Goitein's concluding formulation is worth quoting at length: the Islamic world between 850 and 1250 (his chronology is very different from Hodgson's) was "intermediate in *time* between Hellenism and Renaissance, intermediate in *character* between the largely secular culture of the later Roman period and the thoroughly clerical world of Medieval Europe, and intermediate in *space* between Europe and

synthesis brought about by the "Islamic infusion." But his historical narrative begins on a strong note of discontinuity: "The Islamicate was unique among the great civilizations of its time in failing to maintain the earlier lettered traditions of its region" (Hodgson 1974, 1: 103). In contrast to the survival of Greek, Latin, Sanskrit and classical Chinese in other regions, older languages of the Nile-to-Oxus region were (with the partial exception of Persian) supplanted by Arabic. This linguistic break was, for those who brought it about, only one aspect of a more fundamental rupture with the past, and that point of view has had a lasting influence on Western approaches. Donner's analysis of classical Islamic historiography concludes with reflections on its legacy inside and outside the Islamic world; he argues, in particular, that Western scholarship has "in large measure internalized certain aspects of the traditional Islamic view," especially "the notion of the rise of Islam as a profound break in human history," and that this view is "profoundly misleading, because it obscures (or tempts us to ignore) important continuities spanning the supposed 'divide' between the Islamic and pre-Islamic eras" (Donner 1998: 294). We might add that it also obscures the real discontinuities resulting from the dynamics of interaction between Islamic conquerors and their socio-cultural environment, rather than from a pristine and self-contained religious project. According to Donner, the critical turn in recent scholarship has not been strong enough to dislodge the unwitting traditionalism that still affects the organization and evaluation of research. And although he does not make the point, it could be argued that radical revisionism is a kind of inverted traditionalism. To suggest that evidence and memory were obliterated to the extent needed for the imposition of a whole fabricated past is, if anything, even more implausible than the vision of a mature Islam storming out of Arabia.

If the critique of traditionalism is an unfinished task, further reflection on the construction of the divide between Islamic and pre-Islamic times should be an integral part of it. And an explanation in terms of a single foundational and pre-programming factor would not seem convincing – it would amount to another restatement of the traditionalist premise. The background to early Islamic self-understanding should be seen as a concatenation of historical forces, processes and situations; a few aspects may be noted, but they are only the most salient parts of a complex and still puzzling picture. First and foremost, the notion of a definitive revelation, completing and superseding earlier ones while correcting the errors that had affected their transmission, was *ipso facto* conducive to devaluation of past traditions: the truth behind them had been restored in a more perfect state, and their outward forms were no longer of any positive interest. This conception

> Africa on the one hand and India and China on the other hand, thus forming, for the first time in history, a strong cultural link between all parts of the ancient world" (Goitein 1966: 59). This is obviously an attempt to grasp the discontinuity between the classical phase and later Islamic history, but the culture in question is only defined with reference to other epochs and regions, never in terms of its own logic.

of the revelation cannot be assumed as present from the very beginning. Scholarly opinions seem to have more or less converged on the view that it evolved in the course of Muhammad's prophetic mission and took more definitive shape as the confrontation with other religious communities continued on a larger scale after the early conquests. Nor did it predetermine the whole range of responses to pre-Islamic traditions. Rather, its influence became effective in conjunction with other factors. The shift to a less apocalyptic stance might at first sight appear to have mitigated its impact (the interpretation of earliest Islam as an apocalyptic vision, although not uncontroversial, is clearly more widely accepted than it once was). But conquest became a kind of substitute for the apocalypse, and the ahistorical model of a great divide could thus be maintained in a very different context. The 'sacred history' that served to make sense of the conquests also became an obligatory frame of reference for succession disputes and factional rivalries among the conquerors. As Donner argues, the cumulative impact of such problems eventually led to a more articulate historical consciousness. But he also shows that the resultant vision of history, and the historiography that grew out of it, were dominated by specific themes: those of prophecy, community, leadership and hegemony. This orientation was not likely to favour recognition or discovery of continuities across the divide. The subsequent construction of an empire and a civilizational framework for it was, as we have seen, accompanied and aided by a massive appropriation of intellectual resources, most importantly those of classical antiquity. But the self-defining emphasis on discontinuity was strong enough to maintain a clear-cut distinction between the properly Islamic branches of knowledge and those inherited from the alien world of the ancients. Even if it can be argued that philosophers of the classical period tacitly transcended this division, it remained a dominant cultural pattern; and although it did not block productive use of the classical past when other conditions were propitious, it could be activated in a more exclusivist vein when the broader historical environment changed. There was, moreover, another side to the exceptional effort put into translating Greek texts during the 9th and 10th centuries. Rémi Brague (1992: 85-92) makes a convincing point when he argues that the focus on translation was also a specific way of relating to the past and its legacy, drawing on it while putting it at a distance. And as a later turn of events was to show, this was a fragile relationship: the abrupt and complete end to translation from the Greek is no less striking than the sustained effort had been.

One more aspect of Hodgson's interpretation should be noted. A quasi-cyclical pattern seems to be built into the post-conquest relationship between religion and political power. That notion is anything but unfamiliar to students of Islamic history. Quite a few modern scholars have proposed more or less adapted versions of the cyclical model originally developed by Ibn Khaldun. Although Hodgson does not explicitly argue in such terms, cyclical outlines are clearly visible. It follows from his analysis of absolutism as an inherent tendency of agrarianate societies, reinforced when they are unified on an imperial scale, that the political dynamics of Islamic states will obey a logic of their own. At the same time, political power will remain vulnerable to interventionist challenges from the social and cultural forces that sustain an autonomous religious sphere. Too much is left of the totalizing religious vision for it to be safely neutralized. But to the extent that projects of religious revival become effective on the political level, they expose themselves to a new round of political alienation from their origins. The cycle may also be seen as a widening one. The transformations of political power – cumulation, fragmentation and internal rationalization – can release trends that attenuate the legitimizing links to religion; conversely, the autonomy of religious elites, interests and ideas can lead to further differentiation inside the religious sphere, not least through the divergent directions of law-minded and personal piety. Finally, it would not seem far-fetched to read Hodgson's model as more general than the Khaldunian one and its modern variants. The cycle that involves religious mobilization and political domination of tribal warriors would, on that view, be a particular case of the fundamental relationship between religion and politics.

Hodgson's analysis of the later history of Islamicate civilization is not explicitly guided by the model summarized above. It is, in my opinion, implicit in his analysis of the "development of political and cultural multiplicity" (Hodgson 1974, 2: 12) that characterizes the 'middle periods' (from the middle of the 10th century to the middle of the second millennium CE). Detailed reconstruction of that part of his narrative is beyond the scope of this paper. But to round off the argument, a few words should be said about political and cultural trends during the classical period, and about Hodgson's interpretation of their long-term consequences. A brief overview must begin with the forms and circumstances of the Islamic turn to absolutism: it specific features were reflected in social and cultural reactions, and the whole constellation set the course of later developments. Every account of this crucial period must focus on the respective roles of the two dynasties that established and consolidated absolutist rule, the Umayyads (or, as Hodgson prefers to call the branch in power from 692 onwards, the Marwanids) and the Abbasids.

As Hodgson sees it, the Marwanid caliphate was caught up in a whole series of inescapable dilemmas. It was from the very beginning widely perceived as a reversion to kingship of a pre-Islamic kind, notwithstanding official claims to Islamic legitimacy. Within the Arab power structure, it represented a shift towards more traditional elites, at the expense of the incipient Islamic aristocracy (the companions of the prophet); this relocation of power called for genealogical legitimation, but the traditional criteria were reinforced by a claim to kinship with the prophet. All these aspects of the Marwanid model exposed it to challenges from those who demanded a return to more genuine Islamic rulership, and their credentials were particularly strong when backed up by closer kinship links to the prophet. The Marwanids had risen to power through manipulation of factional (more or less artificially tribalized) alliances and rivalries among the Arab conquerors, and were by the same token vulnerable to ongoing fragmentation and realignment of the forces active in that field. Last but not least, the Syrian power basis of the dynasty was not only inconveniently located at the western margin of the imperial heartland; it was also – and perhaps more importantly – a conquered part of an empire whose centre remained invincible, whereas the whole domain of the Sasanian Empire had been overrun and expansion had even continued beyond its borders. The continuing conflict with the Byzantine Empire, charged with religious significance, was scaled down after the failed siege of Constantinople in 717, but it distracted attention and drained resources; it does not seem to have obstructed learning from the much older imperial tradition of the adversary, but it certainly constrained the overall strategy of the rulers in Damascus. In short, the Marwanid version of absolutism was ideologically, institutionally and geopolitically handicapped; Hodgson portrays it as a balancing act, bound to come unstuck sooner rather than later. This also explains why he does not – in contrast to many other Western historians – refer to an Abbasid revolution. From his point of view, the Abbasid seizure of power in 750 should rather be seen as a step towards a more normal and consistent form of absolutism, and the founders of the new dynasty "were completing the work" (ibid., 1: 284) begun by the Marwanids, "the reconstitution of the state in terms of the long-standing absolutist civic ideals of the region" (ibid., 1: 283).[3] The Abbasid mode of reconstitution entailed a more equal distribution of power and status, both between regions and between the now more ethnically diverse members of the Islamic community. But on this basis they built a superstructure much closer to Persian models of absolute monarchy than the Marwanid state had ever been.

If the 'Abbasid revolution' is a misnomer for a rationalizing and equilibrating twist to an older project, it becomes equally impossible to speak of a betrayal of the revolution. After 750, such accusations came from the more radical Islamic opposition, and they have sometimes found a sympathetic echo in Western scholarship. Hodgson prefers to describe the outcome as an "Abbasid compromise" (ibid., 1: 272) A compromise was already built into the alliance between dynastic pretenders and piety-minded activists that overthrew the Umayyads, but it was worked out in greater detail after the consolidation of Abbasid rule. It may be seen as a mediating framework or a *modus vivendi* imposed on the problematic relationship between religion and politics, outlined above, and in that capacity, it had – as Hodgson argues – a lasting civilizational impact. Three aspects of the institutionalized compromise (as distinct from the initial strategic one) should be noted.

On the political side, the Abbasid settlement enabled first a half-century of

---

3   There is some affinity between Hodgson's argument and Grunebaum's stronger claim that the Abbasids engineered a transition from patrimonial to rational statehood (Grunebaum 1961 [1955]: 16).

vigorous absolutist rule, and then a long-drawn-out process of devolution and fragmentation, very different from the explosive crisis that toppled the Umayyads. The absolutist states of agrarianate civilizations, however rooted in unchanging conditions of social life, were always prone to disintegration, or at least loss of central control, and in imperial states, such processes unfolded on a correspondingly enlarged scale. Hodgson describes the Abbasid pattern of decline as a "dissipation of the absolutist tradition" (ibid., 1: 473) and dates it from 813 (the end of the fourth *fitna* that left al-Mamun in sole control of the caliphate) to 945. Political fragmentation during this period was largely due to bids for power by provincial elites, often without formal rejection of caliphal authority; but in the context of overall devolution, sectarian projects of state-building could also play a certain role. The dissipating process thus produced new models of political power, adapted to local conditions as well as to lower levels of religious legitimacy, and capable of further diffusion throughout an expanding Islamic world. On the religious side, the Abbasids "were willing to accord formal and exclusive status to the representatives of the former Piety-minded opposition" (ibid., 1: 275). In other words, they recognized the autonomy of a relatively large and loosely structured religious elite, barred it from direct intervention in affairs of state but did not obstruct the development of vast doctrinal and legal programmes that translated into mechanisms of comprehensive social control. Apart from a brief early 9th-century attempt (under al-Mamun) to reclaim religious authority for the caliph, this new pattern of relations between the two spheres was left undisturbed and took definitive shape during the 9th and 10th centuries. The ulama as the defining socio-cultural protagonists of Islamicate civilization, the elaboration of Islamic law as later periods were to know it, and the formation of the dominant schools of jurisprudence: these were the key components of a model that could be superimposed on a wide variety of local cultures during the later phases of decentralized expansion.

Hodgson's line of argument is less conclusive when it comes to a third aspect of the Abbasid settlement, but the general thrust of his reflections is reasonably clear: the institutional framework put in place after 750 enabled a certain development of alternative currents within Islamicate civilization, but contained them in such a way that their capacity to affect long-term developmental trends remained strictly limited. Philosophical speculation, often converging with the more speculative kind of Islamic theology, was an important part of intellectual life during the classical period. Several factors seem to have favoured its growth. The interpretive and reflective work undertaken within the now more securely available socio-cultural space was not confined to the boundaries of a clearly demarcated tradition – the demarcating criteria were yet to be defined. Earlier traditions that had developed philosophy as a mode of thought and a way of life were strong enough to provide themes and models for further elaboration within a still flexible Islamic context. The prosperous, mobile and culturally receptive society of the early Abbasid period offered various ways of linking philosophical reflection to more professional activities. For all that, both philosophy and the more rationalistic versions of theology were at a disadvantage when pitted against the currents which Hodgson describes as piety-minded': the latter were both more effectively involved in the regulation of social life and more closely linked to the reconstitution of popular religiosity within a new doctrinal and institutional framework. Similarly, the cosmopolitan court culture (*adab* culture, as Hodgson calls it), most highly developed at the centre of the Abbasid empire, was dependent on a basis more adversely affected by the dissipation of the absolutist tradition' than was the nexus of piety and social order. Court society fostered literary culture and ideals of all-round cultivation, but did not produce a civilizational counterweight to the patterns that coalesced around *hadith,* sacred law and Quranic piety. On this point, Hodgson's conclusions are more negative than those of some other historians; for example, Ira Lapidus (2002 [1988]: 99) refers to "two principal versions of Islamic civilization, the courtly cosmopolitan and the urban religious," and argues that they "represented the political and religious elites thrown up by the Arab conquests."

Hodgson devotes whole chapters to speculative thought and literary culture. By contrast, he has much less to say on a third alternative current that for a while posed a much more overt challenge to mainstream Islam: the Ismaili movement of the 9th and 10th centuries. The most extensive discussion of Ismailism is to be found in the chapter on personal piety (Hodgson 1974, 1: 378-384), where it is described as the esoteric faith of an elite and a refuge for spiritual interests unsatisfied by other answers; its role in the 9th-century political restructuring of the Islamic world is only briefly mentioned. The civilizational dimension of Ismaili heterodoxy is not given its due. This shortcoming of Hodgson's analysis is obviously not unrelated to the general state of research at the time. The question will be revisited in another contribution to this volume.[4] To sum up, the 'classical civilization of the High Caliphate' left a legacy that set its stamp on developments during the 'middle periods.' In particular, Hodgson underlines the distinction between two kinds of trends and patterns: those that developed in ways conducive to further expansion and maintenance of civilizational unity across cultural and political borders, and those more closely bound up with transient conditions and therefore much less transferable – although not *ipso facto* irrelevant – to a different historical context. This is not to suggest that the whole course of Islamic history was predetermined by classical paradigms. Internal factors became effective in conjunction with external ones, and more specifically with massive changes to the global setting of Islamicate civilization. Hodgson notes two major

---

4 Hodgson has more to say on Ismailism elsewhere, especially in his contribution to the *Cambridge History of Iran* (Hodgson 1968; this goes beyond earlier work on the 'order of Assassins.') But the discussion of Iranian Ismailism underlines the paradox that the ideological impact of the movement was more visible within an enclave (and a fragmented one at that) than inthe counter-caliphate of Fatimid Egypt.

shifts of that kind during the early second millennium, although he does not fully spell out the implications. On the one hand, socio-economic, political and cultural transformations in East Asia and Western Europe – unmatched by anything comparable in the Islamic world – brought these two parts of the Eurasian macro-region to new levels of development and of interaction with other civilizations. Neither of these two regional mutations amounted to a global reversal of fortunes for Islamicate civilization, and although one of them did in the long run lead to such consequences, that had less to do with direct confrontation during the middle period than with subsequent outflanking. Western expansion triumphed through the construction of overseas empires, in contrast to the Eurasian arena of Islamic expansion. On the other hand (and, in the short run, much more importantly), the early second millennium saw momentous changes to the balance of power between the main agrarianate civilizations and the largely nomadic Inner Eurasian zone. The Islamic world was directly and massively affected, but the two main waves of Inner Eurasian expansion did not enter Islamic history in the same way. The Turks came as converts and participants in an ongoing process of political fragmentation and restructuring, the Mongols as pagan conquerors who caused widespread destruction before the power structures which they had imposed were assimilated and used to launch a new phase of empire building. It was the upshot of these successive encounters with inner Eurasia that determined the shape and position of Islamicate civilization at the time of global transition to modernity. But the present discussion cannot go beyond a brief acknowledgement of these interrelations between civilizational dynamics and global history.

References

Brague, Rémi (1992) *Europe: la voie romaine*. Paris: Gallimard.
Crone, Patricia (1987) *Meccan Trade and the Rise of Islam*. Princeton: Princeton University Press.
Crone, Patricia and Cook, Michael (1977) *Hagarism. The Making of the Islamic World*. Cambridge: Cambridge University Press.
Décobert, Christian (1991) *Le mendiant et le combatant: L'institution de l'Islam*. Paris: Seuil.
Donner, Fred McGraw (1981) *The Early Islamic Conquests*. Princeton: Princeton University Press.
Donner, Fred McGraw (1998) *Narratives of Islamic Origins. The Beginnings of Islamic Historical Writing*. Princeton: Darwin Press.
Donner, Fred McGraw (2005) "The background to Islam," in Michael Maas (ed.), *The Cambridge Companion to the Age of Justinian*, Cambridge: Cambridge University Press, pp. 510-533.
Fowden, Garth (1993) *Empire to Commonwealth. Consequences of Monotheism in Late Antiquity*. Princeton: Princeton University Press.

Goitein, S.D. (1966) *Studies in Islamic History and Institutions.* Leiden: E.J. Brill.

Grunebaum, Gustave E. von (1969 [1946]) *Medieval Islam. A Study in Cultural Orientation.* Chicago: University of Chicago Press.

Grunebaum, Gustave E. von (1961[1955] *Islam. Essays in the Nature and Growth of a Cultural Tradition.* London: Routledge and Kegan Paul.

Hodgson, Marshall G.S. (1955) "How did the early Shî'a become sectarian?," *Journal of the American Oriental Society* 75, pp. 1-13.

Hodgson, Marshall G.S. (1968) "The Isma'ili state," in *The Cambridge History of Iran,* Vol. 5., Cambridge: Cambridge University Press. pp. 422-482.

Hodgson, Marshall G.S. (1974) *The Venture of Islam. Conscience and History in a World Civilization,* v. 1-3. Chicago: University of Chicago Press.

Hodgson, Marshall G.S. (1993) *Rethinking World History. Essays on Europe, Islam and World History.* Cambridge: Cambridge University Press.

Lapidus, Ira (2002 [1988]) *A History of Islamic Societies.* Cambridge: Cambridge University Press.

Wansbrough, John (1977) *Quranic Studies. Sources and Methods of Scriptural Interpretation.* Oxford: Oxford University Press.

Wansbrough, John (1978) *The Sectarian Milieu: Content and Composition of Islamic Salvation History.* Oxford: Oxford University Press.

Chapter 2

The Middle Period: Islamic Axiality in the Age of Afro-Eurasian Transcultural Hybridity

BABAK RAHIMI

> [...] taking a global perspective does not imply that the world has always been an interconnected one with a single center from which development and progress spread to less-developed regions. Instead, it makes much more sense to think of the world in 1400 as having been composed of several regional systems, or in other words to have been "polycentric" each with densely populated and industrially advanced cores supplied from their own peripheries.
> Robert B. Marks, *The Origins of the Modern World* (Marks 2002: 15)

In his seminal article "the Interrelations of Societies in History," published in 1963, Marshal Hodgson registered a ground-breaking argument against the Eurocentric conception of the past, which traced history in terms of an unfolding development from Mesopotamia and Egypt to Greece and Rome, and finally to the Christian of northwestern Europe, where the medieval life paved the path to modernity (Burke III, 1993: 3-34). In it, he posited the claim that from a global historical perspective the development of civilization is an Asian-based phenomenon, and that it played a crucial role in the rise of the modern world. He also argued that the history of the intersecting stretches of agrarian urbanite societies, which extended across the entire Afro-Eurasian complex – what he called, following Toynbee, the Oikoumene – , was an interrelational one with persistent and interconnecting traditions, from which interaction between these traditions radiated incessantly into wide regions.

According to Hodgson, an understanding of history in interrelational hemispheric terms would allow us to overcome a "classic ethnocentric dichotomy in the main part of the world-ourselves and the others, Jews and Gentiles, Greeks and Barbarians, "West" and "East" (Burke III 1993: 7). In a sense, the history of societies, understood in interrelational terms, acknowledges a mobile and an interactive sphere of cross-regional complex, wherein cultures have continuously depended on the course of development of the Afro-Eurasian civilizational complex as a whole.

If we accept, following Hodgson, the notion of interconnection of societies in history, it is reasonable to claim that the period from the $9^{th}/10^{th}$ centuries to the $13^{th}/14^{th}$ century marks a crucial phase in an increase of global interconnection and integration, involving socio-cultural crystallization of historical significance. Through communication, trade, travel, war and nomadic formations – including, not least, the histories of migration – in the context of rural and urban relations, this period encompasses a set of deep-seated transformations across Afro-Eurasian landmass. Manifested in different forms and yet appearing with an intense degree of mobility and mobilization, fusion and integration, such era of increasingly civilizational intermingling marked a transcultural age of hybridity.[1]

The term "transcultural" refers here to the liminal complexes that signify an intricate set of interdependent and cross-fertilizing constant historical processes in the production of spaces of exchange and negotiation, encounter and communication, travel and migration.[2] The history of transcultural dynamics is an account of global interaction between nomadic rootlessness and urban sedentary complexes, maritime expedition tied to land-based socio-cultural patterns of commercial urbanity and development of cited civilizations. In particular, the term "hybridity" underscores an ongoing historical process of constant fusion between social complexes in such that encounters between different civilizations through the process of cultural encounter leads to processes of identity formation and new ways of communication. As result, such process constitutes the incorporatation of different (already hybridized) structures of consciousness.[3]

---

[1] My claim here is akin to Björn Wittrock's idea of "Ecumenical Renaissance." See Wittrock (2001). However, Wittrock's use of the term "Ecumenical Renaissance" automatically elicits comparison with an earlier ecumenical period, failing to identify the unique significance of this historical epoch. My use of the term "transcultural age of hybridity," however, is more akin to Armando Salvatore's argument that encounter between the Islamic traditions and modernity has constituted of what he refers as "a transcultural Euro-Mediterranean space." See Armando Salvatore (2001).

[2] I borrow the term "transcultural" from A. Höfert and A. Salvatore's (2000) provocative argument that historical flows of people between Europe and the Middle East, inclusive of the elites and masses, have constructed "transcultural" processes in which identity-alterity structures increasingly become dependent on in-between, liminal situations. The notion, they argue, "demonstrates the potential to alter the demarcating boundaries, not only in the sense of displacing them, but also through recomposing markers of identity and alterity in a way that makes it impossible, and even irrelevant, to trace back the original root of a certain identity" (Höfert/Salvatore 2000: 17).

[3] This assertion may also be articulated as the intensification of worldwide social relations in terms of global mélange, pervading from the center to peripheries. With respect to dynamics of culture, hybridization can also be defined as the way in which civilizations become differentiated from existing practices, fuse and remerge

In this view, the age of transcultural hybridity did not mark a sudden or radical redrawing of the outlines of the Afro-Eurasian landmass. Rather, it inaugurated a period in the escalation of shifts in civilizational dynamics towards hemispheric integration, fusion and cross-fertilization that brought about an impressive degree of intense creativity and exceptional broadening of cultural horizons. Increase of contact between societies led to the proliferation of myriad forms of public spaces, social organizations, institutions and new political orders. Yet the upshot of such transcultural interactive zone was determined by conflict, rivalry, exchange, encounter and chronic collision between competing forms of political orders that, in turn, led the way to complex hybridization processes of intercivilizational significance.

The particular case of the Islamic world in the Middle Period (945-1503) serves as an example of such hybridization historical process: an era marked by distinct political fragmentation, cultural cross-fertilization and vernacularization of intercivilizational significance. In the following discussion my primary concern will be to draw a general outline of the global interconnective patterns in the emergence of a transcultural hybrid civilizational complex in the Eurasian landmass from $9^{th}/10^{th}$ to the $13^{th}/14^{th}$ centuries. I will then focus on the Islamic world from the 10th to the 14th centuries and discuss the revolutionary significance in the emergence of new Islamic civilizational complexes with the successive waves of Turkish tribal migration from the steppe grass lands of Central Asia to the settled regions of the Anatolian-Mediterranean and Irano-Mesoptemian plateaus.

While elaborating on certain interconnected patterns of global history, without presuming linearity of historical development or ubiquitousness of cultural hybridities, my argument will evolve around the notion of intermingling of cultures, involving momentous shifts along dimensions of reflexivity and modes of communication. The notion of the "Middle Period Islamic Axiality" denotes, then, a crucial civilizational rupture in Islamic history from 10th to the $13^{th}/14^{th}$ centuries which generated new forms of reflexivity, new world views and imaginative ways in articulating self, knowledge and reality, based on the notion of transcendence. As a result of such civilizational encounters, this age identifies the production of new cultural sites situated in increasing processes of global mélange.

The Afro-Eurasian complex: from $9^{th}/10^{th}$ to 13th centuries

When in 1137-38 Ramisht, a rich Muslim merchant on his way to Mecca, visited his hometown of Sirâf, the bustling Iranian port-city on the Persian Gulf repre-

> with new forms in new practices. Culture, in its hybrid form, is therefore not a coherent system but a process that is generated, maintained and transmitted into new forms in constant process of formation (Hannerz 1987).

sented a cosmopolitan commercial center with a thriving trading basis for merchants to trade directly with China and east Africa (Stern 1967: 10). The port city of Sirâf was matched by an abiding ability for commerce to cities, bustling commercial centers, and maritime urbanities like Aden, Alexandria, Baghdad, Cairo, Constantinople, Guangzhou, Kiev, Quanzhou, Suhâr and Venice, wherein long-distance trade was prevalent to help shape myriad zones of economic exchange and cultural encounter.

Muslim merchants of the 12th and 13th centuries, along with Chinese, Indian and east/north African merchants, in part, unleashed a global system of commerce that signaled the increasing integration of the world into common yet diverse commercial networks of production and exchange. Whereas links with the Mediterranean lands remained sporadic prior to the late 9th century, the centuries that followed the Arab conquest of northern Africa and Iran-Mesopotamia regions saw a quickening of contacts within the Afro-Eurasian zone of cultivation and urban life. Prior to the "rise" of the West to preeminence in the 16th century, by the turn of the first millennium a system of commerce and cultural interaction emerged that reached its apogee toward the end of the 13th century (Abu-Lughod 1989). First, based in Song China, the 11th century witnessed the appearance of a "world economy" with ramifications on a transregional scale. Likewise, the years between *circa* 1250 and 1350 saw a period of expanding international commerce in the regions between China and northwestern Europe, entailing economic growth and cultural developments in the newly integrated areas.

The increase of trade drew Japan, Southeast Asia and Middle East closer together, while a rise in the use of camel caravans led to an expansion of communication with sub-Saharan Africa (Bentley 1998). In the Asian subcontinent, for instance, an extensive commerce reached southern India by land, and mostly around the coastal maritime routes, from Coromandel shores north to the Ganges Delta, to Burma, Vietnam and beyond. Divided in diverse zones of transactions, mainly defined by language and religion, and dominated by imperial and core urban settings, as well as hinterland-less commercial enclaves, interaction between cities became possible by sealanes, rivers and caravan routes. Ports, like Sirâf, and river-based cities, like Baghdad and Cairo, served the important function of bringing goods and people from long distances, enhancing mobility and interaction.

Moreover, along with developments of maritime and land trade, an increase of travel, migration, campaigns of imperial expansion, crossregional religious war (Crusades) and conversion inaugurated an age of long-distance mobility and transportation, as well as large-scale subordination and conquest. Though the expansion of Europe into northeast Germany was a continuous movement that originated with the campaigns of Charlemagne, the 11th century marked the religious conversion and political colonization of the Baltic European settlement to the northwestern and northeastern Europe. From the 1066 Norman conquest of England by Duke William of Normandy to the Spanish campaigns of the Christian knights, from the expedition of the Scandinavian navigators into the northern seas to the Latinization of Hungarians and eastern Europe, the growth of Europe, especially, in the 12th century identified an age of intense interconnection between Germanic, Slavic and Latin Mediterranean-based cultures. "The birth of Europe as a Eurasian phenomenon," in this fashion, brought about an integrated Europe made up of northwestern France, Flanders, lowland England, Spain, northern and southern Italy (Moore 1997). While travel provided the new integrated-hybrid civilization of Europe with the incentive of economic adventure, especially, in the 13th century (Marco Polo), proliferation in European travel writings reflected the increasing importance of movement across homeland as a prelude to further conquest of the new territories.

China experienced similar processes of integration under the Song dynasty (960-1279), as elite culture grew more uniform and political systems became more unified with the continue growth of the imperial urbanite civilization through military-building and interational trade (Haegar 1976). The expansion of the examination system, and the growth of bureaucracy saw the concentration of power in the hand of the emperor – a process that accelerated in later dynasties. Yet the remarkable growth of commercialization and industralization (Hobson 2004: 51) under the Song dynasty opened up the Chinese society to flow of goods, movements of persons, cultures and ideas across Eurasia.

Similarly, in western Asia, in the 10th century the Byzantine-Russian complex ceased being on the defensive and began to aggressively advance its borders east and westwards at the expense of Bulgars, increasingly heading towards greater cultural integration through contact with neighborhing civilizations. Through land and, most important of all, maritime routes that reached Constantinople, the Byzantime-Russian civilization grew closer to the Islamic and Latin Christian cultures.

When in 1279 the Mongols, under the leadership of Genghis Khan's grandson, Kubla Khan, defeated the last outposts of resistance in Song China, the newly established nomadic empire signaled the emergence of a huge imperial network in the Eurasian landmass. This further connected the Islamic world with Southeast Asian societies, a historical process that eventually led to the Islamization of south Asian regions – like the case of Indonesia in the 16th century. Accordingly, in Central and Western Asia before the end of the 13th century most of the khans had become Muslim, and hence initiated a process of blending Central Asian shamanistic religions and Tibetan form of Buddhism with Islamic practices. Although the Mongol conquest of China and Islamdom did not amount to any serious interruptions in the Chinese and Islamic civilization, since it remained essentially a military occupation, the Steppe nomad warriors creatively adapted to the traditional Chinese and Abbâsid administrative systems.[4] This

---

4   Later in the 14th century, when the Mongols showed signs of weakening, the emperor reintroduced the examination system and accommodated Chinese participation in bureaucratic positions.

nomadic imperial process of adaptation is crucial to the transcultural period since it marked a historical event which, according to the W. Barthold, ushered in a turning point in the construction of a creative synthesis between Chinese and Islamic political orders (Barthold 1928).

The rise of nomadic empires in this manner played an important role in the age of transregional integration. This is so since nomadic imperial orders placed high value on trade and diplomacy, which ultimately resulted in, according to Janet Abu-Lughod, an "explosion" that effectively paved the path to "world history" (Abu-Lughod 1989: 154). As Bentley has argued, in the half-millennium from 1000 to 1500 large imperial states, like the Mongols, continued to promote transregional interaction, embarking both on a remarkable set of empire-building processes that expanded from the seas of China to the River Nile (Bentley 1998: 244-45). By linking China with the outside world, mainly through trade networks in Central Asia, the impact of the Mongol conquest facilitated communication over long distances, as nomadic political orders encouraged the spread of religions, the acquisition of knowledge and technological exchanges across inner, eastern and western Asia. In addition, with the centralization of the Mongol state from tributary to sedentary systems of taxation, diverse sectors of economy, namely, agricultural, commercial and pastoral, grew closer together with the advancements in the size of the military and the centralization of administrative control over both sedentary and rural regions. As Di Cosmo explains, "So called steppe empires created fluid environments, suitable for travel and trade that allowed the peripheral civilizations to come into contact with one another" (Di Cosmo 1999: 4). Nomadic conquests identified a major epoch in the greater interrelation of societies not only in Eurasian terms, but also on the rural-urban and nomadic-sedentary scales.

As an outcome of trade, migration, conversion and conquest, such global transformations also involved major breakthroughs of civilizational importance. Similar to the original Axial age civilizational transformation in human reflexivity (roughly from the eighth to the $4^{th}/3^{rd}$ century B.C.E.), the $9^{th}/10^{th}$ to the 13th centuries displayed a momentous shift in reflexive consciousness on an Afro-Eurasian scale.[5] The transcultural age identifies, in a sense, an extension of the original Axial transformation on fundamental basis of human reflexivity and historicity "to reflect upon and give expression to an image of the world as having the potential of being different from what it was perceived to be here and now" (Wittrock 2001: 8). This mode of reflexity and communication ultimately entailed a new way of conceptualizing and articulating the self and reality in terms

---

5   By Axial age civilizations, Eisenstadt explains, "we mean those civilizations that crystallized during the half-millennium from 500 BCE to the first century of the Christian era, within which new types of ontological visions, conceptions of a basic tension between the transcendental and mundane orders emerged and were institutionalized in many parts of the world" (Eisenstadt 2000: 2).

that go beyond the everyday mundane realities. With the increasing hybridization of consciousness (i.e. ways of reflexivity and modes of communication) through contact, exchange and conversion the period, then, saw the emergence of distinct of cultures, ethos and historical consciousness that intensified creative attempts to fuse the gap and, accordingly, overcome the tension between transcendental and mundane realities with the construction and regulation of social interaction.

In the 11th and 12th centuries the gradual appearance of new civilizational complexes in northwestern Europe, in what had previously been a marginal region of the Mediterranean-based civilizations, and the expansion of Italian maritime cities inaugurated a revolutionary development of tighter organization of the church, state and urbanization. The so-called feudal, urban, papal and intellectual revolutions manifested deep-seated changes in economic, political and religious institutions that, consequently, entailed cultural shifts of societal epistemic importance. With the rise of universities, for instance, the intellectual revolution not only introduced education to laymen, but also facilitated the acquisition of Greek knowledge through the intellectual advances made by the Muslims.

In close connection to the urban revolution and the triumph of papal monarchy between 1050 and 1300, the growth of "popular culture," sectarian and monastic orders (like the spread of the Cistercian movement in the 12th century), ushered in an age of carnivalesque practices and mystical movements, which ultimately culminated in the attempt to fuse the mundane and transcendental worlds within mass-popular and church-autonomous fields of social interaction. Although, as Moore argues, the "revolutionary" characteristics of the period between the 9th and 12th centuries were profoundly political in nature, the European experience of the transcultural age entailed transformations that went beyond state-organizational and class structural levels (Moore 2000). In this regard, the proliferation of pluralistic institutions – Church, nobility, city-state, and guilds – led to the formation of cultural spaces that increasingly separated the official from the non-official spheres of publicity.

In the Indic world, until the late 10th century Hindu rajas controlled Afghanistan and parts of eastern Persia to the upper Indus, while Gujerat maritime power limited the colonization of Islam from the sea along Indian Ocean shores. But when in the beginning of the 11th century northern India saw the southward invasion of the Gazna Turks, who owed allegiance to the Sâmânî rulers of Khurâsân, the Indic world began to undergo centuries of civilizational fusion. The 10th to the 12th centuries in this manner marked a crucial phase in the Southeast Asian civilizations, a period that involved a transition from pan-Indic to three interactive civilizations of Hinduism, Indo-Islam and Theravada Buddhism (Krejcí 1990). The transition involved cultural and vernacularization transformation, "a process of change by which the universalistic orders, formations, and practices of the preceding millennium were supplemented and gradually replaced by localized forms" (Eisenstadt/Schluchter/Wittrock 2001: 41). This process of vernacularization not only created new localities of distinct vernacular cultures, but also saw an unprecedented growth of textual production that was unique in its "combination of antiquity, continuity, and multicultural interaction."[6] Central to this Indic case of civilizational interaction was primarily the exchange of Islamic and Hindu vernacular cultures that generated implicit dogmatic and ritualistic intermingling, to which the eventual emergence of the Sikhism in the 15th century would best represent this hybrid historical process.

As for China, the Neo-Confucian movement ushered the reaffirmation of the virtues and the continuity of the Confucian tradition, with its canocial system of belief, in the context of dynamic processes of the centralization under the Song dynasty. Central to the movement was the pursuit of the ideals of sainthood and self-cultivation, a spiritual quest that entailed the overcoming of selfishness and the enchantment of noble virutues inherent to human beings. Moreover, the synthesis of Buddhist dogma (and Daoist metaphyics) with Confucian philosophy created a new body of thought that underscored the creativly paradoxical process of preservation of tradition through the transformation of tradition.[7]

In the puzzling case of Japan, where the country enjoyed the natural protection of its insular position from foreign nomadic incursions, the samurai class, the landed lord and warriors, began to develop a distinct form of "honorific culture" in the 11th and 12th centuries (Ikegami 1995: 72-8). During this period, the samurai's military pride generated the construction of a community of honor, which set up the tradition of honorific individualism of self-discipline to produce a new consciousness on both individual and collective dimensions. As a consequence to the formation of samurai elite collectivity as a formidable ruling class, the emergence of a samurai honorific culture ushered the establishment of Shogunate political order that lasted for the next six and one-half centuries (1192-1867). Japan represents a distinct yet complicated case for the age of transcultural hybridity. As a non-Axial civilization, set apart from the Axial ones (mainly China, India and the Middle East), the dynamics of the Japanense culture was tied to the transformation of the samurai elite and its honorific culture, which effected state-building processes from the medieval to the early modern periods.

Perhaps in its most dynamic center of transcultural age, the Mediterranean

---

6   As Pollock explains, the expansion of literary and political textual production, which "began in South India, Sri Lanka, and Java around 900 and reached maturity by 1200 occurred in northern India at a somewhat later date under conditions of political change different from what obtained in the south" Eisenstadt, Schluchter and Wittrock, 2000: 45-53). Similarly in China, this process of literary production saw its apogee under the reign of Song rule, during which the development of literary vernacular culture marked one of the high point in the history of Chinese literature. Also consider the case of Southeast Asian regions, like Vietnam, that, starting in the 1300s produced similar developments in the production of literary texts.
7   Consider, for instance, the case of Zhu Xi. His attempt to synthesize Buddhism and Confucian philosophy highlights interesting similiarties to Aquinas' fusion of Christian theology with Greek philosophy.

complex emerged to represent networks of commercial exchange, marking a cornerstone of the intercivilizational hybridity. Inseparable from the European agricultural revolution with the emancipation of the serfs, which resulted in the growth of trade and the burgeoning of towns, the budding Mediterranean urbanite civilizations provided an alternative seaborne route of conquest, pilgrimage and trade to traditional land-based means of transportation. Especially through trade and warfare, the region included a heightening of long-term structural conflict between vying local powers and complex exchanges of culture and religion.

This proliferation of encounter was twofold. First, with the growth of cities-states of Genoa, Pisa, and Venice, and the spread of trade, Christianity saw an increase of contact with Islamdom in northern African and eastern Mediterranean coastlines (Ashtar 1983: 3-63). The availability of traversing sea routes not only provided a new route for import of "Oriental" artifacts, but it also served to facilitate the existence of shared taste in architecture and cultural practices, vocabularies, meanings and interests that cut across localities.[8] Second, the pan-European expansionist Crusades, which originally began in France in 1095 and saw its most decisive defeat with the conquest of Acre by the Mamlûks in 1291, opened western Europe to the Islamic world by bringing the Iberian Peninsula, the Muslim north Africa and eastern Mediterranean shores closer together.[9] War and conquest in this fashion brought about commercial activities in such that not only supplied war and colonization materials to the warring regions, but also allowed the western Christian forces to take an active part in the importation of ideas, texts and cultural materials from the Moslem Levant to northern and southern Europe.[10]

At the heart of this Levantine interrelation between South European, North African and Mesopotamian regions was the greater fusion of Christian and Islamic civilizations, as symbols, rituals and popular expectations of imminent transformation, in the form of millenarian cultures, spread throughout the region in unprecedented ways. The consequence of this process of exchange by the turn of the 15th and 16th centuries, as has been noted by Cornell Fleischer, was the in-

---

8   Consider, for instance, the case of Venice. The Arabic influence on Venetian architecture, which in part was heavily influenced by Byzantium, is a powerful reminder of the interregional complex of the Mediterranean realm (Howard 2000: 2-5).
9   The first Crusade started in Clermont with the speech of Pope Urban II in 1095, which called for the conquest of Jerusalem.
10 As a result of the crusades, certain Muslim customs spread into late medieval Western Europe. Dress codes and general taste were imported from the Muslim world (mainly Muslim Spain, Baghdad, Cairo and Damascus) to the northern shores of eastern Mediterranean cities. But the momentum of exchange primarily involved ideas, philosophies and "oriental romance" from "Byzantium, Georgia, Armenia and Arabia/Persia" (Cardini 2001: 84). The first translations from Arabic texts into Latin, for instance, were completed around 1150 in Spain. As Cardini notes, this "was to change the face of Western learning" (Cardini 2001: 84).

terconnection of the northern and southern Mediterranean shores, sharing certain cultural traditions that mainly included common traits of millenarian expectation.[11] In extension, as has been argued in a seminal article by Sanjay Subrahmanyam, the 1500s saw the crystallization of pan-civilizational exchange of millenarian symbols, myths and traditions that helped to develop imperial projects from the Middle East to Southeast Asia (Subrahmanyam 1997: 735-62). In the first-half of the millennium, the Mediterranean domain provided a creative setting for the intermingling of cultures, involving momentous shifts along dimensions of reflexivity in terms of apocalyptic attempts to redefine the relationship between the mundane and transcendental worlds.

The notion of "connected history," coined by Subrahmanyam, invites us to consider the circulation of ideas, myths and rituals, in which cultures relentlessly maintain close proximity in hybrid spaces, wherein identity and alterity vie for power with unyielding intensity. Respective to the broader intercivilizational historical perspective from the $9^{th}/10^{th}$ to the $13^{th}/14^{th}$ centuries, the intracivilizational Islamic experience in the transcultural age of interconnected histories was mainly manifested with the emergence of the Turko-Persian Islamicate cultures, a point that I will expand upon in the following section.

The Turko-Persian ecumene and the rise of sûfî-brotherhoods

When non-Arabs became the rulers and obtained royal authority and control over the whole Muslim realm, the Arabic language suffered corruption. It would almost have disappeared, if the concern of Muslims with the Qur'ân and the Sunnah, which preserves Islam, had not also preserved the Arabic language. This (concern) became an element in favor of the persistence of the sedentary dialect used in the cities. But when the Tartars and Mongols, who were not Muslims, became the rulers of the East, this element in favor of the Arabic language disappeared, and the Arabic language was absolutely doomed. No trace of it has remained in these Muslim provinces: the non-Arab Irâq, Khurâsân, Southern Persia, eastern and western India, Transoxania, the northern countries, and Anatolia. The Arabic style of poetry and speech has disappeared, save for a (remnant) in the provinces of the non-Arab Irâq and beyond to the East, no trace or source of (the Arabic language) has remained. Even scientific books have come to be written in the Persian language, which is also used for teaching in Arabic classes (Ibn Khaldûn 1965: 295).

---

11 Since *A Mediterranean Apocalypse* has not yet been published, I refer to Sanjay Subrahmanyam's brief description of Fleischer's work in "Connected Histories: Notes Towards a Reconfiguration of Early Modern Eurasia," *Modern Asian Studies* (Subrahmanyam 1997: 750).

So wrote Ibn Khaldûn in his famous *Muqddimah*. What characterizes the above-statement is the recognition of the widespread expansion of the Persianate culture in the 14th century, an expansion that caused Ibn Khaldûn to lament as the popularity of Persian replaced Arabic as the *lingua* franca of Islamdom. Although, as Ibn Khaldûn correctly notes, the Mongol conquest of the mid 13th century greatly helped the ongoing vernacular transformations away from Arabic in the Islamicate world, the shift in the choice of making literary and political texts in neo-Persian (*darik*) was, however, first undertaken around the 10th century at the Sâmânî court (819-1004.) in Transoxiana, which later expanded under the rule of Buyids (932-1062) and Persianized Turks, like the Ghaznavîds (989-1149).[12] The rise of the Muslim Persian states as representatives of Arab-Iranian cultural synthesis in the post-High Caliphate age (692-945) characterizes a major shift of civilizational importance; this development signaled the extraordinary efflorescence of the Islamized Persianite cosmopolitan culture that expanded over large areas of Anatolia, Transoxania and western India, where an exemplary instance of Arabic-Persian creolization and vernacularization took place.

Two centuries earlier, Abû-l-Rayhân al-Bîrûnî (973?-1048), the famous Khârazmian-Iranian scientist, in his *Kitâb al-Hind* dates the reign of Sabuktigîna at Ghaznah, Afghanistan, as the 'the days of the Turks' (*'ayyâm at-turk)*, a term that underlines an increase of interconnection between Iran-Mesopotamian, Anatolian-Mediterranean and Central Asian regions with the – gradual – migration of the Turks (Al-Biruni 1953: 16).

To all appearances the 11th century was a time when relations between the sedentary civilizations and the (semi) nomadic populations of Central Asia crossed a major threshold, whereby migration, conquest and conversion set off a critical socio-political and cultural organizational changes in the Islamdom; a process which reached its apogee with the Mongol incursion in the 13th century when nomad power reached the full capacity of its political organizational potential in Eurasia (Lewis 1988: 33-34; 88-89; Saunders 1982: 141). The emergence of the Turkish people, in their both detribalized (Ghaznavîds and Mamluks) and tribalized form (Seljuqs), ultimately opened the way for the establishment of the Persianized-Turkic powers, such as the Ottomans and the Safavis, in Asia Minor and Iran-Mesopotamian steppes, and the establishment of the Sultanate of Delhi in the 13th century in the Panjab and most of the Gangetic plain (Hindustân).

The appearance of the Turkish and Persianate cultures in the Middle Period (945-1503), to use Hodgson's periodization, marks an era of unprecedented po-

---

12 Neo-Persian was a simplified literary form of Pahlavî language (Middle Persian) from the Sâsânian era, written mainly in Arabic scripts. By raising this point, I am not ignoring the 'Abbâsid debt to the Sâsânîan Persian system of administration and government. Rather, I am merely indicating how it was under the Sâmânî power that the neo-Persian language emerged as the idiom of administration and court literary culture.

litical fragmentations and cultural creolization in the context of nomadic and sedentary relations.[13] According to Hodgson, the period of genesis (c. 600-945) saw the replacement of Syriac and Pahlavi ("Irano-Semitic") traditions by an Arabic culture on post-axial, agrariante and urbanite civilization; underpinning an inclusive Muslim community between the Nile and Oxus river developed on this basis. By contrast, the Middle Period was marked by a widening gap between state and society, the diffusion and pluralization of Sûfîsm and the expansion of neo-Persian as a literary language throughout a large part of the Afro-Eurasian landmass. In an article published posthumously in 1970, Hodgson described this period as an age of great cosmopolitan creativity that reached its height by the 16th century, when the main region of Islamdom came under the control of empires (Ottoman, Mughal and Safavi), administrated by military patronage states.[14]

The most critical threshold of the transcultural age in the (early) Middle Period of Islamic history was the Turkish migration from Central Asia. The successive waves of the Turkish migration from the steppe grass lands of Central Asia to the settled regions of Anatolia and the Iran-Mesopotamian plateaus began in the 9th century, when Turkish slaves were recruited in order to create a new military order, loyal to the Byzantine and the early Caliphate state.[15] The Turkish socio-military institution, in its various forms, had been in a sense the backbone of Caliphate, at least, from the end of the 9th century onwards. With the rise of the Ghaznavids, military slave elites of Turkish origin emerged as heirs to the Caliphate political order.[16] The Saljuqs suzerainty in the 11th and the early 12th centuries,

---

13 Hodgson lists six periods of Islamic history: the formative (to 692), the High Caliphate (to 945), the International Civilization (to 1258), the Age of Mongol Prestige (to 1503), the era of Gunpowder Empires (to c. 1800) and Modern Times, with the emergence of nation-states. The "Middle Period" groups together the third and fourth periods of this list (Hodgson 1974, 1: 98).

14 This was the fifth phase of Islamicate history, namely the era of "Gunpowder Empires." In this article, Hodgson argues that egalitarian and cosmopolitan elements in Islam, incorporated and institutionalized in the civilization of the Irano-Semitic societies, have made a lasting impact on interregional developments on a hemispheric-wide base (Hodgson 1970: 99-123).

15 Although they primarily served in the Muslim armies as early as 674 C.E. the systematic introduction of Turkish slaves into the Caliphate army occurred under the reign of Al-Mansûr (745-75) (Pipes 1981: 152). However, the creation of the slave soldier institution consisted of both free mercenaries recruited abroad and captured Turks among the tribes in Transoxnia, known in the Muslim world as Mamlûks (Crone 1980: 74-80).

16 It is important to note that the Persianization of Turkish people was a process already in the making with the rise of the Central-Asian trade in the 5th and early 6th centuries, when the Turks were in constant contact with the pre-Islamic Sâsânîd culture. Apart from pastoral nomads, the pre-Islamic Turkish society was never wholly nomadic; culturally and economically, it also included certain urban elements that had been shaped by commercial interests (Kwanten 1979: 32; 39-40; Cahen 1968: 5-7).

however, marked the establishment of the first non-slave Turkish nomadic empire that led the way to the revival of Orthodox Sunnism. The establishment of a non-military slave Turkish power with vast expansionist aspirations represents the first major nomadic conquest movement with religious renewalist dimensions.

In a sense, the migration of the tribal Turks to the Anatolian regions at the beginning of the 11th century, led to major demographic transformations.[17] This occurred in two major successive historical phases. The Saljuq victory over the Byzantines forces at the battle of Manzikert in 1071 inaugurated the first decisive stage, with major political consequences: the establishment of Turkish-speaking principalities in the western borderland marches as a way to challenge Byzantine control over Anatolia and the Islamic heartland. The ascend of the Tughil to the Caliphate seat of Baghdad in 1055, in this context, marked a combination of decisive leadership and military prowess as well as a deteriorating political and economic situation within the Islamic territories that enabled the first tribal Turks, the Saljuqs, to make themselves the dominante force in the Iran-Mesopotamian plateau. This socio-demographic process, known as "Turkicization," entered a second phase of development with the Mongol invasion of 1258, which intensified the Turkman migration to the western regions of Anatolia, replacing the Greek-Christian peasant population with Turkish groups of nomadic origin. Though sporadic movements occurred throughout the 11th to the 13th centuries, the 14th century highlights the finalization of a major demographical shift in Anatolia that involved radical changes of socio-cultural significance.

The transition from the early to the late Middle Period, as seen in the context of successive Turkish migrations to Anatolia, can be regarded as a revolutionary phase in two important ways. At one level, the complex process of hybridization of Arabic, Persian and Turkish cultural elements from the end of the High Caliphate to the establishment of the Ilkhânâte era in Iran in the 13th century, represents a new period of intense civilizational hybridization, and a new stage of the Turko-Persian ecumene. (Canfield 1991: xiv). The Turko-Persian Islamicate culture that had crystallized in eastern Iranian margin in the 11th century, and was later exported to cultural zones of south Asian India, was a product of intercivilizational encounters and open to further developments of that sort. In the particular case of Turkization of Anatolia from the 11th to the 14th centuries, the regional mixture of agrarian, nomadic tribal and urban settings was particularly favorable to cultural blending.[18] Accordingly, the fusion of Arabic-scriptural, Byzantine-

---

17 Though non-nomadic Turkish settlers were already living in Khurâsân, Khwarazm and Transoxania by the time of Arab conquest in the seventh and eighth centuries, the most expansive southward migration of the Turks, as settlers and pastoralists, occurred mainly in the 11th century, which changed the ethnic composition of the Middle East.
18 Although Claude Cahen has argued that it is obviously impossible to give any figure for the Turkish immigration into Asia Minor, evidence indicates a long-term

Greek, Turkish-nomadic and Persianate-lettered traditions of the Middle Period paved the way for the creation of new cultural complexes.

At another level, this "mixed borderland civilization" also became a meeting ground of different religious traditions (Wittek 1996: 20). With regard to the interdependent process of migration and encounter, the blending of steppe (instrumental) religious practices of the Turkish nomads with the world (soteriological) religions of Iran-Semitic and Byzantine-Greek societies represents the crystallization of new cultural milieus, where nomadic and settled civilizations had to some extent been amalgamated;[19] this leveling of cultural and religious capacities opened the way for the breakdown of civilizational frontiers between steppe and sown. With the Islamization of Turks and the Turkization of Islam, shamanist ritual practices, performances to attain a trance state in order to communicate with the world of spirits for the purpose of fertility, healing, protection and aggression, were creatively fused with Islamic eschatology and the soteriological practices of divine guidance to pass reckoning on judgment day towards salvation.

From the 11th century onwards, the most original expression of this cross-fertilization between shamanistic and soteriological traditions was the emergence of Anatolian Sufism. In its distinct shamanistic form, Darvish Islam or "Islamicized shaman" (*Bâbâ* Islam) marked a dominant aspect of the daily life of the Turkish nomadic population, and indeed the main factor for the conversion of rural Asian Minor to Islam.[20] The strong popularity of spiritual leaders called *Bâbâ*s (whence the name *Bâbâi*s for their followers) reflected the widespread tendency of combining certain elements of Shi'i, Sunni, Persianiate ethos of chivalry (*javânmardî*) and Christian beliefs with shamanistic practices, in which *Bâbâ* Islamist groups like the *Bektâshî* Darvishism best attests (Köprülü 1978: 123).[21] As H.R. Roemer writes, the period marked an age of religious configura-

---

process of conversion of the natives to Islam with the migration of Turkish Muslims to the region from the 11th to the 13th centuries (Cahen: 1968: 143; Levtzion 1979: 52-67).

19 The difference between instrumental and soteriological religions is primarily based on their experiential orientation towards the supernatural: whereas the former type represents the belief in salvation manifested in practices directed towards appeasing the supernatural with the aim of redemption, the later is directed towards making specific things happen in the world through magical practices of shamanism and spirit-possession. In this sense, instrumental religions are not based on faith, but rather on the notions of efficacy of spiritual experience to control the supernatural (Gellner 2001: 69-72).

20 As Kortepeter notes, the notion of "Islamized shaman" was also synonymous with the Turkish term of "bagiji" or sorcerer, which could imply the supernatural ability to illicit magic involving the use of medicines in order to harm others (Kortepeter 1991: 19)

21 The warrior ethos of *Javânmardî* was an ideal life, involving chivalry spirit based on physical masculine strength. Such ethos, originating from the pre-Islamic Per-

tions, in which a "popular religiosity became widespread [...] These included a marked willingness to believe in miracles, a cult of saint with the growth of much frequented places of pilgrimage, and even the veneration of 'Alî, the cousin and son-in-law of the prophet Muhammad [...]" (Jackson/Lockhart 1968, 6: 192). Correspondingly, the popularization of Shi'i saintly figures, like 'Alî as a source of mystical veneration by various Islamic sects, especially the Sûfî-Sunni orders, generated what has been called by C. Cahen as the "Shi'itization of Sunnism."[22]

Although by the 11th century Sufîsm had already played a considerable role in the development of the Islamic faith, leading up to al-Ghazali's legitimation of Sufism with his greatest work *The Revivification of the Religious Sciences* in the 12th century, this variegated mystical movement experienced a growth of popularity with the rise of *Bâbâ* Islam. The fusion of Sûfiesque Shi'isectarianism and millenarian movements in the later Middle Period can in part be credited to this process of religious hybridity, whereby Shi'i, Sunni and Sûfî practices and creeds intermingled in close proximity and at times overlapped in the shifting spaces of everyday interaction.[23] But with the emergence of the Turkish Sûfî-brotherhood orders – the so-called "*ghâzî*" warriors" – such movements gave a political expression to this civilizational fusion. It was at this stage that Sufism began to be transformed from loose associations into organized religious orders (*tariqa*) with their own distinctive cultural practices, forming spiritual brotherhoods in the form of popular mass movements whose leaders where some of the greatest political and religious reformers of Islam.

The origins of these brotherhood associations traces back to the 8th century small ascetic brotherhoods on the island of Abadan in the Persian Gulf (Ayoub 2004: 153) and, later in the 10th century, to the urban-based "pure brethren" of the Qaramati movement. The Qarmati brotherhoods played a great role in the development of the Islamic guilds in the 10th century, and the *futuvvat* associations that were revived under the reign of Caliph An-Nâsî in the late 12th and early 13th centuries, as a consequence of the expansion of trade and revival of towns under the Saljuq rule (Lewis 1937: 20-37).[24] In the early Middle Periods, these rela-

---

sianiate culture, was later incorporated into the *futuvvat* fraternal circles of Middle Period Islamic history (Babayan 2002: 168-69).

22 Quoting C. Cahen in Arjomand's *Shadow of God and the Hidden Imam* (Arjomand 1984: 67).

23 For the best exposition of Sûfî history of later Middle Period, see Arjomand (1981). It is important to note, however, that Sûfîsm and Islamic messianic movements (especially in its Shi'i form of Mahdîsm) existed in earlier periods of Islamic history, and that they were not essentially inclusive of each other. The histories of Abbâsîd and the Isma'ilî (Fâtimîd) revolutions in the 8th and the 10th centuries, for instance, are replete with apocalyptic and messianic beliefs in the Mahdî that "spread widely beyond other extremist Shiite groups" (Amanat & Bernhardson 2002: 114).

24 Although they were consolidated under An-Nâsî, according to Arnakis however, the *futuvvat* associations first appeared in the 9th century in the form of "volunteer war-

tively autonomous movements, in the form of popular militia and volunteer Sûfî-guild associations, played a crucial role in the local governance of eastern Islamdom, which reached maturity as a political and social force from the 11th to the 14th centuries.[25] With their own Sûfî mystical ceremonies and chivalric ritual practices, the *futuvvat* associations combined ethical codes of egalitarianism, in the Persianate form of *Javânmardî* and the *Mazdakî* notions of piety, with non-egalitarian charismatic elitist ethos of master (*pîr*)-disciple and patron-client relations.[26] Ties of blood and kinship affiliations were less important than competition for the sacred status of leadership in the clubs, manifested in the paradoxical notion of "first among equals," which reflected the brotherhood spiritual character of the associations.

Especially in the later Middle Period, 1200-1501, after the Mongol invasion, culminating in the conquest of Baghdad in 1258 and the disintegration of the 'Abbâsid Caliphate, the *futuvvat* associations began to merge with the Anatolian-Sûfî orders, a process that during the 14th century spread further into the Islamdom with the increasing intermingling of rural and urban relations as a consequence of migration and nomadic incursions (Lewis, 1937: 27-28).[27] The blending between *futuvvat* and the Anatolian-Sûfî orders created the *akhîyat al-fityân* or *akhî* movements, which tended to fuse the horseback warrior culture of Central Asia with the sedentary Iran-Semitic Messianic traditions. Recruited mainly among the craftsmen, and composed of associations of young men organized as guilds in Anatolia in the 13th and 14th century, the *akhîs* shared the basic rules of *futuvvat* (Cook 1970: 16-17). Built around the warrior ethos of steppe regions and the Qura`nic notion of justice, the brotherhoods lived by a strict code of masculine honor, an ethic of bravery, embedded in a culture of reference for spiritual sacred persons (shaman) and belief in the potential to unite the mundane

rior guilds" (Arkakis 1953: 232-47). The literal meaning of the term "*futuvvat*" is youthfulness and by implication chivalry (Keyvani 1982: 25). But the term is also associated with the Middle Persian word of *javânmardî* or chivalry (Kâshifî 1983: 9).

25 As Hodgson notes, by the end of the Middle Periods, the *futuvvat* had become the mystical expression of urbanite guild associations with their own political and religious authority (Hodgson 1974, 1: 130-131).

26 The *Mazdakîs* were a Zoroastrian gnostic movement that emerged as a sectarian movement in sixth century pre-Islamic Persia. They advocated radical egalitarian values with strong this-worldly inclinations. The precise influence of the late Sâssâniân tradition of *javânmardî* and *Mazdakîs* on the *futuvvat*, which also included similar youthful masculinist ritual practices and ethical ideals, is unclear. For a good description of the *Mazdakî* movement, see Babayan (2002: 170, 265-271).

27 It is important to note that such process appears to have already occurred with the first wave of Turkish migration to Anatolia and Iran-Mesopotamian regions. The emergence of the Qalândarî-e movement in eastern Khurâsân and western parts of central Asia in the 10th century serves as a good example in the rise of Sûfî-brotherhoods in the early Middle Period (Karamustafa 1994).

with the supernatural world through ritual, ceremony and, above all, war. Throughout Islamdom, the brotherhood orders began to organize themselves with a hierarchy, evolving around the charismatic leader, his deputies *(khalifâh)* and ordinary followers *(murîds)*. With relative autonomy, they constituted a counter political culture that created its own political conception of Islamic justice, contravention of the *sharî'a*, distinctive ceremonies (i.e. dance-trance rituals of *zîkr*), clothing, public spaces *(takkiyah)* and incorporation of various "heterodoxical" beliefs and doctrines, based on what Karamustafa calls "an uncompromising antinomianism" (Karamustafa 1994: 17).

The emergence of the Sûfî-brotherhoods in the 14th century identifies a fascinating example of this civilizational experimentation, a process that led to the formation of new political orders with the establishment of the Ottoman and Safavi Empires from the 14th to the early 16th centuries, reshaping the political cultural landscape of Islamdom. But, with the emergence of the Turko-Persian Islamicate cultures, this new historical configuration also created new ways of reflexivity and modes of communcation, marking a new Axial condition that generated new types of eschatological, cosmological and symbolic realities in vernacular hybrid terms. The Middle Period Islamic Axiality, in this regard, idenitifies an integral part of the transcultural age, in which through encounter, emerging societies reformulated new expressions to defining self and other, knowledge and reality by transcending pre-existing social and cultural boundaries, and integrating new institutional arrangements in transcendental terms.

References

Abu-Lughod, Janet (1989) *Before European Hegemony: The World System AD 1250-1350*, Oxford: Oxford University Press.
Amanat, Abbas/Bernhardson, Magnus (eds.) (2002) *Imagining The End Visions of Apocalypse from the Ancient Middle East to Modern America*. London & New York: I.B. Tauris.
Arjomand, Said Amir (1981) "Religious Extremism (Ghuluww), Sufism and Sunnism in Safavid Iran: 1570-1722." *Journal of Asian History*, 15, pp. 1-35.
Arjomand, Said Amir (1984) *The Shadow of God and the Hidden Imam*, Chicago: Chicago University Press.
Arkakis, G.G. (1953) "Futuwwa Traditions in the Ottoman Empire: Akhis, Bektashi, Dervishes, and Craftsmen." *Journal of Near Eastern Studies*, 12 (4), pp. 232-247.
Ashtor, Eliyahu (1983) *Levant Trade in the Later Middle Ages*, Princeton, NJ: Princeton University Press.
Ayoub, Mahmoud M. (2004) *Islam: Faith and History*. Oxford: One World.

Babayan, Kathryn (2002) *Mystics, Monarchs, and Messiahs: Cultural Landscapes of Early Modern Iran*, Massachusetts: Cambridge, Harvard University Press.
Barthold, W. (1928) *Turkestan Down to the Mongol Invasion*, London: Luzac & Co.
Bentley, Jerry H. (1993) *Old World Encounters: Cross-Cultural and Exchanges in Premodern Times*, Oxford: Oxford University Press.
Bentley, Jerry H. (1998) "Hemispheric Integration, 500-1500 C.E." *Journal of World History,* 9 (2), pp. 237-254.
Birge, John Kingsley (1937) *The Bektashi Order of Dervishes*, Hartford & London: Hartford Seminary Press.
Al-Bîrûnî, Muhammad Ibn Ahmad (1953) *Kitâb fi Tahqîqî mâ Li-l Hind*, Hyderabad.
Burke III, Edmund, (ed) (1993) *Rethinking World History: Essays on Europe, Islam, and World History*, Cambridge: Cambridge University Press.
Cahen, Claude (1968) *Pre-Ottoman Turkey: A General Survey of the Material and Spiritual Culture and History c. 1071-1330,* New York: Taplinger.
Canfield, Robert L, (ed.) (1991) *Turko-Persia in Historical Perspective*, Cambridge: Cambridge University Press.
Cardini, Franco (2001) *Europe and Islam*, transl. by Caroline Beamish, London: Blackwell.
Cook, Michael Allan (ed) (1970) *Studies in the Economic History of the Middle East,* New York & London: Oxford University Press.
Crone, Patricia (1980) *Slaves On Horses: The Evolution of the Islamic Polity*, Cambridge: Cambridge University Press.
Curtin, Philip D. (1984) *Cross-Cultural Trade in World History*, Cambridge: Cambridge University Press.
De Bary, Theodore (1975) *The Unfolding of Neo-Confucianism*, New York: Columbia University Press.
Di Cosmo, Nicola (1999) "State formation and Periodization in Inner Asian history." *Journal of World History*, 10 (1), pp. 1-40.
Eisenstadt, Shmuel N., Schluchter, Wolfgang & Wittrock, Björn (eds.) (2001). *Public Spheres & Collective Identities.* London: Transaction.
Eisenstadt, Shmuel N & Schluchter, Wolfgang (1998) "Introduction: Paths to Early Modernities-A Comparative View." *Daedalus*, 3, pp. 1-18.
Eisenstatdt, Shumuel (2000) "The Civilizational Dimensions in Sociological Analysis." *Thesis Eleven,* 62, pp. 1-22.
Gellner, David (2001) *The Anthropology of Buddhism & Hinduism: Weberian Themes*, Oxford: Oxford University Press.
Haeger, John Winthrop (1976) *Crisis and Prosperity in Sung China,* Tucson: University of Arizona Press.
Hannerz, Ulf (1987) "The World in Creolization,"*Africa*, 57 (4) 546-559.

Hobson, John M (2004) *The Eastern Origins of Western Civilizations*, Cambridge: Cambridge University Press.
Hodgson, Marshall G (1970) "The Role of Islam in World History." *International Journal of Middle Eastern Studies*, 1, pp. 99-123.
Hodgson, Marshal G. (1974) *The Venture of Islam*, 3 Vols., Chicago: Chicago University Press.
Höfert, Almut/Salvatore, Armando (eds.) (2000) *Between Europe and Islam: Shaping Modernity in a Transcultural Space*, Brussels, P.I.E.-Peter Lang.
Howard, Deborah (2000) *Venice & the East: The Impact of the Islamic World on Venetian Architecture 1100-1500*, New Haven & London: Yale University Press.
Ibn Khaldûn, Rosenthal, Franz, trans. (1967) *The Muqaddimah: an Introduction to History*. New Jersey: Princeton University Press.
Ikegami, Eiko (1995) *The Taming of the Samurai: Honorific Individualism and the Making of Modern Japan*, Cambridge, Massachusetts: Harvard University Press.
Jackson, Peter and Lockhart, Laurence (eds.) (1968) *The Cambridge History of Iran*, Vol. 4, Cambridge: Cambridge University Press.
Karammustafa, Ahmet T. (1994) *God's Unruly Friends: Dervish Groups in the Islamic Later Middle Period 1200-1500*, Salt Lake City: University Utah Press.
Kâshifî, Husayn Vâ'iz (1998) *Rawzat ash-Shuhadâ*, Tehran: Senani.
Kayvani, Mehdi (1982) *Artisans and Guild Life in the Later Safavid Period: A Chapter in the Economic and Social History of Iran*, Berlin: K. Schwarz.
Khoury, Philip S. & Kostiner, Joseph (eds.) (1990) *Tribes and State Formation in the Middle East*, California: University California Press.
Köprülü, Mehmed Fuad (1978) *Les Origines de l'Empire Ottoman*, Philadelphia: Porcupine Press.
Kortepeter, Carl Max (1991) *The Ottoman Turks: Nomad Kingdom to World Empire*, Istanbul: Isis Press.
Krejcí, Jaroslav (1990) *The Civilizations of Asia and the Middle East: Before the European Challenge*, Houndmills, Basingstoke, Hampshire: Macmillan.
Kwanten, Luc. (1979) *Imperial Nomads: A History of Central Asia, 500-1500.*, Philadelphia: University Pennsylvania Press.
Lapidus, Ira M. (1999) *A History of Islamic Societies*, Cambridge: University of Cambridge Press.
Levtzion, Nehemia (ed.) (1979) *Conversion to Islam*. London & New York: Holmes & Meier.
Lewis, A.R. (1988) *Nomads and Crusaders, AD 1000-1368*, Bloomington: University Indianapolis Press.
Lewis, Bernard (1937) "Islamic Guilds." *The Economic History Review*, 8 (1) pp. 20-37.

Lewisohen, Leonard (ed.) (1991) *The Heritage of Sufism, Classical Persian Sufism From its Origins to Rumi*, Vol. I Oxford: Oneworld.

Moore, R.I. (1997) "The Birth of Europe as a Eurasian Phenomenon." *Modern Asian Studies* 31(3) pp. 583-601.

Moore, R.I. (2002) *The Origins of the Modern World: A Global and Ecological Narrative*. Lanham, Maryland: Rowman & Littlefield.

Pipes, Daniel (1981) *Slave Soldiers and Islam: The Genesis of A Military System*, New Haven: Cambridge University Press.

Salvatore, Armando (ed.) (2001) *Muslim Traditions and Modern Technologies of Power*, Münster: Lit Verlag.

Sanders, Paula (1994) *Ritual, Politics, and the City in Fatimid Cario*. Albany, New York: New York State University Press.

Saunders, J.J. (1982) *A History of Medieval Islam*, London: Routledge & Pauls.

Schulz-Forberg, Hagen (ed.) (2004) *Unravelling Civilization: European Travel and Travel Writing*. Brussels: P.I.E.-Peter Lang.

Stern, S.M (1967) "Ramisht of Siraf, a Merchant Millionaire of the Twelfth Century." *Journal of the Royal Asiatic Society*, 7, pp. 10-14.

Subrahmanyam, Sanjay (1997), "Connected Histories: Notes Towards a Reconfiguration of Early Modern Eurasia," *Modern Asian Studies* 31 (3), pp. 735-62.

Wittek, Paul (1996) *The Rise of the Ottoman Empire*, London: Royal Asiatic Society of Great Britain and Ireland.

Wittrock, Björn (2001) "Social Theory and Global History: The Three Cultural Crystallizations." *Thesis Eleven*, 65 (1), pp. 27-50.

Chapter 3

Identity Formation in World Religions: A Comparative Analysis of Christianity and Islam

ARPAD SZAKOLCZAI

Introduction

The aim of this paper is to analyse, comparatively, the processes through which the authenticity of the religious founders, extending both to their personality and message, was established in the two main world religions, focusing on the earliest period. Questions of identity formation include the sources of the personal identity of the founding figures, their identification as prophet or saviour, and the way in which the identities of believers and their opponents were characterised and formed in the respective sacred books.

In terms of a theoretical background the paper relies on the works of Max Weber on charisma, and Alessandro Pizzorno on identity formation, emphasising the role of processes of recognition in the formation of identity. Pizzorno's ideas will be complemented in two ways: by Victor Turner's studies on liminality and performative experiences, and René Girard's ideas on the mimetics of desire.

Theoretical background

1. Max Weber: prophetic charisma

The identity of the prophet, or the 'founder of religion' in general,[1] is a problem ridden with difficulties. Max Weber has the unique merit of placing the question of prophecy and prophetic religions, beyond any overall evolutionary scheme or

---

1 Any attempt at a comparative study of Christianity and Islam, and especially their founders, is rendered difficult by a problem that is not merely terminological: while Mohammed is identified as a prophet by his followers, Jesus is considered much more; so the claim that Christianity is a 'prophetic religion' already implies a partisan position that is not compatible with the methodological considerations outlined above. As a result, I will have to use the technical term 'founder of a world religion.'

simplistic contrast between 'traditional' and 'modern' societies, at the centre of historical sociology and social theory, and developed the concept of charisma first of all to analyse this problem. Weber considered prophecy as the clearest example of charisma, and while defining charisma in terms of personal characteristics as a 'gift of grace,' he also emphasised that prophets need to be recognised, connecting identity formation to processes of recognition.

However, in spite of its pioneering achievements, Weber's work on charisma has a series of shortcoming. First of all, Weber never tackled satisfactorily the exact relationship between charisma as a pure gift, a strictly personal quality, and as a result of a process of recognition. This is a serious shortcoming, as highly charismatic persons, even geniuses possessing clearly extraordinary gifts, might go unrecognised under certain conditions, as it happened with the great 'madmen' of the 19th century, like Hölderlin, van Gogh or Nietzsche. Second, concerning the special case of religious charisma, prophets or saviour declare themselves, with considerable effect, as mediators of divine will or messages, not simply possessors of unique personal qualities, whether recognised or not. Finally, while Weber's concept starts with extraordinary situations and the singular ability to resolve them, the founding of a religion requires different qualities: a stable, durable identity which is recognised generally as an authentic carrier of divine will.

It is here the work of Alessandro Pizzorno, focusing on the manner in which identities are recognised, compliments Weber's approach.

2. Alessandro Pizzorno: identity and recognition

The term 'recognition' is increasingly used in contemporary social theory, mostly through the works of Charles Taylor (1994) and Axel Honneth (1995). Pizzorno's approach, however, while compatible with them, was developed earlier and goes much further (see Pizzorno 1986, 1987, 1989, 1991, 1993, 2000). Following Levinas and the early Jena work of Hegel, Taylor and Honneth restrict their attention to the importance of the emotional and moral reconfirmation provided by the recognition of the other, emphasising mutuality, reciprocity, rights, symmetry, and the development of a legalistic moral philosophy. Pizzorno, however, argues that processes of recognition not only reconfirm but form and transform identities, both personal and collective.[2]

Recognising the other in this sense is not restricted to the granting of a positive emotional evaluation or acknowledgement. Illustrating Pizzorno's point through the theoretical framework of Michel Foucault on the three axes of experiences one can argue that processes of recognition involve knowledge, power

---

2   As a particularly pertinent example, he evokes the recognition of states, a central element of the system of international relations after the treaty of Westphalia.

and ethics at the same time (Foucault 1984, 1986). At the cognitive level recognition implies not simply the knowledge of something, close to familiarity, but the identification of an object as belonging to a certain class, or of an unknown phenomenon as being identical to something already familiar. However, the entire Kantian object-subject logic is bypassed by Pizzorno when he introduces the Hegelian dialectic of the master and the slave (or rather serf). Casting a novel eye on this idea worn out by Marx and conflict theory approaches, Pizzorno reads the confrontation as a struggle for recognition. A search for recognition between two subjects always has the aspect of a testing. According to Pizzorno, the 'slave' for Hegel is by no means in a hopeless position, justifying the need for an all or nothing revolution. Quite on the contrary, Hegel's aim is to show that even in such an extreme situation of inequality, the specifically social logic of recognition by itself will lead to an eventual turning of the sides.

This is because the identity of a person can only be acquired if it is recognised by other human beings. Approaches arguing for the eternal fixity of personal identity simply fail to notice, taking for granted, the subtle processes of recognition that contribute to establishing a stable identity. Thus, of course much of our identity is acquired in family; and there is no reason to take up an extreme social constructionist position denying the importance of purely biological factors. But the family is also a main source of emotional recognition. However, as blood relationships and emotional recognition normally coincide in a family, the latter's formative impact on identity often goes unacknowledged. Similarly, rational choice approaches simply take for granted the subtle processes of peer pressure that is exerted on the preferences a person has, extending even to his or her identity, and which are especially strong in certain 'liminal' moments and situations.

While the term recognition is central for Pizzorno's sociology, for a better understanding of the processes of recognition we need to make a subsequent step, moving from 'recognition' to 'circles' of recognition. Given their 'mutual recognition,' human beings 'have received an identity, and they may count on being recognised by some circles of others. These circles make recognition durable and, hence, trust rational. Individual interests grow out of different positions in the networks and circles of recognition' (Pizzorno 1991: 219). This is why Pizzorno's work is foundational for a properly social theory; and why his theoretical considerations end on an ultimately both refreshing and reassuring note: 'A too fierce self-reliance can be scary or pretentious. The principle of autonomy of self, if it is not meant to operate temporarily, cannot stand alone and not be a sham. Behind "autonomy" some other self recognizing me is necessary. I now know that beyond every decision of my current self, "some other kind of otherness" must be sought' (Pizzorno 1986: 372).

At this point Pizzorno's ideas can be complemented by ideas from two other contemporary social thinkers, Victor Turner and René Girard.

3. Victor Turner: liminality and performative experiences

Turner's work focuses on the experiential side of the processes of identity formation and transformation (Turner 1967, 1969). The most important part of his work is based upon Arnold van Gennep's classic study on rites of passage (van Gennep 1960). The most paradigmatic examples are initiation rites, which guide individuals (and their families) through the major moments of transition in the human life cycle, like birth, puberty, marriage, or dying. These rites follow a strict sequential order, starting with the rites of separation in the stage of preparation, consisting of various deprivations, endurance tests and ascetic exercises; followed by the actual ritual performance in which the candidates are tested; and concluded by the rites of re-aggregation that celebrate the successful performance and the return to normality and order. In order to characterise the fluid, malleable character of the ritual, created by the artificial suspension of the normal conditions of everyday life, van Gennep and Turner came up with the concept 'liminality,' which by now gained a very wide use in the social and human sciences.

Much of Turner's later work is devoted to the broader significance of the concept of liminality. Two of these directions are of particular importance for this paper. The first concerns the link between rituals and experiences. Rituals are not simply formal ceremonies, but require involvement and participation; but this is because they themselves are based on experiences. Rituals for Turner have a preventive character; they are deployed to ease transitions, or to prevent the outbreaks of conflict and crisis. However, exactly because of this evocation and incitement of emotions such rituals are dangerous, and can be performed solely under the guidance of special 'masters of ceremonies.'

In some of his last writings Turner recognised basic affinities between his approach and the work of Wilhelm Dilthey on events and experience (Turner 1985a, 1985b). In most of his studies Turner emphasised the creative, transformative potential of liminality, and the sense of community (called *communitas*) created between those who have jointly underwent such rites.

Second, the term liminality can be used in general to characterise fluid, transitory conditions. The collapse of the taken for granted order in real-world conditions creates a genuine betwixt and between situation, one which is not under the control of 'masters of ceremonies,' thus – in Weberian language – requires the emergence of a charismatic leader. Here Turner's work can be used to better understand the dynamics of major crisis moments in world history, including the concept of 'charisma,' and its contrast with its opposite, the Trickster (Horváth 2000; Radin 1972).

In real-world large-scale liminal situations historical events are experienced at the same time by a large number of individuals; thus, the approach can help to study jointly the formation of personal and collective identities.

4. René Girard: the mimetics of desire and rival brothers

If Turner often celebrated liminality, Girard called attention to its dangers (see Girard 1976, 1977, 1987, 1989). If Turner emphasised the preventive aspect of rituals, for Girard they rather only staged, without fully understanding, the original events of a sacrificial crisis. According to Girard, situations of crisis in small-scale communities easily degenerate into full-scale violence, due to the imitative aspect of human nature, and such an escalation of violence can only be stopped by the eventual identification and sacrifice of an innocent victim, or scapegoat. Human culture is founded on such mechanisms of scape-goating, repeated in rituals of sacrifice.

There are two aspects of Girard's framework that will be important for this paper. First, Girard calls attention to the crucial role distinctions play in social life, both at the level of social relations, and concerning the ability of individuals to make such distinctions and thus prevent descent, through imitation and mimetic rivalry, into a full-scale sacrificial crisis. Without social distinctions, and without individuals who have a good sense of judgment and are able to discriminate, society is always on the brink of descending into a liminal crisis. Second, in this context the anxiety created by the birth of twins in any small-scale society becomes intelligible. Due to their indistinguishable identity, twins threaten the delicate balance of social order. On a more general scale the problem is reflected in myths about fraternal rivalries; and for Girard it is by no means accidental or irrelevant that foundation stories very often involve rival brothers, of which one has to die for a successful foundation of the city.[3]

5. The spiral as a model of change

Finally, the paper will make use of the metaphor of the spiral, particularly suitable for a properly social analysis of processes of historical change. The meaning of the term 'social' is taken from Mauss (2002) and Simmel (1971), in distinction to both Durkheim and Marx.

The model of the spiral is different from non-social models of evolution or linear growth, whether taken from biology or from termo-dynamics; and from the anti-social models of conflict. Conflict models are anti-social in the sense that society, or community substance in any meaningful sense, is dissolved in the moment conflict breaks out, and cannot be re-established unless it ends. Conflicts of course do happen, and the study of the rhythm in which conflicts break out and escalate is central for understanding historical processes; but to explain society, and processes of social change, through conflicts as the purported 'engine' of

---

3   See for e.g. Cain and Abel, Romulus and Remus, Joseph and his brothers, or Eteocles and Polyneikes.

social change, thus in some way 'beneficial,' is not simply untenable, but deeply nihilistic in its outcome.

Though rarely if at all theorised explicitly, the metaphor of spiral does surface occasionally in explanations of socio-historical dynamics. It is present in milestone works of arts, written at crucial historical junctures. Thus, it is central for two of the most important poems of the 20th century: 'The Second Coming' by William Butler Yates,[4] and 'I Live in Expanding Rings' by Rainer Maria Rilke.[5] The former was written in January 1919, thus just after WWI, while the latter in 1905, or at the moment when the clouds leading to the storm of WWI started to gather. The metaphor of the storm, by the way, is also central for Thomas Mann's The Magic Mountain, also written during and around WWI. At a different but similarly liminal moment, the Renaissance, Leonardo da Vinci also came to a similar conclusion, when he 'had come to identify every action in nature as occurring along spiral lines' (Pedretti 1973: 15).

The metaphor was also used, and in some crucial junctures of their works, by major contemporary social theorists. Thus, in Volume 1 of his History of Sexuality Michel Foucault talks about the 'perpetual spirals of power and pleasure' (Foucault 1980: 45; emphasis in original); while Norbert Elias introduces the argument of his most important methodological book Involvement and Detachment through Poe's short story about fishermen in the maelstrom (Elias 1987: 45-6). Examples could be continued from various analyses of phenomena like panic, terrorism, the stock market, or the logic of expectations in general.

One might argue that such a model is not specifically social either, as models taken from medical epidemics or chaos theory perfectly capture the spiralling character of events. However, by combining experience-events and processes of recognition it is possible to formulate a specifically social model of spiralling processes. While epidemiology or meteorology provide us with important metaphors for illustrative purposes, there the outburst gathers momentum solely due to an originally random encounter of particles, or a purely physical interaction between viruses and their hosts. In human history, such 'storms' also start with humble beginnings; however, here we have to study the exact manner in which such minute beginnings establish themselves through the unique interaction of human experiences that are always strictly personal; and processes of recognition that contribute to the formation of personal and collective identities, and that are always social.

This paper will apply these considerations for analysing, in so far as it is possible, the very first instances in the rise of Christianity and Islam.

4 'Turning and turning in the widening gyre/The falcon cannot hear the falconer;/Things fall apart; the centre cannot hold;/Mere anarchy is loosed upon the world.'
5 'Round God, the old tower, my gyres I perform,/and I've gyred there centuries long;/and don't know whether I'm falcon or storm/or, maybe, a mighty song.'

The comparative analysis

1. Prelude

A methodological note

There are two guiding methodological principles in this paper that need to be pointed out explicitly, being particularly important for the study of religion: the paper is comparative and non-judgmental. The first is rather obvious, follows from the basic principles of scholarly analysis, and distances itself from the claim that a specific tradition, whether religious, cultural, national or political, can only be understood from the 'inside.' The second may be more controversial, as by this I mean the principle, fundamental for any serious study of religion, that transcendental experiences are accepted as possible. This is not equal to indiscriminate credulity, only recognises the limits of scientific knowledge and the legitimacy of non-scientific traditions which can be genuinely serious, with their own principles of verification; and in this regard it is fully compatible with the basic principles of Kant's thought, not to mention the founding figures of academic reasoning, Socrates, Plato and Aristotle. What it clearly repudiates, however, is the tradition identified by Jonathan Israel (2000) as the 'radical Enlightenment,' and which he traces back to Spinoza. Science must overcome its hubris and re-learn to be humble.

Historical context: liminal conditions

Temporal and spatial liminal conditions exerted a huge impact on the rise of axial age systems of thought.[6] The rise of Christianity, however, took place in a place and time that cannot be defined as liminal. This is already indicated by the fact that it is situated outside the time horizon of the axial age, even in the broad sense of Jaspers. More particularly, Jesus lived at a rather stable and peaceful moment both concerning the Roman Empire in general: the rule of Augustus, the high moment of Rome, and the still relatively stable period under Tiberius; and the case of Palestine in particular: well after the Maccabean revolts of BC 167-4 and the Roman invasion of BC 63, and well before the Jewish wars and the Fall of Jerusalem and the destruction of the Temple in AD 70. In fact, it was exactly due the relative – though always delicate – calmness of the situation that Jesus was considered as a threat to the peace that led to his condemnation and death. One could even situate some of his most startling claims – 'Think not that I am come to send peace on Earth; I came not to send peace but a sword' (Mt 10: 34) –

---

6   For details, see my 'Ecumenic Empires, Global Ages and Prophetic Religions,' in the same volume.

in this particular context. Jesus did not arise out of a liminal moment – he rather created liminality.

In stark contrast, Islam emerged at a particularly liminal moment, and at a specifically liminal location. The moment was the on-dragging war between the two main powers near the Arabian peninsula, the Eastern Roman and the Sassanide Persian empires. Warfare intensified since the middle of the 6th century, with disastrous consequences: 'In Muhammad's lifetime they waged the most destructive of all the wars waged against one another in all their centuries of fighting, and at his death both empires were financially and politically exhausted' (Hodgson 1974: 145). They were therefore ripe to be overrun – and Mecca, due to its liminal location, was in an ideal position to make use of this opportunity. This was because it was not only situated at the intersection point of the main caravan routes (Guzzetti 2004: 20), a central advantage for any trading community; but also because of its equidistance from the three main centres of power surrounding Arabia: Syria in the West, Yemen in the South, and the Persian Empire in the North-East (Hodgson 1974: 158). The rise of Islam, in a certain way, only realised this ripe opportunity.

2. Personal identity

Personal identity is first of all based on family connections, the genealogical lineage in which one is a descendent, and which on its turn is continued by one's own descendants. In the case of Jesus this elementary fact of human existence was broken, and in both directions. The Messiah was expected to come from the house of king David; but Jesus is not a descendent of king David. The Gospel of Matthew makes the point clearly, though obliquely, and thus it is often misunderstood. It seems as if its long genealogical lineage was composed in order to make Jesus appear as the descendant of David (Mt 1). However, the next chapter makes it clear that Joseph was not the father.

This poses the question whether the long genealogical story serves a purpose. The answer is that it indeed offers a lesson: instead of identifying a direct lineage of Jesus, it heralds his coming by the times in which he was born, by dividing the long lineage into three phases of fourteen generations (Mt 1: 17). Genealogy or direct blood descent is thus replaced by generation or the question of context, which will have its consequences for matters of recognition as well.

Furthermore, the birth of Jesus is accompanied by a number of further stories that break radically with expectations concerning a prophet or a saviour. These are exclusively contained in the Gospel of Luke – for the simple and good reason that after the ironic take on genealogical lineage Matthew declines any interest in actual birth and childhood stories. The birth is taken place not only out of home (Nazareth), in Bethlehem, but even outside the house, in the stable. Jesus furthermore receives no education worthy of telling, and we do not even know of any special experience or vision that he would have had, marking his calling as a prophet.

This break is further emphasised in episodes where Jesus would explicitly reject belonging to the lineage of Abraham and David. Thus, he claims that he is lord of David rather than his son (Lk 20: 41-4); even declaring, to much consternation, that 'Before Abraham was, I am' (Jn 8: 58). These claims are significant because they go against 'natural' expectations: one would expect an emphasis on such descent, especially in the case of a people, like the ancient Hebrews, where such descents were held in particularly high regard.

The situation is very different in the case of Muhammad, which is especially significant in light of the fact that his biographers consciously took the Gospels as models for their storylines. Muhammad was born into a leading family of Mecca, even though its relatively less prestigious side, and his father died before birth and he became an orphan at the age of six. On the opposite end, although – strangely – he had no surviving sons, and even most of his daughters died without heirs, claims about his blood descendents would play a major part in the history of Islam, just as similar genealogical lineages would be central for his main disciples and followers.[7]

3. The identity of the religious founder

Matters of personal identity, however, only became relevant due to the identification of these persons as founders of world religions. Here questions of experiences and recognition play a particularly crucial role. A prophet is not born; he or she must be recognised as a prophet (Weber 1978: 242). Such recognition of course become closely entangled with later ideological fabrications, and stories about the announcing of prophets are especially dubious. Still, the manner in which such announcements were construed can be revealing, especially in a comparative analysis. Related stories can also contain elements of truth that can be established with some degree of certainty. Finally, especially important and revealing is the exact dynamics and sequential order of personal experiences and acts of recognition.[8]

---

7   The contrast can be perceived realising that the exact equivalent of the Ismaili myth of the 'true Imam' (Lewis 1967: 26-8) is the *Da Vinci Code*.
8   While the terms 'identity' and 'recognition' are concepts taken from contemporary 'Western' social theory, it is not anachronistic to apply them for the distant past, and neither do they imply acceptance of the Christian tradition as a starting point. Quite on the contrary, these concepts have a general applicability for the problem of how a new type of non-traditional religion or spirituality establishes itself, through converting people, be it Christianity, Islam or Buddhism. Furthermore, the idea that contemporary theories of identity formation are inherently rooted in the Christian tradition, or that the New Testament somehow 'anticipates' these developments,

Concerning the New Testament the first point to notice is that each of the Gospels starts prominently by questions of recognition; and that the manner in which this is done goes way beyond the mere assertion of the status of Jesus, or even the simple story-telling of acts of recognition. There are two particularly important aspects of these acts: the relationship between two prophets and the delicate balance between positive and negative acts of recognition. The Gospels place a particular emphasis on the recognition of Jesus by St John Baptist, a historical figure with disciples on his own, lending further weight to the claim. Thus, there is a direct personal testimony beyond miraculous signs announcing or accompanying recognition. Second, this is underlined by a subtle play with refusals. This first applies to the Baptist, who declines the honour, thus increasing the force of his recognising the other, the real one. But in the Gospel of John this will be applied to the entire age that failed to recognise Jesus; and this age is identified by the same word 'generation.' Jesus is not a descendant of the lineage of David, rather came at the proper 'generational' moment; but it is exactly this generation that fails to recognise his true, non-genealogical identity (see also Mt 11: 16-9; 12: 34, 39; 17: 17).

Even the question of family background is revisited in this context, closing another circle. It is not only the entire 'generation' that fails to recognise Jesus; even more intriguingly, he would be rejected (not recognised as a 'prophet') by exactly those who were closest to him. 'no prophet is accepted in his own country' (Lk 4: 24).[9] This is further reinforced and closed from the other end: far from relying first of all on his own kin, Jesus repudiates blood relationships as being secondary to spiritual ties (Mt 12: 46-9), just as he would identify 'second birth,' spiritual birth or conversion to be more important than physical birth (Jn 3: 3-8)

Thus, positively, the Gospels start by acts of recognition; and negatively, they simply do not contain anything concerning the experiences of Jesus: sources of his call or mission; formal learning, or even endurance tests in the form of hardships and sufferings. The early tribulations told by Luke are all related to his birth and infancy, endured by his parents, thus could not have left a trace on his being.

There were a few visionary experiences referred to in the Bible; allusions to the future tribulations. They are often connected to acts of recognition. The sequential order of experience and recognition, however, is singular, even perplexing, the exact opposite of what one would expect on the basis of Dilthey's or Turner's theories. The starting point is not an experience, followed by the attempts to make sense of it, recognising its exact meaning; quite on the contrary,

    thus that there is some kind of partisan affinity between the religious text and contemporary theorising, outside truth, is simply not tenable.

9 The passage in Matthew is even more striking for the purposes of the paper: 'A prophet is not without honour, save in his own country, and in his own house' (Mt 13: 57).

it is the recognition that is followed by a specific type of experience; even further – and in this sense very close to Turner's framework – this experience has the specific character of a trial or testing.

It is well worth examining a few cases in some detail.

As a first example, let's take the scene of baptism. The three main elements of the episode, the recognition by the Baptist (Mt 3: 14-5), the visionary experience with the voice in the Sky and the bird descending from above (Mt 3: 16-7), and the fasting in the desert and the temptation by the devil, including the travel to the Temple and the invitation to throw himself down (Mt 4: 1-11), are told in a reverse order, compared to the standard narrative of rites of passage. The story is supposed to start with a rite of preparation, the fasting in the desert; crowned by the visionary experience, the rewarding of the ascetic for his labours; and end with the recognition of the authentic quality of the vision by a 'master of ceremony,' the widely recognised prophet of the desert. Still, the initiation ceremony worked, as Jesus starts his preaching mission after this episode, paradoxically concluded by an ascetic rite of preparation (Mt 4: 17).

This is by no means an isolated case. Let's take another important scene of recognition, when Peter would identify Jesus as 'the Christ, the Son of the living God' (Mt 16: 16). The following verses, containing Peter's 'reward,' the foundational narrative of the papacy is famously missing from the other Gospels;[10] however, all three synoptic Gospels agree that this recognition is followed by the first time Jesus announced his own sufferings. The same sequence is repeated in the next chapter, where the Transfiguration is followed by the healing of the sick child, and then with the second announcement of sufferings.

Such an emphatic reversal of the experience-recognition sequence must serve a purpose. This can be explained in the following way. The purpose of the post-recognition trial is not to prepare for a performance-experience or to reaffirm its content, acknowledging the genuine morality or even sanctity of the person, as there is no trace of such experiences in the Gospels. It serves rather to counterbalance the act of recognition that has just happened. Instead of celebrating and thus further confirming this recognition, which might lead to excessive self-confidence and hubris, the events are followed rather by a real tribulation, or allusions to such a trial, in order to prevent emotional loosening and self-relaxation. A further reason can be that each of the three advanced warnings are immediately followed in the text, going further back in the sequence, by a 'birth': the resurrection.

The situation is radically different for the case of Muhammad, where the basic facts of the accepted storyline can be arranged according to the standard sequential pattern, though revealing some unique peculiarities.

---

10 This is not so surprising, given that Luke is connected to Paul, while Mark to those who remained in Jerusalem.

Muhammad had lived the life of a normal merchant until his mid-to-late 30s when he suddenly became preoccupied about living a life of truth and purity (Hodgson 1974: 158). The moment is quite typical, whether identified as a Dantean mid-age crisis, or the time in which the shamans or magicians usually receive their calls.[11] In his exalted state Muhammad performs various ascetic exercises, goes to the desert, meditates in the cave. He is not alone in having such a troubled mind; given the liminal character of the time and place, it should not be surprising that there were several other prophets around engaged in similar activities (Hodgson 1974: 160). For a time he finds no solace, his desperation is increasing, and seriously considers jumping off the mountain. Suddenly, at this very moment, according to the historian at-Tabari (Guzzetti 2004: 46), in the 'night of destiny,' something happens to him: he hears a voice and has a vision (K 93: 3-8).[12]

Thus, eventually, the rite of preparation lead to a result; the experience arrives. But he had gone through everything all by himself, and is terrified by this experience, which further propels him into a tremendous crisis (Guzzetti 2004: 45). It is also accompanied by a series of apocalyptic visions, that belong to the oldest layers of the Koran (K 54: 1, 47-8; also 102: 1-8, 104: 1-9). He has doubts, not being so sure whether he is not just tormented by demons or ginns; he needs reassertion and recognition. But there is no 'master of ceremony' around; no other prophet who would willingly identify his experiences and recognise his status. Other prophets would enter the scene later, but only as his mortal rivals. Instead, he is consoled by his wife, but this is done not due to specific prophetic signs, rather to his general human qualities: as he is sincere and good, he just cannot be visited by demons. Some further recognition is given by a Christian, but even he is a cousin of his wife. Recognition therefore, in exact opposite to the Gospel story, started at the 'most intimate level' (Hodgson 1974: 167).[13]

It also continued there, and for a long time. The first male person believing him was his ten years old cousin, Ali, followed by his adopted son, Zayd, a liberated slave, and his future father-in-law and the first kaliph, Abu Bakr. For a gap of about three years the visions also stopped, and he only privately talked about his revelation. Thus, for a long period Muhammad was exactly a prophet in his own country, and even more, in his own house.

---

11 Dante was about 35 years old when composing the *Divine Comedy*; about the shaman's calling, similarly around the age of 37, see Turner (1975).
12 The abbreviation 'K' will stand for the Koran.
13 While, following the Weberian distinction between ethical and exemplary prophecy, one might argue that in Muhammad's case all that mattered was the recognition of the word of God, and not the person of the messenger, a strict separation along these lines is problematic. The entire question of believing in the Koran has only become possible because Muhammad as a person was first believed to have told the truth about Allah speaking to him.

This storyline must now be interpreted in light of the theoretical perspective outlined. While the relative perspectives of Turner and Pizzorno are quite different, focusing respectively on performative experiences and the struggle for recognition, they both agree that an alteration of identity, which is certainly involved in the calling of a prophet, can only be based on a genuine testing and trial. An initiation rite, or a passage from childhood to adulthood, for example, implies the leaving of the family, the world of the home, and the entry into the world at large: the broader community of the village or the tribe. It cannot be administered by family members; quite on the contrary, in most cases such rites can only be conducted by persons who do not even belong to the village. Similarly, recognition in the sense of Pizzorno implies a challenge and measuring, close to the Biblical sense of mene tekel. As we have seen earlier, the world of the family hides the difference between the genetic and the recognitive aspects of identity, as children receive the strongest emotional recognition exactly from persons to whom they are related by blood ties.

Even once Muhammad had decided to go public, about three years after his first vision, for a long time he failed to secure recognition outside his family, and especially outside his hometown. A particularly important event in this context, especially in light of later developments, retaining significance up to our very day, is the famous episode of the 'Satanic verses.' In the fifth year of his preaching, thus around 618, Muhammad went to Ca'aba and, surrounded by friends and foes, narrated them his first revelation (Guzzetti 2004: 78-9). Then, trying to use the occasion to secure further converts, he posed a question about the assessment of three main female deities of the region, and himself gave the answer: they are brave virgins, and their intercession is much appreciated by God. This was a clear concession towards paganism, but failed to bring success. In consequence the passage was edited out of the Koran, though transmitted by tradition. There are two aspects that I would like to emphasise about this story: the joint evocation of three virgin female goddesses, an image which clearly evokes the Three Graces; and their identification as intercessors or mediators of grace, a role comparable to the Virgin Mary. The editing out of this episode will result in the systematic ignoring of the qualities associated in other (among others, Greek and Christian) traditions with female deities or saints.

The success of his external mission, however, only came after another, and in a way last, experience-recognition complex.

This happened around 619, leading to the extension of his mission out of its local character. There is a quite general scholarly consensus about the exact sequence of events, with a number of striking elements. It starts with a new liminal crisis, this time related to purely this-worldly experiences of sufferings, as within a short time both Muhammad's wife and stepfather have died (Hodgson 1974: 171). While loss of close relatives is always taxing, especially when taking place together, in the case of Muhammad such grievances were exacerbated by the unique character of the loss. Khadijah and Abu-Talib were not just close relatives, but were the two emotionally closest family members for Muhammad; furthermore, the two persons on whom his material existence relied upon; and finally, even his major sources of recognition as prophet. Thus, apart from the emotional hardship caused, and the liminal situation of mourning, the two deaths also forced him to look for new sources of support, trying to move outside Mecca.

He visited the nearby oasis of Ta´if, but the mission proved to be a failure (Hodgson 1974: 171), though one Christian slave there evidently believed in him (Cook 1986: 310). On the way home, however, he encountered a few ginns (sprites), and managed to convert them (K 72: 1-2). Thus, while men repudiated him, the spirits brought him comfort. This is an extremely strange, even disturbing account, with no parallels in the New Testament. Recognition to Jesus was never given by spirits; quite on the contrary, it was very often the driving away of demons that led to his recognition. Another contrast can be given from the life of St Francis, the 'second Christ' and a crucial comparative reference point. Whenever turned away by man, according to his biographers Francis preached to birds or even the fish; never to spirits.

The next episode in the storyline only renders this aspect even more perplexing. As, after meeting the sprites, he also had a new vision that would be 'given a central place in Muhammad's legend' (Hodgson 1974: 171). This vision seems to consist of two parts: in the first part he was ravished to the Temple (K 17: 1; usually identified as Jerusalem); in the second, to the throne of God, or the 7th Heaven (K 53: 13-18).

Once back to home, after such taxing and peculiar experiences, he needed further recognition, both in the sense of confirmation and consolation by human beings, and this he obtained in two different ways. The first came still from the small circle of relative and friends. Becoming a widow, he took two new wives, one being Aishia, the daughter of one of his most faithful disciples, Abu Bakr. Aishia was only six years old then, the only one of his wives who was a virgin, and though Muhammad did not immediately go to her, he did so about three years later – which makes it coincide with another taxing, liminal experience, the flight to Medina – and which still leaves much room for perplexity about this entire affair.

The second type of recognition, finally, came from the outside. A few Muslim converts left already earlier to Medina, a town in which there were three important Jewish clans, and they managed to make some further converts. Between 619 and 622 occasionally, and in increasing numbers, these converts came to visit Muhammad, and this convinced him that, especially given the increasingly hostile atmosphere in his native town, he needed to move there.

The pattern of the sequence is again very clear. The intensification of Muhammad's mission is stimulated through liminal experiences of suffering and uncertainty. He is looking for human recognition and sources of support, but is turned away; and at this very moment, while on the road – another typical liminal situation – he is visited by spirits and visions. Human recognition and consolation only comes later, on the basis of them, and still in a predominantly local setting.

4. Who is recognising?

The missions of Jesus and Muhammad differed not only in the exact sequences of experiences and recognition, but also in the behaviour of the different types of persons involved in these acts.

Prophets

Recognition of a prophet by another prophet carries additional weight. In the case of Christianity, in all Gospels the charisma of Jesus is first recognised by St John Baptist. Even further, the Gospel of Luke makes Jesus and St John Baptist relatives. Irrespective of the veracity of kinship, the story actually reinforces the weight of the recognition. From the perspective Girard's the mimetic theory the Baptist has two strong reasons not to give such recognition: as he is both a rival brother and a rival prophet. In the case of Muhammad, however, the various prophets of the region would become rivals, and the contestation will only end by the complete submission or death of the rivals (Guzzetti 2004: 169-71).

Women

In the case of Muhammad, as we have seen, one woman played an extremely important, pioneering role in recognising his mission: his wife, Khadijah. The other significant women in his life, mostly his later wives, however, had no such roles to play: they only provided sources of support and pleasure. This was much related to the fact that after his move to Medina the defence and proliferation of Islam shifted from questions of recognition to the use of physical force, or from religion to politics.

In the case of Jesus the role played by women in the recognition and proliferation of his mission is widely considered as negligible. After all, the famous genealogy in the opening chapter of Matthew is purely male; he was recognised by the male prophet St John Baptist; and all his disciples were male. Yet, a more careful reading, with the help of the theoretical perspective exposed and used above, leads to a quite significant shift of perspective.

The Gospels start with an act of recognition and submission by a woman, before Jesus is even born. This, of course, is the famous episode of Mary's conception by the Holy Spirit. Two points are relevant in this episode for our purposes. First, recognition not only marks the starting point of the mission of Jesus, but his very existence. According to the Biblical narrative Jesus could only come into the world if the Spirit was recognised by Mary; and if she willingly gave her assent to conceive a child from the Spirit. Free, unforced submission and an unspoilt, childlike innocence capable of recognising is the real starting point of the Biblical narrative, after the ironical male genealogy.

Second, the normal sequential order between experience and recognition is reversed even here. In practically any narrative about the birth of a famous person, recognition follows the actual events. A child is born, and somebody – the midwife, a prophet or a sage – makes some pronouncements about the unusual qualities and future heroics of the newborn. Here, however, recognition is presented as the condition of possibility of birth; and this recognition is given not simply by a close family member but the mother herself, or exactly the person who, in any other narrative, after the childbirth, is disqualified from making such claims.

In concluding this episode I would like to stress that from the perspective of recognition and identity the significance of the female gender in the New Testament narrative must be reassessed. Far from being secondary, overshadowed by male prophets and disciples, this recognition by Mary is the condition of possibility of the entire narrative. The quantitative preponderance of males and the few references to Mary are irrelevant from this perspective; even further, it can be explained by the fact that after the birth, the logic of the narrative required the underplaying of such blood lines. The aim of the narrative was not to replace patriarchal genealogy with matriarchal genealogy.

Still, even though all his disciples were male – and for various reasons had to be – Jesus was also followed, or recognised, by females as well, and some of these recognitions carried exceptional significance. I do not have in mind the general reference to female followers (see Lk 8: 1-3), rather two singular episodes: the case of the Phonician and the Samaritan women (Mt 15: 21-8, Mk 7: 24-30; Jn 4: 5-30). The particular significance of the first encounter is widely recognised, though interestingly enough the episode can be interpreted in two radically different manners. On the one hand, this is one of the cases in which Jesus makes the claim that his mission is restricted to 'the lost sheep of the house of Israel' (Mt 15: 24). It is thus central, together with related passages like Mt (10: 5-8), for the claims of Géza Vermes (2004: 328-9) about the purely Jewish character of the original mission of Jesus.

The passage, however, can be read in the exact opposite manner. For this, we first need to recognised that this episode, the meeting of the Canaanite woman in Tyre, is the first case in Matthew when Jesus leaves the land of Israel. He furthermore does so in a very particular context. Tyre, together with neighbouring Sidon, is already mentioned in Mt (11: 20-1), where Jesus was reproaching the cities of Israel that they failed to repent though he was working miracles there. Further on, and still alongside the same dynamics of failing recognition, a series of events take place: Jesus is not recognised at home (Mt 13: 53-8); St John Baptist, who recognised his mission first, is beheaded (Mt 14: 1-12); Peter lacks faith (Mt 14: 30-1); and his conflicts with the Pharisees get more and more bitter (Mt 15: 1-20). This is the context in which, for the first time, he leaves Israel and enters the region of Tyre and Sidon.

It is by no means insignificant that the first contact Jesus has with the non-Jewish world is actually the city of Tyre, as Tyre has a very special place in mythical history. Tyre is the home-place of Europa, daughter of Agenor, the Phonician king of Tyre. It is from the coast of Tyre that Europa was ravished by Zeus,[14] and taken to Crete. In the text it is specifically emphasised that the woman was pagan, even Greek (Hellenic), or 'Syrophenician by nation' (Mk 7: 26). It is therefore particularly significant that the first step of Jesus outside the boundaries of Israel can be connected with the continent, Europe, that would play a particularly significant role with the further spread of Christianity.

From this perspective the otherwise perplexing aspects of the story become intelligible. After all, Jesus not simply went outside Israel but encountered, all alone, a woman in Tyre, the situation was therefore liminal in multiple ways. The fact that he 'had' to encounter a woman there can be understood by drawing parallels with the case of Mary and the annunciation. There, the emphasis was on breaking the genealogical lineage, underplaying the role of man and giving and exalted place, through a unique act of recognition, to a woman. Here, the problem is identical, the breaking of the exclusive character of the mission. Just as earlier, a woman is put to a test. There, she had to consent to carry the child of the Spirit. Here, she has to persist in her request that Jesus cure his child. In his attempt to prove the purely Jewish character of the entire mission of Jesus Vermes simply fails to understand what is going on: that the character of the encounter is a testing.[15] I need to remind again that the situation is highly liminal, the proper condition for testing: the first time the borderline of Israel is breeched by Jesus, and the first time he is talking after his mission has started, alone, without his disciples, to a woman. The woman, however, passed the test, in opposition to so many of the compatriots of Jesus who failed; so therefore the nature of the mission mutated. Vermes wants to fixate the mission of Jesus, and fails to realise that such fixity, in this case exclusivity, even if it existed before, in liminal conditions becomes malleable.

Finally, it is shortly after this allusion to the extension of the mission that Jesus asks, and receives, recognition by Peter in the famous scene (Mt 16: 15-9), and which would be interpreted as the foundation of the Church. The sequential order is the same in Mark; and it is important to underline here that exactly Matthew and Mark are considered as the more traditional or 'Jewish' Gospels, in opposition to the more 'Greek' Luke and John.

What has been stated about the encounter with the Phonician woman is Tyre

---

14 In many European languages rape, ecstatic-mystic rapture, and kidnapping/ravishing have the same etymological root.
15 About Vermes, see the following recently made claim, amazing in many ways: 'As a former Catholic priest who has returned to his Jewish roots, he tends to see the events described without party political bias.' See Peter Stanford, 'The Jesus jigsaw,' in *The Sunday Times*, 20 March 2005, Culture, p. 41.

is fully confirmed by another major and quite unique Biblical episode, the encounter with the Samaritan woman in the city of Sychar (Jn 4: 5-30). This episode, in many of its details, is so stunning that its authenticity is often questioned. Following the excellent discussion of Michel Henry (2002), who calls attention to the exceptional significance of this passage, I will only focus on a few aspects of the episode.

Henry starts by recognising the problematic, late character of the episode, but argues that the message it contains is supported by a series of passages in the Synoptic Gospels (Henry 2002: 64-6). Its significance is also undermined by aspects of physical and literary context. In the Gospel of John this is the first time Jesus leaves Israel, meeting all alone a woman who is also a foreigner, member of a hostile ethnic group, the Samaritans. The meeting furthermore takes place at Jacob's well, obtained by the Patriarch on the occasion of a peculiar episode in the Book of Genesis, the rape of his daughter Dina (Gen 33: 19). Jesus asks the women to give him drink from the well, and it is in the ensuing conversation that one of the most striking words of the Gospel are uttered, with Jesus identifying himself as the Messiah: 'I am who are speaking to you' (Jn 4: 26) – a statement whose significance is only underlined by the abruptness of its uttering (Henry 2002: 63-4).

The passage directly evokes the famous tetragrammaton YHWH, or 'I am that I am' (Ex 3: 14). The self-definition, however, is altered, and in two significant ways. Definition by being is changed to definition by speech (logos); and furthermore, the speech is addressed to a second person, this person being female, and non-Jewish.

Due to this emphatic reference to words, the verbal context of the statement should be carefully revisited. While the self-revelation is about words, the passage is satiated with references to the most physical needs: Jesus asks for water; from a woman; and immediately after references are made to bread and eating (Jn 4: 30-4). All this serves to undermine the extraordinary revaluation the passage operates (Henry 2002: 66). Finally, the episode starts and ends with problems related to recognition: the conflicts with the Pharisees (Jn 2: 25, 3: 1, 4: 1), and one of the most famous declarations about the failure of recognition: 'A prophet is not valued in his own country' (Jn 4: 44) – a claim which, strikingly, is immediately qualified by the evangelist (4: 45).

The significance of this episode is further underlined by broader issues of context: the episode serves as a conclusion to the long 'recognitive' part of the Gospel of John. The question of recognising the identity of Jesus is central for all four Gospels, discussed at the very beginning of each, taking up increasingly more and more space. It is dealt with by Mark in a few verses at the start (Mk 1: 7-11), while in Matthew and Luke in their first two chapters. In John, this extends to four chapters, thus a significant part of the entire book. These four chapters summarise and further elaborate the arguments of the previous evangelists. Mark starts in the middle, placing the emphasis on the Baptist. Matthew and

Luke take the storyline further, singling out for attention the break in the genealogical lineage and the importance of Mary. John takes the argument even further, giving a particularly Greek twist. Each of the first three chapters focuses around a single concept, or phenomenon, that is specifically Greek. Chapter 1 is about logos, and it is this logos that is at the origins, thus replacing the genealogical-patriarchic lineages and the emphasis on blood or 'seed;' the logos that is associated with the Holy Spirit. It is this Greek-philosophical lineage that is carried further in Chapter 3, with its emphasis on second birth, or conversion, another central term of Greek philosophy, and another area in which Christian theology would decisively rely on such philosophical sources, crowned by the work of St Augustine. Chapter 2 on the wedding in Cana and the transfiguration of water into wine, seemingly breaks this smooth link between Chapters 1 and 3, and is often considered as being out of the narrative line. Its position, however, can be understood together with Chapter 4, to which it rhymes, and with which it closes the introductory-initiatory circle of recognition. Taken together Chapters 2 and 4 are clearly Greek, though not so much philosophical as Minoan-Dionysian.

Children

The role played by children in recognising charisma is again radically different in the two cases. In the case of Jesus, they simply have no such role. Of course, children are extremely important for the message of the Gospel, and are often identified as favourite themes for Jesus, either in concrete physical reality when Jesus plays with them or indicates them as model for behaviour (Mt 19: 13-4, 21: 16; Lk 18: 15-7); or, in a sense related to the latter, when he exhorts the listeners to be like children (Mt 11: 25, 18: 2-10; Mk 9: 36-7). But children never feature among his disciples, which is really as it should be, as children have no business of identifying a prophet as a prophet. The recognition of charisma is a matter for adults.

It is all the more surprising then that children do play a fundamental role in the recognition of Muhammad as a prophet. This is even underlined in the most authoritative narratives, stating that his first male disciple was a child of mere ten years of age, and who was by the way his cousin. This is further reinforced by the fact that the first female person who recognised him was his wife Khadijah; and that upon her loss, and in another the context of liminal experience of suffering, it was again a child who would comfort him – this time Aishia who would become her wife at the age of six. It needs to be emphasised that such a conflation of personal recognition by family members – and especially by children – is highly problematic if at stake is the recognition of the prophet as a prophet. Children, of course, are extremely important sources of support, and do have a quite sharp sense of distinguishing good and bad persons. However, apart from their volatility and defencelessness, they simply cannot be relied upon in identifying the qualities of a prophet.

Disciples

For Jesus, three instances will be stressed. First, disciples have a central role in recognising and identifying the charisma of Jesus. In this role they are not only outside the circle of family members or immediate personal acquaintances, but the distinction is explicitly emphasised. The contrast is so strong that one could even take offence of it, especially if Mary is pictured among those 'rejected' in this way (Mt 12: 46-50); but the scene only draws the implications of the very first chapters of Matthew, and is therefore a fundamental part of the message.

Second, while Jesus is recognised and followed by the disciples as an unquestioned master, elements of mutuality and reciprocity are introduced in the narrative. Occasionally this is explicit (see Jn 1: 35-41). More importantly, at least some of them are called by Jesus in some central episodes to share with him the experience and the burden (transfiguration at Mount Tabor, vigil at the Gethsemane garden), while in others to follow his actions (Peter walking over the sea), though they usually fail, leading him to exhortation. The structure of these episodes, and the moral of the exhortations, is very specific. The disciples are not threatened by choice punishments for failing to evaluate his special qualities, or unique and distinct character; rather they are taken to task for not being like him. They are offered equal status, but fail to capture and maintain the opportunity. These are part of the failings identified at the start of John (1: 7-11).

Finally, though only in John, the first disciples of Jesus are also identified as former disciples of St John Baptist. Whether the episode is authentic or not, the crucial point is the emphasis on mutual recognition, this time between prophets; instead of a rivalry, the earlier prophet is identified as bowing to the more recent one. Thus, from the recognition of disciples, we are back to our first point, the recognition of the heralding prophet with which our analysis, and the Gospels, start. The circle is closed.

The case again could not be more different from Muhammad. The recruitment of disciples, especially outside the closely-knit family circle, was very slow.[16] Even after the move to Medina, stimulated by increasing number of people coming from Medina converting to his prophecy, progress was slow. Its pace only increased once Muhammad started to organise raids on caravans, in order to support himself; and even then, after initial failures, the radical breakthrough happened when – in violation of the holy truce – his men attacked and defeated a caravan (Hodgson 1974: 175). In response to widespread initial outcry, Muhammad justified the blatant breach of agreements on the basis of a new revelation that 'while violation of the truce was bad, persecution of the faith was worse and

---

16 In contrast, in his recent book Vermes estimates that the entire preaching of Jesus was about six months' long (Vermes 2002: 371). Whether it is true or not, the point concerns the *possibility* of making such a claim; and at any rate even the classical account is only talking about three years.

justified the violation' (Hodgson 1974: 175). On this basis he then succeeded to recruit, for the first time, a larger raid force, and at the wells of Badr inflicted a huge defeat on Quraysh opponents of vastly superior numbers. This victory was considered to confirm divine support for Muhammad, and from now onwards the march of Islam was more or less unstoppable. The significance of events is shown by the fact that presence at Badr would be later considered as 'a patent of nobility' (Hodgson 1974: 176).

Thus, in contradistinction to Jesus, the main external disciples of Muhammad were recruited not through the recognition of a prophet but of a successful raider; they were never offered an equal status, only unconditional submission to accepting him as the one and only messenger of Allah; and they were not disciples of other prophets – these other prophets rather were forced to submit, or were simply murdered (Guzzetti 2004: 170).

The image of the enemy

In his theory of recognition Pizzorno emphasises the importance of rivalry and adversity. Contrary to the approach of Honneth, recognition is not necessarily identical with positive acknowledgement and emotional support; it might well be given by accepting the person as a rival, even as an enemy. From a different angle, this approach can be supported by the theoretisation of labelling or stigmatisation offered by Goffman. In both approaches a central question is the exact balance between the identity of the self and the other. What is the exact dynamics of recognition? Is it a contest, an agonistic duel, in which the other provides a way to test oneself, to measure oneself against an opposition which is respected, and therefore ends by the acceptance of the other, which does not necessary imply full-scale victory, not to mention the annihilation of the opponent, being rather a re-confirmation of self-esteem; or is the other vilified and blamed, threatened with all kinds of punishments, torture and death, forcing a life-and-death struggle?

In the case of Jesus, exhortations against the unbelievers are rare, and not connected inherently to the message. They remain vague and general, blamed on inherent human weaknesses, and connected to not those who are actually physically present – as most of them, according to the narrative, are instantly converted by his miracles – but rather to the weakness in maintaining and transmitting faith, or what they have witnessed or heard. The contents of his speech, and the targets of his acts, are hardly ever the unbelievers or the unfaithful, those who fail to recognise him; they are only identified afterwards, and usually only for the disciples. Even when perhaps the strongest of such threats of punishments is issued in instructing the disciples, they are only advised to 'shake off the dust of [their] feet' (Mt 10: 14); the punishment is left to God and the Day of Judgment. The punishment is therefore not physical violence, just a parting of ways, whether it is the leaving of the city, as advised in this passage, or the excommunication of the 'sinners,' as practised by the Church. This practice is a return to the very old communal practice of ban or exile,[17] in opposition to the capital punishment characteristic of large-scale bureaucratic empires.[18]

There is one crucial difference from this general practice; one case in which Jesus is going out of his way to attack and vilify a particular opponent: these are the Pharisees. This is a practice that at a first look seems strange, aggressive, intolerant, even incantatory, highly incompatible with the mostly non-violent and non-conflictual message of the Gospels. Luckily, we can start our analysis with one of the most underused writings of Max Weber, who interprets the Pharisees as sect religiosity whose main character was a reaction against Hellenisation, especially the Sophists.[19]

The Pharisees are neither prophets nor priests. They do not show or even pretend the attributes of prophets, and are also different from the Sadducees, the high priests, who were their main opponents. They possess three distinct identifying features. They are the pious purists, maintaining tradition in the strictest possible sense, and separating themselves, physically and morally, from those who do not live according to the letter of their strict moralising rules. The novelty in this respect is that they no longer do so only with respect to the Hellenes, but also the Jews (Weber 1952: 386-7).[20] Second, they are mostly members of the literate intellectual elite, often referred to as the Scribes. Due to these two factors, and their joint hostility to both the high priests and the broad populace, they would build up structures alternative to the Synagogue, devaluing priestly rituals, as if transforming themselves into an alternative elite, waiting in the shadows to capture power. In fact, according to Weber, the true significance of the Pharisees would only become visible after the Fall of the Temple, when 'all Judaism became Pharisaic' (ibid.: 391). Finally, because of their education and skills, in

---

17 There is a close parallel here between punishment meted out by the Pygmies of the rainforest (Turnbull 1968), exile by ostracism in democratic Athens, and ban in ancient German or Roman legal practices (Agamben 1998).
18 Inquisition is mostly a legacy of Spain, and therefore an often ignored consequence of the 'multicultural' situation of the peninsula, the joint presence of Christians, Muslims and Jews. Furthermore, the crucial issue in this case, just as with the end of the Renaissance in general, is the collapse of the separation between temporal and spiritual powers, the foundation of medieval European culture, and the ensuing power invested in secular authorities to further persecute religious heretics, after their excommunication.
19 It is little short of a miracle that this text is available, one of the very few surviving manuscripts from Weber's *Nachlass*, somehow escaping the 'treatment' of Marianne Weber.
20 It is important to notice that up to the very last scene of the Gospels, the Passion, if occasionally Jesus uses the word 'Jew,' it always refers to the Pharisees. This is partly because only they spoke Hebrew (the populace used Aramaic); and partly an ironic take on their pretence of being the only 'true' Jews.

spite of their critical stance they had easy access to the central corridors of power.[21]

The attacks by Jesus start with the excessive importance attributed by them to the law and ritual purity, but go much further and turn directly against their own character, reaching its highest pitch and coherence in Matthew 23. Though putting excessive burden on common people (Mt 23: 4), they themselves often fail to live according to their own principles (see also Mt 7: 4). This is because they confuse the letter and the spirit of the law: being preoccupied with the former, lose the latter: 'Ye fools and blind, for whether is greater, the gift, or the altar that sanctifieth the gift?' (Mt 23: 19). This is why they are repeatedly identified as hypocrites, charged with the highest possible sin, the unique that cannot be forgiven: 'whosoever speaketh a word against the Son of man, it shall be forgiven him; but whosoever speaketh against the Spirit, it shall not be forgiven him, neither in this world, neither in the world to come' (Mt 12: 32). In the framework of this paper it is especially important to emphasise that this highest of charges is explicitly made not concerning offences committed against the person of Jesus.

This already shows that these attacks cannot be identified as charges voiced against rivals. Jesus is not trying to out-perform the Pharisees in what they are doing, rather preaches something completely different. It is true that he attacks them exactly as false guides, offering a different kind of guidance; but does so not by using existing liminal conditions of confusion, rather by creating a liminal storm on its own in order to overtake spiritual leadership from the hands of a pseudo-elite that in a way tries to make use the best of both worlds, being comfortably inside power and still pretending outsider status, criticising everybody and not taking responsibility for anything. The attempt, by conventional measures, completely fails. Jesus only manages to bring together former enemies, like the Pharisees and the Sadducees who conspire in his death sentence, or Pilate and Herod (Lk 23: 12), and ends his life on the cross, derided as 'king of the Jews.' Yet, exactly in this way, through complete failure and dejection, somehow the momentum was generated for the rise of a new world religion.

The situation again could not be more different in the case of Islam. First of all, since the earliest revelations (see Suras 102, 104) the Koran is exhorting in

---

21 The unique characteristics of the Pharisees invite broader generalisation and contemporary comparison. They condense, in a genuinely archetypical sense, two types that would have a huge impact of the dynamics of the modern world: the Puritanic sects, already mentioned by Weber, and the educated elites of court societies (like 18th-century France or Communist East-Central Europe) who stay close to the centres of power, enjoying all the privileges, though maybe having some frills out of mocking and criticising the dictatorial rules, while being convinced of their own special status and deeply despising the general populace, considered at best the passive targets of the enlightening mission. For some details in this regard, see Szakolczai (2005).

the strongest possible sense against those who failed to believe in the prophet. In the original language these exhortations are delivered in an extremely powerful, poetic, incantatory language, where the content of the message, the evocation of strong choice punishment; the formal artistic devices used, the rhymes, repetitions and alliterations; and the fact that this was hurled at a loud language against the opponents all contributed to intimidate or force the opponent into submission, and where such verbal violence could always easily turn into actual physical conflict. In fact, it is not an exaggeration to say that the message of the Koran operates at two levels: one is the actual call for a pious, pure, chaste, upright, moral life; and the other is the reinforcement of this message by the rewards and punishments to be meted out each according to what they deserve. The reference point is singular and always the same: the person of Muhammad as the unique voice of God and the revelations transmitted by him as the sole fountain of truth; and violence should be applied, as a duty, to those who fail.

The contrasts are stark even related to the concrete example discussed. There were no Pharisees in early Islam, but the adjective 'hypocrite' is often used to translate the term munafiqun, denoting a group of Muhammad's opponents who were supposedly particularly vicious (Hodgson 1974: 178). They are, however, not an established group pre-existing the preaching of Muhammad, with access to the official circles; rather those who have only superficially adhered to the new faith.[22] Far from being a powerful group external to the prophet, challenged purely due to fundamental questions of religious and practical conduct, even character, they are a group of people who were forced to submit to the new faith, but trying to maintain a degree of independence under external conformity. The attacks on the hypocrites is therefore part of a powerful but extremely questionable two-step strategy of oppression that would be used by many similar regimes to hammer opponents into full submission: the first step is physical conquest, the subduing of an entire population by force; while the second step is the gradual extermination of all inner sources of resistance, by requiring a genuine belief in the conquerors. It was this two-step strategy that, as shown by Goddard (2000: 68-74), led to the gradual Islamisation and Arabisation of the entire near East and North Africa.

With this point, however, the paper moved from the dynamics of experience and recognition, central for the early stages of the new religion, to the subsequent question of the dynamics of conversion and conquest, which is outside its proper theme, though to which it hopefully prepares the ground. The analysis suggests that even here, the radical contrast between Christianity and Islam can be clearly observed. While in the latter case conversion followed conquest, already in the life of the prophet, in the former case, for about three centuries after the death of

---

22 A main sign of this hypocrisy was the failure to take part in warfare. I thank Stefan Leder for this comment.

Jesus, conversion took place without any coercive force; rather, on the contrary, in the face of mortal risks. The situation would change later; and given that this change happened almost 1700 years ago, it is all-too easy to forget the exact dynamics of emergence.

References

Agamben, Giorgio (1998) *Homo Sacer: Sovereign Power and Bare Life*, Stanford: Stanford University Press.
Elias, Norbert (1987) *Involvement and Detachment*, Oxford: Blackwell.
Foucault, Michel (1980) *History of Sexuality, Vol. 1*, New York: Vintage.
Foucault, Michel (1984) "What Is Enlightenment?" In: Paul Rabinow (ed.) *The Foucault Reader*, New York: Pantheon.
Foucault, Michel (1986) *The Care of the Self*, New York: Vintage.
Girard, René (1976) *Deceit, Desire and the Novel: Self and Other in Literary Structure*, Baltimore: John Hopkins University Press.
Girard, René (1977) *Violence and the Sacred*, Baltimore: John Hopkins University Press.
Girard, René (1987) *Things Hidden since the Foundation of the World*, London: Athlone.
Girard, René (1989) *The Scapegoat*, Baltimore: John Hopkins University Press.
Goddard, Hugh (2000) *A History of Christian-Muslim Relations*, Edinburgh: Edinburgh University Press.
Guzzetti, Cherubino Mario (2004) *Muhammad: La vita di Maometto, profeta di Allah*, Cinisello Balsamo (Milano): Edizioni San Paolo.
Henry, Michel (2002) *Paroles du Christ*. Paris: Seuil.
Hodgson, Marshall (1995) *The Venture of Islam: Conscience and History in a World Civilisation, Volume One: The Classical Age of Islam*, Chicago: University of Chicago Press.
Honneth, Axel (1995) *The Struggle for Recognition: The Moral Grammar of Social Conflicts*, Cambridge, Mass.: Polity Press.
Horvath, Agnes (2000) *The Nature of the Trickster's Game*, PhD thesis, European University Institute, Florence, Italy.
The Koran (1955), translated by Arthus J. Arberry, Oxford: Oxford University Press.
A Koran (1987), translated by Róbert Simon, Budapest: Helikon.
Lewis, Bernard (1967) *The Assassins: A Radical Sect in Islam*, London: Weidenfeld & Nicholson.
Lewis, Bernard (2003) *The Crisis of Islam: Holy War and Unholy Terror*, London: Weidenfeld & Nicholson.
Mauss, Marcel (2002) *The Gift*, London: Routledge.
Pace, Enzo (1999) *Sociologia dell'Islam*, Rome: Carocci.

Patocka, Jan (2002) *Plato and Europe*, Stanford: Stanford University Press.
Pedretti, Carlo (1973) *Leonardo: A Study in Chronology and Style*, London: Thames and Hudson.
Pizzorno, Alessandro (1987) "Some Other Kinds of Otherness: A Critique of "Rational Choice" Theories." In: A. Foxley/M.S. McPherson/G. O'Donnell (eds.), *Development, Democracy and the Art of Trespassing: Essays in Honor of Albert O. Hirschman*, Notre Dame: University of Notre Dame Press, pp. 355-73.
Pizzorno, Alessandro (1987) "Politics Unbound." In: Charles S. Maier (ed.) *Changing Boundaries of the Political*, Cambridge: Cambridge University Press, pp. 27-62.
Pizzorno, Alessandro (1989) "Spiegazione come reidentificazione." *Rassegna Italiana di Sociologia 30/2*, pp. 161-84.
Pizzorno, Alessandro (1991) "On the Individualistic Theory of Social Order." In: Pierre Bourdieu/James S. Coleman (eds.) *Social Theory for a Changing Society*, Boulder and Oxford, Westview Press, pp. 209-231.
Pizzorno, Alessandro (1993) *Le radici della politica assoluta*, Milano, Feltrinelli.
Pizzorno, Alessandro (2000) "Risposte e proposte." In: Donatella Della Porta/Monica Greco/Arpad Szakolczai (eds.) *Identità, riconoscimento e scambio: Saggi in onore di Alessandro Pizzorno*, Bari, Laterza, pp. 197-245.
Radin, Paul (1972) *The Trickster. A Study in American Indian Mythology*, with commentary by Karl Kerényi and Carl G. Jung, New York: Schocken.
Simmel, Georg (1971) "Sociability." In: Donald N. Levine (ed.) *On Individuality and Social Forms: Selected Writings*, Chicago: University of Chicago Press.
Simon, Róbert (1987) *A Korán világa*, Budapest: Helikon.
Szakolczai, Arpad (2005) "Moving Beyond the Sophists: Intellectuals in East Central Europe and the Return of Transcendence." *The European Journal of Social Theory 8 (4)*.
Taylor, Charles (1994) *Multiculturalism: Examining the Politics of Recognition*, Princeton: Princeton University Press.
Turnbull, Colin M. (1968) *The Forest People*, New York: Simon & Schuster.
Turner, Victor (1967) "Betwixt and Between: The Liminal Period in *Rites de Passage*." In: idem *The Forest of Symbols,* New York: Cornell University Press.
Turner, Victor (1969) *The Ritual Process,* Chicago: Aldine.
Turner, Victor (1975) *Revelation and Divination in Ndembu Ritual*, Ithaca: Cornell University Press.
Turner, Victor (1985a) "Experience and Performance: Towards a New Processual Anthropology." In: Edith Turner (ed.) *On the Edge of the Bush*, Tucson, Arizona: The University of Arizona Press, pp. 205-226.
Turner, Victor (1985b) "The Anthropology of Performance." In: Edith Turner (ed.) *On the Edge of the Bush*, Tucson, Arizona: The University of Arizona Press, pp. 177-204.

van Gennep, Arnold (1960 [1909]) *The Rites of Passage,* Chicago: University of Chicago Press.
Vermes, Geza (2004) *The Authentic Gospel of Jesus*, London: Penguin.
Weber, Max (1952) *Ancient Judaism*, New York: The Free Press.
Weber, Max (1978) *Economy and Society,* Berkeley: University of California Press.

Chapter 4

The Emergence of Islam as a Case of Cultural Crystallization: Historical and Comparative Reflections

JOHANN P. ARNASON

The concept of cultural crystallization (first introduced, if I am not mistaken, by Björn Wittrock) has been used in the context of comparative historical-sociological research, most prominently in debates about the Axial Age and the civilizations that took off from it, but also in connection with the question whether comparable transformations occurred at other times and in other settings (see especially Wittrock 2005; also the discussion in Arnason/Eisenstadt/Wittrock 2005). Here I will not attempt to define it in precise and detailed terms; I will treat it as an orientative device, serving to link together several key themes. Most obviously, it refers to the formation of distinctive cultural orientations or premises, more precisely: clusters of such orientations, interconnected but often conducive to internal tensions and interpretive conflicts; innovative transformations of religious traditions are prime cases in point, but not the only ones. But the concept also implies an institutional dimension: a translation of cultural patterns into institutional frameworks, not to be understood as standing above or outside social change, but as giving specific directions to it. Finally, the interplay of cultural and institutional factors involves specific relationships and more or less effective coalitions between intellectual and political elites; at the same time, traditions in the sense of enduring frameworks for discourse, interpretation and dispute take shape.

Civilizational dimensions

So far, I have outlined the idea of cultural crystallization at its most elementary level without any particular reference to civilizational analysis. What happens when we apply it to that field? Since any discussion of the civilizational dimension must start with the point that we are dealing with large-scale-units and long-term trajectories, the first answer that suggests itself is that cultural crystallization on the civilizational level – i.e. the formation of civilizations, or the transformations radical enough for us to speak of a new civilization – enacts the model summed up above on a particularly large scale. But on closer inspection, and if some note is taken of variations, it becomes possible to suggest differentiations that will turn out to have some bearing on Islam in comparative perspective. Two considerations of this kind seem especially relevant.

There is, first, a marked contrast between different patterns of the relationship between cultural orientations and institutional frameworks. There are cases where cultural orientations are articulated, elaborated and transformed within enduring civilizational complexes, whose institutional formations and power structures in particular evolve alongside the cultural and intellectual changes. China would seem to be the most obvious example. On the other hand, there are historical experiences of the kind Talcott Parsons had in mind when he coined the concept of 'seedbed societies' (which we may take to be an echo of the axial model). Here cultural orientations of a particularly innovative kind emerge in settings that do not allow full realization of their institutional potential, and the resulting cultural legacies are later appropriated by other societies on a broader scale. Parsons wanted to put both Ancient Greece and Ancient Israel into this category. It seems to fit the latter case much better: here the discrepancy between a cultural breakthrough and a restricting social and geopolitical context is at its most marked. In the short run and in the original environment, the Jewish invention (or reorientation; here I will bypass the debate as to which concept is most adequate) of monotheism found a very limited institutional expression: after the destruction of the monarchy and an interlude in exile, it became the foundation for a small hierocratic community, later exposed to cultural and political pressures from Hellenistic civilization, and to internal conflicts resulting from that; there seems to have been an enduring tension between the ongoing religious development and the power structure oscillating between theocratic and monarchic models. A more comprehensive and far-reaching institutional dynamic, generated by monotheism, could only unfold after further transformations of the religious premises in new socio-cultural settings. The Greek case is less clear-cut: here the distinctive cultural orientations were inseparable from – indeed largely identical with – a very specific institutional context, the polis and the corresponding type of city-state culture. But this civilizational complex was a particularly fragile and conflict-prone one, torn between rival and incompatible developmental paths (not just Athens and Sparta, but also Corinth and Syracuse, and perhaps other *polis* communities may be seen as representatives of such directions), and in the end, its self-destructive dynamics paved the way for absorption into more composite civilizational formations – first the perhaps mislabelled Hellenistic and then the Roman one – where cultural aspects of the Greek legacy had a much more formative impact than the strictly political ones. There is thus at least a grain of truth in Parsons's thesis.

But if, with these two examples in mind, we take another look at the Chinese case, the contrast may seem less stark than it appeared at first sight. The most innovative and also the most conflict-ridden period in the history of Chinese civilization, the Age of the Warring States (roughly the third quarter of the last millennium BCE), saw the emergence of sharply divergent intellectual currents as well as new strategies for state-building, some of which represented a more overt break with the traditions of an existing civilizational complex than others. The current – or rather the combination of currents – that won out was a rationalized version of traditionalism, centred on a restoration of sacred rulership and a re-elaboration of the notions of intertwined cosmic and social orders that served to underpin and transfigure it. But for some time, the relationship between cultural orientations and institutional frameworks had been more uncertain and contested than at any other moment, before or after, in the history of Chinese civilization.

To sum up, it might be more useful to conceptualize this issue in terms of a continuum of varying relationships, rather than a dichotomy of polar contrasts. The distinction I have in mind is perhaps best described as one between civilizational patterns and civilizational complexes, and the historical connections between them vary in significant ways. The embodiment of civilizational patterns in civilizational complexes takes more circuitous forms and involves more long-drawn-out processes in some cases than others; conversely, some breakthroughs to new civilizational patterns occur in situations less favourable to implementation on the multiple levels of social life than others.

The second issue to be considered has to do with intercivilizational relations and their role in the emergence of new civilizational formations. If we accept that recent work on global history has shown interactions and exchanges of all kinds, often over long distances, to have been a much more significant factor in the destinies of human societies than earlier historians tended to assume, we must conclude that it has become implausible to think of any civilizational formation (in the sense of *Hochkultur* – I am using the concept in a sense that restricts it to history after the beginnings of civilization in the singular) in terms of complete isolation. But the role of intercivilizational contacts is very much more salient and significant in some cases than others. It seems to have been least important – at any rate least evident – in the case of pre-Columbian American civilizations (the Meso-American and Andean complexes). As for the Eurasian or Afro-Eurasian macro-region, recent scholarship has thrown light on early contacts between China and more western regions. They were clearly more significant than earlier accounts had suggested. But it still seems legitimate to describe the early trajectory of Chinese civilization as relatively isolated by comparison with other parts of Eurasia: there was, from very early on, a Mediterranean-Levantine-Iranian-South Asian zone of intensified intercivilizational contacts. At the beginning, the Mesopotamian complex – clearly more central than any other – develops together with more derivative but not merely imitative peripheral formations around it. At a much later stage, the intertwined composite civilizations of Hellenism (Assmann 2000: 277) argues, to my mind persuasively, that this is a bit of a misnomer) and the Roman Empire emerge out of a long history of intercivilizational encounters. One further implication of that development should be noted: the question of the relationship between civilizations and historical regions comes to the fore. As civilizational unity becomes more problematic, regional unity becomes by the same token more salient.

Let us now try to situate the emergence of Islam and Islamicate civilization (I prefer this term, coined by Marshall Hodgson, to 'Islamic civilization') within this twofold frame of reference. It happened at the very core (or, more precisely, through the interaction of a core and an inner periphery) of the above-mentioned zone of intensified contacts. And as I will try to show, it represents a specific version of the relationship between civilizational patterns and civilizational complexes.

A first glance at the historical record would suggest that we are dealing with a prime case of cultural crystallization – indeed of multiple crystallizations. At the religious level, a new – and, on its own terms, definitive – version of monotheistic prophecy crystallized through demarcation from the pre-existing ones. It seems clear that the radicalized monotheistic message was intended as an alternative to the troubles and schisms that Christology had produced within the Christian Church (Fowden [1993, 2005] has stressed this point); by the same token, it drew in some ways closer to Judaism, and perhaps especially to the Judeo-Christian currents (how important that affinity was seems to be a matter of debate among scholars in the field); but notwithstanding the surviving elements of primordialism (S.N. Eisenstadt has drawn attention to this aspect), the message was not to be confined within ethnic boundaries. Second, this religious crystallization became the foundation for a new civilizational formation – whether we prefer the label 'Islamic' or 'Islamicate,' there is no denying the relatively rapid emergence of this new civilization, and its internal unity is so pronounced that it seems more apposite to speak of a civilizational synthesis than a composite civilization. Third, there is a geocultural side to the process that merits separate mention: as Hodgson noted, Islamicate civilization imposes for the first time a cultural unity on the Ancient Near East, or the 'Nile-to-Oxus region,' as he preferred to call it. The character of a whole region – the most central of the Old World – is thus redefined. Moreover, the civilizational patterns that established this new unity also proved uniquely capable of expansion into other parts of Afro-Eurasia. Islamicate civilization became the premodern globalizing civilization par excellence. Finally, this whole crystallizing process was, on the level of the self-understanding of the new civilization, condensed into a narrative that seems best described as sacred history. This point can be conceded to the sceptics that cast doubt on the traditional accounts of Islamic origins – without accepting all the conclusions that the more radical sceptics want to draw from it. It does not follow that this narrative results from a wholesale suppression of the record and the construction of an imaginary alternative; there is no a priori answer to questions about the relationship of sacred history to historical experience.

At this point, it may be useful to digress briefly and note a few theoretical and methodological problems with the line of argument proposed by the radical revisionists. First, they like to present their approach as a result of progressive and logical radicalization of the critical stance that goes back to Goldziher and Schacht (this is, for example, apparent in one of the most recent exercises in this genre, Nevo and Koren 2003). But this divorce of critical logic from substantive issues will not do. There is, to borrow a formulation from Said Arjomand's unpublished paper on theoretical issues in discussions about early Islam, no straight path from the 'higher criticism' pioneered by Goldziher and the 'higher deconstruction' practiced by the radical revisionists. Second (as I have already hinted), their sweeping claims about the construction and closure of sacred history bring in strong and unexamined theoretical assumptions about cultural genres and their interrelations. Third, when developing an alternative account of Islamic origins, they seem to face a dilemma: They either leave the question of the historical background to the assumed large-scale rewriting of history unanswered, or – if they try to answer it – they come up with historical scenarios of such complexity that that it becomes increasingly difficult to accept their disappearance from cultural memory (the latter would seem to apply to the Nevo-Koren version).

However, we do not face a choice between traditionalism and radical revisionism. Not only is there a large body of work produced by moderate revisionists; there are also meta-critiques of the revisionist critique, reacting against what they see as unwarranted scepticism about the traditional sources, but sufficiently responsive to issues raised by the revisionists to take the debate to a new level. A good example of this genre is Fred M. Donner's study of early Islamic historiography (Donner 1998). On the basis of detailed comparison of the Quran with other early sources (especially *hadith* records), he argues that the Quran must be accepted as an early and singular text, rather than a part of a broader ex post construction of sacred history. This is obviously not the same line as that taken by one of the most respected Western translators of the Quran, who claims in a preface that "we have no reason to believe that the whole Quran contains a single verse that does not come from Muhammad" (Paret 2001 [1966]: 5). Donner's argument has to do with the relative chronology rather than the authorship of the Quran: it seems clear that the acculturation of monotheism in Arabia was a project pursued from many quarters, and it does not seem inconceivable that the canonized text incorporated borrowings from rival prophets who were at the same time portrayed as precursors or rebels. But given the nature and limits of the evidence, it is very unlikely that such questions will ever be settled, and it is more important to assess the evidence for prophetic innovation and authority prior to conquest on an imperial scale. Donner also analyzes the early Islamic transition from ahistorical piety to historical consciousness, and concludes that the overall picture is more nuanced than either traditionalists or radical revisionists would have it: On the one hand, memories and records of the crucial early decades became a battlefield for rival factions and interpretations, rather than a tabula rasa for orthodox constructs; on the other hand, agreement on key themes and central events among otherwise conflicting camps is significant enough to provide some footholds for historical inquiry. A critical history, as distinct from a wholesale rejection of the tradition, is possible, but the results so far are piecemeal and provisional.

Another illustration of the metacritical approach is Garth Fowden's study of the ruins of Qusayr Amra, seen as a key to the court culture of the Umayyad period (Fowden 2004). Here the stated intention is to confront the literary sources with other kinds of evidence (excavations, inscriptions and monuments), and the results suggest a complex cultural synthesis in the making: "In preferring an effective rearrangement of preexisting elements, sealed by a process of appropriation to itself and denial to others, rather than some more thoroughgoing originality, early Islam was conforming to a model of transition that is common enough in cultural history. Under the Umayyads it conditioned the ideology of kingship quite as much as the biography of the prophet" (ibid.: 307). The Umayyad phase of this formative process was more open to multiple options than the pattern that took shape after 750. In a more speculative vein, Fowden conjectures that "congruities of Mediterranean and pre-Islamic Arab culture" (ibid.: 310) may have been of some importance for further acculturation in the wake of conquest.

Excursus: Weber and Eisenstadt on Islam

Drawing on all this work, it may be possible to sketch a picture of the Islamic crystallization that will amplify – and in some respects modify – the one outlined above. But before moving in that direction, let us take a look at earlier Western approaches to the field. Although Western scholars could never take the traditionalist account at absolute face value (to do so would have amounted to conversion), its indirect influence is evident in interpretations that stress the formation of Islam as a self-contained religious world-view and civilizational model in Arabia prior to the conquest of the Near East. The most extreme version of that view can be found in the work of the anthropologist most interested in the comparative analysis of civilizations, Alfred Kroeber (1952: 381): he refers to Islam as a civilization born in the head of one man, the prophet Muhammad, and goes on to suggest that something analogous might have happened if Nazi Germany had won the second world war, and Hitler thus been enabled to impose his vision of a new world order. Nobody else seems to have gone quite as far as that; but on an altogether different level, there are echoes of the traditionalist account in Max Weber's comments on Islam; and given the importance of his work for comparative civilizational analysis, a brief outline of basic assumptions may be useful.

As is well known, Weber planned but did not write a comparative study of Islam as a world religion and its impact on social life, with particular reference to its economic ethic and the preconditions for capitalist development. Recent attempts to piece together Weber's picture of Islam have shown that the problem is not simply due to an unfinished project. At a deeper level, Weber's image of Islam is internally fragmented, and this explains the absence of a comprehensive civilizational profile comparable to his analyses of India and China. In his concluding reflections on the two latter cultural areas and their place in world history, he draws a geocultural boundary that separates India and China from what he calls the Occidental-Near Asian (*vorderasiatisch*) world. Although this enlarged version of the West has something to do with geographical and ecological settings, the most salient unifying factor is obviously the predominance of monotheistic religions that can be traced back to a common source. On this view, Islam should be included in the 'greater West' which Weber contrasts with East and South Asia. But when it comes to the comparative analysis of traditional domination and its structural variants, he describes Islamic feudalism as 'Oriental.' This shift reflects an ambiguous view of Islamic religious orientations as such. Weber's most focused analysis of early Islam begins with the claim that Muhammad's retreat from Mecca to Medina changed the whole character of his religious vision: the eschatological religiosity of "pietistic urban conventicles" mutated into a "national Arabic warrior religion" (Weber 1968, 2: 624). When the community organized around this new message embarked on expansion and conquest, it was bound to move further away from its original stance. The commitment to holy war was rooted in this-worldly aspirations to wealth, power and prestige; the other world was portrayed as a "soldier's sensual paradise" (ibid.: 625). Weber concludes that the very idea of salvation in the ethical sense is alien to this triumphant form of Islam, and that the foundations of its economic ethic are "purely feudal" (ibid.: 624).

But why should this uninhibited warrior religion be compared (as Weber does in the last section of his Sociology of Religion) to the world religions that centre on ethical visions of salvation? Conquest alone would not be enough for Islam to constitute a world religion in the emphatic Weberian sense. Weber hints at an answer when he refers to elements of ethical religiosity in early Islam, but adds that they were overshadowed by the dominant warrior ethos (ibid.: 474). The marginalized ethical message seems more or less identical with the eschatological religiosity that Muhammad abandoned when he left Mecca. This may be taken to show that Weber did not simply equate Islam with a warrior religion; it is less clear whether he saw the ethical potential as relevant to later developments, or identified any specific socio-cultural forces a representative of its spirit. Sufism does not qualify for that role: it was, in Weber's opinion, of Indian origin and entered the Islamic world through Persia. It did not bring Islamic societies any closer to the distinctive urban religiosity of Judaism and Christianity;" for Islam, the city had only political importance" (ibid.: 626) – but as a centre of patrimonial rule, not as a site of collective autonomy. The implications are clear: for Weber, urban religiosity never became a serious rival to the dominant warrior version of Islam. In view of this background, Weber's approach to Islamic feudalism is easier to understand. There is in fact – if we follow Weber's description – nothing distinctively Islamic about this institutional complex. Its only significant connection with religious traditions is historical: the early and irreversible empowerment of a military elite through a warrior religion. Military rulers and their governing associates respond to the omnipresent and self-perpetuating problems of patrimonial power structures – the intertwined dilemmas of centralization and decentralization – in distinctive ways. More precisely, mercenary armies and tax farming are the cornerstones of the particular kind of feudalism that develops under these conditions. It differs markedly from the complex "cosmos of rights and duties" (ibid., 3: 1070) characteristic of Occidental feudalism. Together with the structural features of Islamic law (an uncontested predominance of sacred law, obstructing rationalization of the secular component as such), the political structures based on this Oriental feudalism were – as Weber saw it – the most salient obstacles to capitalist development.

Weber's observations on later Islamic states – from Seljuks to Ottomans – have been analyzed in detail, and there is no need for further comments. For present purposes, a brief glance at his much less explicit view of the earliest period may be more useful. In terms of the framework outlined above, this period represents the phase of crystallization. It might seem gratuitous to dwell on obsolete ideas, conclusively rejected by later scholarship. Weber was dependent on sources available at the time, and probably less familiar with the most advanced research than in the fields of Indian and Chinese studies. But his errors are instructive: they provide a particularly striking counterpoint to perspectives emerging from current debates. To begin with the question of religion and expansion, Weber does not deny that religious energies were mobilized for the purpose of conquest, but he insists on their complete subordination to the usual worldly goals of warfare (to use the language of his own formulation, this would be an extreme case of material interests absorbing ideal ones), and to make this view more plausible, the pre-conquest politicization that took place in Medina is construed as a break with eschatological origins. In short, salvationist visions do not enter into Weber's account of the early Islamic conquests. As for the results of the conquests, it comes as no surprise that he does not deal with the specific imperial formations of early Islam. This is in line with the the general neglect of empires as such in his sociology of domination: they vanish into the patrimonial night where all cows are black. His comments on the two early imperial dynasties are more interesting. The Umayyads appear as representative of a feudal aristocracy that acpitalized on the conquests, and the only ethical motive mentioned in connection with the Arab resistance to them is the "asceticism of the warriors' camp" (ibid., 2: 627 – translation amended: the quoted text mistranslates *Kriegslager* as "military caste"). The power struggles that accompanied the rise and fall of a dynasty were thus – on Weber's view – essentially due to internal differentiation of the warrior elite that had spearheaded the conquests. Neither the problem of reconciling a universal religion with ethnic privileges, nor the dynamic of adaptation to pre-existing cultural patterns in the conquered territories seem to count as explanatory factors. But when it comes to the Abbasids, external influences are as overwhelming as they are absent from references to the Umayyads.

For Weber, the Abbasid revolution is nothing less than a transplantation of "the caesaropapist principles of the Zoroastrian Sasanids [...] into Islam in the name of a return to the sacred tradition." (ibid., 2: 819) In retrospect, we can see the two extremes as pointers to a problem that Weber did not raise: the role of inter-civilizational encounters in the phase of crystallization.

S.N. Eisenstadt's interpretation of Islam (Eisenstadt 1987), although very condensed, is more systematic than Weber's, and the following discussion will not attempt to cover all its aspects. The main question to be considered is whether Eisenstadt's critique of Weber leads to more adequate perspectives on the phase of crystallization. Eisenstadt begins with two critical observations on Weber's civilizational analysis in general and his understanding of Islam in particular; in both cases, basic conceptual problems are aggravated by inherent difficulties in theorizing Islam, as well as by shortcomings of Weber's approach to that particular field. First, a levelling conception of premodern societies (most evident in general definitions of traditional action and traditional domination) prevents Weber from grasping the meaning of and impact of the radical cultural transformations which Eisenstadt first defined with reference to the Axial Age, and later in terms of axiality as a type of cultural framework for social life. To cut a long story short, the axial turn occurs in varying contexts at different moments, but the common pattern is a new way of distinguishing between higher and lower orders of reality and translating such distinctions into visions of social order. This is the background to the formation of world religions, and Islam may be seen as a late case of axial transformation, superimposed on the results of several earlier ones (Greek, Judaic, Christian and Iranian). The axial perspective would thus be pre-eminently relevant to Islamic history; but as we have seen, Weber's view of the conquests that created an Islamic world was very far removed form such considerations. Second, Eisenstadt criticizes Weber for failing to distinguish between religion as one complex of social meanings and practices, and religion as an articulation of cultural premises for a whole civilizational pattern (to use a more Durkheimian language, this point has to do with the difference between institutional and meta-institutional aspects of religion). Although the criticism applies to the whole project of comparative sociology of world religions, Eisenstadt stresses its particular importance for understanding Islam. As he argues, a comparison of the classical phase of expansion with some later ones will highlight the difference: in the first case, a dominant civilizational pattern was imposed on a whole region (which in due course became the Islamic heartland), before mass conversion to Islam marginalized other religions, whereas – for example – the diffusion of Islam in Southeast Asia was more a matter of religious beliefs and practices spreading without transforming the whole civilizational pattern, and often taking syncretic forms through adaptation to indigenous traditions. This argument is convincing, and one might add that Eisenstadt's point has an obvious bearing on some more specific aspects of the classical phase. Neither the historically marginal but intrinsically interesting attempts of philosophers to develop alternative readings of revealed truths, nor the more massive Ismaili challenge to established Islam (briefly discussed below), can be properly understood without reference to the civilizational dimensions of religion.

But there was yet another side to the phase of crystallization. The civilizational impact of an expanding religion was, at this stage, inseparable from imperial power. The imperial formations of early Islam – those ruled by the Umayyad and Abbasid dynasties – were essential to the crystallizing process: their role exemplifies the more general point that the civilizational potential of religious traditions and transformations is most effectively realized in conjunction with political structures. However, Eisenstadt does not pursue this part of the question. After hinting at a general affinity between axial cultural premises and imperial forms of power, he goes on to note that only "very few Islamic regimes – the Abbasids, the Fatimids, less so the Safavids, but most of all the Ottomans – developed imperial characteristics; and even so, they remained imperial regimes of the traditional kind" (ibid.: 344). This somewhat puzzling formulation calls for comment. In light of Eisenstadt's objections to Weber, the term 'traditional' should probably be taken to denote the archaic patterns that precede axial changes, and thus to suggest an enduring tendency of Islamic empires to lag behind their cultural-religious self-definitions. But apart from the omission of the Umayyads, the list obscures the fact that the empires in question related to the religious and civilizational context in different ways. The Abbasids were directly and decisively involved in the formative phase of a civilizational complex, and the Fatimids belong – as will be seen – to a later chapter of the same story, whereas the Safavids and the Ottomans rose to power in a very different historical environment.

Beyond traditionalism and revisionism

To continue the argument signalled above, it seems that analyses of the more constructively revisionist kind, combined with other work, have now made it possible to distinguish between the intra- and extra-Arabian phases of crystallization. To begin with the first phase, it seems clear that Patricia Crone's reevaluation of the role of long-distance trade – and the corresponding impact of commercialization on Arabian society – has been widely accepted (cf. Crone 1987; this was a much more disciplined kind of revisionism than Crone and Cook 1977). To downgrade that factor is, by the same token, to shift attention to the intertwining of political and religious ones. The intra-Arabian emergence of Islam was clearly a case of state formation, but of a peculiarly self-cancelling kind: it involved the mobilization of nomad warriors for expansion and conquest, but did not result in durable state structures within the peninsula. It took place in a broader geopolitical context: against the background of inter-imperial rivalry

(Roman vs. Iranian) that in the 6th century CE had affected the peninsula more deeply than before, and in response to a conjuncture that had left the two imperial centres more vulnerable to counter-challenge from the periphery than before. To stress these political aspects is not to reduce the religious factor to an epiphenomenon of state formation. The whole record suggests that the religious mutation had a history and a dynamic of its own, but any reconstruction of details is problematic. A cautious revisionist concludes that "we can only accept as an established fact that a prophet, among others, preached Abrahamic monotheism in an Arabic milieu, in a social context marked by fragmentation, weak integration, and against organic polytheism" (Décobert 1991: 42). 'Organic polytheism' is a somewhat puzzling expression, and should not be taken as a reference to a pristine archaic religious culture (among other things, G.W. Bowersock 1990 draws attention to Hellenistic influences reflected in restructurings of Arabian polytheism). The culminating phase of the monotheistic turn also linked up with earlier moves in the same direction, and echoes of rivalries persisting on the eve of expansion are preserved in the record of false claimants to prophecy after Muhammad's death.

But perhaps the most interesting – and most recently recognized – aspect of the intra-Arabian crystallization is the role played by the South Arabian civilization, centred in today's Yemen. Jan Retsö has discussed this question in various recent writings (2003, 2005); the following remarks draw on his work. It is only in the most recent decades that we have become aware of the dimensions and the distinctive character of this civilization. In relation to the older centres of the Near East, it belonged to the category of peripheral formations, and it was a relative latecomer (it developed in the main after the crisis of the late Bronze Age); but it was more remote than the other peripheries, and therefore had a more independent political history; furthermore, it was in closer contact with the Northeast African periphery of Egyptian civilization, and this became especially important after the Christianization of Northeast Africa. Enough is now known about the record of state formation in South Arabia to conclude that the last stages (the Himyarite kingdom in particular) represent an imperial turn; but this path was then blocked and the South Arabian region thrown into turmoil by the repercussions of the Roman-Iranian conflict. Alongside the development of states with imperial aspirations, a monotheistic trend in South Arabian religion became more pronounced; although borrowings from (even conversion to) Judaism were obviously important, there does seem to have been an indigenous side to this development. Last but not least (Retsö places particularly heavy emphasis on this point), there are significant traces of a Yemeni eschatological tradition.

If we accept that this legacy was incorporated into emergent Islam, that is bound to affect our view of the whole problematic. At this point, the intra-Arabian crystallization begins to look like a much more complex process: it could perhaps – in the context of the whole Near Eastern region – be described as an integration of three peripheries: the civilizational domain of South Arabia, the townships of Northern and Western Arabia, and the more nomadic (perhaps re-nomadized) periphery that covered much of the peninsula. Obviously, the identity that emerged from this process drew on older sources, but the background is difficult to trace. According to Retsö (this is perhaps the most controversial part of his argument), an original non-ethnic or trans-ethnic Arab identity, linked to specialized groups with military and religious tasks and seen as the guardians of a language endowed with sacral and poetic properties (distinct from everyday speech), was adapted to the new purposes of the Islamic community. Further discussion of this thesis must be left to specialists. But from an outsider's point of view, it has at least the merit that it helps to account for what Goitein (1966: 7) calls the "miraculous linguistic process by which the Arab nation came into being."

Our understanding of the post-conquest crystallization – on a much enlarged regional scale – will depend on the view taken of the preparatory phase inside Arabia. For one thing – as Décobert (1991: 51-52) notes – , if we admit that there was, from the move to Medina onwards, a power structure with a fusion of political and religious authority at the top, it follows that the expansion must be seen as a conquest directed from a centre, rather than a "barbarian" invasion. Furthermore, the pre-existence of this institutional structure means that here is, if not a fully-fledged civilizational model, at least a core (a politico-religious one) around which such a model can be constructed. This rules out the view of Islam as wholly made up of borrowings from conquered cultures.

Décobert (ibid.: 47) sums up the approach pioneered by Goldziher and Schacht (and which he thinks the radical revisionists have abandoned) as an attempt to "suivre les traces de l'élaboration islamique à partir d'un substrat arabe primitive, de superstrats (romains, chrétiens, judaïques …) et d'adstrats (hellénistiques, rabbiniques …) étrangers." The term 'primitive' is obviously not being used in the invidious sense: it does not rule out the development of the original religious-political nexus mentioned above. As for the distinction between 'superstrats' and 'adstrats,' it is not clarified, but I would assume the former to refer to refer to cultural orientations of a more fundamental kind, the latter to more specific (and perhaps variable, from one part of the conquered region to others) ingredients of the Islamicate synthesis. But the most surprising aspect of this formulation, with its heavy emphasis on Roman-Hellenistic-Judaic sources (three interpenetrating traditions) is the absence of the other imperial-civilizational domain: the Iranian one. As it happened, political conquest was more complete where – at the outset – religious and civilizational affinities were more limited (the Byzantine civilizational centre survived, the Iranian one did not); but in the long run, this also led to a more comprehensive incorporation of political traditions.

Post-conquest crystallization

There are no self-evident chronological markers for the phase of crystallization; the choice of dates depends on overall visions (pre-comprehension, to use the proper hermeneutical language) of the whole process, as well as on specific assumptions about the course and meaning of events. As Donner (1998: 1) notes in his discussion of early Islamic historiography, traditional views – widely shared by Western historians – tended to focus on the half-century between 610 and 660. From an intra-Islamic point of view, the prime importance of this period is beyond dispute: it encompasses Muhammad's preaching of a new religion and the subsequent rise of an empire dominated by his followers, but also the internal conflicts that shaped Islamic cultural memory and defined the basic terms of later disputes between orthodoxy and heterodoxy. If the main emphasis is on the formation of a new religion and on its foundational experience of discord, historians coming from outside the Islamic community can take a similar view, especially if they accept (as Donner does, on the basis of careful consideration of the evidence) an early date for the Quranic text. When the focus shifts to the emergence of a whole civilizational pattern and the precondition for its global expansion, the chronological framework must also be modified. Marshall Hodgson's reasons for dating the formative phase from the end of the 7th to the middle of the 10th century are discussed in another paper in this volume; here I shall briefly summarize some arguments in favour of a different periodization. They emerge from new approaches and unfolding debates in recent scholarship.

As noted above, we can speak of an initial intra-Arabic prelude to crystallization, much more structured than Hodgson's picture of a long transition would indicate. On the cultural side, the intra-Arabian legacy now seems more important than earlier accounts had suggested – not least because of growing insight into the achievements and original characteristics of South Arabian civilization. On the political side, a 6th-century geopolitical upheaval, due to changing relations and power balances between the imperial states that surrounded the peninsula, was followed by new initiatives in state formation, of which the Islamic proto-state in Medina proved to be the most decisive. It is unlikely to have been the only one of its kind, but the Islamic tradition preserved only a very selective record of the earliest beginnings. Following Donner's analysis, several aspects of the Medinese polity may be distinguished. It invented a new form of sacral rulership, vested in a prophet; in fact, this was probably the most total fusion of religious and political authority that had yet been achieved anywhere. But the consolidation of this new and inherently expansive centre also entailed state-building strategies of a more conventional kind. Donner lists three crucial aspects of the process: "a more systematic approach to taxation than had hitherto prevailed in northern Arabia," (1981: 69), the "extension of a centralized legal authority over those areas controlled by Muhammad and the *umma*," (ibid.: 72) and "agents [...] appointed by Muhammad to oversee various tribal groups that had submitted to Islamic rule" (ibid.: 73). Incipient processes of state formation are always confronted with and at the same time dependent on tribal structures; the over-dramatized image of statehood as involving an abrupt and total break with tribal institutions is misleading, but specific features and dynamics of the relationship vary widely. The early Islamic state imposed a particularly self-contained and demanding model of political community, defined as a community of believers submitting to an exclusive and universal god (if we want to describe this innovation in terms of the axial model, it represents a more direct and thoroughgoing infusion of the transcendent into the mundane than any other socio-cultural pattern of that kind). But this radically de-particularizing model was also capable of harnessing tribal identities and loyalties to its own purposes. How the two levels of collective identity interacted is still a matter of debate; it is, at any rate, clear that the conquering Islamic armies combined tribal and supra-tribal principles of organization in very efficient ways. On the other hand, the conditional accommodation of tribal values was to affect the subsequent history of the Islamic polity and community in a manner not envisaged at the beginning: through disputes over the succession to the prophet.

The reconquest of Arabia after the rebellions and secessions following Muhammad's death marked a new stage. By reaffirming control over the peninsula at the very moment when an exceptionally difficult succession problem had to be solved, the emerging Islamic centre took a decisive step towards durable statehood. At the same time, the logic of its strategy led to further expansion. A unified peninsular state could not but interfere with the politically and territorially fluid power structures on the margins of neighbouring empires, all the more so since escalating warfare had destroyed the traditional mechanisms of control on the Byzantine as well as the Persian side. The forcibly reintegrated nomadic and semi-nomadic tribes (a disproportionately important minority of the population) were most easily kept in line through mobilization for conquest. The new religious revelation lent meaning and legitimacy to visions of indefinite expansion, and the combination of emphatic universalism with enhanced ethnic particularism was a massive motivating force before it became a source of tensions and oppositional movements. In short, an open-ended imperial project was the most natural option for the post-prophetic Islamic state. Because of the strong and original religious component of the conquering movement, as well as the complexity of cultural and political traditions indigenous to the conquered regions, the whole process resulted in the crystallization of new patterns on a civilizational scale.

Scholarly work on the comparative analysis of civilizations has shown that the religious-political nexus ('le théologico-politique,' as some French authors have called it) is a particularly rewarding starting-point for strategies of comparison. This seems to be eminently true of Islamicate civilization, where the exceptionally complex and contested issue of defining relations between religious and political authority became central to a broader configuration of formative trends.

The historical context of these developments is best understood in light of the problem of succession to prophetic rule. In Weberian terms, this was a case of transition from charismatic to traditional rulership, but complicated by several more specific factors. The charismatic centre was of quite unusual dimensions: a critical approach to the details of Muhammad's biography does not necessarily cast doubt on the view of the Islamic state as a very close union of religious and political power. Those who succeeded to supreme authority had to claim legitimacy through conformity with the prophetic message, but aspirations to maintain the same level of authority were bound to encounter resistance from the defenders of prophetic closure. The charismatic origin continued to command obedience in a profoundly altered situation, and to forbid imitation while tempting both rulers and rebels to test the limits thus imposed. These dilemmas became more acute in conjunction with the rapid shift to imperial domination of a whole region and expansion beyond its borders. Moreover, the new imperial state inherited territories, multi-ethnic societies and traditions from two older empires with whose legacies it had to come to terms. For a power structure based on a delicate and dynamic balance between settled and nomadic groups integrated through expansion, this swift transition to empire was a particularly challenging task. As Donner notes (ibid.: 273-278), the Arabian-Islamic state proved less viable than the larger formation which it had built up, and the political integration of Arabia went out of sight for a very long time to come. The empire eventually succumbed to a more long-drawn-out process of fragmentation, but a surviving shadow version of the caliphate retained some symbolic weight, and later empire-builders could still unify important parts of the Islamic world. The Islamicate civilizational framework outlived its original political basis and maintained its continuity across political ruptures and reversals.

In short, the Islamic invention – the Medinese paradigm of comprehensive sacral authority – faced problems of maintenance, extension and elaboration, and the solutions to them had ramifications that affected all domains of socio-cultural life. The following comments will centre on three successive aspects of the crystallizing phase: the early caliphate, including the first Islamic dynasty (1); the 8th-century upheaval traditionally known as the Abbasid revolution (2); and the Ismaili movement, which may be seen as a failed but far from inconsequential counter-paradigm taking shape in opposition to the Abbasid settlement (3). This is a very selective approach, but the thematic foci are chosen with a view to their key significance in a broader context.

1. It is now a commonplace among historians of Islam that the image of the four 'rightly guided' caliphs – from 632 to 661 – is a pious construct of much later origin, designed to smooth over succession disputes as well as controversies about the very meaning of the caliphate. In a sense, Western scholarship tended until recently to accept a secularized version of the same view: a broadly shared and continuous model of rulership after prophecy was taken for granted. More recent critical approaches to early Islamic history have undermined this assump-

tion. There are, however, no signs of scholarly consensus on a new interpretation; reappraisals of the historical evidence have led to widely divergent conclusions. A comparison of the two most seminal works on the subject, by Crone and Hinds (1986) and by Wilfred Madelung (1997), may help to clarify the main points at issue. Crone and Hinds begin with a discussion of the caliphal title. Its ambiguity (it can mean both deputy and successor) made it adaptable to changing aims and circumstances, but could by the same token serve to disguise the meaning of such adjustments. Crone and Hinds show – this would seem to be the most uncontroversial part of their argument – that early and continuous use of the title *khalifat allah*, which can only mean 'deputy of God,' is well attested at least from Uthman onwards. They then go on to draw far-reaching conclusions. The original version of the caliphate, with its strong component of religious authority, now seems closer to *Shi`ite* conceptions of authority than to Sunni ones, and the former might in that sense have a better claim to represent an orthodox current. Far from having shifted to a more traditional form of kingship, the Umayyads continued to claim the emphatically religious and distinctively Islamic legitimacy inherent in the idea of 'God's caliph;' this enabled them to assert jurisdiction over doctrinal as well as legal matters. The first Abbasids strove to maintain the same status, but in the longer run, they failed. As Crone and Hinds see it, both the historical shift towards a downgrading of caliphal authority in the religious sphere and the historiographical misrepresentation of the early caliphate reflect the growing strength of the 'ulama, whose ability to translate religious expertise into social power thus resulted in a definitive curtailment of the political centre.

According to Crone and Hinds, the early caliphate represented a uniquely radical form of theocracy (this Weberian term is used without any further discussion of its conceptual underpinnings). There are no obvious links to earlier models: both the Byzantine and the Sasanian paradigms of kingship have been described as caesaropapist, but neither of them unified political, legal and religious authority to the same degree as the Islamic alternative. Speculations about Samaritan origins are, as the authors admit, wholly gratuitous. Although Crone and Hinds do not explicitly say so, their line of argument would suggest that the theocratic project of the conquerors was designed to surpass the less consistent institutional principles of the two empires with which they were confronted, and it is tempting to take this hypothesis one step further. An attempt to transcend existing models of sacral rulership might be seen as a logical continuation of the prophecy that had announced the most perfect form of monotheism and begun to harness it to the accumulation of political power. This Arabian innovation preceded expansion into the Fertile Crescent, and acknowledgement of this historical priority should perhaps be seen as the limit beyond which revisionism goes off the rails. More importantly, the reference to Islamic origins highlights another side of the transition to empire, not taken into account by Crone and Hinds but in my opinion easily linked to Madelung's much more detailed reconstruction of the early caliphate and its vicissitudes. The earliest conquests beyond Arabia entailed on the one hand a retreat from the Medinese model, both because of the absence of the prophet and due to the new problems posed by imperial rule and ongoing military expansion; on the other hand, the same process demanded both the construction of an imperial self-image to counter those of the adversaries, and an effort to appropriate the imperial legacies on both sides of the Mesopotamian divide. In this context, it is a plausible assumption that the institution of the caliphate evolved through attempts to maintain a strong religio-political centre, disputed redefinitions of its role, and conflicts between forces that articulated and legitimized their strategies in relation to this central issue. Such perspectives fit in with Madelung's narrative: he stresses the unsettled character of the early caliphate, the improvised succession arrangements, and the polarizing dynamic of elite rivalries. Ali's brief and contested rule (656-661) is described as a counter-caliphate,' a reaction against the ascendancy of the Meccan aristocracy and its Quraysh core under Uthman. In that capacity, it was a logical choice for later constructions of heterodox genealogies, however anachronistic it may be to project fully-fledged sectarian demarcations back into Islam's first century.

To sum up, the case for putting more religious authority back into our image of the early caliphate seems compatible with a more discontinuous and multilinear story than the one proposed by Crone and Hinds. And if the institution that joined the religious to the political sphere was shaped by interpretive and practical conflicts, it was by the same token exposed to challenges from those who aimed at closer approximation to the ideal of prophetic rule (or, to put it another way, at minimizing the distance between God's messenger and God's deputy). That kind of opposition became most potent when the theocratic theme was combined with a stronger emphasis on the universalist message of the revelation and when the religious concerns were linked to socio-political protest against exclusion and privilege. Such a constellation was clearly at hand when the Umayyad regime entered its terminal phase towards the middle of the 8th century.

2. As we have seen, some interpretations have stressed the continuity of historical patterns across the dynastic divide between Umayyads and Abbasids. In each case, the analysis of trends and events reflects specific views of the period as a whole. For Hodgson, long-term continuity is due to the irresistible logic of absolutism and its imperial apogee; for Crone and Hinds, the early Abbasid caliphate represents an ambitious but ultimately unsuccessful effort to maintain the early Islamic model of rulership. Constructions of continuity have, however, not been the most typical way to make sense of the events in question. The rise of the Abbasids has frequently been seen as a revolution. Among non-Western examples of political transformation, it stands out as one of very few cases where Western scholars have been most willing to apply a concept of revolution derived from European experience. One author even refers to it as "one of the best organized revolutions in history;" (Sharon 1983: 16) another considers it "a most appropriate example of the method by which a loosely controlled revolutionary apparatus is transformed into an established government of imperial capabilities"

(Lassner 1980: 7). More concrete parallels have been suggested. In a critical review of the literature on the subject, R. Stephen Humphreys (1991: 109) argues that "many of the questions we ask about the Bolsheviks would be equally significant in regard to the Abbasids." This broad agreement on the revolutionary dimensions of dynastic change has not precluded dispute about the specific character of the revolution. Some basic features are uncontested. The Abbasid revolution was prepared by a clandestine organization which in due course launched an armed rebellion on the eastern periphery of the empire, overthrew the central government, and established a new geopolitical balance of power. The leaders and activists of the revolution shared a strong but ambiguous ideological orientation. On the one hand, supreme power was to be restored to closer kinsmen of the prophet, but this demand could still leave the field open to several contenders, and neither the timing nor the operative details of the Abbasid takeover have been easy to explain. On the other hand, the appeal to a broader community of believers marked a decisive step beyond the ethnic particularism of earlier Islamic regimes. Taken together, the two aspects exemplify one of Eisenstadt's observations about Islam: the fusion of a strong universalism with limited but crucial primordialist elements. The practical meaning of this ideology in the context of a revolutionary transformation is a good deal more controversial.

It seems clear that the debate on the Abbasid revolution has, most recently, taken a turn that revives traditional views against the revisionist positions defended by later 20th-century scholars. The traditional interpretation was stated in classic terms by Julius Wellhausen (1973 [1927]: 558): "Under the guise of the international Islam, Iranianism triumphed over the Arabs." Although Wellhausen was not very explicit about his underlying conceptual framework, this formulation clearly suggests a vision of history as the realm of one *Volksgeist* in contest with another, with religion – universal or not – reduced to a 'superstructural' role. But other statements would seem to throw doubt on that assumption, and to imply a more autonomous role for religion. At the end of the book, Wellhausen contrasts the Abbasids with the dynasty they had overthrown: "While the Umaiyids [sic] had essentially rested upon a nationality, they [the Abbasids] supported their government upon a guard and upon the religion. Their Khaliphate may be described as a Caesareopapy" (ibid.: 564). He also notes that the supposed triumph of the Iranians, who were eventually ousted by the Turks, was more short-lived than that of "international Islam." All this points to the conclusion that the Abbasid revolution might have had less to do with one ethnic category replacing another than with a new relationship between religion and political power, as well as between religious and political community. The second thoughts thus indicated were taken much further by later historians who found it difficult to locate the Iranian factor. Moshe Sharon, summing up his analysis of the Abbasid revolution with particular reference to the rebellion in Khurasan, stresses "the Arabism of its leadership and the Islamism of its ideas," (Sharon 1983: 198) and although this opinion was never uncontested, it was shared by many other scholars in the field. Following its lead, the Abbasid revolution would be best understood as a reactivation of the Arabic-Islamic nexus that had already given an impetus to conquest and empire-building.

If the 'Iranianist' interpretation is regaining ground, this is less a matter of returning to Wellhausen's position than of revisiting the whole problematic from angle more conducive to adequate grasp of the civilizational questions at issue. Saleh Said Agha's analysis of the "revolution that toppled the Umayyads," (2003) by far the most detailed of its kind, goes beyond earlier scholarship in distinguishing between the activists of the revolutionary organization and the forces involved in the revolutionary process. On both levels, careful scrutiny of the sources confirms the preponderance of Iranians, but not of the same type: Islamicized clients *(mâwalî)* of Iranian (and other non-Arabic) origin were the backbone of the organization, whereas more recent converts were mobilized for revolutionary action and gave it the character of a popular revolt. As Agha argues, historians have often disregarded ethnic stratification and conflict for no better reason than an a priori commitment to oversimplified modernist theories of nationalism. Once the latter are subjected to due criticism, collective identities (in this case Arab and Iranian, allowing for internal differentiation on both sides) can be taken more seriously as a ubiquitous but context-dependent historical factor. They can in some constellations give rise to premodern nationalism, but circumstances can also channel them in more self-transcending directions. In the specific conditions of the early Islamic world, the problems posed by an increasingly explosive ethnic divide were susceptible to integrative and universalistic solutions. Conversion was, as Agha puts it, a Trojan horse: the non-Arab converts could turn the "moralistic, egalitarian and inclusive aspects" (ibid.: 170) of Islam against an Arab establishment that was also vulnerable to accusations of having betrayed both the principles and the family of the prophet. But the Trojan horse was also a transforming factor for those who used it: their success made membership in the universal community of believers more important than any pre-Islamic identities.

It is now widely accepted that the anti-Umayyad revolt in Khurasan, prepared by an organization first active in Kufa, was one of several movements that tore the Umayyad empire apart in the 740s. Some of them had distinctive regional and/or ethnic backgrounds. A Berber rebellion in North Africa, linked to Kharijite dissent, foreshadowed later upheavals in the region. Yemeni connections seem to have been important for a briefly successful Umayyad pretender. However, the movement that brought the Abbasids to power stands out – not just as the most successful one, but also as endowed with a transformative dynamic that can hardly be claimed for other cases. This explains the attractivity of the idea of the 'Abbasid revolution.' But if that interpretation is to be upheld, on more conclusive grounds, further specifications to the concept of revolution are needed. Said Arjomand (1994) defines the 8th-century transformation of the Islamic empire as an 'integrative revolution.' In a general sense, this term refers to an enlargement and restructuring of the political community; subtypes, including the 'constitutive revolution' that brings statehood to previously stateless societies, can be distinguished on the basis of various criteria (cf. also Arjomand's contribution to this volume, as well as a forthcoming book). With regard to the Abbasid revolution, several interconnected aspects of an integrative dynamic may be noted. Arjomand's main emphasis is on the integration of non-Arab Muslims into the elites as well as the religio-political community at large (as he notes (Arjomand 1994: 20), "the Abbasid revolution was accompanied by massive conversions of the non-Muslim subject population to Islam"). In this respect, the Abbasids in power continued along the lines envisaged by the organizers of the revolution. But in the present context, the processes of intercivilizational integration are particularly noteworthy. Here, too, recent work has vindicated the Iranianist approach, albeit in a modified sense. There was no abrupt or wholesale Iranianization of central state structures after 750; earlier accounts tended to exaggerate the difference between the two dynastic regimes. Nor did the borrowing of Iranian techniques and traditions begin with the Abbasids. The Umayyads had already taken interest in Persian statecraft and relied on specialists trained in that tradition. Arjomand stresses "the permanent mark left on the Islamic civilization by Ibn al-Muqaffa and the generation of Persian secretaries that supplied strong elements of continuity between the two eras divided by the Abbasid revolution;" (ibid.: 36) as he also shows, with particular reference to Ibn al-Muqaffa, these intercivilizational architects of a new order could develop projects that were only in part adaptable to the practical strategies of the rulers. But the trend was certainly accelerated by the integrative dynamic of the Abbasid revolution. The more inclusive definition of the community made for a more receptive attitude to cultural legacies of the region (at least during the formative phase), and the Iranian connection was crucial in both respects – not least because of the transfer of the geopolitical centre to a former core domain of the Sasanian Empire. The concomitant changes to the style and symbolism of monarchic rule paved the way for the incorporation of an old and rich tradition of discourse on kingship. On the other hand, the revolutionary movement had drawn on Iranian traditions in a different way. Agha (2003: 212), drawing on Madelung and others, refers to "an Iranian para-Islamic continuum:" a whole counterculture of dissent, protest and revolt, with elusive but undoubtedly significant links to memories and surviving elements of Mazdakism. Translation into Islamic terms was not yet the only outlet open to traditions with an older pedigree in the region: the 8th-century upheaval was accompanied by millennial revivals within other religious communities (Arjomand 1994: 21). The overall picture is unclear and the record very fragmented, but the appeal to a 'continuum' seems to have been essential to the successful rebellion in Khurasan. As the new regime consolidated its hold on power, it cracked down on erstwhile allies and agents, often with extreme brutality; some of the currents first mobilized and then suppressed entered into the making of new heterodoxies.

Finally, integrative developments in the aftermath of the revolution also had to do with the socio-cultural constitution of the Islamicate world. Marshall Hodgson's seminal treatment of that problematic is discussed elsewhere in this volume, and the field will only be briefly revisited here. Four main aspects of the socio-cultural integrative process may be distinguished. The construction of an Islamic tradition in a strong and systematic sense through collected (and very often invented) reports on the founding phase and its protagonists, was in the main an achievement of the early Abbasid era. As Arjomand notes, this resulted in a distinctively Islamic link between revolution and tradition, and more specifically in the canonization of the Medinese paradigm as a model for radical political change, conceived as a return to pristine principles. The elaboration of Islamic law went hand in hand with the formation of tradition. Opinions differ on the importance of the earliest decades and the Umayyad period for both *hadith* and law, but the crucial contributions of legal scholars during the ascendant phase of Abbasid rule are undisputed: this period saw both the systematization of law and the differentiation of approaches that found embodiment in schools of jurisprudence and their respective sub-traditions. Law and tradition, together with the interpretation of the Quran, became the reserved domain and defining concern of the 'ulama, who thus established themselves as a civilizational elite. Finally, the social constellation that prevailed during the later classical period – the 9th and 10th centuries – fostered strong links between 'ulama and merchants. S.D. Goitein (1966: 217-241, 242-254) saw the merchants as a 'Muslim bourgeoisie,' capable of social self-assertion and self-expression through an articulate economic ethic, but not of the kind of organization needed for the pursuit of political power. His terminology now seems somewhat anachronistic, but there is no doubt about the importance of the merchant-'ulama nexus, It shaped the distinctive features of the public sphere in Islamicate societies, including those that insulated it from the exercise of political power.

As Hodgson and other historians of the 'High Caliphate' have stressed, the internal structuring of Islamicate civilization was – in the first instance – compatible with openness towards other civilizations and creative appropriation of their achievements. This does not settle the question whether the internal logic of integration was in the longer run conducive to closure and detrimental to transformative capacities. That issue opens up a vast field of inquiry, far beyond the formative period, and therefore beyond the scope of this paper. It may, however, be noted in passing that no answer to the question can justify a purely internalist reconstruction of Islamic history. The defining patterns that crystallized during the period discussed here affected all later developments, but only in conjunction with a complex set of external factors.

In light of the broader implications and long-term consequences discussed above, the term 'Abbasid revolution' seems justified. It might still be objected that the description is less applicable to the revolutionary process as such. The subtitle of Agha's book (2003), "neither Arab nor Abbasid," sums up a complex analysis of both issues. No further comment is needed on reasons for rejecting the Arabist interpretation; as for the other point, Agha argues – to my mind convincingly – that the Abbasid takeover was engineered on the eve of final victory over the Umayyads, and thus later than most historians have wanted to admit; that it was a coup within the revolution; and that it imposed hereditary dynastic rule on a movement that had wanted to link succession within the family of the prophet to election by the community (without a clear delimitation of the latter). The dynamic of this takeover and the need to consolidate its results were obviously central to Abbasid policies in the aftermath of victory. But Agha's interpretation does not disconnect this factor from the broader context. In that regard, a brief comparison with a view from the other side may be useful. Jacob Lassner's work on the formation of Abbasid rule (1980) has mostly been aligned with the Arabist position. As far as the preparatory phase is concerned, that seems to be true, but when it comes to the revolutionary process as such, Lassner is less interested in ethnic backgrounds and cultural borrowings (as he sees it, speculations on the latter will never get beyond vague conjectures) than in the internal logic of a power structure being adapted to specific goals. The Abbasid way of consolidating revolutionary power was, first and foremost, based on generalized and innovative use of the institution of clientage. Lassner takes this explanatory model very far: for him, the 9th- and 10th-century shift to massive use of slave soldiers was the "logical conclusion" (ibid.: 16) of Abbasid-style clientage. At this point, critical comments are in order. Arguments about intercultural borrowing may sometimes be unavoidably vague, but the notion of power-seeking strategies and their unintended consequences unfolding in a cultural vacuum is thoroughly implausible, and doubly so when applied to rival factions within a conquering elite with a very distinctive ethnic profile, operating in the kind of intercivilizational environment characteristic of the 7th- and 8th-century Near East. An interpretation which disregards that part of the picture is a priori unconvincing.

To conclude, it should be noted that the debate on the Abbasid revolution goes beyond controversies about ethnic or social background and ideological content. Recent scholarship on states and social revolutions has shown a general tendency to take geopolitical conditions and dynamics more seriously. In the Abbasid case, that line of argument was to some extent anticipated by those who stressed changing power balances between provinces, but there is at least one attempt to develop it in a broader context. Khalid Yahya Blankinship's analysis of the Umayyad 'jihâd state' and its collapse draws attention to the Eurasian geopolitical setting that first facilitated rapid conquest and then proved fatal to a regime bent on further all-round expansion. In the first phase, the emerging Islamic empire made huge gains at the expense of the Byzantine one and destroyed its Sasanian rival; further offensives led to the conquest of Berber North Africa (where conversion seems to have played a greater role than elsewhere at this stage), the overthrow of a particularly fragile post-Roman regime in Visigothic Spain, and the establishment of a first foothold in India. Let us note in passing that this pattern of sustained expansion makes the absence of any serious action against the declining Axum empire rather puzzling. But a second round, beginning in the late 720s, brought the Umayyad state face to face with a whole series of much more resilient adversaries: the Franks in the west, a reinvigorated Byzantine Empire, the Khazars in South Russia, the Turks in Central Asia, and the stronger Indian kingdoms east of the Indus. Efforts to overcome these new obstacles proved fruitless, and the strain was too much for the Umayyad regime. Blankinship thus agrees with Hodgson on a fundamental point: the Marwanid power structure had collapsed before the Abbasid revolution, and the Abbasid leadership was one of several contenders in the field. But his analysis leads to further claims. He underlines the impact of the great Berber revolt in the last stage of Marwanid rule, which caused "the breakup of Muslim political unity and the end of the universal jihad," (Blankinship 1994: 203) he also suggests that "with the failure of the universal war jihâd, more emphasis began to be placed on the peaceful quest," and that thus "the doors were opened for the already extant spiritual element of Islam to undergo a development which has greatly enhanced the attractiveness of Islam to non-Muslims" (1994: 4).

3. According to Marshall Hodgson's periodization of Islamic history, the classical phase ended in the middle of the 10th century. For present purposes, we do not need a precise date, and a strict chronological delimitation would in fact seem implausible. But there are good reasons to regard the crystallizing phase as continuing well into the 10th century, all the more so if we include the formation of the most ambitious and most widely active heterodoxy of the Islamic world: the Ismaili movement. Some historians (Western and Islamic) would question this categorization. As they see it, the term 'heterodoxy' prejudges a question that should still be open to debate: whether the Ismailis or their established adversaries were closer in spirit to the original Islamic message. But in the given context, the concept of heterodoxy can be defined in less loaded terms. It can, in other words, be used to describe a movement centred on a far-flung clandestine organization, committed to religious ideas incompatible with the enforced standards of orthodoxy, and capable of translating religious dissent into strategies for revolt and conquest on several fronts. As Eisenstadt has argued in both theoretical and empirical contexts, the dynamics of interaction between orthodoxies and heterodoxies are a particularly promising theme for comparative civilizational analysis. In that regard, the Ismaili movement stands out as one of the most interesting cases.

The Ismaili movement was, as a recent history of Islamic political thought puts it, an attempt to "take over the Muslim world in the name of a new creed" (Crone 2004: 197). This happened at a stage when Islamic religious ideas were being institutionalized as civilizational premises in a more sustained fashion than before (cf. Eisenstadt's distinction between the two aspects of religion). In that regard, the Ismaili project invites comparison not only with other major religious heterodoxies, but also with civilizational divisions in a more general sense. Internal conflicts of interpretations are a recurrent civilizational phenomenon, but in some cases they go so deep that it seems appropriate to speak of civilizational schisms: radically different versions of shared cultural premises, with implications translating into alternative institutional patterns and historical trajectories. If this concept is to be applied for comparative purposes, we must allow for considerable variation within its range of meaning. The institutional impact of cultural interpretations is less significant in some cases than others, and even when it reaches relatively high levels, the dynamic of the schism as such may be inflected or overlaid by other factors. It would be hard to find a more convincing example of civilizational schism than the 16th-century bifurcation of Western Christendom. But the interplay and the divergent paths of the two reformations (one of them somewhat misleadingly known as the Reformation and the other as the Counter-Reformation) were complicated by a simultaneous civilizational mutation that involved a broader spectrum of forces: the Western European transition to modernity. Earlier cases to be considered include the Indian trajectory during the Axial Age, which led to the separation of Buddhism from the evolving traditions that later crystallized into Hinduism, but views on the civilizational significance of this schism will to some extent depend on the disputed question whether Buddhism was linked to an alternative conception of kingship. At any rate, the contest ended with the virtual disappearance of Buddhism from its original homeland, and its diffusion elsewhere took place in a different institutional environment. Finally, it should be noted that civilizational schisms do not ipso facto take a religious form. It is tempting – and certainly not incompatible with classic accounts left by contemporaries – to see the conflict between Athens and Sparta as a schism within Hellenic civilization. In this case, the outcome was self-destructive from the broader civilizational point of view: a fatal weakening vis-à-vis neighbouring powers with imperial ambitions.

The case for understanding the Ismaili movement as a civilizational schism can begin with its reinterpretation of the Islamic revelation. The Ismailis relativized the prophetic paradigm by inserting it into a more complex cyclical scheme where the last prophet is succeeded by a whole sequence of imams; the authority of the latter was more emphatically related to an esoteric spiritual meaning of the divine message, and this soteriological remodelling was linked to an eschatological vision that brought the apocalypticism of early Islam back in a new setting. When taken to its extreme conclusion, the Ismaili conception of the imam – and especially of the Mahdi, the ultimate redeemer – tended to overshadow the prophet. Disagreement on that issue was one of the major causes of division within the movement. The most telling way to relativize the status of the prophet was to downgrade his role as a lawgiver. The esoteric core of Ismailism was, in general, conducive to antinomian tendencies, but their strength depended on circumstances; only two small-scale and short-lived attempts to abrogate the official version Islamic law are known (under the Qarmati regime in Bahrein in the 10th century and in an Ismaili stronghold in northwestern Iran in the 12th century).

The association of the imamate with esoteric knowledge was anchored in gnostic traditions and modes of thought. Islamic gnosticism was, however elusively, affiliated to late antique gnosticism, and scholarly approaches to the former are bound to reflect interpretations of the latter. The most recent work (cf. especially Williams 1999 and Stroumsa 1992) tends to stress the heterogeneity of the gnostic field. A cluster of religious countercurrents responded to the problems and perceived shortcomings of both Judaism and Christianity; they overlapped in significant ways, but can hardly be reduced to a common denominator. However, no better term has so far been suggested for the complex of elective affinities that gave rise to the notion of gnosticism. On this view, the idea of a continuous gnostic tradition persisting within Islam becomes untenable. On the other hand, the sources do not seem to allow a reconstruction of specific links to particular traditions. As for the overall picture, B.S. Amoretti (1975: 488) suggests that an Islamic mould for Gnostic themes might have been constructed in a manner somewhat analogous to the surpassing of the older monotheisms, with "the Quranic message itself viewed as deriving from and re-interpreting the Hellenistic-Christian-Iranian gnostic culture of the age." The Ismaili movement linked this re-interpreted gnostic heritage to political messianism based on two principles: an emphatic re-unification of religious and political authority through the imamate, and legitimation through a direct dynastic connection to the prophet. No more pronounced case of politicized gnosticism has ever been recorded (by comparison, the reconstruction of gnostic trends in modern politics depends on more complex and problematic assumptions). According to Patricia Crone, this "odd mixture testifies to the extraordinary impact of Muhammad's career on the Middle East: even Gnostics came to see religious state formation and conquest to be the way out of their problems" (Crone 2004: 117). The suggestion is no less plausible because it comes from an author who had previously gone very far indeed in impugning the historicity of Muhammad's career. But if the mixture helped to mobilize opposition to the Abbasid regime and its representatives throughout the Islamic world, it was (as Crone also shows) not a solid foundation for an alternative model.

Bernard Lewis's early work on the origins of Ismailism – one of the first attempts to relate the movement to its historical context – stressed two aspects: the religious expression of a social protest movement, most strongly rooted among artisans, and the active interest in other religious traditions that could, at its most articulate, develop into a "strong strain of interconfessionalism, verging at times on complete rationalism" attitude (Lewis 1975 [1940]: 94). Later scholarship does not seem to have refuted these claims, but it has relativized them through stronger emphasis on other points. In its heyday, Ismailism appealed to individuals and groups with very diverse social and cultural backgrounds, and this broad basis highlights the unifying force of the religious message that held it together. There is evidence of unorthodox openness to traditions long established and still active in the region, but this stance was subordinate to the quest for a final perfection of the revelation. Measured against the claims made on that basis, the political results were conclusively disappointing. The Ismailis were at first remarkably successful in organizing a clandestine counter-community, on a civilizational scale and throughout the Islamic world. When they moved on to open revolt, it proved difficult to maintain the ideological bond between local power centres established in places separated by vast distances. Conquest on a larger scale, firstv in the Maghreb and then, much more significantly, in Egypt, was followed by rapid adjustment to the existing mainstream techniques and frameworks of state building. In fact, the Ismaili (Fatimid) regime in Egypt became a prime example of state power based on slave soldiers, with early signs of all the attendant problems of this institutional complex. Apart from the claim to represent a more legitimate succession to the prophet, and a more authentic union of religious and political authority than the Abbasid caliphate, there was next to nothing distinctively Ismaili about this state. This is not to deny that it played an important role in Islamic history. The Fatimid caliphate in Cairo was a major power in the Mediterranean region, and it was – after an interval of thousand years – the first fully independent state centred on Egypt. As such, it also laid the foundations for Egypt's later cultural pre-eminence in the Islamic world. But this was not what the Ismaili activists had aimed at.

On the intellectual level, some offshoots of the Ismaili movement may be seen as major landmarks of the dialogue between philosophy and religion within Islamicate civilization. The two cases most familiar to Western scholars are the 10th-century "Brethren of Purity" in Basra and the 11th-century work of Nasir-e Khosraw (1990). But the long-term pattern of sectarian survival after political failure was a very different matter (for a comprehensive history of Ismailism from the beginnings to modern times, cf. Daftary 1990). Small communities, often in remote places, perpetuated Ismaili traditions but abandoned the political activism that had once been associated with them. If early Ismailism had the potential to develop into a civilizational schism, it was contained during the decisive phase and thoroughly neutralized in subsequent centuries.

References

Agha, Saleh Said (2003) *The Revolution which toppled the Umayyads: Neither Arab nor Abbasid.* Leiden: E.J. Brill.
Amoretti, B.S. (1975) "Sects and heresies." In: *The Cambridge History of Iran*, Vol. 4, Cambridge: Cambridge University Press, pp. 481-519.
Arjomand, Said Amir (1994) "Abd Allah Ibn al-Muqaffa and the Abbasid revolution," *Iranian Studies* 27: 1-4, 9-36.
Arnason, Johann P./Eisenstadt, S.N./Wittrock, Björn (eds.) (2005) *Axial Civilizations and World History.* Leiden: E.J. Brill.
Assmann, Jan (2000) *Das kulturelle Gedächtnis.* München: C.H. Beck.

Blankinship, Khalid Yahya (1994) *The End of the Jihâd State – The Reign of Hishâm ibn 'Abd al-Malik and the Collapse of the Umayyads.* Albany: Suny Press.

Bowersock, G. W (1990) *Hellenism in Late Antiquity.* Cambridge: Cambridge University Press.

Crone, Patricia (1987) *Meccan Trade and the Rise of Islam.* Princeton: Princeton University Press.

Crone, Patricia (2004) *Medieval Islamic Political Thought.* Edinburgh: Edinburgh University Press.

Crone, Patricia and Cook, Michael (1977) *Hagarism. The Making of the Islamic World.* Cambridge: Cambridge University Press.

Crone, Patricia and Hinds, Martin (1986) *God's Caliph. Religious and Political Authority in the First Centuries of Islam.* Cambridge: Cambridge University Press.

Daftary, Farhad (1990) *The Ismailis: Their History and Doctrines.* Cambridge: Cambridge University Press.

Donner, Fred McGraw (1981) *The Early Islamic Conquests.* Princeton: Princeton University Press.

Donner, Fred McGraw (1998) *Narratives of Islamic Origins. The Beginnings of Islamic Historical Writing.* Princeton: Darwin Press.

Eisenstadt, S N (1987) "Webers Analyse des Islams und die Gestalt der islamischen Zivilisation." In: Wolfgang Schluchter (ed.) *Max Webers Sicht des Islams. Interpretation und Kritik.* Frankfurt: Suhrkamp, pp. 342-359.

Fowden, Garth (1993) *Empire to Commonwealth. Consequences of Monotheism in Late Antiquity.* Princeton: Princeton University Press.

Fowden, Garth (2004) *Qusayr Amra. Art and the Umayyad Elite in Late Antique Syria.* Berkeley; University of California Press.

Fowden, Garth (2005) "Late Antiquity: Period or idea?," unpublished paper presented to a workshop on "Comparative perspectives on the Roman Empire," European University Institute, Firenze, May 2005.

Goitein, S.D. (1966) *Studies in Islamic History and Institutions.* Leiden: E.J. Brill.

Humphreys, R. Stephen (1991) Islamic History. A Framework for Inquiry (Revised Edition). Princeton: Princeton University Press.

Kroeber, Alfred L. (1952) *The Nature of Culture.* Chicago: Chicago University Press.

Lassner, Jacob (1980) *The Shaping of 'Abbâsid Rule.* Princeton: Princeton University Press.

Lewis, Bernard (1975[1940]) *The Origins of Ismailism.* New York: AMS Press.

Madelung, Wilferd (1997) *The Succession to Muhammad. A Study of the Early Caliphate.* Cambridge: Cambridge University Press.

Nasir-e Khosraw (1990) *Le livre réunissant les deux sagesses (Kitâb-e Jâmi'al-Hikmatayn),* tr. by Isabelle de Gastines. Paris: Fayard.

Paret, Rudi (2001[1966]) "Vorwort," In: *Der Koran. Übersetzung von Rudi Paret*. Stuttgart: Kohlhammer.

Retsö, Jan (2003) *The Arabs in Antiquity: Their History from the Assyrians to the Umayyads*. New York: Routledge.

Retsö, Jan (2005) "Arabia and the heritage of the Axial Age." In: Johann P. Arnason/S.N. Eisenstadt/Björn Wittrock, *Axial Civilizations and World History*, Leiden: E.J. Brill, pp. 337-358.

Stroumsa. Guy Gedaliahou (1992) *Savoir et salut*. Paris: Editions du Cerf.

Weber, Max (1968[1956]) *Economy and Society. An Outline of Interpretive Sociology*, Vols. 1-3, ed. by Claus Wittich and Guenther Roth. New York: Bedminster Press.

Wellhausen, Julius (1973[1927]) *The Arab Kingdom and its Fall*. London: Curzon Press.

Williams, Michael Allen (1999) *Rethinking 'Gnosticism': An Argument for Dismantling a Dubious Category*. Princeton: Princeton University Press.

Wittrock, Björn (2005) "Cultural crystallization and civilization change: Axiality and modernity." In: Eliezer Ben-Rafael and Yitzhak Sternberg (eds.) *Comparing Modernities: Pluralism Versus Homogeneity. Essays in Homage to Shmuel N. Eisenstadt*. Leiden: E.J. Brill, pp. 83-124.

Crossroads and Turning Points

Chapter 5

Revolution in Early Islam: The Rise of Islam as a Constitutive Revolution

SAÏD AMIR ARJOMAND

We conceive of revolution in terms of its great social and political consequences. In a forthcoming comparative and historical study of revolutions, I contrast to the state-centered revolutions of modern times with another ideal-type of revolution which I call the 'integrative' revolution (see the Appendix). This ideal type of revolution – which is an aspect of all revolutions – expresses two simple ideas: revolutions 1) bring to power a previously excluded revolutionary elite, and 2) enlarge the social basis of the political regime. This makes integrative revolutions not just political but also 'social revolutions.' Integrative revolution is in turn divided into three subtypes, the two sub-types I derive from Aristotle-Pareto and Ibn Khaldun are so labeled. The 'constitutive' type is my own invention, offering the sharpest contrast to the state-centered or 'Tocquevillian' type in that it is the typical pattern of radical change in the political order through the enlargement of political community in 'stateless societies,' be they of 6th century BCE Greece or 7th century CE Arabia.

In addition to this structural typology, we need to come to terms with the motives and goals of the revolutionaries as historical actors, and here I do what may be politically incorrect from the viewpoint of the theory community by using the term teleology, not in the strict Aristotelian sense but rather as a term denoting the directionality of revolution. Through teleology, I seek to capture the distinctive direction of a revolution, its intended or intentionally prefigured consequences. This ideal-typical characterization of revolutions as historical individuals is intended as a substitute for the putatively general or generic teleology of all revolutions as steps in the forward march of mankind in historical materialism and the popular 20th-century conception of revolution.

The constitutive revolution of Sargon of Akkad had unified the city-temple-states of Mesopotamia on the basis of the idea of universal monarchy. What Cleisthenes similarly achieved in Athens eighteen centuries later by means of democratic political reform, was done by Muhammad in the 7th century of the Common Era as a by-product of a religious revolution: the unification of the tribes of Arabia on the basis of Islam. In this essay I draw on the vast primary and secondary literature on the subject only for details that illuminate (a) the rise of Islam as a 'constitutive' revolution, and (b) its teleology as set off by an apocalyptic vision and given its distinctive direction by a transcendental monotheism.

The pre-conditions of a constitutive revolution: The Arabian tribal society on the periphery of the two empires. Its cultural and religious unity and economic integration

In the 7th century, one can speak of an Arabian religion *(din al'arab)* whose beliefs and rituals were centred on a pantheon of interrelated tribal gods. These gods had their sanctuaries in the territory of a tribe, and were usually shared by allied tribes or those in the vicinity able to visit them. Such sharing of the divinities, and participation in common fairs and festivals around their sanctuaries, made for religio-cultural unity (Chelhod 1955: 123-25). The sacred enclave was called *hijr,* where common rituals of initiation, pilgrimage to and circumambulation of the sanctuary shrine with shaven heads were performed (Retsö 2002: 587, 624). The most important divinities were *Manât,* the goddess of the tribes of Aws, *Khazraj* and *Ghassân,* the *Lât,* goddess of the *Thaqif,* and the *'Uzzâ,* goddess of Muhammad's tribe, the *Quraysh,* as well as the *Kinâna,* the *Khuzâ'a* and all of the *Mudar* confederacy.[1] The three goddesses were considered the daughters of the paramount god, *Allâh.* Muhammad's ancestor, *Qusayy,* had settled the *Quraysh* in the sacred enclave *(haram)* of Mecca just over a century before his birth. The custodianship *(hijâba)* of the House of *Allâh,* the *Ka'ba,* was secured for the *Quraysh,* and made them beneficiary of sacred immunity from attacks by other tribes (Peters 1994: 26, 69). Even though the custodial functions became divided among his descendants through the lines of Hâshim and 'Abd al-Dâr, *Qusayy*'s cultic reforms had a lasting effect, making him the "unifier" *(mujamma')* of the tribal union of the *Quraysh* on behalf of *Allâh* (Dostal 1991: 193-98). Furthermore, *Qusayy*'s descendants succeeded in creating a supra-tribal collective identity by founding or reconstructing a cultic union, the hums. Fabietti (1988: 32) considers this union a response "to the unreliability of a system based on the kinship model," consisting in the superimposition on the tribal kinship system of a form of solidarity and cohesion based on religion (din), and Dostal (1991: 215-16) sees it as a response to the unsuccessful invasion of Mecca by Abraha, the Christian Ethiopian viceroy of Yemen in mid-6th-century CE. Be that as it may, the *Quraysh* linked their claim to be "the people *(ahl)* of Allah" to a

---

1   The Arabian gods could be identified with those of the ecumenical pantheon of the antiquity. The 'Uzzâ, in particular, was already identified with Aphrodite at Petra in the 1st century CE (Bowersock 2003: 2).

covenant *('ahd)* of their putative ancestor, Abraham, whose image, holding arrows for the ritual of casting arrows in front of the idol Hubal, was only to be erased by Muhammad's order (Rubin 1990: 104-107).

The fact that the gods and their sanctuaries were usually shared by tribes made for a measure of religious and cultural unification. The religious unity of the Arab tribes of the *Hijâz*, Western Arabia, was thus periodically reaffirmed by their pilgrimages to the divine sanctuaries around Mecca. These gods offered their worshippers protection (Q. 8: 72), and could intercede on their behalf with the higher god, *Allâh* (Q. 10: 18; 30: 12) (Watt 1988: 32-33). Invaluable information preserved in the pilgrimage formula of ritual invocation *(talbiya)* for the pre-Islamic Arab tribes proves that the relationship between the supreme god, *Allâh* and the gods of the other tribes was conceived as partnership (shirk). Each tribe had its own invocation formula. That of the *Nizâr* was: "Here I am, O God, here I am; Thou hast no partners except such partners as Thou hast; Thou possessest him and all that is his [i.e., the partner's]" (Kalbi 1924: 7; Kister 1980: 33, 50-51), while *Quraysh*'s was cited in the *Qur'ân* (and became known as 'the Satanic Verse'): "To the Lat and the *'Uzza*, and *Manât*, the third and the other! Verily they are the high-flying cranes; and their intercession [with *Allâh*] is to be hoped for" (Kalbi: 19). The idol of the tribe of *Khawlân*, *'Umyânus*, appears to have been associated with *Allâh* on a more equal footing, as the *Khawlân* were dividing their cattle and harvest between the two (Kalbi. 43-44). The *Qur'ân* characterizes the Arabian form of polytheism as 'associationism' *(shirk)*, and its description of the Arabian tribes as "associationists" or believers in divine partnership *(mushrikun)* is quite precise. They admitted the supreme authority of Allah but associated other tribal deities with him (Kister 1980: 48-49) Associationism was thus the linchpin of the religious unity of the segmented society of politically autonomous Arabian tribes.

The polytheistic cult of idols that persisted beneath the *Allâh*-dominated associationism was deeply rooted in the social organization of tribal Arabia and cemented it. Not only each tribe, but each clan *(batn)* within it had its own idol. Lesser idols pertained to the lower echelons of social organization: noblemen of the clans had their own idols, and domestic idols symbolized and cemented the unity of the family (Kalbi 1924; Lecker 1993: 332, 342). This polytheistic tribal idolatry was hedged by a cult of vengeance *(tha'r)* with elaborate rituals than fostered clan solidarity (Chelhod 1955: 101-104). Furthermore, their social grounding gave the idols great political significance: in each clan, the idol was associated with its leader and with the clan assembly *(majlis)* (Lecker 1993: 342).

The religious unification of Arabia was sustained by a modicum of linguistic unity. The tribes of the Hijaz were unified by one of the two lingue franche of the peninsula, the other being the language of the Northern and Central Arabian tribes. During the century preceding the rise of Islam, the organization of the local trade by the *Quraysh* in the linguistically unified Hijaz had made for considerable economic integration of Western Arabia. Trade fairs had grown in the protected environs of the divine sanctuaries in Western Arabia, especially those around Mecca in conjunction with pilgrimage rites (Kister 1972: 76-77; Crone 1987: 177-85). The *Quraysh* became traders under the leadership of *Qusayy*'s grandson, *Hâshim*, and played an important role in the growth of the caravan trade in the region. Meccan trade was "a trade conducted overwhelmingly with Arabs and generated by Arab [...] needs" (Crone 1987: 149). The *Quraysh* were thus "the merchants of Arabs," (Crone 1987: 153) and their trade acted as a force for economic unification of the Hijaz. Furthermore, it had important political implications. The *Quraysh* created a military force consisting of mercenary Bedouins and Ethiopians *(ahâbish)* to protect the caravans, which also enhanced its political predominance[2] (Fahd 1989). Meccan trade was also based on pacts *(ilâf)* among the clans of the *Quraysh* and the Bedouin tribes, not only of mutual help and protection but also the guarding of caravan on a profit-sharing basis (Peters 1994: 58-59, 68-69). The pacts amounted to a "Pax Meccana" in the Hijaz (Kister 1965: 120-21). The situation was, however, rife with tension and conflict. The disparate and heterogeneous coexistence of the commercial ethos of the city of Mecca, and the superimposition of religious unions on kingship ties did not always work smoothly. Rival religious and tribal cleavages could overlap, producing intermittent conflict, as they did between Mecca and *Tâ'if* (Chelhod 1958: 97, 113). This was inevitable as long as the religio-culturally unified and economically integrated tribal society of Western Arabia remained segmented and without any central or otherwise unified political authority structure.

Foreign political domination of Arabia is an important feature of the historical background of the rise of Islam. Arabia was on the periphery of three completing empires, the Persian, the Byzantine, and let us not forget, the Ethiopian.[3] The royal house of Himyar in southern Arabia had converted to Judaism in the 5th century. The Persians had conquered Southern Arabia toward the end of the 6th century, driving out the Ethiopians, and left a Persian colony, known as "the sons" *(al-abnâ')* whose predominance had become truly tenuous by the time of the rise of Muhammad. Down to the end of the 6th century, the Persians also dominated much of north-eastern and northern-central Arabia, including Yathrib (the future Medina) through their Lakhmid Arab client state in the Hira (near the future Kufa).[4] The Byzantines dominated north-western Arabia through their

---

2 Some Ethiopian military presence is still found in Mecca during the 2nd Civil War, half a century after Muhammad's death (Bashear 1997: 99-100).
3 In the earlier centuries, the Ethiopian empire had been dominant in Southern Arabia, but by the seventh century, it plays a subordinate role as an ally of the Byzantines.
4 The Sasanian empire was meanwhile undergoing the most serious crisis of its history. Military defeat by the Byzantines resulted in the deposition of Khosraw II by a praetorian coup in 628. Subsequent militarization of government produced a severe dynastic crisis in the Persian empire. Khosraw's son, Shiruya, having killed all his

Ghassanid client tribal dynasty, and their influence in the south seems to have been growing through the Ethiopians (Hoyland 2001: 236-42). "And remember when you were few and abased in the land and were fearful that the people *(al-nâs)* would snatch you away," so the *Qur`ân* (8: 26) reminds the Arabs. 'The people' was taken by the earliest commentators to refer to the Persians (or the Persians and the Byzantines; Kister 1968. 143-44). The poet *Qatâda* affirms: "the Arabs were confined between the lions of Persia and Byzantium" (cited by Crone 1987: 249).

Persian authorities or their Lakhmid clients in Hira favoured the Jews of Yathrib for much of the 6th century. The Jewish tribes of Nadir and *Qurayza* dominated Yathrib (they were said to be its "kings") as agents of the Persian emperor for whom they collected taxes. When the Nadir and the *Qurayza* lost this important fiscal function, which was given to an Arab from the Khazraj tribe about the beginning of the last quarter of the 6th century, their economic power declined (Kister 1968: 147; 1979: 330). The political status of the Jews declined more sharply. By the time of the migration of Muhammad in 622, though still considerably richer than the Arabs (Serjeant 1978: 3; Newby 1988: 17), the Jews of Yathrib were either the allies or clients of the Arab tribes of Aws and Khazraj. The Christians of Najran and southern Arabia were under Byzantine domination. It does not seem too unreasonable to conclude from our admittedly scanty evidence that when Muhammad brought the Koran in Arabic, Judaism and the various forms of Christianity were already hopelessly compromised by the strong identification with foreign domination, taxation and warfare" (Newby 1988: 47-48). References in the *Qur`ân* (Kassis 1983: 274) to itself as the "Arabic Recitation *(Qur`ân)*" (Q. 20: 113; 42: 7; 43: 3) and an "Arabic judgment" (Q. 13: 37), and to "Arabic tongue" (Q. 16: 103; 26: 195; 46: 12) effectively present Islam as an alternative to foreign religions[5] (Watt 1956: 143). Muhammad thus began his prophetic career in Mecca as God's messenger to the Arabs (Welch 1983: 196), "a people *(qaum)* to whom no warner came before thee" (Q. 32: 3). "And so We

> brothers, died in less than a year, and was succeeded by a minor son. In 630, the year of victory for Islam when Muhammad took Mecca, the commander of the palace guards opened the gates of the capital, Ctesiphon, to a usurper who was in turn killed by the spear of a guardsman shortly afterwards (Morony 1984: 92). Another minor was put on the throne but soon left it vacant for a woman, Khosraw II's daughter, Bôrân, who failed to revive the glory of divine Sasanian kinship and was assassinated by a general. (Daryaee 1999). She was further to take the blame of subsequent historians for the disintegration of the empire: "and with that – she being the ruler of Persia, their dominion weakened and their glory lapsed [...]. The word spread throughout the world that the land of Persia did not have a king, and that they were seeking shelter at the gates of a woman" (Dinawari: 111). Severe political crisis in the Sasanian empire left the Persian agents in eastern Arabia and the Persian colonists in the Yemen helplessly vulnerable to their local opponents and eager to court the rising power of Muhammad.

5 The adjective *'arabi* (Arabic) is aid to occur in the *Qur`ân* for the first time.

have revealed to thee an Arabic Recitation, that thou mayest warn the Mother of Cities and those who dwell about it [...]" (Q. 42: 7).

Transcendent monotheism and apocalyptic messianism

The two or three empires for which Arabia was a common periphery were centers of two axial civilizations which were witnessing vigorous growth of universalist religions of transcendence, or 'world religions' in Max Weber's terms: Zoroastrianism, Christianity, and Manichaeism crossing the two. The Arabian religion embedded in peninsular kinship and tribal institutions, as depicted above, had in fact not remained immune from ecumenical religious aspirations to transcendence and universalism. Muhammad drew two critical components of Islam from the ecumenical culture of the late antiquity: apocalyptic messianism and transcendent monotheism. Both components are essential for understanding the rise of Islam as a revolution. Apocalyptic messianism supplied the key factor in the causation of the revolutionary break with embedded religion, the second in its long-term teleology or the subsequent evolution of Islam. In other words, the first explains the motivation of his revolution in Arabia, the second its global consequences – the new empire and axial civilization it gave birth to.

In the forthcoming book, I also present apocalyptic messianism as the contribution of the Maccabean revolt to world history, a contribution made not by the winners of the revolution but by the losers who withdrew to the desert to form the Qumran community. Although the Qumran settlement was destroyed by the Roman army of Vespasian, the Messianism they has sustained in institutionalized form for two centuries survived them and was passed on to Christianity, Rabbinical Judaism and Islam. The broader apocalyptic frame of Messianism was carried by them and by other sectarian groups through the intertestamental period, and was taken up by the Christians. The Enochic circles effected the other-worldly transposition of political Messianism in the Similitudes of Enoch (Enoch, 1, 37-71), as did the Christians gradually after the destruction of the Temple in 70 CE. Other apocalyptic notions survived and coalesced with Messianism, notably that of the prophet of the end of time, which informs the apocalyptic reconstruction of Elijah as the returning prophet. The apocalyptic perspective of the Book of Daniel was especially privileged, as the Maccabean winners of the revolutionary power struggle had appropriated its ideas and effected its inclusion in the Old Testament canon. Centuries later, the apocalyptic world-view found a forceful statement in the early, Meccan, verses of the Koran on the coming of the Hour. These marked the inception of some two decades of revolutionary "absolute politics"[6] in the remote Arabian periphery of the empires that changed the course of world history.

There can be little doubt that the apocalyptic notions of the Enochic circle were known to the Jews of Arabia in the 7th century, as was the Danielic tradition. The Book of Enoch has survived in Ethiopian. Its notions may well have penetrated Southern Arabia through their domination.[7] It is certain that the Karaite Jews of the 9th century were called Sadduccees by their opponents, while considering themselves the Righteous *(saddiqin)* and the sons of Righteousness *(sâdôq)*, that their missionaries called themselves the wise *(maœkilim)* in the Danielic tradition, and that they carried the religious tradition of the Essenes in the Islamic era[8] (Erder 1994). It is also more than probable that the Essenes, or unorthodox Jewish sectarians influenced by them, were present in 7th-century Arabia (Erder 1990: 349-50). The religious leaders of these sectarians were evidently not called Rabbis but *ahbâr* (*haberim* in Hebrew; Rabin 1957: 123); and incidentally, quite a number of them converted to Islam (Newby 1988: 86). Most apocalyptic notions of early Islam can be traced to Jewish sectarian sources, even though the central messianic idea of the paraclete came from Christianity. There may also have been some Manichaean influence, as we have record of an attempt to introduce it to Arabia through the teaching of Mazdak at the end of the 5th century that left behind a number of "Mazdakites/Manichaeans *(zanâdiqa)* of Mecca" (Gil 1992: 19 33, 42). The Manichoans, too, had been receptive to the Enochic and Christian apocalyptic lore.

The Enochic idea of the heavenly tablet (Enoch, 1, 90), as the archetype of all revealed books, is crucial in informing the *Qur`ânic* conception of revelation according to which the heavenly archetype and eternal source of all revelation is "the preserved tablet" or "the Mother of Books." The Koran (19: 57-58; 21: 85-86) mentions Enoch twice as *Idris,* which is etymologically traceable to the *Qumranic dôrçsh ha-Torah* (Interpreter of the Law) (Erder 1990; Gill 1992: 34-35), uses the epithet *siddiq* whose Zadokite connotation is evident, and alludes to

---

6   As defined in Pizzorno 1994.
7   The eighty-two early Muslim converts who took refuge in Ethiopia during the Meccan persecution may also have brought back some Enochic notions. Furthermore, we find twenty-two Christians from Ethiopia or Najran among other early converts (Life: 146-48, 179-80).
8   Erder (1994: 197, 210-12) goes further and argues that the name *'qârâ'im* (Karaites)' was derived from *qeri'è ha-šem* associated with "the Sons of Sâdôq" in the Damascus Covenant, which was, incidentally, found among the Geniza documents in Cairo and published as a Zadokitte work in 1910. What Erder calls the Karaites "Sadduccee dilemma" ceases to be dilemma if we adopt the most obvious interpretation of the evidence – namely that the Karaites and the Zadokites, both of whom rejected the Oral Law of the Rabbis, are the same group separated by a few centuries. In my forthcoming book, I emphasize the Zadokite/Sadduccee identity of the Qumran leaders.

his heavenly ascension (Q. 19: 57). There are traces of influence of the oldest section of the Book of Enoch, the Book of Watchers, in the *Qur'ân* (Crone unpublished), and Ezra, another major figure of the Enochic and Judaeo-Christian apocalyptic lore, is mentioned once in the *Qur'ân* in the diminutive form of 'Uzayr. By the time of the Fourth Ezra and in the subsequent literature, Ezra the scribe had become Ezra the prophet. Ezra was identified with Enoch and appears as the key figure in the mystical speculations of the Jewish communities of Arabia[9] (Newby 1988: 60-61). At the beginning of Ezra IV, which circulated not only in Syriac but also in Arabic, Ezra is clearly presented as a Second Moses (Ezra, 4, 14: 1-6); and it is as the messianic "prophet like Moses" that he enters into Islam. The phrase occurs in a poem attributed to Muhammad's uncle and protector, Abu Tâlib: "We have found Muhammad, a prophet like Moses, described in the oldest books."[10] (Life: 160)

The paraclete is referred to in Q. 61: 6, where Jesus son of Mary gives the children of Israel "good tidings of a messenger who shall come after me and whose name shall be more praised/Ahmad *(ismuhu ahmadu)*." The Koranic statement is a reasonable paraphrase of the promise of the coming of the paraclete in Jn 16: 13-14[11] (Life: 104; Arjomand 1998: 241-42). The paracletic term, *ahmad*, also occurs in the above-mentioned poem by Abu Tâlib.

Daniel is not mentioned in the Koran. This is surprising in view of the evident influence of the Book of Daniel. The reference to Abraham as the friend of God (Dan. 3: 35), which also occurs in the Essene Damascus Covenant, is carried over to the Koran (4: 124). Gabriel and Michael, the two archangels who are introduced to the Hebrew Bible in the Book of Daniel are both mentioned in the Koran. In fact, Gabriel's role in hierophany and audition (Dan. 10: 4-11.1) becomes central; Gabriel is not only as the angel of revelation but is also seen by the Islamic tradition as Muhammad's frequent counselor. Last but not least, the Danielic notion of setting the seal on prophecy (Dan. 9: 24), crucially influenced Muhammad's idea of final prophecy.

9   The assertion in the *Qur'ân* (9: 30) that "the Jews say 'Uzayr is the son of God as the Christians say the Messiah is the son of God" should be understood in this light, especially as we have Ibn Hazm's gloss that the referent is the Sadduccee sect of the Yemen (cited in Erder 1990: 349). An interesting refutation of the divine status of the prophets in the apocalyptic lore is found in an inscription dated 786/170 that asserts that Muhammad, Jesus and 'Uzayr are just servants of God, like all other creatures (Nevo and Koren 2003: 398).
10 See also Ibn Ishâq: 353; Life: 240.
11 The influence of the Gospel of John may have been reinforced through Manichaeism. Indeed, Biruni's (1879: 190) statement is a striking presentation of the great Babylonian prophet, Mâni (d. 277) as the forerunner of Muhammad: "In his gospel [...] he says that he is the paraclete announced by the Messiah, and that he is the seal of the prophets (i.e. the last of them)." Be that as it may, the Muslim tradition came to consider Ahmad ("more praised") a variant of Muhammad and another name for the Prophet, and identified him with the paraclete.

There can be little doubt that the notion of Seal *(khâtam)* is apocalyptic, as is its Hebrew cognate, *khotam*.[12] The basic tenet of primitive Islam, according to Casanova (1911: 8) was that "the time announced by Daniel and Jesus had come. Muhammad was the last prophet chosen by God to preside, at the end of time, over the universal resurrection and Last Judgement." His argument for equating the expression "Seal of the Prophets" *(khâtam al-nabiyyin)* with "the prophet/messenger of the end of time" *(nabiy/rasul âkhir al-zamân)* is persuasive (Casanova 1911: 18, 207-13, 228). It should also be noted that the early traditions consider the seal of prophecy a physical mark of prophecy between Muhammad's shoulders, variously described as a dark mole or a lump the size of a pigeon's egg (Life, 80; Ibn Sa'd 1: 106-7, 2: 131-32), or alternatively on his chest. According to one well-known tradition, the finality of Muhammad's prophecy itself is apocalyptic: "I am Muhammad, and I am the Paraclete *(ahmad)*, and I am the resurrector *(hâshir)* – the people are resurrected upon my steps – and I am the final one – there is no prophet after me" (Mas'udi, 3: 7). An earlier variant includes "and the prophet of the *malhama* (tribulations of the end of time)" (Tabari, 9: 156n, 1066). The epithet "Prophet/Messenger of the *malhama*" is even more decisive, and is attested for Muhammad in several other early traditions as well (Ibn Sa'd, 1: 65; Casanova 1911: 49-53). *Malhama*, a loan word from the Hebrew *milhâmâ* (war), is the same as notion as the one we find in the apocalyptic War Rule and other texts from the Qumran[13] (Rabin 1957: 118-19). Let us close with one last apocalyptic tradition which has Muhammad saying: "I was chosen prophet together with the Hour; it almost came ahead of me" (Cited, together with some other similar ones in Arjomand 1998: 246).

In contrast to the apocalyptic beginning of Islam, which is largely ignored, its monotheism is obvious and generally acknowledged. We shall bring it to our analysis of the teleology of Muhammad's revolution in Arabia. What needs to be emphasized at this point is that the Jewish and Christian communities of Arabia were not the only bearers of monotheism. There was a third group known as the *Hanifiyya*. Given the scanty references found to the Arab monotheism identified by the *Qur'ân* as the remnant of the religion of Abraham, the *hanif*, we can only speculate on their probable role in the transmission of the above-outlined *apoca-*

---

12 The Hebrew cognate *khotam* is the messianic signet-ring of Haggai 2:23, where Yahwe declares to Zerubbabel: "I shall take you […] and make you like a signet-ring; for I have chosen you." The apocalyptic connotation of the term is made explicit, and is, furthermore, applied to prophecy by Daniel who speaks of the time for setting the seal on prophecy (Dan. 9: 24) and is told by Gabriel to "keep the book sealed until the end of time" (Dan. 12: 1).
13 Rabin (1957: 119) also traces the Qumranic origins of the Islamic apocalyptic terms *hashr*, mentioned above, and *harj* (Hebrew, *heregh* [slaughter]).

lyptic lore to Islam.[14] We can, however, be certain that the religion of *the hanif*'s was a form of monotheism associated with the belief in foundation of the *Ka'ba* by Abraham and the settlement in Mecca of his son Ishmael, with the ritual of hajj, and with the sacrifice of animals consecrated to the *Ka'ba* (Rubin 1990: 92, 102; Bashear 2004). Their *tabliya formula* for the ritual of hajj, however, was significantly monotheistic, and unlike those of the other tribes mentioned above, did not identify any partners for God (Rubin 1990: 100; Bashear 2004: 5-6). Muhammad very successful in identify with it and appropriating its core Abrahamic tenet and ritual for Islam. There remained, however, a group of *hanifs* who refused to convert to Islam, and were led by the monk Abu 'Âmir, who had fought against the Muslims in the battle of Uhud, as an opposition group to Muhammad in Medina in the last years of the Prophet's life (Watt 1956: 189-90; Gil 1987, 1992).

The new revelation and Islam as submission to one universally-acknowledged God

One day in the month of Ramadhan at the end of the first decade of the 7th century, when in seclusion following the ancient custom of the *Quraysh*,[15] Muhammad b. *'AbdAllâh*, a trader with skins about forty years of age, received the call to prophecy. He was shaken until reassured by his wife's cousin, Zayd b. 'Amr b. Nufayl, a *hanif* monotheist, who swore by the God who held his soul that "thou art the prophet of this people" (Life: 105-107). According to another report, Zayd had said: "I expect a prophet from the descendants of Ishmael [...] who has the seal of prophethood between his shoulders. His name is Ahmad" (Tabari, 6: 64). The *Qur'ân* was later to confirm that God sends to the 'gentiles' of the 'unscriptured' *(ummiyyun)* "a messenger, (one) of themselves, to recite to them His signs [...]" (Q. 62: 2; Watt 1988: 53). And Muhammad was indeed "the gentile prophet" *(al-nabiyy al-ummi)*, whom they find written down with them in the Torah and the Gospel [...]. Believe then in God, and in his messenger, the gentile prophet [...]" (Q. 7: 156, 158).

The attestation of messianic expectations among the Jews of Arabia in Muslim traditions (Life: 197-98, 240; Ibn Sa'd, 1: 103-104) cannot be dismissed as an Islamic version of praeparatio evangelicorum, as it is corroborated by Jewish and Syriac sources (Lewis 1953; Cook & Crone 1977: ch. 1). It is worth noting that one particular tradition, doctored to suggest the Jews of Medina expected it to

---

14 There is some indication that they expected a new prophet (*Life*: 98), and that one *hanif*, Umayya b. Abi'l-Salt of *Tâ'if*, claimed to be one (Rubin 1990: 90, 96; 1995: 72-75).
15 The custom of *tahannuth*: seclusion in mount Hirâ,' followed by feeding the poor and ending with the circumambulation of the *Ka'ba* (Kister 1968).

become "the sacred enclave/place of migration *(muhâjar)* for a prophet from the *Quraysh*" retains the significant (and inconvenient) phrase "at the end of time *(fi âkhir al-zamân)*" (Ibn Ishâq: 13-14; Life: 7, translation misleading). Furthermore, it is clear from the *Qur`ân* that the acceptance of Muhammad messianic claim by the few converts among the "people of the book" was of great psychological importance to his early in his career. Two elements from the Judaeo-Christian apocalyptic tradition thus stand out in Muhammad's earliest messages: he was the gentile prophet sent to the people of Arabia, and he was the prophet of the end of time.

In this Meccan period, as he encountered mounting opposition from his own oligarchic clan of *Quraysh*, Muhammad was repeatedly told in the *Qur`ân* to distance himself from them and to seek confirmation from the people to whom the Book or Knowledge has already been given (Rahman 1976: 11-12). In addition to reports of the acceptance of Muhammad as the prophet of the end of time by Jewish converts in his biography (Life: 240-41), the *Qur`ân* itself contains evidence of the acceptance of Muhammad's messianic claim in the course of the emotional experience of conversion:

Say to them [i.e., to the recalcitrant Meccans], O Muhammad, 'Whether you believe in [the *Qur`ân*] or not, those who have been given the Knowledge before it, when it is recited to them, fall upon their faces in prostration. And they say, 'Glory be to our Lord! Our Lord's promise has been fulfilled.' And they fall upon their faces weeping [...] (Q. 17: 107).

There is ample evidence of apocalypticism in the early, Meccan, verses of the *Qur`ân* which speak of the coming of the Hour as the prelude to Resurrection: "The Hour has drawn near and the moon is split;" (Q. 54: 1) "The Hour is coming, no doubt of it;" (Q. 22: 7; 40: 59[61]) "Haply the Hour is near;" (Q. 33: 63; 42: 17[16]) and "surely the earthquake of the Hour is a mighty thing" (Q. 22: 1). The apocalyptic Hour is the earthly prelude to eschatology. It is the hour of calamity that precedes Resurrection.[16] The appearance of the Beast (Q. 27: 82) and such cosmic cataclysms as the smoke *(dukhân;* Q. 44: 10), the rolling up *(takwir;* Q. 81) of the sun, the darkening of the stars and the movement of the mountains (Q. 81: 2-4), the splitting *(infitâr;* Q. 82) of the sky, the scattering of the stars and the swarming over of the seas (Q. 82: 2-4) are evidently the signs of the Day of Resurrection "when the tombs are overthrown" (Q. 82: 5). The *Qur`ân* also

---

16 A number of mostly obscure catastrophic terms for the occurrence at the Hour are identified by the early commentators with the Day of Resurrection. These include *âzifa* (the imminent) (Q. 40:18, 53:58), *wâqi'a* (terror) (Q. 56; 69: 15), *râjifa* and *râdifa* (quake and second quake) (Q. 79: 6-7), *âkhkha* (blast) (Q. 80: 34-36), *ghâshiya* (enveloper) (Q. 88), *zilzila* and *zalzâl* (earthquake) (Q. 99; 99: 1) and *qâri'a* (clatterer) (Q. 69:4, 101; 101:1-3).

speaks (14: 49) of "the day the earth shall be transformed to other than the earth." The mountains will be pulverized into dust (Q. 56: 4-6), or become like plucked tufts of wool (Q. 70: 9). A few signs of social disorder accompany cosmic cataclysms: "And when the Blast shall sound, upon the day when a man shall flee from his brother, his mother, his father, his consort, his sons" (Q. 80: 33-36).

At the Hour, "the Trumpet *(sur)* shall be blown; that is the Day of the Threat [...]. And listen thou for the day when the caller shall call from a near place. On the day they hear the Cry *(sayha)* in truth, that is the day of coming forth" (Q. 50: 19, 40-41). The Cry is not unprecedented; it is a portent of God's physical destruction of the nations which had disowned their prophets in sacred history (Q. 11: 67, 94). But the final day has no precedent. It is indeed "the day when the earth is split asunder about them as they hasten forth" (Q. 50: 43). "For the Trumpet shall be blown, and whosoever is in the heavens and whosoever is in the earth shall swoon, save whom God wills. Then it shall be blown again, and lo, they shall stand, beholding. And the earth shall shine with the light of its Lord [...]" (Q. 39: 69-70). This final transfiguration of the earth is presumably "the new creation" (Q. 14: 22).

Muhammad also preached the absolute transcendence of *Allâh* as the One God who came to sublimate other divinities. Muhammad's Lord *(rabb)* in the earliest verses of the *Qur`ân* (Watt 1988: 87-88), is identified with the Lord of All Being/the worlds *(rabb al-'âlamin)* "who sent Moses as his Messenger (Q. 7: 61, 67, 104; 26: 16). This ecumenical "One God" or "the lord of all," attested in Greek funerary inscriptions in Palestine from the 4th, 5th and 6th centuries was identified, much more frequently in the later verses, with *Allâh* as the Lord of the *Ka'ba* and God of Abraham, Moses and Jesus. It followed that the mission of the Messenger of the God of universe was also universal:

We have not sent thee, save as a mercy to all being/the worlds (Q. 21: 107).

Say: "O mankind (al-nâs) I am the Messenger of God to You all,[17] of Him to whom belongs the kingdom of heavens and the earth. There is no god but He. (Q. 7: 158).

Muhammad also assimilated the transcendent, universal god of southern Arabia, the *Rahmân* (Merciful One), to *Allâh*. The *Rahmân* is attested in late 4th-century Himyarite inscriptions as the "Lord of heaven and earth," and in the mid-6th inscription recording the expedition of Abraha, the Ethiopian viceroy whose Christianity is attested in other sources, begins in the name of the Merciful One and "his Anointed One *(messiah),* king Arbaha" (cited in Hoyland 2001: 556). The

---

17 Q. 34: 28 is more emphatic in this respect: "We have sent thee not except to all of the people *(illa kâffatan li'l-nâs).*" For a discussion of all these verses, see Welch 49-51).

Rahmân was also known closer to Mecca in the Yamâma in central Arabia, and his angels were believed to be all female (Q. 43: 19). Muhammad appropriated him as an epithet of *Allâh* or one of his "most beautiful names" (Q. 17: 110) despite the resistance of the Meccans, who professed "unbelief at the mention of the *Rahmân*."[18] (Q. 21: 36; also Q. 13: 30; Peters 1994: 48, 156-57; Kister 2002: 5-6) With less resistance, some lesser divinities would be transformed to God's beautiful names, others demoted to the rank of angels (Watt: 1988: 90-91) and a few discarded as mere names (Q. 53: 23). Just as Abraham had submitted, or surrendered himself to the Lord of all Being (Q. 2: 131), those who accepted Muhammad's new revelation of monotheism and thereby became 'Muslims' were sternly required to worship the One God exclusively.

Starting point was the predominant position of *Allâh* in the associationists' pantheon, Muhammad considered anyone who rejected partners for God and declared his/her exclusive belonging to Him had submitted to the Lord of all Being (Q. 40: 66) or "undergone Islam *(aslama)*" (the term '*islâm*' soon assumed the congruent meaning of submission; Baneth 1971: 188-89). His message of transcendental monotheism thus struck at the heart of associationism (shirk) – the social or embedded religion[19] of segmented Arabia whose main beneficiary, his own tribe of *Quraysh*, began to persecute him and his followers.

Muhammad began to look for a sacred enclave *(hjr, muhajar, dâr al-hijra)*,[20] and began making discreet enquiries among visitors to the trade fairs at the divine sanctuaries around Mecca. At that time, after just over a decade of preaching in Mecca, Muhammad had built a small community of the faithful numbering barely over a hundred.

Mobilization for Holy Struggle *(jihâd)* and the construction of a new community

The evident demise of mediated Persian authority in Yathrib had aggravated the endemic violence typical of segmented "stateless societies," setting its main tribes of Aws and Khazraj in unresolved deadly conflict. What was needed for its resolution was a holy judge-arbiter *(hakam)*, the only native extra-tribal authority known in Arabia and one similar to the judges of the Old Testament. A number

---

18 According to one report, a presumably early convert who had changed his name upon conversation to ʼAbd al-Rahmân was asked by a Meccan friend to adopt a different name because "I don't know al-Rahmân!" (Life: 302).
19 'Social," as conceived by W. Robertson Smith and E. Durkheim, and 'embedded' in contrast to world or transcendental religion, as conceived by M. Weber and S.N. Eisenstadt.
20 See Serjeant (1982: 26-27) for the pre-Islamic attestation and meaning of the notion.

of aldermen *(naqibs)* from Yathrib were in charge of the search for one, and met Muhammad at the trade fair. According to the earliest account of a meeting between Muhammad and the Yathribites in 'Aqaba by 'Urwa b. al-Zubair, the aldermen gave Muhammad the following pledge: "We are of you and you are of us, whoever comes to us of your companions, or you yourself if you come to us, we shall defend you *(numni'ka)* as we would defend ourselves" (Tabari 6: 136; Mèlaméde 1934). They probably also gave him an armed escort of 4 or 5 bodyguards who later migrated with Muhammad (Lecker 2000: 164-65). As the heavenly counterpart to the pledge of the 'Aqaba, Muhammad received permission to fight (Q. 22: 40-42), whereupon he ordered his companions to migrate from Mecca to the future Medina (Life: 213). The prophet thus chose his sacred enclave, and embarked on the "migration" [to a sacred enclave] *(hijra)* that was to mark the beginning of the Islamic era. Those who undertook *hijra* and joined him in the sacred enclave had the special status of Migrant *(muhâjir)*. God's permission to fight was probably first given to the Migrants "who have been expelled from their dwellings without any cause," (Q. 22: 39) and then to all Muslims "to fight in the way of God" (Q. 2: 244).[21] The coincidence of the two orders is not an accidental event in Muhammad's biography but was essential to his struggle for this-worldly translation of the apocalyptic vision that began in Medina. This is proven by the striking association between migration *(hijra)* and the struggle *(jihâd)* "in the path of God" (Q. 8: 71-73; 9: 19-20) in the *Qur`ân* (Crone 1994: 354-55).

Migrating to the sacred enclave of Allah meant foregoing the protection of the partner-god and thus discarding associationism with monotheism (Watt 1988: 20, 25). This was the condition sine qua non of Islam or submission to God: "To those who believed but did not make the *hijra* it is not for you (pl. to give 'protection' *(wilâya)* until they do make the *hijra*" (Q. 8: 72). Muhammad also had to derive his own authority exclusively from God. It is striking the very frequent references to Muhammad as the Messenger of God occur exclusively in the Medinan verses of the *Qur`ân* (Welch 1983: 43).

Upon his arrival, Muhammad found the inhabitants of Medina "a mixed lot, consisting of the believers united by the mission *(da'wa)* of the Messenger of God, the polytheists who worshiped idols, and the Jews who were the armored people of the forts and the allies *(halifs)* of the tribes of Aws and Khazraj, and wished to establish concord among all of them" (Report from Bayhaqi reproduced in Lecker 1995: 31) Muhammad's emigrants were supporter by the Medinan believers, and organized several raids against the caravans of the *Quraysh*, typically by a handful of Muslims, to sustain themselves from booty.

Muhammad, the prophet of the end of time, did begin the conquest of Arabia

---

21 Other – presumably somewhat later – verses promise paradise as a reward (Watt 1956: 4-5).

as the Prophet of the *malhama*; his apocalyptic battle was no other than the battle of Badr in Ramadan of year 2/March 624 when God, according to the *Qur'ân* (3: 123-25), sent down three thousand angels to fight alongside his army.[22] Just as God had sent Michael to help in the great apocalyptic battle of the Book of Daniel, the Muslim tradition has Gabriel and Michael each lead a thousand angelic troops to the right and the left of Muhammad (and archangel *Isrâfîl* is added at the head of another thousand to reach the number given in the *Qur'ân*; Wâqidi, 1: 57-71, 113; Ibn Sa'd, 3: 9), and considers the battle of Badr as "the day of redemption/deliverance *(furqân)*" mentioned in Q. 8: 41 as a parallel to Ex. 14: 13. With the help of the angelic host, Muhammad's three hundred or so holy warriors, who constituted almost the entire body of male Muslims at the time, defeated an army consisting of three times as many Meccans and their allies. The rich booty was distributed among the 313 or 314 holy warriors, three quarters of whom were Medinan converts[23] (Wâqidi, 1: 23; Life: 336).

The battle of Badr also sealed the institutionalization of holy warfare as the distinctive Islamic path of revolutionary struggle for the religion of God *(din Allâh)*: "Fight them until there is no more persecution and religion, all of it, is God's" (Q. 8: 39). In fact, Sura 8 of the *Qur'ân (Anfâl)*, believed to have been revealed as divine commentary on the battle of Badr (Wâqidi, 1: 131-31), or a section thereof, was often read to the Muslim armies before battle during the Muslim conquests.

Most of the Badr prisoners were ransomed to support the new Muslim community, but two anti-Muhammad pagan intellectuals were executed. The victory was also used by Muhammad to have two Medinan pagan intellectual opponents of Islam executed by their own converted clansmen (to avoid vengeance and payment of blood money)[24] (Watt 1956: 178-79). A few months later (625/3), Muhammad besieged the fortification of the Jewish clan of *Qaynuqâ'*, whose strength is put at three hundred armored men and four hundred men without mail (Life: 363), until they surrendered unconditionally. Their Arab protector from the tribe of Khazraj, 'Abd Allâh b. Ubayy, who almost passed for a king before Muhammad's arrival (Life: 279), interceded for them. He reportedly felt confident enough to grab the Prophet by the neck until the latter said: "You can have them!" (Life: 363) The lives of the Jewish clan were spared, but they were expropriated and expelled from the Medina settlement. This alarmed a half-Arab nobleman of the Jewish clan of Nadir, Ka'b b. al-Ashraf, who went to Mecca to

---

22 According to 'Abdallâb b. 'Abbâs, the angels wore white turbans in the battle of Badr and red turbans a few years later at Hunayn (where they helped but without fighting; Life: 303-4).
23 According to Wâqidi, their number was 313, 5 of whom were not present during the distribution of booty.
24 They belonged to the Aws Manât, the majority of whose clans broke their idols and converted to Islam, changing its name to Aws *Allâh* (Watt 1956: 178-79).

confer with the *Quraysh* and began composing anti-Muslim satires. Muhammad sanctioned a conspiracy involving Ka'b's half-brother to assassinate him and absolved the conspirators from the sin of lying. After the assassination of Ka'b b. al-Ashraf, he reportedly added the injunction, "Kill any Jew that falls into you power," whereupon an Arab wantonly murdered his Jewish ally. The murder of Ka'b b. al-Ashraf "cast terror among the Jews, and there was not a Jew in Medina who did not fear for him life" (Life: 367-69). At this point some Jewish leaders approached Muhammad, and he seized the opportunity to conclude a pact with them that reaffirmed the status of the Jews as members of the unified community of Medina but also obligated them to pay the war tax (Serjeant 1978: 32). The pact, which was kept by 'Ali b. Abi Tâlib (Lecker 1995: 26), formed the nucleus of what modern scholars have referred to as "the constitution of Medina" (CM; Wellhausen 1975; Humphreys 1991: 92-98).

While proselytizing and winning new converts who would accept his prophetic authority on the basis of the new revelation, Muhammad wasted no time consolidating his authority as a judge-arbiter *(hakam)* according to Arabian customary law, which included legislative authority (Serjeant 1978: 1-2). In doing so, he needed divine succor, and the phrase "obey God and His messenger" appears some forty times in the *Qur`ân* in Verses that are mostly dated to his first three years in Medina (Watt 1956: 233). In this series of pacts, which were correctly executed, "Muhammad the Prophet *(al-nabi)*" (CM: A.1) secured recognition of his authority as the judge-arbiter to whom all disputes were to be referred on behalf of *Allâh* (CM: B.4). One of the later Clauses reiterates the requirement of referring disputes "to *Allâh* and to Muhammad, the Messenger of *Allâh*" (CM; F4). The potentially expansive quality of this authority is evident. Those subject to this authority are constituted "a unified community *(umma wâhida)* set apart from [other] people" (CM: A.2a). The *Qur`ân* (21: 92) duly sanctioned the new social compact for the believers: "This community of yours is a unified community, and I am your Lord, so worship me."[25] Although the unified community was religiously plural and "a rather loose heterogeneous political entity," comprising not only the Muslims but also non-Muslim clans. As the Muslims were its soul, "the more the new faith grew, the more the *umma* overshadowed the clans" (Wellhausen 1975: 131).

Medina was still tribally organized, with each clan "in charge of the management of its affairs," joint payment of blood-monies and collective responsibility for ransoming its prisoners (CM: A.2c-j). The Migrants of *Quraysh* were constituted into a clan alongside those of the Aws and the Khazraj. Individuals who would lose the protection of their tribes by joining the united community were

---

25 Serjeant (1978: 5-7) sees Q. 3: 101-103 as a further reference to the new social pact. The term *"umma wâhida"* occurs eight times in the Qur`ân. See Rubin 1985: 134-38 for citations.

compensated according to the customary blood-money and ransom rates (CM: A.3a); and the Jews joining it were assured parity (CM: A.8). All covenanters with Muhammad *(mu'minin)*[26] were declared to be under the security *(dhimma)* of God, which the least of them could extend on behalf of all (as any member of a clan could pledge protection on its behalf; CM: A.7) A covenanter was, on the other hand, forbidden to kill another in retaliation for an infidel (among his kinsmen; CM: A.6); and the united community was given collective responsibility for the punishment of crimes against its members and for treason (CM: A.5). The inner part of Medina was declared a sacred *(harâm)* for the covenanters (CM: F, H; Denny 1977: 45), just as Abraham had reportedly declared Mecca a sacred area (Rubin 1985: 11). A pact of tolerance allowed the Jewish covenanters of the united community to have their religion, as the Muslims had theirs, as long as they paid the war levy *(nafaqa)* alongside the other covenanters and refrained from treason (CM: E.3-3b, G; Rubin 1985: 12).

This last clause points to the crucial fact that, from the moment of constitution of a new community, Muhammad was also making constitutional provisions for the (revolutionary) struggle in the path of God. That a levy was imposed on the covenanters and their Jewish affiliates for the purpose is a minor aspect of this development. The general peace and security of God eliminated the legitimacy of the use of violence by politically autonomous segments of the Arabian tribal society. The monopoly of the legitimate use of violence was in principle invested in the united community, thereby laying the foundation for a unified structure of authority – a state – devoted to the realization of the final end of the prophetic mission:

The covenanters shall make peace only in unity. No covenanter shall make peace apart from other covenanters in fighting (qitâl) in the path of God – and that only as a just and equitable decision by them. And all raiding parties shall fight with us one after another. And the covenanters shall execute retaliation on behalf of one another with respect to their blood shed in the path of God (CM: A.9-11, my translation).

The Migrants had been aided by the Medinan hosts – the 'Helpers' *(ansâr)*, with whom Muhammad had instituted artificial kinship by a pact of Brotherhood. The Helpers had provided their emigrant 'brothers' with land and palm trees (Life: 231-35).

The next battle, 'Uhud, in March 625/3,[27] went badly for the Muslims. The Helpers, who bore the brunt of casualties found the support of their Muslim brethren more burdensome. 'Abd Allâh b. Ubayy openly criticized Muhammad

---

26 I am following Serjeant's (1978: 12-15) suggestion that the term '*mu'minin,*' which later acquired the meaning of the 'faithful,' originally meant parties to/beneficiaries of the covenant (*amân*).

27 I follow the chronology of Jones (1957), which is basically al-Wâqidi's.

for following the hot-headed youths against his own better judgment and Ibn Ubayy's advice and thereby bringing disaster to the Medinan Helpers, seventy of whom were killed. The power struggle between 'Abd Allâh b. 'Ubayy and Muhammad intensified as the tension between his Jewish clients and the Prophet increased. No longer trusting the Jews of Medina, Muhammad asked his secretary, Zayd b. Thabit to learn Hebrew and the Jewish script in 625/4, which the latter reported did in 17 days of intensive study (Abbott 1967: 247, 257). Some five months after the battle of Uhud Muhammad decided to expel Ibn Ubayy's other Jewish allies, the Banu al-Nadir, and sent them an ultimatum. Ibn Ubayy encouraged the Jewish clan to resist, saying to them, according a common in *Qur'ân* interpretation, "Surely, if you are expelled, we shall go out with you, and if you are attacked in war, we shall help you." This is immediately denied by the Book: "God testifieth that they are lying" (Q. 59: 11). Following two serious set-backs which cost the lives of nearly 50 missionaries sent by Muhammad to the nomads, he accused Banu al-Nadir of conspiracy to kill him, and attacked their oasis, destroying their palm trees. The Nadir were one of the two former "kings" or fiscal agents of the Persian empire. They surrendered in August 625/4, on the condition that they would keep their movable property, except for arms, and were deported, some to Syria others to Khaybar. Two of them reportedly "became Muslims in order to retain their property." The rest packed their belongings on camels and left "with such pomp and splendor as had never been seen in any tribe in their days." Their land was distributed among the Migrants. The Medinan Helpers were excluded, presumably because they did not need land, except for two who pleaded poverty (Life: 437-38).

The Nadir exiles from the Jewish settlement of Khaybar approached the Meccan pagans in the hope of being restored to Medina, and Muhammad dispatched a team including a converted son of a Jewish woman of Khaybar to assassinate their leader, Abu Rafi' Sallâm b. Abi'l-Huqayq, most probably in 626/5 (Watt 1956: 30-31; Newby 1971: 217-20). Meanwhile, Ibn Ubayy persisted in his opposition, and over a year or so later, spread scandalous rumors about Muhammad's young wife, 'Âyisha. Muhammad summoned a meeting of Ibn Ubayy's fellow Khazraj tribesmen to strip him from tribal protection from punishment but did not succeed. But soon thereafter, Ibn Ubayy ceased his opposition and Muhammad himself eventually performed his funeral rites (Watt 1956: 185-87).

As the mobilization for holy struggle continued and the number of holy warriors increased from some 300 in 624 (Badr) to 3000, with thirty-six horsemen in 627, the war levy and booty from raids on the *Quraysh* caravans became inadequate and there was an evident need for additional fiscal prey *(tu'ma)* (Kister 1986: 88-89). According to some reports, the other kingly Jewish clan, Banu *Qurayza* had also first joined Banu al-Nadir in the summer of 625/4 but had come to terms with Muhammad, concluding a pact of peaceful coexistence *(muwâda'a*; Kister 1986: 82-85). Coexistence, however, turned out to be neither easy nor peaceful, and the Quryaza, the strongest of the Jewish clans of Medina, became Muhammad's most lucrative fiscal prey in 627/5, immediately after the battle of the Trench. Perhaps as a vestige of their former status as the agents of Persia, the *Qurayza* possessed a large number of weapons in their storehouses, and lent the Muslims tools to dig a tend around Medina when was besieged by the *Quraysh* and its allied tribes. However, the *Qurayza* also established contacts with the *Quraysh* through instigators from the Nadir exiles. After some inconclusive fighting, the *Quraysh* and their allied lifted the siege and left in disarray. Muhammad at once laid siege to the fortification of the *Qurayza* two miles from Medina. The *Qurayza* surrendered unconditionally after two or three weeks, even though one companion of the Prophet had indicated by a gesture that their lives would not be spared. The number of Muhammad's holy warriorsnow exceeded three thousand. He confiscated the 1500 swords and shields, 300 coats of arm and 200 spears from Banu *Qurayza* for them. Insisting on observance of the legal formality of arbitration by a man from the protecting Arab tribe of Aws, Muhammad Sa'd b. Mu'âdh, a man who had previously managed the assassination of Ka'b b. al-Ashraf and was severely wounded during the siege, to decide the judicial murder of the Jewish captives. Some 400 men constituting the entire male population were executed by the Migrants, except for six by their three Medinan Arab confederate clans so as to avoid vengeance and payment of blood mono (Watt 1956: 214 16). The *Qurayza* women and children, numbering about one thousand, taken captive and sold into slavery. The procceds went to his new treasury, while Muhammad made grants on their land and palm trees to the Migrants who were to give back the tree given to them by the Medinan Helper (Kister 1986: 90-96). Medina was thus cleared by the Jewish clans and Muhammad became the undisputed ruler of the united community he had set up in it.

Political success did not lessen Muhammad's sense of living at the end of time and preparing for the Last Judgment. For this reason, he insisted that his mosque be built, in accordance with Gabriel's instructions, as a "booth like the booth of Moses thy brother," (Kister 1962: 154) and without a roof. When the palm branches were replaced by bricks as its wall about the time of the battle of the Trench, he refused to add a roof and retained the Mosaic form appropriate for the end of time. Nevertheless, success also sharpened the Prophet's political pragmatism. After the battle of the Trench, Muhammad married the widowed Muslim daughter his distant cousin Abu Sufiyân, the leader of the pagan *Quraysh*, who gradually ceased to take part in its military operations, and was conspicuously absent during the negotiations for the treaty of al-Hudaybiyya in March 628/6 between Muhammad and the *Quraysh*. Some three months later, Muhammad attacked the rich Jewish settlement of Khaybar, rewarding some 1600 Muslims who had pledge their steadfastness in anxious moment before the truce of Hudaybiyya with booty and land.[28] Despite its disadvantages, notably the undertaking to return Muslim refugees to the *Quraysh* the latter did not capitalize (Görke 2000), the truce of Hudaybiyya enabled Muhammad to take part in a pilgrimage and thus paved the way for the taking of Mecca in January 630/8, and to realize his dream of the believers "entering the Holy Mosque in security, God willing, with your heads shaven, not fearing" (Q. 48: 27). The importance of appropriating the hajj for clearing Islam of the suspicion of foreignness and making it firmly Arabian cannot be overemphasized. Muhammad marched into Mecca with some 10,000 armed men (as compared to the 3,000 he could muster three years earlier). Abu Sufiyân visited his camp secretly and arranged for a general amnesty. Within a month of the conquest of Mecca, Muhammad added some two thousand men to his army and defeated a coalition of the old opponents of the *Quraysh* in Hunayn at the end of the same month. The wholesale conversion of the old *Quraysh* oligarchy took place rapidly, with the "winning of [their] hearts" with generous distribution of the booty from Hunayn, which caused considerable resentment among old Muslims, especially the Medinan helpers who reportedly got nothing (Life: 594-97). Muhammad was now the most powerful man in Arabia, and its close and distant tribes hastened to send him "delegations' to join him as confederates (Ibn Sa'd, I, 2: 38-86). In the last months of 630/9, he was able to send an army of 30,000 to Tabuk.

From the viewpoint of the teleology of Muhammad's revolution, this unification of Arabian was an incidental result of the triumph of the religion of God. Muhammad undertook the breaking of the idols of the *Ka'ba* himself, beginning with the destruction of Hubal, the red amber statue in human form in whose name Abu Sufiyân had led the pagan Meccans in 'Uhud, their most successful battle against Muhammad, with the cry: "*Allâh* is greater and more glorious!" He sent 'Ali b. Abi Talib, Mughira b. Shu'ba and Khâlid b. al-Walid to destroy, respectively, the three goddesses, *Manât*, the *Lât* and the *'Uzza*. The tribes of Khath'am and Bâhila fiercely defended their idol, Dhu'l-Khalsa, and one hundred of them were killed before the idol was destroyed (Kalbi: 15-17, 25-28, 36). The destruction of the idols meant the liquidation of the social organization of tribal Arabia, and above all, of autonomous tribal political leadership (Lecker 1993: 343). What was left to complete the unfolding of the religious telos of Muhammad's revolution was the destruction of a handful of rival Arabian monotheistic prophet, the most important and powerful being Musaylima of Yamâma, the prophet of al-*Rahmân*, the area close to Mecca (around present-day Riad). This was done by his successor, Abu Bakr 632-634 (Kister 2002).

---

28 The division of booty and fiscal levies imposed on the Khaybar were formally recorded, and served as the legal model for treaties with the Jewish colonies of Fadak, which followed immediately, and with those of Wadi al-Qurâ' and Taymâ' later, all of which stipulated payment of regular levies to the Muslim state (Life: 521-23; Watt 1956: 218).

The destruction of the old, segmentary political order was thus complete. The construction of a new political community and government, has barely begun, however. As we shall see, these task, especially the second – namely the construction of a new authority structure and government, remained incomplete at Muhammad's death. The unfolding of the teleology of the revolution thus continued under his successors.

The unification of Arabia, and the emergence of a composite Muslim polity

The idea of the *umma* as a community designated for salvation through a prophet is already strongly present in the Meccan verses of the *Qur`ân* (Denny 1977: 44, 52). Such a community, however, could not be constituted in Arabia without a revolution as we have defined the term: it required a radical transformation of the politically segmented tribal society and the structure of authority that held them apart. Although the Meccan converts had been individuals, Medina witnessed the phenomenon of acceptance of Islam by whole clans (Watt 1956: 170-71). The constitutive revolution began with Muhammad's migration to Medina. Muhammad had taken cognizance of the existing kinship and tribal solidarities and sought to harness them for the propagation of his religious mission. His missionaries to Medina had been sent to the Banu al-Najjâr clan of and Khazraj, clan of his maternal grandmother (Life: 199; Mélamêde 1934: 48), and himself resided with them when he migrated, and built his mosque in their quarter (Tabari, 8: xvii, 4-5). But the decade of struggle and warfare in the path of God had set sons against fathers and kinsman against kinsman. The cult of vengeance was transformed into holy warfare. The believers were "each other's avengers of blood on the war path of God, but tribal law and family sentiment are wholly ignored" (Wolf 1951: 147). Membership in the new community of believers displaced, desacralized and subordinated the old ties of kinship: "Verily, they who have believed and fled their homes and spent their substance for the cause of God, and they who have taken in the Prophet and been helpful to him, shall be near of kin to the other" (Q. 8: 73).

Muhammad's tribal policy was an aspect of creating a society and polity on a religious foundation around the belief in one God and Muhammad as His messenger. Arabian tribes could put themselves under the protection of God and His messenger without professing Islam. In this way, Muhammad created an intertribal security system, a *Pax Islamica*, around the growing polity in Medina. *Pax Islamica* had a religious kernel: it was a system based on 'the security of God and his messenger.' As he grew stronger, he demanded Islam from prospective allies brought under God's protection, but continued to make purely political alliances with distant and powerful tribes which came to submit to *Pax Islamica* on the basis of the Arab norms of tribal alliance (Watt 1956: 144-46). In the year 626/5, he made a special arrangement with 400 men from the Muzayna tribe, granting them the status of "emigrants" (muhajirun) within their own territories – which meant they would not have to join the *jihâd*, thereby making an exception to coupling of *hijra* with *jihâd* as a condition of Islam (Madelung 1986: 231-32). The *umma* was not a suitable term to apply to this confederate polity, and as Watt (1956: 247) points out, it no longer appears in the *Qur`ân* or the treaties.

The reason was the radical change in the basis of Muhammad's domination in Arabia. Khâlid b. al-Walid and 'Amr b. 'Âs, two important tribal leaders of the *Quraysh*, who were late converts like Abu Sufyân, had already joined Muhammad in Mecca during the summer before the fall of Mecca, and taken part with 3,000 men in the campaign of Mu'ta in September and October of 629/8. Only 700 of the 12,000 men who fought in Hunayn, the decisive battle for unification of Arabia under Muhammad, were Migrants (Watt 1956: 53-59). Although their number had multiplied almost tenfold since the battle of Badr six years earlier, these early Muslims or members of Muhammad's charismatic religious movement were now a small minority in his armed forces.

Muhammad, however, did not live long enough to settle the constitution of the new polity. Nor did he have the time to lay down the constitution of its government. This contrast sharply with Muhammad's regulation of warfare, which formed the basis of the Muslim conquests or what we might call "the export of the Islamic revolution" that resulted from the mobilization of the Arab tribes. One curious consequence of this failure is that, by the middle of the 7th century, the Muslim state appears as a huge army accompanied by the most rudimentary civil bureaucracy" (Donner 1993: 312).

Succession to charismatic leadership and the consequences of Muhammad's constitutive revolution in Arabia

The social background of the first Muslims who comprised the core of Muhammad's charismatic movement was very different from those of either the *Quraysh* oligarchs or the tribesmen of Arabia who pledged allegiance to Muhammad in his last years. The first Muslims were individual converts. They included 6 or 7 slaves, 5 women, 4 lowly brothers and one man (Bilâl) freed by Abu Bakr. One of the slaves was of foreign (Ethiopian) tongue and a Christian, and was said to teach Muhammad the *Qur`ân* by his detractors. Of the 82 who migrated to Ethiopia from Meccan persecution, 5 were freedmen or clients *(mawâli)*, the rest were from Meccan clans and included some of Muhammad's cousins (Life: 143-48, 179-80; Ibn Sa'd, 3/1: 282-83). The Migrants who fought in the battle of Badr included 11 slaves and freedmen (Watt 1956: 344). Abu Bakr and 'Umar were merchants who, unlike Muhammad himself and his cousin 'Ali and his son-in-law 'Uthmân, did not belong to the tribal elite. The first change in the recruitment pattern was conversion by clan is reported in Medina a little before the Prophet's migration, when, following their above-mentioned leader, Sa'd B. Mu'adh, "every man and woman among the Banu 'Adbu'l-Ashhal joined Islam" (Life: 201). Conversion by clans in Medina and among the northern Arabs continued under Muhammad. The second major change came after the conquest of Mecca and the battle of Hunayn, when tribes of southern Arabia and other region pledged allegiance to Muhammad. As the wars immediately following the death of the Prophet demonstrated, quite a few of these tribes did not acknowledge Muhammad's prophecy and did not convert to Islam, some of them professed Islam but did not want to pay taxes to the nascent Islamic state, and yet others were followers of rival 'false prophets' (Kister 2002: 13-26).

With the change in the composition of Muhammad's polity came a corresponding change in the pattern of motivation. As in any socioreligious movement, Muhammad had always had to overcome the typical dilemma of 'mixed motivation' by offering his followers rewards in both this and the other world.[29] According to Ibn Ishâq (Life: 395), this mixture of rewards in both worlds had been reinforced after the disastrous battle of Uhud: "And he who desires the reward of this world We will give him it; and he who desires the reward of the next world We will give him it and We shall reward the thankful" (Q. 3: 145).

Now the mix of motives had to be made considerably this-worldly for the tribesmen who had joined the original holy warriors. Furthermore, the holy warrior/migrants had been maintained on booty from the tribes, but as *Pax Islamica* expanded, and the confiscation of Jewish settlements was completed, northward expansion was the only remaining outlet for raids and booty (Watt 1956: 145). Here we have the crucial factor behind the export of revolution from Arabia, which also explains why, contrary to a widespread misperception, it was not accompanied by the mass conversion of the conquered populations.

The biggest unsettled questions at the time of the Prophet's death were those of legitimate rulership and organization of the state. The absence of reference to the form of government and political leadership in the *Qur'ân* is truly astonishing. Donner explains it as a consequence of Muhammad's apocalyptic expectation of the Day of Judgment, which would obviate the need for laying down norms of government. This forced his successors "to develop a theory of political legitimacy with almost no *Qur'ân*ic basis" (Donner 1998: 45). Madelung (1997: 16-17), by contrast, argues that Muhammad saw the precedent of the rulership of the families of the earlier prophets mentioned in the *Qur'ân* as applying to his

---

29 Sa'd b. Khaythama had insisted on drawing lots with his father because only one of them could participate in the battle of Badr, saying he would have let his father go had it not been for the promise of going to heaven (Waqidi, 1: 20). By contrast, a holy warrior evidently not so impressed by the latter promise during the battle of the Trench complained that "Muhammad used to promise that we would eat the treasures of Khosraw and Caesar [the Persian and Roman emperors]" (Life: 454).

family as well, seeing a Hashimite monarchy as the obvious solution to the problem of succession after his death. Although Madelung may be right in arguing that this hierocratic principle of kinship to the Prophet was closest to Muhammad's intention of transforming his prophetic charisma to the charisma of his lineage by establishing a House of Muhammad on the biblical model of the House of David and the House of *'Imrân* (Moses') for him *umma*, three other principles were also imperfectly adumbrated in the sayings and deeds, which had a potential for further logical development and corresponding institutionalization. The most important of these was the principle of seniority or precedence *(sâbiqa)* in Islam. There was also the entirely principle of consensus (rida wa'l-jamâ'a). The weakest in terms of Prophetic endorsement was the surviving pre-Islamic principle nobility and leadership (sharaf wa'l-riyâsa) (Sharon 1984). This last principle was, however, favored by the *Quraysh* oligarchy of late converts whose hearts Muhammad had won at the finalstage of unification of Arabia.

As Muhammad's male offspring had predeceased him, Madelung (1997: 253) follows the *Shi'a* in seeing his famous designation of his son-in-law and cousin, 'Ali at Ghadir Khumm – "'Ali is the patron *(mawlâ)* of whomever I am a patron of" – as his succession appointment, and points out that the oath of allegiance to 'Ali as the fourth caliph matched this formula. The position argued by Madelung became the principle of Hâshimite legitimism when 'Ali's son succeeded his as the Caliph after his assassination with the proclamation, "I am al-Hasan, the son of Muhammad," and was so addressed by the leading member of the Hâshimite clan, 'Abd Allâh b. 'Abbas somewhat later during his brief tenure of the caliphate (Madelung 1997: 311, 313). Paradoxically, however, the hierocratic model found relatively little support in the revolutionary power struggle after Muhammad's death, and was only developed much later by the *Shi'ite* sects into the doctrine of Imamate. 'Ali, its main beneficiary, in fact gave his pledge of allegiance to Abu Bakr and 'Umar, and it was his precedence in Islam that primarily assured his succession as the fourth Caliph, though he also claimed consensus as the basis of his legitimacy in the civil war with *Mu'âwiya* (Sharon 1984: 130-32). The latter, greatly reinforcing the policy of the third Caliph, 'Uthman, subordinated the principle of precedence in Islam to that of nobility and leadership, and was accused by later generations of thus turning the Caliphate into kingship *(mulk)* with the establishment of the Umayyad dynasty.

Immediately after the death of the Prophet, Abu Bakr and 'Umar were clearly apprehensive of the hierocratic principle, which would result in the caliphate and prophethood being reunited in the same family, meaning that the Banu Hâshim' would have the monopoly of both (Lammens 1910: 16-17; Madelung 1997: 22). Abu Bakr and 'Umar were of very modest origins, and must have counted on the support of "the disinherited" *(mustad'afun)* who, as we have seen, were numerous among the early converts. They broke into a meeting of the Ansâr and pushed them into accepting Abu Bakr as the *khalifa* (successor) of the Messenger of God, and made an alliance with the obscure Fihrite on the margin of *Quraysh*,

Abu ʻUbayda b. al-Jarrah, who was ʻUmar's friend and was later designated as his successor but was killed in battle, to create the 'triumvirate' that took power after the death of the Prophet (Lammens 1910) and the *Umayyads*. Later, after succeeding Abu Bakr to the Caliphate, ʻUmar ordered the murder of the leader of the Medinan Helpers, Saʻd b. ʻUbâda (Lammens 1910: 116-17, 142). Like the Hâshimites, the Ansâr "tried to restore their faded fortune by backing" ʻAli, and when he lost the First Civil War, they were no longer part of the political elite (Donner 1981: 274). The Hashimite clan had the satisfaction of burying Muhammad and excluding Abu Bakr and his daughter ʻÂyisha from attending his funeral.

Abu Bakr, seconded by ʻUmar and supported by the early Muslims claimed legitimacy on the basis of their precedence in Islam and developed the idea of the successorship *(khilâfat)* of the Prophet. They thus instituted the Caliphate and fought the Arab tribes which refused to accept that the Prophet had founded a state authorized to receive taxes as well as those how followed rival Arabian prophets in what became known anachronistically as the wars of apostasy *(ridda)*. When readmitting the defeated 'apostate' tribes, Abu Bakr, the first Caliph, and ʻUmar, his successor, exacted from their members, upon (re)conversion to Islam, the pledge to obey "whomever God had invested with authority" *(wallâ Allâh ʼl-amr)* (Kister 1994: 100-101).

Like the Hâshimites, the old oligarchy of late converts opposed ʻUmar's caliphate with the appeal to "O, House of *Qusayy*," and gained ascendancy under the third caliph, ʻUthmân. After persuading ʻAli's son, al-Hasan to abdicate the Caliphate, Muʻâwiya greatly reinforced ʻUthman's policy and subordinated the principle of precedence in Islam to that of nobility and leadership, and was accused by later generations of thus turning the Caliphate into kingship *(mulk)* with the establishment of the Umayyad dynasty.

In contrast to his lack of attention to the normative regulation of the political order, Muhammad did institute a system of religious pluralism as a part of the realistic modification of the Meccan apocalyptic vision. The gentile prophet of the Meccan period, devoted to the restoration of the primal religion of Abraham whose "recitation" *(Qurʼân)* consisted of the communication of the Enochic "preserved tablet," becomes "the Messenger of God" in the Medinan Verses, and the Torah and the Gospel are explicitly recognized as holy scriptures: "For each of you [i.e., Jews, Christians, Muslims] We have appointed a path and a way, and if God had so willed, He would have made you but one community [...]" (Q. 5: 48). The *Qurʼân* (3: 64) also came up with the formula for integrating the Jews as anti-associationist monotheists into the united community: "Say: 'O People of the Book, come to a word (which is) fair between us and you, (to wit) that we serve no one but God, *that we associate nothing with Him*, and that none of us take others as Lords beside God" (Emphasis added).

This accommodative pluralism was endorsed by divine revelation: "There is no compulsion in religion *(lâ ikrâh fiʼl-din)*" (Q. 2: 256). According to one important tradition, this verse was revealed on the occasion of the Prophet's decision to accept poll tax from the Magians (Zoroastrians) rather than requiring their forced conversion. This gave the Zoroastrians the same de facto status as the "people of the Book" *(ahl al-kitâb)*. This decision provoked the indignation of a group of Muslims, including 'Abd Allâh b. Ubayy, who criticized the Muhammad for granting the Zoroastrians the privilege he had denied the Arab polytheists and were called the 'hypocrites' *(munâfiqun)* on account of this opposition. Muhammad remained adamant, however, and reaffirmed that the Arab polytheists would be fought until they professed Islam (Kister 1994: 89-91).

The Islamicization of Arabia was completed 'Umar, the second Caliph, who completed the wars of 'apostasy' and eradicated polytheism and the religion of the prophet of al-Rahmân and other rival prophets among the Arabs. He also expropriated and expelled the Jews of Khaybar and the Christians of Najran. He legitimated this final revolutionary step with a tradition of the Prophet saying during his terminal illness that "two faiths will not live together in the land of the Arabs (variant, *Hijâz*)." (Kister 1994: 94-95).

There is no evidence, however, that 'Umar or anyone else used the term *umma* to refer to the unified Islamic Arabia, nor, a fortiori, to the vast political society unified by the Muslim state after the conquests. The notion of *umma* reverted to it original meaning of a community designated for salvation through a Prophet (Denny: 44, 52). Competing proselytizing religious communities were the striking feature of the religious situation in late antiquity and Muhammad conceived his own *umma* or community of believers in the same line, albeit as the best of them (Q. 3: 110) and their (golden) mean (Q. 2: 143). The *Qur`ân* also links the notion of religious community with the "people of the Book" (Q. 2: 63, 65; 5: 69-70; 22: 18). According to the earliest *Qur`ân* commentaries, the *umma* of Muhammad consisted of the Muslims not contaminated by a pre-Islamic birth" (Bashear 1997: 44). The Muslim *umma* was thus completely distinct from the society ruled by the Caliphate, which comprised other religious communities of the peoples of the Book. This enabled Muhammad's successors to turn the de facto recognition of different religious communities in the late Sasanian empire into the pluralistic system of autonomous "protected" religious communities that was distinctively Islamic and eventually developed into the Ottoman millet system (Fowden 2001: 97-98). The notion of a political community subject to a ruler entered Islam much later and with the reception of the Persian political lore. It was the ancient idea of the subjects as the flock *(ra'iyya)* of their ruler who was to govern them with justice (Arjomand 2003).

Appendix: A typology of revolutions from revolution in world history

Type I: Integrative Revolution

Integrative Revolution is subdivided it into three of our ideal types or models, Types I. 1-3 , which are designed to cover the range of variation in the relation between revolution and the enlargement of the political community: 1) the revolutionary construction of an integrated political community from segmentary tribal societies or self-contained city-states; 2) the opening of oligarchies in the course of expansion of city-states into empires; and 3) the integration through the invasion of the center from a mobilized political island in the periphery. A fourth model will represent the better explored relationship between centralization of power and revolution, and constitute our second type of revolution (Type II).

(i) Integrative Revolution 1 (I.1): Constitutive Revolution.

Radical change in the political order may result from the incongruence between cultural and political integration. This can arise in a culturally unified society where the structure of authority remains segmented – confined to tribes or city-states. The larger society is culturally unified while political authority is segmented, except under martial emergency, and political integration remains either intermittent, in the form of *ad hoc* confederations of tribes and city-states, or weak, based solely on networks of personal ties among patrons and clients across the segments (Balandier 1985: 318-322). Such societies, including the "segmentary states" that are found to be prone to rebellions (Fallers 1968: 80), can be restructured through revolution. The type of revolution that belongs to these societies is an integrative revolution that constitutes a new political order by institutionalizing central political authority and unifying the segments into a more integrated political community. Its ideal type will accordingly be called 'Constitutive Revolution.' The first revolution in world history, the Akkadian revolution, belongs to this Constitutive type, as does the rise of Islam.

(ii) Integrative Revolution 2 (I.2): Aristotelian-Paretan Revolution.

Aristotle's idea of integrative revolution in oligarchies can serve as the starting point for our second model. According to Aristotle, oligarchies and aristocracies are prone to revolution because of those they *exclude* from the political society. Impoverished members of the governing class become revolutionary leaders; the regime is undermined by persons who are wealthy but excluded from office; and sedition arises when the circle of government is too narrow and "the masses of a people consists of men animated by the conviction that they are as good as their masters in quality" (*Politics*). From these considerations it would follow that the type of revolution to which oligarchies and aristocracies are prone is what we shall call *integrative revolution*, revolution that enlarges the political community, broadens the franchise and/or other political rights, notably access to power.

Among the moderns, Pareto's theory of revolution comes closest to Aristotle's idea. Put simply, his theory is as follows: If access to the political class, the ruling elite, is blocked to energetic and resolute individuals – lions – from the lower classes, and if the ruling elite becomes weak and incapable of stern repression because of an increase in the proportion of foxes over lions in its composition, a revolution is likely to occur (Pareto 1968[1917-19]: 2227). In this situation, socially upwardly mobile individuals who are excluded from power develop into a revolutionary counter-elite that eventually seizes power and makes history the graveyard of yet another aristocracy (Pareto 1968[1917-19]: pp. 1304-1305, 2053-2057).

(iii) Integrative Revolution 3 (I.3): Khaldunian Revolution.

Integrative revolutions can begin at the center, or they can begin in the periphery. The latter constitute a distinct type which students of contemporary revolutions have often misconstrued as "peasant revolution." Huntington (1968) called it simply "the Eastern type" of revolution. Medieval Islam offers us the possibility of a better understanding of this type of integrative revolution which I propose to call Khaldunian and put forward as our third structural ideal type of integrative revolution.

Ibn Khaldun, as we have seen, offers as a structural pre-condition of dynastic change, the endemic translocation of ruling authority and group solidarity between the periphery and the center in a dual social structure. He also paves the way for a theoretical move from dynastic change to revolution by considering the *superimposition* of new religiously (or ideologically) based solidarity upon existing, tribal group solidarity *('asabiyya).*

The essentials of the Khaldunian type of revolution are the following. It begins in the periphery with a militarized solidary group that is united on the basis of a religious cause. The key factor for explaining the failure of the regime and the success of the insurgents is differential solidarity. The urban base of the regime lacks social cohesion while the already strong group solidarity of the insurgents is strengthened by a unifying religious cause. The revolutionaries progress gradually with a series of attacks on governmental forces. The end comes after a long time with the military defeat of the dynasty and the capture of its capital and other major cities.

Type II: Tocquevillian Revolution

Huntington's "Western" type of revolution, which I will call the Tocquevillian ideal type, is the one most familiar to us. In this modern type of revolution, a centralized state is already in place. In fact, revolution takes the form of the disintegration of the authority of the state and the collapse of the established political order at the center. As we shall see, most Integrative Revolutions have centralization as a consequence of the termination of revolutionary power struggle. What is distinctive of our Type II of revolution is that centralization also appears as a *cause* of revolution. The notion of the state, however, needs to be modified to the structure of domination or authority structure, especially if we wish to apply it to pre-modern revolutions.

Historically-specific Ideal-types of Teleology of Revolution.

The distinctive direction of a revolution as shaped by its intended or intentionally prefigured consequences will be called its teleology. Teleology can also be modeled by highlighting the distinctive features of each case. This ideal-typical characterization of consequences of revolutions as historical individuals is intended as a substitute for the putatively general or generic teleology of all revolutions as steps in the forward march of mankind in historical materialism and the popular 20th-century conception of revolution.

Abbreviations

Life: A. Guillaume, The Life of Muhammad. A translation of Ibn Ishaq's Sirat Rasul Allah, Oxford University Press, 1955 (Page references to the original Arabic text of Ibn Ishâq's Sira are given on the margin of Guillaume's translation).

CM: Constitution of Medina (References are to the paragraphs of Documents A-H as edited in Serjeant 1978)

Tabari: Tabari al-Tabari, Muhammad b. Jarir, 1879-1901/1985-2000, Ta'rikh al-rusul va'l-muluk, ed. by M.J. de Goeje, 15 Vols. (Leiden, 1879-1901); annotated English translation: The History of al-Tabari, Albany, 38 vols., NY 1985-2002: SUNY Press. References are to the English translation. Page references to the original Arabic text are given on the margin of this translation.

References

Abbott, N. (1967) *Studies in Arabic Literary Papyri II: Qur'ānic Commentary and Tradition*, The University of Chicago Press.

Arjomand, S.A. (1998) "Islamic Apocalypticism in the Classical Period." In: B. McGinn (ed.) *The Encyclopedia of Apocalypticism*, Vol 2., New York: Continuum, pp. 238-83.

Arjomand, S.A. (2003) "Medieval Persianate Political Ethic." *Studies on Persianate Societies 1*, pp. 5-31.

Baneth, D.Z.H. (1971) "What Did Muhammad Mean When He Called His Religion Islam? The original meaning of *Aslama* and its Derivatives." *Israel Oriental Studies 1*.

Bashear, S. (1997) *Arabs and Others in Early Islam*, Princeton: The Darwin Press.

Bashear, S. (2004) "*Hanifiyya* and *Hajj*," *Studies in Early Islamic Tradition*, Jerusalem: The Max Schloessinger Foundation.

Bowersock, G.W. (2003) "The Nabataeans in Historical Context." In: G. Markoe (ed.) *Petra Reconsidered*, New York: Abrams.

Cahen, C. (1961) "La Changeante portée sociale de quelques doctrines religieuses." In: *L'Élaboration de l'Islam (Colloque de Strasbourg)*, Presses Universitaires de France.

Chelhod, J. (1955) *Le Sacrifice chez les Arabes*, Paris: Presses Universitaires de France.

Chelhod, J (1958) *Introduction à la sociologie de l'Islam*, Paris: G.-P. Maisonneuve.

Crone, P. (1987) *Meccan Trade and the Rise of Islam*, Princeton: Princeton University Press.

Crone, P. (1994) "The First-Century Concept of *Hiğra*." *Arabica 41*, pp. 352-87.

Crone, P. (n.d.) "'Uzayr and the Fallen Angels: Reflections on the *Book of Watchers* in the Qur'ān." Unpublished paper.

Daryaee T. (1999) "The Coinage of Queen Bōrān and Its Significance for Late Sāsānian Imperial Ideology." *Bulletin of the Asia Institute, n.s., 13*, pp. 77-82.

al-Dinawari, Abu Hanifa Ahmad b. Dawud (1960) *Akhbār al-tiwāl* (ed. by `A. `Amir, Cairo.

Denny, F.M. (1977) "*Umma* in the Constitution of Medina." *Journal of Near Eastern Studies, 36/1*, pp. 37-47.

Denny, F.M. (1981) *The Early Islamic Conquests*, Princeton: Princeton University Press.

Denny, F.M. (1986) "The Formation of the Islamic State." *Journal of the American Oriental Society 106*.

Denny, F.M. (1993) "The Growth of Military Institutions in the Early Caliphate and their Relation to Civilian Authority." *Al-Qantara. Revista de Estudios Árabes 14*, pp. 311-326.

Denny, F.M. (1998) *Narrative of Islamic Origins. The Beginning of Islamic Historical Writing*, Princeton: The Darwin Press.

Dostal, W. (1991) "Mecca before the Time of the Prophet – Attempt of an Anthropological Interpretation." *Der Islam, 68/2*, pp. 193-231.

Erder, Y. (1990) "The Origins of the Name Idris in the Qur'ān: A Study of the Influence of Qumran Literature on Early Islam." *Journal of Near Eastern Studies 49/4*, pp. 339-50.

Erder, Y. (1994) "The Karaites' Sadducee Dilemma." *Israel Oriental Studies 14*, pp. 195-226.

Fahd, T. (1989) "Rapports de la Mekke préislamique avec l'Abyssinie: Le Cas des ahâbîš." In: T. Fahd (ed.) *L'Arabie préislamique et son environnement historique et culturel*, Strasbourg: E.J. Brill.
Fowden, G. (2001) "Varieties of Religious Community." In: G.W. Bowersock/P. Brown/O. Grabar (eds.) *Interpreting Late Antiquity*, Cambridge, MA: Harvard University Press.
Gil, M. (1987) "The Medinan Opposition to the Prophet." *Jerusalem Studies in Arabic and Islam 10*, pp. 65-96.
Gil, M. (1992) "The Creed of Abu `Āmir," *Israel Oriental Studies 11*, pp. 9-57.
Görke, A. (2000) "The Historical Tradition about al-hudaybiya. A Study of `urwa b. al-Zubayr's Account." In: H. Motzki (ed.) *The Biography of Muhammad*, Leiden: Brill, pp. 240-70.
Hoyland, R.G. (2001) *Arabia and the Arabs. From the Bronze Age to the Coming of Islam*, London and New York: Routledge.
Ibn Sa`d (1917) *Kitāb al-Tabaqāt al-Kabir (Biographien)*, 8 Vols. (ed. by E. Mittwoch/E. Sachau), Leiden: E.J. Brill.
Jones, J.M.B. (1957) "The Chronology of the *Maghāzi* – a Textual Survey." *Bulletin of the School of Oriental and African Studies 19*, pp. 245-80.
al-Kalbi, Hishām b. Muhammad b. al-Sā'ib (1924) *Kitāb al-asnām* (ed. by Ahmad Zaki Pasha), Cairo.
Kassis, H.E. (1983) *A Concordance of the Qur'an*, University of California Press.
Khoury, R.G. (1983) "Sources islamiques de la '*sîra*,'" *La Vie du prophête Mahomet*. (Colloque de Strasbourg), Presses Universitaires de France.
Kister, M.J. (1962), "'A Booth like the Booth of Moses': a Study of an Early Hadith." *Bulletin of the School of Oriental and African Studies 25*, pp. 150-55.
Kister, M.J. (1965) "Mecca and Tamim (Aspects of their Relations)." *Journal of the Economic and Social History of the Orient 8*, pp. 113-63.
Kister, M.J. (1968a) "Al-Hira: Notes on its Relations with Arabia." *Arabica 15*, pp. 143-69.
Kister, M.J. (1968b) "*Al-tahannuth*: an Inquiry into the Meaning of a Term." *Bulletin of the School of Oriental and African Studies 31*, pp. 223-36.
Kister, M.J. (1972) "Some Reports Concerning Mecca. From Jāhiliyya to Islam." *Journal of the Economic and Social History of the Orient 15*, pp. 61-93.
Kister, M.J. (1979) "On the Wife of the Goldsmith of Fadak and her Progeny: A Study in Genealogical Tradition." *Muséon 92*, pp. 321-330.
Kister, M.J. (1980) "*Labbayka all-humma, labbayka* : On a Monotheistic Aspect of a Jāhiliyya Practice." *Jerusalem Studies in Arabic and Islam 2*, pp. 33-57.
Kister, M.J. (1981) "'O God, tighten Thy grip on the Mudar ... : some socio-economic and religious aspects of an early hadith," Journal of the Economic and Social History of the Orient, 24: 242-73.

Kister, M.J. (1984) "... ill_ bihaqqihi ... A Study of an Early Hadith." *Jerusalem Studies in Arabic and Islam 5*, pp. 33-52.
Kister, M.J. (1986) "The Massacre of the Banu Qurayza." *Jerusalem Studies in Arabic and Islam 8*, pp. 61-96.
Kister, M.J. (1994) "Social and Religious Concepts of Authority in Islam." *Jerusalem Studies in Arabic and Islam 18*, pp. 84-127.
Kister, M.J. (2002) "The Struggle against Musaylima and the Conquest of Yamāma." *Jerusalem Studies in Arabic and Islam 27*, pp. 1-56.
Lecker, M. (1993) "Idol Worship in Pre-Islamic Medina (*Yathrib*)." *Le Muséon 106*, pp. 331-46.
Lecker, M. (1995) "Wāqidi's Account of the Status of the Jews of Medina: A Study of a Combined Report." *Journal of Near Eastern Studies 54*, pp. 15-32.
Lecker, M. (2000) "Did the Quraysh Conclude a Treaty with the Ansār prior to the Hijra?" In: H. Motzki (ed.) *The Biography of Muhammad*, Leiden: Brill, pp. 157-69.
Madelung, W. (1986) "Has the *Hijra* Come to an End?" *Revue des Études Islamiques 54*, pp. 225-37.
Madelung, W. (1997) *The Succession to Muhammad. A Study of Early Caliphate*, Cambridge University Press.
Mélamède, G. (1934) "The Meeting at al-`Akaba." *Le Monde Oriental 28*, pp. 17-58.
Al-Mas`udi, Abu'l-`Ali b. al-Husayn (1970) *Muruj al-Dhahab wa Ma-din al-Jawhar*, ed. by Ch. Pellat, 11 Vols., Beirut.
Morony. M.G. (1984) *Iraq after the Muslim Conquest*, Princeton University Press.
Nevo, Y./Koren, J. (2003) *Crossroads to Islam. The Origins of the Arab Religion and the Arab State*, New York: Prometheus Books.
Newby, G.D. (1971) "Observations about an Early Judaeo-Arabic." *Jewish Quarterly Review 61*, pp. 212-221.
Newby, G.D. (1988) *A History of the Jews of Arabia*, Columbia: University of South Carolina Press.
Pizzorno, A. (1994) *Le Radici della Politica Assoluta e altri Saggi*, Milan: Feltrinelli.
Rabin, C. (1957) *Qumran Studies*, Oxford: Oxford University Press.
Retsö, J. (2002) *Arabs in Antiquity: Their History from the Assyrians to the Umayyads*, New York, NY: Routledge Curzon.
Rubin, U. (1985) "The 'Constitution of Medina.' Some Notes." *Studia Islamica 52*, pp. 5-23.
Rubin, U. (1990) "*Hanifiyya* and Ka`ba." *Jerusalem Studies in Arabic and Islam 13*, pp. 85-112.
Rubin, U. (1995) *The Eye of the Beholder. The Life of Muhammad as Viewed by Early Muslims*, Princeton: The Darwin Press.

Serjeant, R.B. (1978) "The *Sunnah Jāmi'a*, Pacts with the Yathrib Jews, and the *Tahrim* of Yathrib: Analysis and Translation of the Documents Comprised in the So-called 'Constitution of Medina.'" *Bulletin of the School of Oriental and African Studies, 41/1*, pp. 1-42.

Serjeant, R.B. (1982) "The Interplay between Tribal Affinities and Religious (Zaydi) Authority in the Yemen." *Al-Abhāth 30*, pp. 11-48.

Sharon, M. (1984) "The Development of the Debate around the Legitimacy of Authority in Early Islam." *Jerusalem Studies in Arabic and Islam 5*, pp. 121-41.

al-Wāqidi, Muhammad b. 'Umar (1966) *The Kitāb al-maghāzi*, 3 Vols. (ed. by M. Jones), London: Oxford University Press.

Watt, W.M. (1953) *Muhammad at Mecca*, Oxford University Press.

Watt, W.M. (1956) *Muhammad at Medina*, Oxford University Press.

Watt, W.M. (1988) *Muhammad's Mecca. History in the Qur'ān*, Edinburg University Press.

Welch, A.T. (1983) "Muhammad's Understanding of Himself: The Koranic Data." In: R.G. Hovannisian/S. Vryonis Jr. (eds.) *Islam's Understanding of Itself*, Malibu, CA: Undena Publications, pp. 15-52.

Wellhausen, J. (1975) "Muhammad's Constitution of Median" (ed. and transl. by W. Behn). In: A.J. Wensinck, *Muhammad and the Jews of Medina*, Freiburg: Klaus Schwarz Verlag, [Orig.: "Muhammads Gemeindeordnung von Medina." In: idem *Skizzen und Vorarbeiten*, Berlin: Reimer, 1884-99, Vol. 4: 67-83).

Chapter 6

ʿAbdallah b. Salam: Egypt, Late Antiquity and Islamic Sainthood

GEORG STAUTH

1. "Egypt" – The Arabs and Early Islam

The general interest with Islam among those who theorised its position with respect to the genealogy of modernity lies with the so called "classical heritage." This question which Franz Rosenthal (1992) pursued in greater detail was inherited from the German or German educated Orientalists like Ignaz Goldziher and C.H. Becker, H.H. Schaeder and later of course in America from G.E. von Grunebaum. Rosenthal speaks of "Fortleben" (survival) which rather seeks for continuities then for Islamic reconstructions based on classical ideas.

If one focuses on the importance of the aura of inherited religious narratives and metaphors of thought, one would ask, how far Mecca and Medina were related in their cultural worlds to the higher civilisations which surrounded the Arabian Peninsula. This includes the question, how far Muhammad and Early Islamic religious discourse were influenced by the religious ideas which were prevalent in the Hellenistic world, Gnosticism, Christianism and Judaism and Greek and Roman Philosophy and science. Both ways, Greek and Roman and at the utmost some Persian influence are considered to be predominant. So in both perspectives continuities, whether religious or philosophic, are traced as the dominant sources of later Islamic discourse.

A third dimension has recently shaped much of our perspective on Islam, this is the one on the originality of Muhammad's revelation and the type of striking effects this brought in breaking with all types of prevalent cultural constructions. There is more and more convincing ground that the language of revelation in a lost time and location had in itself a stunning revolutionary effect (Ammann 2001). It should be noted, indeed, that this later view comes close to the self-perceived idea of Arabs, acknowledging "that their race did not share in philosophy, although they surpassed other nations in rhetoric and poetry" (El-Elwany 1957: 1).

As is with all religions, the myth seems to have been the important ideological motive, not logic or philosophy. The predominant myths in Central Arabia, if not deriving from bare Arab Tribal History, depended largely on Ancient Judaism and Pharaonism.

This is where I would maintain that "Egypt" figures as a sort of hidden inner pattern of constructions in Early Islamic narrations, re-phrasing something which was since long a subject of Christian dogmatic discourse, namely in that – in contrast to Jewish, Greek and Roman perceptions – the Christians, and perhaps here lies the specific importance of the Alexandrian school, engaged in a strong dialogue, if not in a sometimes latent state of heretic prosecution,[1] with old Egyptian culture.

The first wave of Islamic conquests (632-641) of Palestine, Syria and Egypt secured the domination over largely Hellenised areas (Rosenthal 1992: 2). It is generally assumed that the Arabs being separated from the dominated populations in language and religion, largely opposed, or neglected any knowledge of predominant local cultural traits, imposing their own language and religion as the ruling pattern. They only later fell at hand to the pre-eminence of the achievements of the higher civilisation (ibid.).

That Egypt was also a very important place at the roots of Hellenism is not only due to Alexander's conquests and his foundation of Alexandria. Many Greek scholars had travelled to Egypt, students of Pythagoras living there and Plato spending some time among them before going to Sicily and then returning to Athens (Rosenthal 1992: 28). Egypt was the must of great Greek scholars to visit Egypt (ibid.).

The more general problem, however, which relates to Early Islam, is the one of the rise of monotheism and the problem in which relation the prophetic revelations of Muhammad stand with the monotheistic forerunners, Judaism and Christianity. We may argue, that, if not for the immediate preaching of Muhammad, then for the later evolving dogmatic discourse, Islam was dependent on these prevalent religions. "Egypt" was of great importance for any evolving monotheistic discourse. Certainly, if we place the birth of Islam fully in a "native North-Arabian prophetic tradition," a "native monotheistic tradition," then it will be impossible to think of any cross-culture-contact discourse in relation to "Egypt," as appears from Gibb (1978: 26-7).

In fact, Gibb's general idea was, that Muhammad out of a certain resentment as a prophet with his antecedents Moses and Jesus, "went back behind both to the figure of Abraham 'the Hanif'" (ibid.: 31). Here, I wish to put some doubt on Gibb's perception that "Islam appeared, not as a new religion, but as a revival of pure Abrahamic monotheism, purified at once of the accretions of Judaism and Christianity and superseding them as the final revelation" (ibid.: 32).

---

1   I should admit that Karlheinz Deschner's "Kriminalgeschichte" and specifically his Chapters on Kyrill and Schenute of Alexandria remain stimulating and revealing in this respect (Deschner 1988: 156-212).

2. The question of Egypt in Late Antiquity and the rise of Islam

There is general agreement that in the rise of Europe and the West – as Brague (2002: 27) takes it from Paul Valéry – Rome, Greece and Christianity were made the basic sources of European self-understanding. Whether in this view "Israel," the "sub-basement in the Old Testament," includes Egypt remains doubtful. In focussing the case of an Egyptian saint, I wish, here, to raise some very hypothetical questions with respect to "Egypt" and its cultural and political influence in Late antiquity, including the question of its possible effects on Early Islamic religious and social developments.

There is rising awareness of the modern intricacies of Egypt's impact on Judaism and Christianity (cf. Assmann 1997; Said 2003). However, when it comes to Islam, and specifically to the first 200 years of Islamic developments, Egypt's impact on Islamic history appears to be less than a black spot on the cultural landscape. This is partly due to the fact that the mainstream literature – after the *futûh*, the Arab conquest – is primarily concerned with the emerging sectarian tendencies in Islam and with the historiography of the related political clashes or with the – often very closely related – issue of tradition and theology and its sources. Since the scene for these clashes was largely limited to the Arab core regions on the peninsula as well as in Palestine, Syria and Iraq, the "Egyptian" affairs and their potential influences were beyond the mainstream interest, naturally because, obviously, also there was a limited amount of sources.

There are recently – perhaps not just recently, however, recently with greater vigour – some new perspectives opened on the subject. I do hope, as my point is related to the modern significance of a Jewish convert in early Islam and a witness of Mohammad as a Prophet, to raise some questions with respect to positioning of Islam and 'Egypt' in an axial age perspective and monotheist breakthroughs.

First of all, certainly, the issue of Egypt widens the perspective into a much broader area of interest, namely, the question of the comparative or even interactive narration of a shared idea of the golden, however, now darkened and suppressed arch-culture of the Nile. It is not possible to follow this up here, however we should note, that Alexandrian philosophy and theology in the third and fourth century, indeed, became strongly involved in finding solutions to the immediacy of the old world of Egyptian Gods. New sublime constructions of symbols and ideas were developed. However, in terms of lifestyle, health, marketing, and solutions to everydayness by way of "sacred tourism," the old ritual places seem to have been alive in the 6th and 7th century as much as they have been before.

With respect to Early Islam, the question of break and continuity was recently again put in terms of "radical singularity" and "total alterity" (Cheddadi 2004). However, as "Islamwissenschft" before, Cheddadi understands this only with respect to role and development of "scripture" in Early Islam. However, we know too little about the interactive process of emerging ideas and the changes and continuities in religious instincts, style of life and mentality. In general, this idea of the totally other and new was always linked to Muhammad's revelation and his personal abilities in life and the simplicity of his message of men of all ranks and colours standing equal judgement in front of an un-attainable God.

On the other hand, certainly, the perspective on "singularity" and "alterity" always included the question, to what does all this refer, to whom does it speak, what does it deny, from where does it depart? From this angle, it seems to me, that there is an alternative to absolute break and abrupt change in that the ideas of origin gained the power of an umbrella not only through political and military strength, but rather gradually took shape in being exposed to a dialogical process with and within the cultures in the occupied territories over a period of 150 years. To be sure, the issue of "Egypt" at that time – if ever – had not ended.

The idea of the retarded fixation of scripture and Islamic style never fully and never materially engaged with what Christianity, what Judaism, what Hellenism meant in terms of material life and life perspectives and cultural instincts of people in the 7th and 8th century.

This later question of popular instincts, psychology and life-perspective emerges as a very important one, it is a question which goes far beyond "text" and the problematic of what we have to treat as more or less authentic sources of Islam. The cultic practice, the local mediatic relation to cults, and what the situation was in the different pre-existing religions in treating cultic necessities, seems to me similarly important. It is interesting to mention in this context of preludes to Islam that Peter Brown's and Ian Wood's discussions on the dramatic changes in Christian imagination in the late 6th century could be taken as evidence of the development of strong inner tensions related to rituals and their perception in popular mass contexts (Brown 1999; Wood 1999). This is in fact immanent with respect to the current problem of positioning Islam in the more general framework of developments leading to the modern processes of nation state formation, national culture and return to religion.

Certainly, Freud's Moses instigated a lively debate, reminding us of the importance of Pharaonic Egypt with respect to Judaism and Christianity. However, that monotheism should be a one way path to rationality, initiating the lead to the steady decline of superstition, has since long been doubted. The issue of "Egypt" poses a much deeper question on the effects of pre-existing local traditions. If we consider that the focus on Early Islam has been shifted, from the pure question of authenticity of sources to the question of culture contact and dialogue, then the question of "Egypt" becomes even more important. The event of Islam has to be related to these questions within the broader – if you wish – the global context of late antiquity.

Considering what Nock (1972) has called "Later Egyptian Piety" there the recurrent topic is, that Egypt in terms of culture, religion and spiritual life remained, despite the influx of Hellenism and Christianity, a world apart in Late antiquity. This peculiarity of "Egypt" as a culture undergoing strong, externally imposed changes and foreign impingements, with continuous resistance and without any comparable depth of internal transformation, is a point well taken (cf. Fowden 1986). However, this dimension could also be reversed. The perplexity of this inner resistance, could also be made a point of cultural force influencing the spiritual, ritual and symbolic attitudes of the world outside. In this respect, I can only propose to take the works of Alfred Hermann more serious and specifically his point on the long continuities of the described "Culture of the Nile" (cf. Hermann 1960; 1959; n.d.). The narratives of this Nil-culture are still waiting to be fully recognised with respect to the developments of Hellenism, of Christianity, and of Islam. My point is that "Egypt" can hardly be understood as a world apart without effect, a world of a coherent long term internal cultural production without change and effecting change to the world outside.

Certainly, if one argues that the arrival of Islam has constituted a marking effect for the eastern Mediterranean region as a whole, the question remains what the position of Egypt is in this transformation process. What has Egypt contributed to the development of Islam, dogma, ritual, and learning? Egypt, certainly, has to be focussed as a main issue specifically in relation to the birth of monotheism and the early Christian theology. However, the emergence of Islam is a different story, and it is difficult to understand this event purely within the framework of the political and intellectual constellations of Late Antiquity. Extending the influence of Hellenism further to the South and the East could be counted just as another expression of the mode to frame out new sources of modernity and/or of Islam. However, my concern is a different one, I wish to stress the dialogical patterns in the construction of monotheism, the dialogue with pre-existent Egypt and perceptions of order, in which monotheism and Islam became engaged and played the dominant role in later power and state formation in the region.

3. The 'longue durée' of Egyptian saints

It should be noted that 'late antique Egypt' is a field of highly specialised historical and archaeological research which is difficult to approach from the site of the non-specialist, the transposition of themes and results from one field to another, therefore, seems a very complicated affair. Perhaps we can gain a more solid ground on struggles over continuities and breaks in the literature on "pilgrimages" and on the early ascetics, the "saintly fathers of the desert."

It is true, my questions arise from a background of struggles which were constitutive to the "Protestant notion of distinguishing and even polarizing an interior 'spirituality' from the exterior devotions and images of traditional piety" (Frankfurter 1998: 5). However, these are perhaps questions that were probably firstly raised in a radical missionary, converting in other words modern sense by early Muslims.

In looking to the different historical and dialogical conditions of the relation between absolute monotheism and personal interiority, Egypt seems to have been preserved in the religious mind as the power of the past, combining broader concepts of Goddess with strong local ritual and symbolic practices on the one hand, and on the other hand as a direct constraint to the conceptual construction of personal piety and the idea of an abstract transcendence in early Christianity.

This is certainly true with respect to the development of theology and theological discourse and the foundation of philosophical "heresies" which then more or less became part of the cultural constructions and church development. Thus the fundamental structures of Early Christianity in Egypt have been aptly described as "the constant and vital interplay between Christianity as emerging from the cosmopolitan religiosity proper to the Hellenistic city of Alexandria and Christianity as bound to the spiritual landscape of the Nile valley (Kannengiesser 1986: 212).

Guy Stroumsa (2005) showed that Clemens of Alexandria was not only a theological enemy of the Egyptian cults, but also a spiritual integrator and in a real modern sense an ethnographer of old cultic practices. This perspective, certainly with respect to early Islam, presumes a new tenuous field of understanding: Early Christianity was as late as into its 4th century largely build on a diaological basis of coexistence with the old Egyptian religion, local cults and symbolic worlds.

One becomes even more assured of a potentially hidden role of "Egypt" in this double-sided construction of monotheism, including the event of Islam, in considering Dominic Montserrat's observations of the "pilgrimage to the shrine of SS Cyrus and John at Menouthis in late antiquity" (1986: 256-279). These are specifically revealing the local tensions specifically about saintly places, the shrines of the saints, showing "that the status and development of the shrine is closely tied up with religious controversies that troubled Egypt between the early fifth and the mid-seventh century CE" and that "the shrine certainly survived the depredations of the Persians in around 618 CE and seems to have been functioning after Egypt became Muslim"(ibid.: 259). Montserrat speaks of the "coexistence of the pagan and Christian" interpretation of the "divine place" of Menouthis until the mid-seventh century. However, Montserrat makes also clear, that the veneration at Menouthis, northeast of Alexandria, and specifically its form, interpretation and administration was strongly linked to the political and theological discourse in Alexandria, now however about two hundred years after Clemens.

This tendency that a certain revival of old Egyptian cults could be observed even after six hundred years of spread of Christianism, could be affirmed if one looks to evidence gathered by Volokhine, namely showing that coptic shrines were often displaced back to old places of veneration for either Isis or Osiris in the 6th and 7th century and that there seems to have operated a sort of "Zeitgeist" of re-inventing the powers of ancient gods within a framework of Christendom. These movements, obviously, were related to the emerging theological debates, secterian struggles and ascetic communities. It is within this framework, that we can today gain some ground for understanding the Egyptian continuities Certainly, "Egypt" did not end after the destruction of the Serapeum in Alexandria in 391. Volokhine argues that the motivation for a reinspiration of old places of temples through Christian pilgrimage was based on functional grounds with respect to aspirations of good health, marketing, and everyday needs. There was a reinvention of oracles in Christian terms even in the 7th and 8th century which only, according to Volokhine was ended with the advent of Islam (Volokhine 1998: 96)[2]

There are two questions unanswered with respect to this evidence: First, it seems that there remains something incomplete in Monosyphism which the teaching of Muhammad attempts to come to grips with. Could one say that the early Muslims stand in direct connection with the idea of Monosyphist rejections of cult sublimation, or, more directly that Early Islam poses a sort of solution to the Monosyphist struggles in ending the cultic reality of late antiquity. Second, and directly related to the first question, one could ask how far the Christian theological discourse – with "Egypt" as its subject – had influenced the theological discourse in Early Islam. Is Early Islam the main event of the definite end of "Egypt" in late antiquity?

A different angle could be traced. With the Muslim conquest of Egypt, the fact is that while the Alexandrian Christians were involved in highly sophisticated religious, theological and factional political quarrels, the Muslims advanced their forces. If Alfred Butler, in an early attempt of simultaneous reading of Byzantine and Arabic sources is right, the fall of Byzantine rule in Egypt given its enormous structural and military superiority was largely due to an irresolvable struggle between Egyptian Coptic and Byzantine theological schools, the later holding worldly power, the earlier maintaining old beliefs and practices. According to Butler, there was, however, no Coptic betrayal, but internal ideological confusion that caused the final defeat in front of the Muslims. In the period of the last ten years before the Arab intrusion of Egypt Cyrus, Governor and Patriarch of Egypt, al-Muqauqas, persecuted perniciously the Copts of Egypt. This persecution was directed against both, the continuity of the practice of ven-

---

2 Volokhine writes here: "La motivation qui préside aux déplacements vers les temples concerne des soucis courants, et non pas une quête des salut : la santé, la bonne marche des affaires, le quotidien. Dans cette mesure, le développement des oracles, le recours aux dieux sauveurs, sont significatifs. Comme le remarquait J. Cerny, la teneur des pétitions écrites en grec adressées aux oracles correspond aux demendes égyptiennes; de même, les papyrus coptes du VIIe ou du VIIIe siècle confirment que la pratique de l'oracle ne disparaît pas avec le paganisme. On s'adressait à Sérapis, à Sobek: on s'adresse à présent au dieu chrétien. L'Islam seul mettra fin à des millénaires de pratique. De même, on ne verra pas forcement de césure entre l'époque paienne et chrétienne en ce qui concerne les habitudes de déplacements vers les sanctuaires."

eration at local Egyptian cultic places as much as of the anti-Chalaedonian theological Elite (Butler 1978: 168-206). It should be said – and very strikingly so it was – that on the side of the Muslims no word of religion or religious quarrel can be traced, (certainly apart of one all embracing word: *Allahu akbar)* in negotiations with the patriarchal powers. Here, it is very interesting to see, the absence of religious language in formulating the treaties of surrender first of Babylon and then of Alexandria (Butler 1978: 256-274, 318-327). There is this anecdote of the encounter and negotiations of Cyrus, the Archbishop and ʿUbâdah b. as-Sâmit, a powerful Negro who was earlier in close relation to Muhammad and later quite involved in the religious party-struggle between Muʿawiya, first "Meccan Calif," and the Ansâr, the Medinan followers of Muhammad (van Ess 2001: 248-259). ʿUbâdah is far from indulging on religious terms. Religious is, if anything far from theology, the simplicity of expression of this black Muslim confronting the Alexandrian Archbishop who refused to negotiate with a black man: "There are a thousand blacks, as black as myself, among our companions. I and they would be ready each to meet and fight a hundred enemies together. We live only to fight for God, and to follow His will. We care not for wealth, so long as we have wherewithal to stay our hunger and to clothe our bodies. This world is not to us, the next world is all" (Butler 1978: 257).

Can we say that perhaps the one-dimensional simplicity in advertising their religion in these early times of conquest, in fact, delivered the basis on which both the Christian parties could see a way for themselves to view the future? Was this future, indeed, a sort of continuation of the theological debate on the back of the simplicity and clarity of the original Islamic message?

The point of Early Islam confronting Egypt and the Egyptian Christians, leave aside the philosophically inclined Jewish community in Alexandria, seems to be one of military straightforwardness and theological simplicity. Certainly, Fowden's idea, that "Islam offered not just an umbrella political regime which protected all those who acknowledged a revealed scripture, but also a strictly monotheist doctrine of God which gave renewed energy to discussions seemingly stalled for ever in the hardened ruts of the Christianological controversies" (Fowden 2005: 10), is well taken. Perhaps from here we can understand, that "Egypt" in Early Islam seems to have been reduced to the practices related to the Qisas al-Anbiyâ, the wide spread popular practice of narratives of the prophets and old Egyptian topics, while only in medieval Islam and from there on, pilgrimages and the veneration of local saints took a fully new shape in Islamic terms.

Taking these dimensions into account, we will be able to view the case of a Jewish man, who was conversant with Jewish myths and legends of the prophets, and an important witness for Muhammad to stand in their tradition. Conversing to Islam he became a pillar of orthodox monotheism, and possibly through his imaginative and magic stories being made part of the Islamic Tradition, he also entered into the broad field of practices related to popular story telling, even after the taste for popular legends of the prophets had faded. He now survives in the memory of people as a strongly venerated saint in the district of Mansura in the north-eastern Nile Delta.

4. ʿAbdallah b. Salam: the early Jewish convert and Egyptian saint

The case that I wish to develop in the following pages stands in a mediating position between "Late Antiquity" and Islam: ʿAbdallah b. Salam is the first Jewish companion to the Prophet Muhammad, he was a well educated Jew with deep genealogical traits in a clan of priests and scholars, he converted to Islam in 622 AD when Muhammad arrived in Medina. He later was an advisor to the Caliphs Umar, Uthman and Muʿawiya and is considered a pillar of early orthodoxy. Second the way in which he is venerated today and since an unknown number of centuries is important. He has his main places of veneration at sites with relics of the Pharaonic past. There, his sainthood seems to have been constructed and reconstructed in relation with his testifying Islamic monotheism as against performing non-Islamic traditions. However, his legends – obviously transmitted by way of local Sufi channels – also entail references to Pharaonic and Jewish material. We should note that he was probably the first Jewish convert to Islam in Medina.

This case is significant with respect to how Islam in a perspective of long duration has dealt with the non-Islamic. This implies the specific story of the impact of monotheism on local beliefs, the construction and maintenance of sacred places and the ambivalent treatment of local beliefs by the orthodoxy and in recent years by often insurgent reformist Salafi-groups.

4.1 Topography and essence

A critical description of historical and symbolic arrangements of the saint necessitates a view on the geography and topography of his places[3].

In general, saintly places are the places of the dead. The ambiguity of genealogical nearness to the sites of the Ancients is quite common practice in both Islam and Christianity. Christians have often built the churches for their patrons on grave yards and cult places of the Romans, similarly the Muslim Saints in the Nile Delta are often very close to the Pharaonic places or places of Egyptian antiquity in general. The religious theory of saintly places dating back to Ernest

---

3 More detailed description of three places in the Mansura-region are presented in Stauth (2005), Ägyptische Heilige Orte I: Konstruktionen, Inszenierungen und Landschaften der Heiligen im Nildelta: ʿAbdallah b. Salam. Bielefeld: transcript.

Renan, therefore, strongly claimed that humanity prayed always at the same places. We may say so, that there is nothing special about ʿAbdallah b. Salam having his place close or on top of a Tell, as the Egyptians call those red and brown mounds of ruins of antiquity, rising up from the dark or green regularly inundated moulds of Delta agricultural land. However, remaining in the – potentially misleading – first glance perspective of geography and Topography, here, the question turns to the fact that ʿAbdallah b. Salam who is the most prominent figure among early Jewish converts to Islam, has not only one, but many places in this region which was a region of Jewish settlement and in the Late Dynastic Period had witnessed many invasions of "Asian" people. In the larger context of the Nile Delta today huge metropolitan cities, relating to times before the Hyksos and settling Jews, have been found (the admirable work of Edgar Pusch and his crew in Qantîr seems to find too little support by his colleagues in this respect). It is astonishing that in other regions no places of ʿAbdallah are to be found. Here, in the the Daqahliyya province with the city of Mansura as its centre the saying goes that ʿAbdallah has more than 3, some say 13, some 39, some 40 places. As I said, it potentially misleading to give this local fixation an over-essential meaning with respect to history. However, ʿAbdallah, connected with Early Islam, the latest of the revealed monotheistic religions, and with Judaism, the first of the religions of monotheism, puts him in a very ambiguous historical place which reminds us that the idea of the one God rose as an idea which became influential in various cultic and ethnic communities and even nations and, indeed, this region was one of culture contact since the early days of human history.

However, from what follows it will become clear, that any attempt to explain the local importance of ʿAbdallah from the angle of continuity of Jewish settlement will fail. There is strong evidence that ʿAbdallah' was, first, perhaps in the 18th century, a place of a tribal leader who was buried near the Tell. Gradually, perhaps in the course of intensive veneration there emerged the need of official orthodox recognition and the place was named and venerated as the one of ʿAbdallah b. Salam, the pillar of Orthodoxy in Early Islam. His Jewish origin was potentially later linked with the Tell in local legends among the Fellaheen who also called and still call the Tell today: "Tell" or "*qasr bint al-yahudi*" (castle of the daughter of the Jew). However, putting ʿAbdallah b. Salam, the Jew and the Muslim saint, and his location, into the one-dimensional essentialist track of a functional and mono-causal explanation, would be misleading again. And I have described in greater detail that nothing is definite with respect to the local arrangements, religious functions and symbolic productions of this saint and in his relation to the collective memory and religious history of monotheism. Nevertheless, the case itself symbolises the very type of constructions and antagonisms which are historically linked with the local presence of Islam and its need of strengthening of monotheism as places, practises, and ideas of the Ancient past. At the same time for today it is important to note, that against and within modernist streams of Islam, the place turns to be continuously rearranged and adapted among local people and followers of 'Abdallah.

Beyond the essentialism of topography, 'Abdallah b. Salam (d. 43 H.) is a Jewish and later Islamic scholar who converted to Islam at Muhammad's arrival in Medina. He has many saintly places in Daqahliyya, the region of the Egyptian provincial capital al-Mansura in the eastern part of the Nile Delta. These places are considered to be his tombs, although in fact nobody – perhaps except the children of the village – would belief in the saint to be really buried here. A saint has his place (*maqam*), indeed, and venerating him here, does not necessarily mean the testified physical presence of his dead body or of any of his relics. This does not challenge the idea of his immediate presence at the place and the veneration of one saint at different places is quite normal practice (Goldziher 1968: 71; Franke 2004). 'Abdallah b. Salam's case, however, is significant in that he has many Maqams just in one specific region with amble prove that he never physically has been in Egypt. He is extraordinary with his Maqams being distributed in this specific north-eastern part of the Nile Delta. The case seems to be unparalleled in the literature, because he is a historical figure of the early days of Islam in Medina, Jerusalem and southern Syria, however, his fantastic presence as a saint is reserved to this specific region in the eastern Delta.

Goldziher took Ka'b al-Ahbar, a contemporary of 'Abdallah b. Salam and a Jewish convert like him, to whom Egyptians have given a place of veneration in Cairo. He considered him as an example for this Egyptian habit to venerate an "absent" saint (cf. Muh. Stud. II, 336-343). This "Egyptian habit," however, does not help to answer our question: Why is 'Abdallah b. Salam, one of the first Jewish converts to Islam venerated in this specific province of Egypt, why is he venerated at so many places in this province, and why – to our knowledge – is he not venerated at any other place in rural or urban Egypt? Here, the question of the "place" of the saint quickly turns into the many questions related to Egypt, Islam, monotheism and the construction of modernity. Certainly, the starting question is how the local conditions of "memory" relate to the historical and symbolic forms of constructing the Saintly. However, in a much broader sense, I think, this case certainly includes the question about the prophetic traditions and early dialogue in the construction of monotheism and its significance for cross-civilsational dialogue today.

4.2 'Abdallah b. Salam – the historical figure

This observation with 'Abdallah b. Salam's places reveals that the appearance of historical relics is linked to the fight of Islamic monotheism against continuities or survivals or reinventions of the Ancients. This is also the present function of this saint and his shrines. Islamology knows generally nothing about his role as a contemporary local saint in Egypt. Islamology presents 'Abdallah through the eyes of history and literary books confirming his factual existence in Islamic sources, mainly the *maghazi-* and *hadith-*Literature. A sort of change in paradigm can be noted, however, in a recent study by Josef van Ess, who actually visited the place of his scholar/saint, the Maqam of Mu'adh b. Gabal in El-Ekseir near al-Hamma in Jordan (van Ess 2001: 365) and took note of a place of the same person in Cairo (ibid.: 376). As will be noted in greater detail below, this is an astonishing exception of an Islamic philologist's modern recognition of a companion of the Prophet as a contemporary saint (van Ess 2001: 359-380). Certainly, van Ess here opens a new landscape for the study of the modern significance of early Islamic history. My own contention is sociological, i.e. limited and simple and to a great extent reductionist: 'Abdallah b. Salam b. al- Harith the person and modern saint will be presented here only in terms of a short summary of his biography: His original name in the time before his conversion was al- Husayn from the Banu Qaynuqa'. He died in 43 H. (664) in Medina. His fame is linked to his "Questions to the Prophet," provoking answers by the Prophet which – as reported were so convincing for him that he converted to Islam. It is also reported that the Islamic tradition gives him great importance, because 'Abdallah belonged to a group of a few Jews who converted and stood with the Prophet and while many of them charged Muhammad with ignorance of the old testament versions of his time, it seems to have been 'Abdallah who may have acknowledged the fact to which Ilse Lichtenstaedter points, namely that Muhammad "in the early times of his mission [...] was not telling Biblical stories, he was dipping deep into the reservoir of Ancient Near Eastern myth from which those Biblical stories themselves had originally arisen" (Lichtenstaeder 1976: 38). It was, obviously, 'Abdallah the specialist of "ancient myth" who identified Muhammad as a specialist in this very field. Not the factual, i.e. textual, but the mythological knowledge led to the recognition of Muhammad as the true and announced Prophet in the line of the ancient Near Eastern religious tradition.

Taking these terms of understanding, 'Abdallah's questions where only to be answered by a Jewish Prophet. As Horowitz tells us, the contents of the Hadiths which figure under 'Abdallah's name in the early Islamic source books and specifically the story of Buluqya, which al-Tha'labi, a well recognized traditioner, traces back to 'Abdallah b. Salam, are mostly originating from Jewish sources and even if 'Abdallah is not the author, the stories derive from the circles of Jewish converts (Horowitz EI/1, I: 32). There always seems to have been a certain uneasiness about 'Abdallah's Jewish descent, certainly among his Muslim contemporaries. However, Horowitz believes that it were traditions that were circulated later in which Muhammad affirms 'Abdallah as one of those who have a secure place in paradise or in which is stated that certain verses of the Qur'an relate to 'Abdallah b. Salam. Fuat Sezgin maintains that the "Questions" of 'Abdallah were later expanded to whole books and other writings which seem to paraphrase the stories which are contained in the Hadith-source books. "He was one of the first converts and had great knowledge of the Jewisch tradition of the world history and the early Prophets etc. (Sezgin 1967, I: 304). The *Masa'il* were later translated into Latin and circulated as *Doctrina Mahumet* and *Theologia Mahometis* in late medieval Europe (Bobzin 1995: 50, 332; Kritzeck 1964: 89-96). According to the sources 'Abdallah was accompanying 'Umar the second Caliph in his raids to Jabiya and Jerusalem. Possibly this relates also to his function as a potential missionary of Jews and we may suspect that his *"Kitab Masa`il Sidi 'Abdallah"* (Sezgin ibid.) points into this direction. In the following struggles for the Caliphat 'Abdallah b. Salam stood firm with 'Uthman, the third Calif. There are reports that he was present when 'Uthman was murdered, however, could not prevent the murder. Later he was a follower of the Caliph Mu'awiya. Perhaps his later importance in Sufi circles derives from his mythological stories about the old traditions of the Prophets and Muhammads own prophecy, the *qissas annabawi*, which often combine old Jewish themes with old Pharaonic materials (Horovitz 1901). As said above many such stories – like the one of Buluqya – also appear in the oldest *maghazi*- and *hadith*-books, Qur`an-commentaries and world histories (Sezgin 1967,I: 304). Brockelmann refers to the *Kitab fi `Azamat allah wa mahluqatih* of Abu Muh. `Aal. B. M. Ja`far b. Haiyan b. ash-Shaikh al-Isphahani (d. 979), who "in the introduction refers to 'Al. B. as-Sallam his using the writings of Daniel, which he took from the tables of Adam preserved in Serendib (Ceylon; Berlin 6159)" (Brockelmann 1942, I: 209). 'Abdallah's main sources in tradition seem to have been such famous authorities like Abu Hurayra und Anas b. Malik (EI/2, I: 52).

This is in short a summary of textual biography of 'Abdallah b. Salam. There is no reference to his veneration as an Egyptian saint. However, it should be noted that his Maqams, which we visited, assemble – in different forms and with different ways of giving importance – a variety of writings taken from religious sources. It would need a very specific analysis to work out in detail these textual representations, and I certainly do encourage the specialists in early Islamic philology to do so. In the following, I will only refer to them in as much they are of interest for the questions which I am developing here.

5. 'Abdallah b. Salam with a view on his pre-Islamic stories and legends

A new "reality" of the historical existence of 'Abdallah b. Salam seems to emerge if we leave the today existing Maqams and the local entourage and enter – with some sociological restraint indeed – into the world of texts. In fact, we have no clear cut understanding of the historical figure: Was he a religious scholar, a specialist in religious mythology, a politico-religious convert and then a missionary? As we showed it is not unusual to have one and the same saint at various places and even at places where he in historical reality never could have been. However, what makes this saint so unusual is the very different character of his local functioning: a variety of "appearances" in one and the same region of the Delta: we may call this a very normal phenomenon of "translocality." However, once we turn to the realm of texts we may state that the question what makes this saint so important and meaningful in this local context gains quite a different turn. 'Abdallah never was in Egypt and so he had no immediate impact on the Arab Conquest of Egypt, the Futuh. However, even if the signs for his historical physical presence are nil, we may uphold the question of a potential inner historical relationship of 'Abdallah b. Salam to his places in Mendes/Manzala. This is merely hypothetical, and we take 'Abdallah's local fictionality only as a point of strategic interest, delimiting our textual investigations

First, there are his miracle-stories and legends which are of interest: As mentioned above, 'Abdallah b. Salam has a name as author of such stories in the early Islamic literary history and it is important to know that such stories of the old prophets and wonders played and until today play an important role in both the local Sufi culture and the popular tradition (Horovitz 1901; Sezgin 1967, I, 304). In his little note on the story of Buluqya, Horovitz refers to a story of 'Abdallah b. Salam in ath-Tha'labi's *qisas al-anbiya* (Horovitz 1901: 519; ath-Tha'labi 1325/1907-8). The early schools of interpretation of Qur'an, responding to questions about historical events which were only vaguely referd to in the Qur'an were often influenced by recent converts who with their knowledge of the Torah were able to answer them. Thus the early Christian or Jewish converts often functioned to explain certain contradictions in naming the event in the history of the early Prophets for example. This is also clearly a reference to the fact that so many biblical and pseudo-biblical material was assembled in the Hadith, narratives of the old religious history with a quite often irrational, miraculous and fictional character. These narratives were often refused by orthodox authorities and modern reformists (Jansen 1980: 27).

The story of Buluqiya belongs to this genre which combines in metaphor and content the myths of pre-Islamic history with the stories of miracles of the Prophets and historical facts. Certainly, the stories also had a certain effect in religious propaganda since they were aimed at a foundational genealogy of the Prophet Muhammad in the line of the old prophets of the Thorah. The story of Buluqiya is a fantastic story which assembles historical and geographical names, however, in a way that remains vague and unrealistic, where factual details turn out to be of a purely metaphorical nature. We may – in line with our modest sociological interests – refer to the story here, only based on Horowitz' presentation. Perhaps, we can trace out, here, three separate dimensions of "reality" as represented in the story's mythological and metaphorical return to the past:

1. Jews in Egypt: The story mentions a certain "King of the Banu Isra'il in Egypt." This is not to reflect in the very sense of "reality" the Jewish presence in Egypt. However, as much as the "real" history of this presence takes a very fictional character, we may only refer to it in a very "loose" way: The story of Jewish settlement always relates to the sons of Jacob in the land of Goshen which only recently is re-identifies with Pithom or Patoumos, today Tell Maskhuta

(Retsö 2003: 250 f.) in the southeast of the Delta (Wadi Tumalat). In what archeologists have attempted to trace as this presence of the Jews remains – when it comes to "real" places – very vague (Hoffmeier 1996: 107-134; Bietak 1986). Adding to the confusion would be to take the story of Ka'b al-Ahbar, (transmitted through ath-Tha'labi/Qisa'i) as "real" which – as local peasants in the Fayyum until today do locate the treasure of Salomon in the lake of Qarun – speaks of the treasure in the "lake" and as reported thus refers to the fact that the Fayyum was always as the settlement of the descendents of Josef resembling a wrong but nevertheless until today in Egypt vital Jewish tradition story, that the land Goshen was located in the Fayyum (Wolfensohn 1933: 81).

2. Torah and Muhammad: The Buluqya-story of 'Abdallah b. Salam also refers to a "book" in which the appearance of the Propheten Muhammad was announced and his personality was described: the Torah. This is obviously referring to similar traditions as transmitted in Ibn Hishams Sira (live story) of the Prophet: 'Abdallah b. Salam is reported to state to the Jews of Medina: "You know, that Muhammed is the messanger of God, you find his name written in the Taurat and dedscribed" (Ibn Hisham 1860: 353/2002: 240). Interestingly enough, we find today this Hadith being part of the collection of sources on 'Abdallah b. Salam at his mausoleum in the village Kafr al-Amir 'Abdallah b. Salam south of Mansura.

3. Myths and metaphors of Pharaonic Egypt: The story refers metaphorically to the thematic of an old Egyptian fairy tale of the "shipwrecked seaman" which is also present in Flinders-Petrie's "Egyptian Tales" (1st series, pp. 88) to which Horovitz (1901: 519) refers. This includes an old thematic of the queen of the snakes which embraces the movement of jinn and snakes with reference to ancient Egypt. Miracles and the powers of magic are often related to some types of references to old Egyptian cultic metaphors and the secrets of the temples in later medieval literature (e.g. U. Sezgin 1994: 12-17). According to Fuat Sezgin there also exists a manuscript (Paris 2954, pp. 113-116) including some magics and amulettes of 'Aballah b. Salam (Sezgin 1967: 304). Mohamad el-Gawhary (1968: 51-54) mentions that specifically the early Jewish converts like Ka'b al-Ahbar and 'Abdallah b. Salam were often refered to in the works of al-Buni (st. 622 H./1225 AD.) when dealing with the names of God used in magic. We may wonder whether the metaphor used in the following Hadith of 'Abdallah b. Salam concerning the arrival of the Prophet in Medina engages with another metaphoric allusion: "a man came with the message of his arrival when I was working in the top of a palm tree and my aunt Khalida bt. Al-Harith was sitting below" (Ibn Hisham 1860: 353/2002: 241). The layer of later reference to 'Abdallah b. Salam in Islamic literature referring to Pharaonic culture seems to explain also his popularity when it comes to jinn and magic. In nucleus we may see here also a different dimension namely the powerful missionary who is able to deal with such practices, a function which could relate directly to his official position in orthodox Islam since his participation in the conquest of Palestine and Syria.

6. Early Islamic knowledge: translating biblical legends and Qur'anic myths

Obviously this later point of the missionary, discursive and psychological power of this saint and his potentially significant role as "translator" and "accountant" of the old Jewish and the Pharaonic myths and legends in the context of the "birth" of Islam and Islamic theology is significant with respect to his image as a pillar of orthodox wisdom. As much as Pharaonic stories, metaphors and histories flourished still in medieval times, as much, however, they were also subject to suppression by religiously inclined people (Haarmann 1978: 371). Nevertheless, the orthodox tradition gave 'Abdallah b. Salam a great intellectual and spiritual position as one of the *al-'urwa al-wuthqa,* the category of steadily trustful believers (Dhahabi, Tadhkirat, I, 26, see also Ibn Sa'd II, pp. 352). 'Abdallah has put his weight on serious religious ground and his position among the early commentators of Qur'an seems unquestioned:

"Unter den bevorzugten Belehrungsquellen des Ibn 'Abbas finden wir vielfach die jüdischen Konvertiten Ka'b al-Ahbar (Ibn Sa'd VII/1, 161, 15 ff.) und 'Abdallah b. Salam, sowie im allgemeinen Ahl al-Kitab, also Leuten aus Klassen, vor deren Mitteilungen sonst auch in Sprüchen, die auf Ibn 'Abbas selbst zurückgeführt sind, gewarnt wird. Nicht mit Unrecht warnt Loth vor der jüdisch gefärbten Schule des Ibn al- Abbas" (Goldziher 1952. 67).

(Among the favorable sources of learning of Ibn 'Abbas we often find the Jewish converts Ka'b al-Ahbar (Ibn Sa'd VII/1, 161, 15 pp.) and 'Abdallah b. Salam, as well as in general traditions from Ahl al-Kitab, people of such strata, the traditions of which even with respect to those which are transmitted from Ibn 'Abbas were otherwise doubted. Loth does not unjustly refer to the Jewish flavoured school of Ibn 'Abbas.)

Another respected commentator of the school of Ibn al-'Abbas is Mujahid b. Jabr, who often quotes 'Abdallah b. Salam as the witness for the Qur'anic verse: "*wa shahida shahidun min bani isra'il 'ala mithlihi*": qala Mujahid: ismuhu 'Abdallah b. Salam (Ibn Sa'd (1985, II: 353, see also adh-Dhahabi, Tadhkirat al-Huffaz, I, 26). Mujahid was well respected among the orthodoxy "weil er sich von den Ahl al-Kitab belehren ließ" (because he was informed by the Ahl al-Kitab" (Ibn Sa'd V, 344; Wolfensohn 1933: 37).

Another Hadith refers to 'Abdallah b. Salam as a very eager convert, it goes back to 'Abdallah b. 'Umar: 'Abdallah b. Salam insisted – against his own former brothers in the Jewish religion – that the tradition of stoning goes back to the real text of the Torah to be considered as Law, this insisting then lead to the death of a young couple punished for adultary. 'Abdallah b. Salam through this episode belongs to the history of introducing of stoning as Punishment in Islam (cf. Ibn Hisham 2002: 241 ff.; Mingana n.d.). It is quite symptomatic that this episode – as a quick view to the respective pages of the internet shows – plays an important role in inter-religious discourse until today.

A subtle background for the otherwise orthodox refuse to fully acknowledge the Jewish converts (e.g. van Ess 2001: 79) seems to refer to the general hostility of the Jews towards the new Prophet: "l'ostilitá degli Ebrei," because Muhammad was not a Jew "fosse generata dall'invidia, perché Dio non aveva preferito di mandare un Profeta ebraico. L'opposizione degli Ebrei sia un travisamento dei fatti e che il motivo fondamentale fosse invece sopratutto politico" (Caetani 1905, I: 413, fn 1).

Similar reactions are vital until today in modern Egyptian interpretations of the Qur`an most notably by Rashid Rida, who opposed the "Isra`iliyat," the Hadiths originating from early converts and speeks of false traditions which were fabricated to undermine Islam (vgl. Jansen 1980: 27). The Isra`iliyat, the "traditions and reports that contain elements of the legendary and religious literature of the Jews," as Juynboll (1969: 121) tells us, found always a very ambiguous reception among orthodox scholars. However, it should be noted that despite the motive of Queen of the Snake in the Buluqya-story for example, ´Abdallah b. Salam was well praised by Rashid Rida (Juynboll 1969: 129). This is astonishing, because otherwise it is known that "Rida contended that all the stories woven around the snake were forgeries and belonged to the *isra`iliyat*" (Juynboll 1969: 122).

We can also learn from Ibn Khaldun how definite the refutation of the Isra`iliat where generally by the Orthodoxy. However, it seems that all this had not affected the well-settled position of ´Abdallah b. Salam as a figure of vigour and belief in early Islam. In Ibn Khaldun´s Muqaddima we find him being honoured as one of the refuters of Ali´s Khalifa and as one of the trustees of the Umayyads (Ibn Khaldun 1958, I: 439). However, Ibn Khaldun warned of the traditions of the biblical interpretations of the Qur`an because they "clung to the (information) they possessed, such as information about the beginning of creation and the information of the type of forecasts and predictions" (Ibn Khaldun 1958, III: 445). Nevertheless, they could also be considered "as people of rank in (their) religion and religious group" (Ibn Khaldun 1958, III: 446). Ilse Lichtstadter seems to give us a sound explanation for the interpretative role of the early converts: Muhammad "was dipping deep into the reservoir of ancient Hear eastern myth from which those Biblical stories themselves had originally arisen. Thus, these variants represent several parallel streams of myth and legend independently from this ancient well of Near Eastern mythology, gradually becoming "history." They were identical in their underlying symbolic meaning but not in the way they were remembered and told in the various cultural and religious environments" (1976: 38). The new religion, therefore, had its own necessities to explain the differences between knowledge of text and knowledge of myth. In fact, there was the need to close the gap due to the historical break with traditions and myth. However, at the same time there arose the necessity to stabilize the sense for cultural continuity and to mobilize it in a missionary sense, or even of instrumentalizing the images and symbols of continuity for the religious metaphoric and mentality of the masses.

Wolfensohn clearly shows that the prophetic stories, deriving from the Isra`iliyat were – in opposition to their refutation by the orthodoxy – already in the first century Hijra – a mass phenomenon. The popular story tellors (qas, pl. qussas), and re-interpretors, wanderers between mosques and public places attracted masses of people listening to the Qisas the mixed legends of the Qur`an and the Bible, explaining the textual discrepancies between both (Goldziher 1969, II: pp. 161). In the event of the recitation in front of a huge audience men and women were applauding the Qas intervening with questions and statements or just raising their hands as they do it until today when listening to poets and singers. The ability of quick response to questions and of inventing of "real" details was part of their profession. Certainly, confronting "the people" they were regarded as the real "scholars" and often better repuded as their rivals the scholars of profession ond of disciplinary studies (Goldziher 1969: II, 167). Certainly, the Isra`iliat took a special part in these legends on biblical figures (Wolfensohn 1933: 62).

Ka´b al-Ahbar is a convert who is often mentioned together with 'Abdallah b. Salam and who like him was a follower of 'Umar, of 'Uthman and Mu'awiya, and who has never travelled to Egypt. He functioned , like 'Abdallah as a councillor and a visionary, however, unlike 'Abdallah his Maqams in Egypt are acknowledged in the literature, for example in Lane's Manners and Customs of Modern Egyptians (quote from Wolfensohn 1933: 32).

Wolfensohn explains the veneration olf Ka´b in Egypt that his name is related to the Jusuf-Legends in the later collections and that these legends have their places in Egypt, therefore finding great interest among the people there (Wolfensohn, 1933: 33). He also points to Ali Bascha Mubarak (al-Hitat al-Taufiqiyya, II: 96) and his mentioning of a Cairean mosque were other saints are burried in the Sajida Zainab quarter, the Shari´a 'l-Nasiriyya street and also entering from the small Harat al-Sayis" (ibid.).

7. Between early Islamic politics and mission

As we have seen, despite all critique against the Isra`iliyat and the Qussas, 'Abdallah b. Salam remains a trustworthy pillar of the Orthodoxy and his traditions are officially presented at his Maqam, specifically in the one near Tell Thmuis in Kafr al-Amir. This fact needs further explanation. Possibly, we may ask, whether in all the textual arrangements there is potentially beyond the all magic, metaphors and legends, quite separately a dimension of the missionary, discursive and psychological power of these early Jewish converts in Islam and specifically of 'Abdallah b. Salam. The most critical authors against all early Islamic sources could give us here an interesting turn in understanding the specific climate of the struggle of ideas in the early time of Islamic conquest of Palestine and Syria. Patricia Crone and Michael Cook in "Hagarism" (1977) develop their critique from the stand against Islam as the late-comer of the prophetic religions as "an unusual, and for a number of related reasons a peculiar historical event" (1977: VII). By way of abolishing the *maghazi-* and *hadith*-literature from the horizon of "real" sources, Crone und Cook are implementing a small number of non-Islamic sources to develop a diverse picture of the early history of Islamic expansion. This finds our interest, because they include some important points on the psychology of religious propaganda and the potential role of the Jewish converts in it. The point is that Jewish Messianism played a role in the expansion of Islam in the times of the Calif 'Umar and that this idea contributed to the later reworking of the life history of Muhammad and his entourage in Medina. With this point Crone and Cook, however, remain mainly interested in the critique of the authenticity claims of the Islamic sources. They contribute little to further our understanding of the coincidence of Messianism, religious intellectualism and scholarship in early Islam. There is, as they claim, the "messianic aspect of the conquest of Palestine" and the respective "warmth of the Jewish reaction to the Arab conquest" (Crone/Cook 1977: 6). However, to merely discuss the metaphor of the Jewish idea of "'Umar al-Faruq" representing the picture of "the one who will come," in terms of a regressive imagery of reworking the sources in the 8th century, is a mere methodological question and out of tune with Islamic self-definition in early Islam.

The question for us is, whether the "Jews who mix with the Saracens" (Crone/Cook 1977: 6) played an important role in the dialogue between the conquering Arabs and the local populations and in which way this dialogue opened new fields of spiritual and ritual orientation. 'Abdallah b. Salam is reported to have accompanied the Caliph 'Umar at his raid to Jerusalem and that he later on was close to 'Uthman and Mu'awiya. The report that in 35 H. an Egyptian military unit came to Medina to support 'Uthman – it came too late – gives some space for speculation with respect to a possible link to Egypt and its political and theological elite.

There are more speculations: Wolfensohn knows that Ka'b al-Ahbar had already left Medina at the time of the murder of 'Uthman and there were other influential persons who did not want to engage in the struggle over the Caliph-ship and left the town. Ibn 'Abbas for example, who was in Mecca. 'Amr b. al-'As was in Palestine; only 'Abdallah b. Salam seems to have stood on the side of the Caliph when the rebels came to murder him (Tab, Ann. I, 3017 cf. Wolfenson 1933: 31). Such reports show the local differences in influence of individual leaders and their different spheres of influence. It is interesting here to know, that the Medinese community of Jews had close "rapporti spirituali e forse anche commerciali con le comunità ebraiche della Palestina e della Babilonia" (Caetani 1905,I: 414).

Furthermore 'Abdallah b. Salam seems to have explained individual names of biblical and qur'anic places in Jerusalem in terms of their significance for the new religion:

"In fact, eschatological descriptions assign a special role to the Temple Mount, the Valley of Hinnom and the Mount of Olives. According to 'Abdallah ibn Salam, a Jew from Medina who embraced Islam after Mohammed's arrival in that city, the sirat – the narrow bridge over the valley on Hinnom which all creatures must cross on Judgement Day – extends between the Mount of Olives and the Temple-area" (e.g. Muslim Iman III, 20/21; Hirschberg 1951/2: 342-3).

We could believe that such stories and reports belong to a type that was recently categorized as "lenkendes historisches Erzählen" (directing historical narrative) which is recently discovered among Arabists and Philologists as playing a major part in the cultural constructions of early Islam (e.g. van Ess 2001). Stefan Leder's study on the narrative of Abu Sufyan's questioning by Heraklios (2001: 1-42; 4) gives us an excellent account of the type of such narratives. However, all this is far beyond explaining why there exists a type of symbolic "networking" of 'Abdallah b. Salam in the Eastern Nile-delta today and in the past. This is not to be explained with the few examples of "thematics" and traditions. However, the very local presence of today seems to have some significance with respect to monotheism and the past. It is this point that perhaps is another layer of his veneration, namely, that the typology of his functioning could also tell us something about his role in history.

8. The modern functioning of the Maqams

There is not one generally applied pattern of local saints in Egypt. Perhaps, however, one could attempt – for the sake of clarity and with a view on "history" and "continuity" – to construct a variety of ideal types based on clusters of different external and internal factors constituting the vitality of their contemporary veneration. Could one speak in this context of a certain ranking of the saints? And, certainly, if the construction of sainthood is about hierarchy and order, then, how do saints relate back to local social order?

To start with, the Maqams of the members of the Prophet's family, the *ahl al-bayt*, all seem to be located in Cairo, the metropolis: Al-Husayn, Sayyida Zaynab, Sayyida Nafisa etc. However, the mere fact of their belonging to the *ahl al-bayt* would not automatically give them the very high rank in estimation and popularity. This is a similar pattern also to be observed with the Maqams of the Sahaba, the companions of the Prophet.

In the case of the great scholar and founder of one of the most important orthodox legal schools Imam al-Shafi'i (150-204 H./767-819 AD) who has his tomb in the City of the Death, the great southern cemetery, it is perhaps his role and influence in Egypt and the Islamic world as a scholar and not belonging to the Sa'ada or even to the Sahaba, that counts for his great popularity. However, it should also be noted that not every Tomb of a great scholar of early Islam is given a similar significance and veneration as a saint.

Of immediate interest in the view of the masses are the tombs of the Egyptian saints and spring offs of the Sufi movement: Sayyid Ahmad al-Badawi (596-675 H./1200-1276 AD) in Tanta and Ibrahim al-Desuqi in Desuq (633-676 H./1236-1277 AD; (Goldziher 1969, II: 338 pp.; Mayeur-Jaouen 1994; Hallenberg 1997). They represent the Egyptian half in the "clan" of the four great figures – the four poles – of Sufism besides the Iraqian al-Jilani (470-561 H./1077-1165 AD) und al-Rifa'i (512-578 H./1118-1182 AD). However, rural Egypt has its own landscape of saints of all strands: martyrs of the Futuh, the time of Islamic conquest of Egypt, others belonging to the Sa'ada, martyrs in the struggle against the crusaders, local Sufi shaykhs, however often only small men, 'symbols' of the *rajul salih*, the 'true' man, who with some very general name only signify their historical anonymity, a category which was already referred to by Goldziher (1969, II: 384).

This variety of types of saints clearly shows that there is no short cut pattern in the veneration of local saints, and that even over periods of time tombs and places changed their local or even regional importance by changing the name of the saint. It is also clear that the intensity of veneration and the popularity of a saint does not depend exclusively on religious factors. There is a certain affinity of saints with Pharaonic places, however this affinity is not exclusive and in the last instance not decisive. We also should keep in mind that this affinity does not relate to the Sabakheen and the search for treasures and gold in the mounds and Pharaonic Tells, as some crude reading of some archaeological reports would suggest. "Low" saints in the religious hagiography can have nevertheless a high esteem and popularity (and later attract a certain "high" religious interest), however, the contrary is perhaps more decisive. It is therefore most important to state, that the question , why a certain tomb is at a certain place, why this tomb is then turned into a Maqam, then a mosque added, and finally perhaps turned into religious centre of regional importance, is in most cases very difficult to answer. The question of the functioning of gaining a definite place in the Pantheon of Egyptian saints is therefore oblivious. This question towards the authenticity of a saint or his pseudo-character as a historical figure belonging to "his" historical place, remains buried in the process of local practice and arrangements and the related potentials and powers of emerging scenarios of an emerging convergence of local interests related to the creative material and symbolic worlds of "memory" in religion, family, village and the state. The creativity there often depends on the potentials of "bricolage" immanent in these factors at the moment of their appearance and potential coincidence. Definitely, as the "archaeological" dimension clearly shows "bricolage" needs an interplay of both the internal perspective of local players and the external perspective of observing outsiders.

With respect to the social function of the Maqams, Catherine Mayeur-Jaouen (2004) points to three factors at work which all include the secular dimension in the construction of the saint. First, she draws on the importance of the institution of the *rizaq ihbasiyya* (a rural type of *waqf*), the religious donation, functioning to administer and maintain the Maqam, with small-scale family networks from Maqam to Maqam from village to village. Thus, the extreme orientation to the saint is part of a process of embedding the communities into a landscape structured by trade and pilgrimage over centuries. Second and often related to the first factor, there is the flourishing of local Sufi-Tariqas. This is a factor for maintaining the patterns of the saint's succession and with it of village identity. We may add the building of a Zawiya near the Maqam, serving as a place for Sufi meditation and practice, which also contributes to the ritual importance of a place attracting the *ziyarat, mawalid, and nudhur* etc. Third the mythological function of a saint, relating him to the state and to official religious schools which support the financial and structural setting of a Maqam and its strategic function within the collective memory in the local and national context.

Perhaps there are some further important factors in operation. The state and the official religious institutions, namely local or national schools of the al-Azhar, are – if not immediately present – always a sort of an absent centre in all matters of public religious events. In the local vernacular for example the *mulid* (mawlid), the feast of the *shaykh* is a standard expression for chaos and confusion. Samuli Schielke (2004: 180, fn. 6) most interestingly observed how this is expressed with the metaphor *"mulid wi-sahbu ghayib"* (a mawlid without its master, i.e. the saint). I think it is important to note the ambiguity of this metaphor with respect to "disorder," it is the absence of the shaykh/saint, not the absence of *hukuma* (government) which creates disorder, despite however, that the Maqams, once they are actively venerated, are registered, and thus administered and controlled. Maqams are often the very place of interaction between government and local interests. As with respect to 'Abdallah's shrine near Tell Thmuis, the "text" representation of the saint is part of this interplay, not to speak of architecture, location and the organisation of attention of the Maqam. In this interplay there is a steadily changing pattern of codification and recognition of the "sacredness" of the saint and his place. Certainly, what Schielke has observed, shows a changing pattern of obsession about formal ritual and control of public space which relates to the arrangements of the *mawalid* (pl.) of the major saints.

There is one further significant element in the construction and maintenance of saints and their Maqams which lies in the nature of what Egyptian writers like Ali Fahmy call *"din sha'abi"* which incorporates more than popular beliefs but rather a whole system of knowledge and mentalities linking the metaphysical problem of deepest everydayness to the place and the shrine. In addition this includes, of course, the flourishing of local markets and the growth of the attendance of the saint, linking his success ambitiously to his transcendental powers. Thus, *"din sha'abi"* is much responsible for the flourishing of such saints in the Delta like al-Badawi (Tanta), al-Disuqi (Disuq) and Sidi Shibl (Shuhada), and the respective steady growth of the towns and markets which they maintain. It is within these fields that we have to re-consider the role of the saint in constructing and spiritually incorporating certain historical locations and spatial arrangements with respect to specific historical events. Furthermore, there relates a certain metaphorical empowerment of speech and action to the saint as representing a sort of eternal continuity of early Islamic history in style. Examples of this are well found in scriptural expressions of early Islam (cf. Leder 2001; van Ess 2001) and with no less importance in medieval Islam with a much stronger presence of expressions of the Pharaonic period (Sezgin 1994, 2001, 2002/3; Haarmann 1990, 1995).

As with respect to *din sha'abi* today these constructions follow a similar dialogical principle, namely, the popular narrative of the saint re-instituting his miracles by way of linking his own fate to everyday feelings and judgements of the people. Thus the popular narrative of the saint embodies an understanding of everydayness linked to the transcendental world which includes an immense pool of transmitted oral and written stories and legends of the saint. The vitality of local spirit among the impoverished peasant population and their psychology of immediacy of world encounter and fantasy develops a pattern of cultural memory beyond modern ethics of authenticity in "text," "descent" and "loacality." The empowering of the saint in the immediacy of "his" event can be directly linked to the empowering of the local "Islamic" way of life of the attending masses.

There is no doubt about this immanent secular power of the saint and his metaphysical rank. This is his direct linkage to the understanding of chaos or order. Furthermore, there is a clear cut economic sense related to his cult and the place of his veneration. This is not only a matter of the closeness of the bazaar as in the case of great saints like Sayyidna Husayn or Sayyida Zaynab in metropolitan Cairo, it emerges deeply on the barns around the Maqams in any little village.

9. The historical psychology of the place

Islamologists – as mentioned above – consider the veneration of saints as contradicting dogma and scriptural tradition. As much there is 'dogma' of the light of divine revelation as in the "Light Verse" (XXIV, 35) related to this-worldly spirituality, however, there is also no doubt about the pure secular nature of the Prophet himself as a human actor. Ignaz Goldziher made it quite clear that puritan Sunnis and 'enlightened' sceptics opposed strongly the idea of sainthood in Islam. He insists on the "influence of inherited instincts of the believers" (1969, II: 277) and on a variety of "psychological factors" (ibid.: 286) as being responsible for the cultic continuity from pre-Islamic periods. He quotes a formula of Ernest Renan, that humanity always from its beginning preached at the same place (ibid., II: 334/303), as a good example explaining this local continuities of the sacred. Certainly, as we have mentioned above, the Eastern Delta of the Nile being as John Holloday noticed "an important culture contact zone between Asia and Egypt" (Holloday 1982: 9), is overloaded with such "transhistorical" places of prayer. Would this aspect of transhistoricality contribute to explain the very specific presence of 'Abdallah b. Salam in this region? Goldziher also already explained to us the unworried practice of the popular tradition to place the tomb of one and the same person at different places. (Goldziher 1987: 336-40). So, certainly, that we have a multiplicity of Maqams may not be irritating. However, certainly it remains of significance that we have so many Maqams of 'Abdallah b. Salam in one region, and that there is no evidence of other places and shrines of his in Egypt, nor in the rest of the Muslim world.

The ambiguity of the place is further revealed in looking at the historical significance of three different locations of the tombs of 'Abdallah b. Salam. The Egyptian cultural geographers of the 19th century already pointed to the astonishing vicinity of Islamic saints and Pharaonic places. Ali Mubarak Pasha for example in his *al-Khittat al-tawfiqiyya al-jadida* mentions – as Goldziher made it a point – mentions the fact of a tomb of Osiris which was turned into a *zawiya al-maslub* (Goldziher 1968, II: 384). At the Tell of Thmuis, south of Mansura, we are told by archaeologists, that there have been relicts from the 4th century B.C. and from the late 9th century AD relicts of Islamic ceramics (EAAE 1999: 663). This could be taken as indicating the hights of the cultural activity at the place in the time of nearly one and a half Millenium before and after Christ. Amélineau (1893: 500 pp.) seems to have found this as a Coptic place in Daqahliyya, however with obviously diminishing importance over time, it has been ultimately destroyed in the times of the Turkish conquest. De Meulenaere (1976) collects reports which date back to the 18th century AD of western travellers and archaeologists in Mendes and Thmuis. The Qubba of 'Abdallah b. Salam was always there, a place of shelter and peace – and sometimes for the storage of relicts found on the tell. The official Egyptian geography of 1945 categorizes Kafr al-Amir 'Abdallah as one of the *bilad al-qadima* – old villages – of the destrict of Sinbilawin. It is stated that its original name was Bani 'Abdallah in the Ottoman Period and that in 1228 H. it was first named as Kafr al-Amir 'Abdallah (Ramzi 1945, II/1: 194). If this is reality, then the story of 1869 by Daninos Pasha on his visit at "tell Tmay (village d'Abdallah-ben Salam)" mentioning a certain Salem as a local leader and as his helper and guide could well fit (de Meulenaere 1976: 92). What, however, has this Salem to do with 'Abdallah b. Salam. Could it be that a local clan of Salams, representatives of which until today lead as Khalifs in the Zaffa (the Friday procession) of the Mawlid at the Maqam of 'Abdallahb. Salam today? Are all this fictive allusions? Maybe!

On the other hand we are told that among the people of the village, *'anda al-'amma,* the place is named Kafr Ibn Salam and that this is meant to be al-'Amir, namely 'Abdallah b. Salam, the *ashab al-nabi* , compagnion of the Prophet. The Maqam is his and they do the pilgrimage for him in great belief (*yazurunahu da'iman*). However, the story ends with a laconic: Only God knows the truth (*wa allahu 'a'lam bil-haqiqa*) (Ramzi 1945, II/1: 194-5). The Tell is mentioned here in relation to Tumai al-'Imdid the village south east and as part of the twin town Mendes (ibid. 187-9; see also al-Rub': 197). And certainly asserting Goldziher, the "psychology of the people" could have easily mixed up both, speaking for each place as the "*Tell bint al-yahudi,*" and in their believe a town of a Jewish Queen which was justly destroyed. Does this have something to do with the Jewish convert to Islam as a religious witness and protector abolishing the *shubahat* of the people on the Tell? Is this something new in the age of fundamentalism or rather a sort of repetition of collective memory of the strength of Islam in earlier periods?

A second place, in the small village Barq al-'Izz very near to Mansura, the situation is completely different. The village has a short mentioning in the "Qamus al-jugrafya" of Ramzi. The village was originally called "Barbansaqa" or (coptic) "Birqinqis" (see also Halm 1982: 710) oder "Bir Bansaqa" oder "Bir Bansafa." Its popular name was "Birqinqis," 1228 H. it was officially registered as Barq Naqs. By the initiative of alocal Shaykh it was renamed in 1930 "Barq al-'Izz" (Lightning of Glory; Ramzi 1994, II, 1: 218). This is the short mentioning of the place – no knowledge of the Maqam of our 'Abdallah, nothing about the reasons behind changing the name. Similarly, at a third place situated in the Lake Manzala near Matariyya, although the Maqam of 'Abdallah stands on a Tell, there is no real history of the place. Ramzi again is primarily concerned with the name of places and their historically official registration (although he sometimes goes back to the Geography of Antiquity), here we only read of two places put together as Matariyya in 1903. The Maqam of 'Abdallah is not mentioned, not the Tell of the Gezira (ibid.: 209). Whether there is something like the "islamized" Coptic saint like the one on the Island of "Tuna" (vgl. Mayeur-Jaouen 1994: 98, fn 70; 258, 262) is not known among the local fishermen. The English traveller Hamilton has at the beginning of the 19th century found a Tell by this name. However, not seen any Maqam. Later on Burton does not find the Tell near Matariyya, however the fishermen bring him there and remember the place in high estime (de Meulenaere 1976: 51, 74).

10. Some conclusive remarks

The local arrangements of the places of the Islamic saint 'Abdallah b. Salam – and his Maqams in the region of Mansura in one way or another show signs of ongoing and obviously very intensive antagonisms – seem to bear the signs of a inner Islamic struggle over orthodox, and then Salafite or heterodox and popular Sufi orientations with respect to an 'inner religious good,' namely, the diverse forms of treatment of the continuity of pre-Islamic and Pharaonic culture in Islamic terms. The momentums and ritual potentials of the old world have been absorbed and reworked and re-activated. It is always the shrine, the Maqam, which is the place of reworking. The places symbolically express this struggle over continuity and monotheistic purity and break with history. The potential regression into pagan practices and Polytheism is counteracted first by the construction of the Maqam, the place of the saint and its public recognition. This is at the same time a place of memory of the past, where symbolic, ritual and scriptural performances of past and the saint entail divergent arrangements with respect to functional interests, communal traditions or for religious purity. The shrines are places for observing of the past. However, specifically in the last 30 years with the emergence of Salafite purism on the local scene, the places turn into arenas of a steady fight over ritual and Islamic form of veneration. This discourse of Islamic purity and popular memory, originated in the far a way metropoles, however, they are now fought sometimes at the most remote and marginal places, turning the local shrine into a place of cultural reconstruction under conditions of strong marginality. The modern re-arrangement of the shrines of ʿAbdallah b. Salam took place in this time. However, the current re-arrangements are only rephrasing discourses and symbolic expressions which were already active in former times.

The great Mulid as it is performed in the village near Tell Thmuis is powerful and the strong tradition here helped the modern reconstruction of the shrine. In the collection of texts locally assembled texts, the saint is presented as the scholar of Early Islam par excellence. However, in the sacred procession (*zaffa*) he figures as an incarnative part of a spiritual feast longing close to the presence of God (resembling the Kyrios of the old times). Furthermore, there remains, the magic figure, the mythical sailor in heaven and between the worlds, symbolizing the presence of an "alien," an "absent" people, in his tales, which are part pf popular literature. All this is ambiguous, tenuous and culturally productive. Despite these contradictions, there is continuity in the overpowering imagination and symbolic representation of the "physical" presence which is expressed in the metaphorical details of the presented "reality" of the sacred. This multi-polar form of the presence of the sacred subject then is the real focus of the perspectivism which is necessary for understanding the sacred as a momentum and a condition of the local world and its immediate recognition.

Methodologically, therefore the different directions of this presence are to be made subject of multiple layers of observation: Text, time, locus, symbol and form. Only in this multiplicity we may be able to understand the actuality of the phenomenon of the "sacred" as it has become part of the modern world.

Constructions of sainthood and the specific meaning of it acquires at one specific place and in one specific region the dialog and co-operation of Egyptologists, specialists in Islamic Studies and Ethnologists, as Haarmann (1990: 57) has already suggested for at least the first two of the named disciplines. It would, however, be too short cut to interpret the need for such a dialog purely in terms of the more recent attempts of Egyptians to cope with both, their "Islamic" and their "Pharaonic identity" as a national task. It is also the ambiguous "religious" continuity of the place which contributes to give the religious Islamic reconstruction a turn in which the Maqam distinguishes itself against a seemingly secular world of the past: a distinction which in many ways rephrases the historical struggles related to the emergence of monotheism and modern religion.

I am proposing with this paper a sociological perspective which, focusing on processes of reconstruction of the Sacred, combines the different disciplinary fields of tackling the relationship between the Saint and his place. The various disciplinary perceptions of the Sacred today cannot be administered separately, rather we have to include them as part and parcel of the modern event of the Sacred at its place. The place itself evolves as a discursive field in which essential elements of it turn out to be made present and exchanged. The place combines the history of "origin" with its own significance as well as with the various historical layers of conditions, actions and intensions and of its symbolic design. The Maqam thus reassures fictional realities of the saint: his live story, the authored texts of the saint, the hagiographic texts, the forms of their authentication. As already mentioned by Goldziher, the multiplicity of places and appearances of one and the same saint is a common feature of Islamc saints. In deed, I am proposing a multiple lecture of all this which relates to diverse layers of inner experience of the saint through the eyes of modern venerators as much as to the history of the factual verification of his existence. There is something factual in attempting to make "present" someone who is "absent": the relationship between time and symbol, ideas and events, forms of embodiment, metaphor, image and magic.

References

Amélineau, E. (1893) *Géographie de l'Égypte à l'époque copte*. Paris: Imprimerie Nationale.

Ammann, Ludwig (2001) *Die Geburt des Islam. Historische Innovation durch Offenbarung*. Göttingen: Wallstein.

Assmann, Jan (1997) *Moses the Egyptian. The Memory of Egypt in Western Monotheism*. Cambridge, Mass.: Harvard University Press.

ath-Tha'labi, Abu Ishaq Ahmad b. Muhammad (1325/1907) *Qisas al-anbiya*. Cairo.

Bobzin, Hartmut (1995) *Der Koran im Zeitalter der Reformation. Studien zur Frühgeschichte der Arabistik und Islamkunde in Europa*. Beirut: Beiruter Texte und Studien 42.

Brague, Rémi (2002) *Eccentric Culture. A Theory of Western Civilization*. South Bend, Indiana: St. Augustine's Press.

Brockelmann, Carl (1942) *Geschichte der arabischen Literatur*, 2 Vols., 3 Suppl. Vols. Leiden: Brill.

Brown, Peter (1999) "Images as a Substitute for Writing." In: Evangelos Chrysos and Ian Wood (eds.) *East and West: Modes of Communication*, Leiden/Boston/Köln: Brill, pp. 15-34.

Butler, Alfred J. (1978[1912] *The Arab Conquest of Egypt and the Last Thirty Years of the Roman Dominion,* Oxford: Clarendon Press.

Caetani, Leone (1972 [1905]) *Annali dell'Islam,* Vol. I, Milano: Ulrico Hoepli. (Nachdr. Hildesheim/New York: Olms).

Cheddadi, Abdesselam (2004) *Les Arabes et l'appropriation de l'histoire. Émergenc et premiers développements de l'historiogrphie musulmane jusqu'au IIe/VIIIe siècle.* Paris: Sindbad/Actes Sud.

Crone, Patricia/Michal Cook (1977) *Hagarism. The Making of the Islamic World.* Cambridge: CUP.

Deschner, Karlheinz (1988) *Kriminalgeschichte des Christentums, Vol. 2. Die Spätantike.* Reinbek bei Hamburg: Rowohlt.

EAAE (Encyclopedia of Archeology and Egyptology) (1999), ed. by Kathrin A. Bard. London: Routledge.

El-Ehwany, Ahmad Foad (1957) *Islamic Philosophy.* Cairo.

El-Gawhary, Mohamad M. (1968) *Die Gottesnamen im magischen Gebrauch in den al-Buni zugeschriebenen Werken,* Diss. Bonn.

Fowden, Garth (1986) *The Egyptian Hermes. A Historical Approach to the Late Pagan Mind.* Cambridge: Cambridge University Press.

Fowden, Garth (2005) "Beyond Late Antiquity: The First Millenim Globalised," Paper for the Florence conference on "Late Antiquity and Axial Changes," 10-11 May 2005.

Franke, Patrick (2004) "Khidr in Istanbul: Observations on the Symbolic Construction of Sacred Spaces in Traditional Islam." In: Georg Stauth (ed.) *On Archaeology of Sainthood and Local Spirituality in Islam. Past and Present Crossroads of Events and Ideas. Yearbook of the Sociology of Islam,* ed. by Georg Stauth and Armando Salvatore, Vol. 5. Bielefeld: transcript Verlag; New Brunswick: Transactions Publishers.

Frankfurter, David (1998) "Introduction, Approaches to Coptic Pilgrimage." In: Idem, *Pilgrimage and Holy Space in Late Antique Egypt,* pp. 3-50.

Gibb, H.A.R. (1978) *Islam.* Oxford: Oxford University Press.

Goldziher, Ignaz (1952[1910]) *Die Richtungen der islamischen Koranauslegung.* Leipzig/Leiden: E.J. Brill.

Goldziher, Ignaz (1968) "Muslimische Traditionen über den Grabesort des Joshua." In: *Gesammelte Schriften II,* ed. by Joseph Desmogyi. Hildesheim: Olms, pp. 71-75.

Goldziher, Ignaz (1968a) "Ali Bascha Mubarak." In: Gesammelte Schriften II, ed. by Joseph Desmogyi. Hildesheim: Olms, pp. 381-384. (WZKM, IV, 1890).

Goldziher, Ignaz (1969[1890]) *Muhammedanische Studien, Vol. II.,* Hildesheim: Olms (Engl. ed. by S.M. Stern, transl. by C.R. Barber und S.M. Stern, London: George Allen & Unwin 1971).

Goldziher, Igmaz (1987[1876]) *Der Mythos bei den Hebräern und seine geschichtliche Entwickelung. Untersuchungen zur Mythologie und Religionswissenschaft*, Wiesbdaden: Fourier.

Haarmann, Ulrich (1978) "Die Sphinx. Synkretistische Volksreligiosität im spätmittelalterlichen islamischen Ägypten." In: *Saeculum 29*, pp. 367-384.

Haarmann, Ulrich (1995) *Das Pyramidenbuch des Abu Ja'far al-Idrisi*. Beirut: DOI.

Haarmann, Ulrich 1990) "Das pharaonische Ägypten bei islamischen Autoren des Mittelalters." *Orbis Biblicus et Orientalis*, Vol. XLV.

Hallenberg, Helena (1997) *Ibrahim al-Dasuqi (1255-96) – A Saint Invented*. Helsinki: Yliopistopaino.

Halm, Heinz (1982) *Ägypten nach den mamelukischen Lehensregistern, Vol. II: Das Delta*. Wiesbaden: L. Reichert Verlag.

Hermann, Alfred (1959) "Der Nil und die Christen." *Jahrbuch für Antike und Christentum*, Vol. 2, pp. 30-69.

Hermann, Alfred (1960) "Die Ankunft des Nils." *Zeitschrift für Ägyptische Sprache und Altertumskunde* (ZÄS) 85, pp. 35-42.

Hermann, Alfred (n. d.) "Rilkes ägyptische Gesichte." *Symposium*, Vol. IV, 24, pp. 371-461.

Hirschberg, J.W. (1951-2) "The sources of Moslem traditions concerning Jerusalem." In: Rocznik Orientalistyczny (Krakau), 314-350.

Hirschfeld, Hartwig (1883) "Essai sur l'Histoire des Juifs de Médine." *R.E.J.*, Vol. VII, pp. 167-193; (1985), Vol. X, pp. 10-31.

Hirschfeld, Hartwig (1902) *New Reserches into the Composition and Exegisis of the Qur'an*. London: Royal Asiatic Society. (Asiatic Monographs, Vol. III)

Hoffmeier, James K. (1996) *Israel in Egypt*. New York and Oxford: Oxford University Press.

Holloday, John S. Jr. (1982) *Cities of the Delta*, Part. III, Tell el-Maskhuta. Preliminary Report on the Wadi Tumilat Project, 1978-1979. Malibu, Udena Publ. (American Research Centre in Egypt Reports, Vol. 6).

Horowitz, Josef (1901) "Buluqja." *Zeitschrift der Deutsch-Morgenländischen Gesellschaft* (ZDMG), 55, pp. 519-521.

Ibn Hisham, Abd al-Malik (1860/1865) *Kitab Sira Rasul Allah. Das Leben Muhammed's nach Muhammed b. Ishak,* Vol 1, Vol. 2. Ed. by Ferdinand Wüstenfeld. Leipzig: Diedrich'sche Verlagsanstalt. Bd. I, Bd. II 1865. (in Engl.: The Life of Muhammad, Oxford: Oxford University Press 2002, transl. by F. Guillaume).

Ibn Khaldun (1958) *The Muqaddimah. An Introduction to History*. Transl. by Franz Rosenthal, 3 Vols. London: Routledge & Kegan Paul.

Ibn Sa'd (1985) *Tabaqat al-Kubra* (8 Vols), Vol. 2. Beirut.

Jansen, J.J.G.(1980) *The Interpretation of the Koran in Modern Egypt*. Leiden: E.J. Brill.

Juynboll, G.H.A. (1969) *The Authenticity of the Tradition Literature. Discussions in Modern Egypt.* Leiden: E.J. Brill.

Kannengiesser, Charles (1986) "Athanasius of Alexandria vs. Arius: The Alexandrian Crisis." In: Birger A. Pearson/James E. Goehring (eds.) *The Roots of Egyptian Christianity*, (Studies in Antiquity & Christianity), Philadelphia: Fortress Press, pp. 204-215.

Kritzeck, J. (1964) *Peter the Venerable and Islam.* Princeton: Princeton Oriental Studies 23.

Leder, Stefan (2001) "Herklios erkennt den Propheten. Ein Beispiel für Form und Entstehungsweise narrativer Geschichtskonstruktionen." *Zeitschrift der Deutschen Morgenländischen Gesellschaft*, Vol. 151, 1, pp. 1-42.

Lichtenstaeder, Ilse (1976) *Introduction to Classical Arabic Literature.* New York: Schocken Books.

Mayeur-Jaouen, Katherine (1994) *Al-Sayyid al-Badawi. Un grand saint de l'islam égyptien.* Le Caire: Institut Francais d'Archéologie Orientale. (Textes Arabes et Etudes Islamiques, Tomes XXXII).

Mayeur-Jaouen, Katherine (2004) "Holy Ancestors, Sufi Shaykhs and Founding Myths: Networks of Religious Geography in the Central Nile Delta." In: Georg Stauth (ed.) *On Archeology of Sainthood and Local Spirituality in Islam. Past and present Crossroads of Ideas. Yearbook of the Sociology of Islam*, ed. by Georg Stauth and Armando Salvatore, Vol. 5. Diclefeld: tran script Verlag; New Brunswick: Transactions Publishers, pp. 24-35.

Meulenaire, Herman de (1976) "Scholarly Exploration." In: Herman de Meulenaire and Pierre MacKay, *Mendes II*, ed. by Emma Swan Hall and Bernard v. Bothmer. Warminster: Aris & Phillips Ltd., pp. 19-169.

Mingana, Alphonse (n.d.) "Notes upon some of the Kuranic Manuscripts in the John Rylands Library," http://answering-islam.org.uk/Books/Mingana/Rylands.

Montserat, Dominique (1986) "Pilgrimage to the shrine of SS Cyrus and John at Menouthis in late antiquity." In: David Frankfurter, *Pilgrimage and Holy Space in Late Antique Egypt*, Leiden etc: Brill, 1998, pp. 256-279.

Nock, Arthur Davis (1972) "Later Egyptian Piety." In: Idem, *Essays on Religion and the Ancient World,* selected and edited, with an introduction, bibliography of Nock's writings, and indexes by Zeph Stewart, II. Oxford: Clarendon Press, pp. 566-574.

Ramzi, Muhammad (1994) *al-Qamus al jugharfi lil-bilad al-misr min 'asr qudama` almisriyin ila sana 1945*, Vol. I, Part 2, al-Qahira: al-Hai`a al-Misriyya al-'amma lil-kitab.

Retsö, Jan (2003) *The Arabs in Antiquity. Their History from the Assyrians to the Ummayads.* London and New York: Routledge Curzon.

Rosenthal, Franz (1992) *The Classical Heritage in Islam.* London: Routledge.

Said, Edward (2003) *Freud and the Non-European.* London: Verso.

Schielke, Samuli (2004) "On Snacks and Saints: When Discourses of Rationality and Order Enter the Egyptian *Mawlid*." In: Georg Stauth (ed.) *On Archeology of Sainthood and Local Spirituality in Islam. Past and Present Crossroads of Events and Ideas.* Bielefeld: Transcript-Verlag/New Brunswick: Transactions Publishers.

Sedgwick, Mark (2000) "The Primacy of the Milieu: The Dandarawiyya's unsuccessful attempt to change ist identity." In: Rachida Chih/Denis Gril (eds.) *Le saint et son milieu.* Cairo: IFAO – Cahiers des Annales Islamologiques 19, pp. 203-214.

Sezgin, Fuat (1967) *Geschichte des Arabischen Schrifttums*, Vol. I. Leiden: E.J. Brill.

Sezgin, Ursula (1994) "al-Mas'udi, Ibrahim b. Wasifshah und das Kitab al-Aja'ib. Aigyptika in arabischen Texten des 10. Jahrhunderts n. Chr." *Zeitschrift für Geschichte der Arabisch-Islamischen Wissenschaften,* Vol. 8, pp. 1-70.

Stauth, Georg (2001) "Skizzen zur materiellen Kultur des religiösen Ortes (Islam) – Kulturelle Immanenz." In: Heiko Schrader/Markus Kaiser/Rüdiger Korff (eds.), Markt, Kultur und Gesellschaft, Münster: Lit-Verlag, pp. 149-166.

Stauth, Georg (2004) "Der Drang zum Heiligen unter 'kleinen Sheikhs' – Heiligenverehrung und islamische Modernisierung unter Beduinen und Fellachen. Vergleichende Untersuchungen im Nord Sinai, im Ostdelta und in Rashid (Rosetta)." In: Walter Bisang/Detlev Kreikenbom/Thomas Bierschenk/Ursula Verhoeven (eds.) *Kulturelle und sprachliche Kontakte. Prozesse des Wandels in Historischen Spannungsfeldern Nordostafrikas/Westasiens. Akten zum 2. Symposium des SFB 295 der Johannes Gutenberg-Universität Mainz, 15-17.10.2001,* Würzburg: Ergon, pp. 367-382.

Stauth, Georg (2005) *Ägyptische heilige Orte I. Konstruktionen, Inszenierungen und Landschaften der Heiligen im Nildelta: Abdallah b. Salam.* Fotographische Begleitung von Axel Krause. Bielefeld: transcript Verlag.

Stroumsa, Guy G. (2001) "Cultural Memory in Early Christianity: Clement of Alexandria and the History of Religions." Conference on Axial Transformations. Florence: European University Institute. December.

Stroumsa, Guy G. (2005) "Cultural Memory in Early Christianity: Clement of Alexandria and the History of Religions." In: Johann P. Arnason, S.N. Eisenstadt and Björn Wittrock (eds.) *Axial Age Civilisations and World History.* Leiden, Boston: Brill, pp. 295-318.

Volokhine, Youri (1998) "Les déplacements pieux en Égypte pharaonique." In: David Frankfurter, *Pilgrimage and Holy Space in Late Antique Egypt,* Leiden etc.: Brill, pp. S. 51-98.

Watt, M. (1956) *Muhammed at Medina.* Oxford: Clarendon Press.

Watt, Montgomery (1952) "The condemnation of the Jews of Banu Quraizah. A Study in the Sources of the Sirah." *Muslim World,* Vol. 42, pp. 160-171.

Watt, Montgomery (1990) *Early Islam: Collected Articles*. Edinburgh.

Wellhausen, Jacob (1961[1897]) *Reste arabischen Heidentums*. Berlin.

Wolfensohn, Israel (1933) *Ka'b al-Ahbar und seine Stellung im Hadith und in der islamischen Legendenliteratur*. Diss. Frankfurt am Main.

Wolfenson, Isra`il (1345/1928) Tarikh al-Yahud fi Bilad al 'Arab. Al-Qahira.

Wood, Ian (1999) "Images as a Substitute for Writing: A Reply." In: Evangelos Chrysos/Ian Wood (eds.) *East and West: Modes of Communication*, Leiden, Boston, Köln: Brill, pp. 35-46.

Chapter 7

Story, Wisdom and Spirituality: Yemen as the Hub between the Persian, Arabic and Biblical Traditions

RAIF GEORGES KHOURY

The Yemen, *al-Yaman* in Arabic, is associated with many images and evocations which inspire dreams: *Arabia felix*, which incorporates the meaning of the country's name in Arabic; this is clearly expressed by the verb *yamana*, *yamina* and *yamuna* (to be happy etc.) in its triple form. *Yaman*, *yamna* and *yamīn* also refer to the right side or right hand which has a preferential position in the ancient and particularly biblical cultures, to which the Arab-Islamic culture belongs as their continuation; one only needs to think of the Last Judgement, *Yaum al-ba'th* ("day of waking from the graves") which consolidates this image. Yāqūt, the author of the classical encyclopaedia of the Muslim world *Mu'djam al-buldān*, explores such interpretations before dealing with the geographical and other information about the country.[1] Much has, moreover, been published about this country, in particular in relation to the division of the country in the early 1960s and after its reunification in the early 1990s. A series of studies by Joseph Chelhod, published in Paris around 20 years ago, on this subject are particularly worthy of mention.[2]

The fact that the Yemen has been repeatedly subject to neglect is a question related to the development of Islamic history and culture, whose heyday is associated with the Umayyad and, in particular, the Abbasid dynasties. Many studies have now been published which demonstrate the importance of the first Islamic generation of the Ist/7th and 2nd/8th centuries of Islam/AD within this process. The question arises here as to where the drive – both military and spiritual – for the gradual conquest of the country originated. I stress the significance of this country – otherwise virtually neglected in the specialist literature – which consisted of diverse regions in early Islam with a merging of influences originating from all of the important orientations of that period. I would not like people to come to the conclusion that the Yemen was important in early Islam because I have com-

---

1   Yāqūt, *Mu'djam al-buldān*, V, 447 ff.
2   Chelhod, Joseph et al. (1984-985), 3 Vols: L'Arabie du Sud, histoire et civilisation. 1: Le peuple yéménite et ses racines. 2: La société yéménite de l'Hégire aux idéologies modernes. 3: Cultures et institutions du Yémen.

piled monographs on scholars such as Wahb Ibn Munabbih,[3] 'Abd Allāh Ibn Lahī'a[4] and others; on no account would this be correct! The Yemen increasingly appears to me as a country, in which the roots of many early Islamic movements lie which, however, were gradually replaced by other undoubtedly more solid movements. Nonetheless, the personalities and lasting influences, without which it is impossible to explain subsequent developments, should not simply be set aside.[5]

In the first volume of his study, Chelhod stresses the inadequacy of the information that is generally conveyed, for example, on the actual contributions of the Yemenis to Islamic military expansion. He makes the following comments in this regard:

"Les chroniqueurs et les historiens arabes reconnaissent généralement que les Yéménites avaient contribué efficacement au succès des armées arabes. Nous estimons, quant à nous, qu'ils sont bien en deçà de la vérité et que la part des Yéménites dans la conquête arabe fut prépondérante. Il ne serait pas exagéré de dire que sans leur concours, l'Empire arabe n'aurait pas du tout été aussi loin, ni édifié aussi rapidement."[6]

("The Arab chroniclers and historians generally acknowledge that the Yemenis made an effective contribution to the success of the Arab armies. We ourselves estimate that they are here on the side of truth and that the Yemenis played a predominant role in the Arab conquest. It would not be exaggerating to say that without their support, the Arab Empire would not at all have got so far or been established so quickly.")

I would like to examine more here than these ideas of an acknowledged expert on southern Arabia. I would like to stress the significance of this area in connection with the role of story, wisdom and spirituality in Islamic culture and present further important arguments as proof of this.[7] Unfortunately, the article about Yemen in the Encyclopaedia of Islam does not fulfil the task of providing a comprehensive account of the country,[8] as newly acquired insights are inadequately represented or not included at all. However, these are dependent on the analysis of the oldest sources on the Yemen which were introduced into circulation di-

---

3   See Khoury, R.G. (1972) "Wahb B. Munabbih."
4   See Khoury, R.G. (1986) "Abd Allāh Ibn Lahī'a. Juge et grand maître de l'Ecole Egyptienne."
5   On the question of the enchantment and disenchantment of the world, see Gauchet, Marcel (1985) "Le désenchantement du monde."
6   Chelhod, Joseph (1984), L'Arabie du Sud, histoire et civilisation, Vol. 1: Le peuple yéménite et ses racines, p. 41; see also the paragraph titled "Le Yémen et la conquête arabe."
7   Many of my contributions have substantiated this belief for many years and are referred to or quoted in detail in this paper.
8   On this, see Encyclopaedia of Islam (1960), in the following written as EI^2, XI, pp. 269-280 (A. Grohmann/W.C. Brice et al.).

rectly or indirectly by Yemeni authors, starting, of course, with Wahb Ibn Munabbih who undoubtedly represents a key figure in this context.

I. The history of pre-Islam and early Islam

The meaning of *Arabia felix* emerges reveals itself most clearly here, as the books on these early Arab centuries were written by Yemenis and in association with the Yemen. Like every historical beginning in the past, this history, if one can call it that, was a vision of the world, which incorporated simultaneously history and fiction as emerges clearly in the anthology "Story-telling in the framework of non-fictional Arabic literature," edited by S. Leder.[9] In my contribution to this anthology, I highlighted both of these sides, *inter alia* by highlighting the problem of orality.[10] Everything was initially passed on orally before later being recorded in writing, *ne varietur*, as noted by R. Blachère.[11] Thus, everything bears the hallmark of orality whose ideal form of transmission was story-telling. Story-telling was a common genre in the old oriental cultures and displays similar traits there to those it displays in Islam. In Islam it is associated with the oldest books about Arabia which bear witness to early events in the lives of the tribes who lived there. It is known that from the second half of the $2^{nd}/8^{th}$ century the Islamic period was the first to begin to summarize, expand and systematically record these accounts in writing with new material from the newly-emerged Islamic Empire. Poetry was the dominant form here and accompanied the entire culture with its omnipotent presence. Everything in cultural development was influenced by it, and above all history.

Some key terms are of extreme significance here, particularly as the entire Islamic culture, its great development and precipitous rise, is a culture of words.[12] By way of introduction to the topic, let us now look at some of the terms which have been in use since the beginning of the Arab-Islamic culture and which lead us to the core of the subject under discussion here:

1. Adab is the oldest substantiated expression which was common from at least the $2^{nd}/8^{th}$ century and on which it would be possible to hold long lectures without ever exhausting the rich history of its development.[13] The experts associate this term with education and educational literature because it is intended to be

---

9   See Leder, Stefan, ed. (1998) "Story-telling in the framework of non-fictional Arabic literature."
10 Khoury, R.G. (1998) "Geschichte oder Fiktion. Zur erzählerischen Gattung der ältesten Bücher über Arabien," in: Leder (1998), pp. 370-387.
11 Blachère, Régis (1952) "Histoire de la littérature arabe," I: 86 pp., 117 pp.
12 These include terms such as: *Adab, Tahdhīb, Tathqīf, Thaqāfa* etc., which are briefly presented above.
13 See EI^2, I, pp. 175.

used in the creation of literature that is defined in this way, thus primarily spirit and character, so that this genre best represents the entire Arabian culture. A very distinguished literature emerged around this word which originally also had a special meaning (see below), but was increasingly transferred to what is known as educational literature, which spread as early as the 8th century and was represented by Arabized Persian authors. The most famous of these was ʿAbd Allāh Ibn al-Muqaffaʿ (720-756 AD),[14] the author of the oldest collection of animal fables in Islam, *Kalīla wa-Dimna*. He wrote many books which featured the word *Adab* in their titles: *Al-Adab al-kabīr* ("The Big *Adab* Work"), *al-Adab as-saghīr* ("The Small *Adab* Work"). It was the same Ibn al Muqaffaʿ who addressed a treatise to the caliph of his time in a concealed form, in which presented to the Islamic leader and his followers the norms of truly educated rule and the good behaviour towards the subjects; the treatise was entitled *Risālat fī l-sahāba*[15] ("Treatise on the Companions of the Caliph"). As we can see, this important concept found its point of entry into Arabian-Islamic society through the mediation of the non-Arabs who came to Arabia and whose role in the area of the education of the Islamic authorities was truly considerable. The initiated path was significantly extended and systematically classified in the 3rd/9th century.

Tāhā Husayn (1889-1973), the Egyptian scholar and most renowned critic of modern Arabic literature referred to the history of the development of this concept for the first time in the modern era in one of his first books, *Fī l adab al djāhilī* (On Pre-Islamic Literature),[16] before analysing the purely philological categories of thought.[17] He repeatedly examines the history of this term in a way that is not possible to demonstrate here.

After Ibn al-Muqaffaʿ, the concept of *adab* became a key one, in particular in the general education of Islamic scholars as demonstrated in detail by the authors of the 3rd/9th century, such as al-Djāhiā (777-869) and Ibn Qutayba (828-889), who also professed their commitment to a humanist education which became a matter of course in the Islamic Middle Ages. Thus, as he too adopted this credo, the aforementioned T. Husayn could state that: *Al-adabu huwa l-akhdhu min kulli shayʾin bi-tarafin*[18] ("Literature consists in taking something from every corner [of a discipline]"). *Felix Arabia!* Nowadays, the term is used to define the literature but retains however its meaning of 'education,' 'good manners' etc. in the everyday life of the Arabs.

2. A second concept soon emerged: to the present day, *Thaqāfa* is the techni-

---

14 See EI², III, p. 883 ff.
15 Kurd ʿAlī, M. (ed. 1913, 3. 1946 edition); also in the author's collected works, Abū l-Nasr, ʿUmar (published in 1966); French translation with commentary and detailed glossary by Charles Pellat (1976).
16 Husayn, Tāhā (1968) *Fī l-adab al-djāhilī* Kairo.
17 Loc. cit., p. 37 ff.
18 Loc. cit., p. 19, 16.

cal term for culture in the Arabian world. However, this word also developed from a purely material meaning, i.e. from the verb *thaqafa/thaqqafa*, to smooth or polish stones etc. Reference can be made here again to the ancient Arabian and early Islamic worlds, in which proper names with professional connotations or similar were derived from this verbal stem, as demonstrated in many instances by names of individuals from the early Islamic period.

3. *A third concept* with the same original meaning as *Thaqāfa* is *Tahdhīb* from *hadhdhaba*, i.e. smooth, polish etc. (initially stones and material substances like the previous verb); it was soon used as a basis for major works on the refinement of character, i.e. about education. The most famous of these is the work of the philosopher and historian Miskawayh (932-1030 AD): *Tahdhīb al-akhlāq* (i.e. "Education or the Education of Characters").[19]

4. Another term is *Hadāra*, used by the greatest historian of Islam, Ibn Khaldūn (1332-1406)[20] in the sense of civilization, i.e. *hadara*, to be present or settled, hence in the meaning of an urban way of life and all that is associated with it in contrast to Bedouinism. Also *Madaniyya* or *Tamaddun* are used in the same sense and express precisely the same view of urban life and lifestyle, but are derived from the term *Madīna* or town which is of Aramaic origin. Both terms refer in different ways to the way of life that emerges in the town, the exposure to urban concentration; however, whereas the former refers to the concentration itself, i.e. the agglomeration, the second refers to the commitment to a ruler (also religious leader as *Diyāna*, i.e. religious devotion, means religion itself, as is the case for the other word *Dīn* for this last term).

Nowadays, *Hadāra* and *Thaqāfa* are almost identical, the first refers more frequently to historical-cultural representation in association with the past, whereas the second, *Thaqāfa*, best corresponds to our contemporary requirements. Given that I repeatedly refer here to earlier periods in Islamic culture, I will keep this last term in mind, but also intend the visions these earlier periods had in association with the term culture, even if these terms appear to differ to us today. In particular as the term culture, which is derived from the Latin *colere/cultum* in the sense of to build on, reside in, maintain, actually leads more in the direction of the aforementioned historian, Ibn Khaldūn, who refers to *'umrān*, i.e. of residing, building on and hence of civilization in urban life. We can see that behind all of these common terms with their various nuances, one common

---

19 Arkoun, Mohamed (1982) "L'Humanisme arabe au IXe/Xe siècle. Miskawayh, philosophe et historien." The full title of the work analyzed by Arkoun is: *Tahdhīb al-akhlāq wa-tathīr al-a'rāq*, see pp. 115, in which the first part refers to the "die Kunstfertigkeit der Bildung der Charaktere" (*sinā'at tahdīb al-akhlāq*), an expression from the ethical literature, according to Arkoun, which was very common. Yahyā Ibn 'Adī is supposed to have already used this title, see *Rasā'il al-bulaghā'*, ed. Kurd 'Alī; Arkoun, 115, note 3.

20 See EI², III, p. 825 ff.

link is important: i.e. the concept of building, processing, cultivating. The path from here to the dominating social and political systems is an easy one.

This was vocabulary which provided a basis for the development of the classical literature of Islam, however in the case of the story-telling tradition, an older vocabulary existed which was associated with story-telling, reporting etc., e.g. *Khabar* (pl. *Akhbār*) (report), *Qissa* (pl. *Qisas*), *Hadīth* (history, story) – and derived from these: the participle form *Qāss* (pl. *Qussās*) (storyteller) and *Muhaddith* (narrator, traditionary, story-teller). The first two of these terms are found in the oldest books about Yemen in pre-Islamic times and assume a special place in this context, as nothing original has come down to us from the old Arabian literature apart from the poetry and a few fragments, which in their original form cannot be of prime significance for the entire literary production of the generation of early Islamic scholars. The works in question are:

1. *Kitāb al-Tīdjān* by Ibn Hishām, author of the official Sīra of the Prophet Muhammad[21]

2. *Akhbār 'Abīd (or) 'Ubayd Ibn Sharya al-Djurhumī al-Yamanī*.[22]

The book by Ibn Hishām would be unimaginable without the main source, which was provided to him by a small document on the same topic by Wahb Ibn Munabbih: *Kitāb al-Mulūk al-mutawwadja min Himyar wa-akhbārihim wa-qisasihim wa-qubūrihim wa-ash'ārihim* ("Book of the Crowned Kings of Himyar, their Histories and Stories and their Tombs and Poems").[23] In the transmission of Asad Ibn Mūsā (132-212/750-827) this book was adopted and expanded from the aforementioned version after a grandson of Ibn Munabbih.[24]

The work of Ibn Sharya is particularly interesting and enables many observations concerning not only the book itself, but also the person of the narrator and the monarch who features in it, i.e. Mu'āwiya, the founder of the Umayyad Dynasty. The fact that the title betrays certain external similarities with the work by Ibn Munabbih, which was based on Ibn Hishām's "*Kitāb al-Tīdjān*" should not

---

21 The oldest surviving parts of the Sīra or Maghāzī (both names were interchangeable) go back to Ibn Munabbih and are found on a few papyrus sheets as is the case with most documents from the first century of Islam/7th century AD; on this, see Khoury, R.G. (1972) "Wahb B. Munabbih," Arabic text. Based on this old version on papyrus, it would appear that the later versions increased significantly in terms of scope; the first of these which had an official character is that of Ibn Hishām (8th to early 9th century), the main parts of which were recently translated into French by Wahib Atallah: "Ibn Hichâm. La biographie du prophète Mahomet. Texte traduit et annoté par Wahib Atallah." Paris, Fayard 2004.

22 *Kitāb al-Tīdjān fī mulūk himyar* and *Akhbār 'Ubayd (or 'Abīd) Ibn Sharya al-Djurhumī fī akhbār al-Yaman wa-ash'ārihā wa-ansābihā* first appeared together in Haidarabad in 1347/1928; new edition, San'ā` 1978, with a foreword and notes by 'Abd al-'Azīz al-Maqālih, professor at the University of Haidarabad also author, poet (and politician for some years now).

23 See Khoury, R.G. (1972) "Wahb B. Munabbih," p. 286 ff.

24 On Asad, see Khoury, R.G. (1976) "Asad B. Mūsā," *Kitāb az-Zuhd*.

be dismissed out of hand; however there are some fundamental differences which concern, in particular, the content and structure of the work. Ibn Hishām's text is longer and more biblical in its roots; in other words, unlike 'Ubayd Ibn Sharya, as the author of Biblical history in Islam, Wahb Ibn Munabbih, the author of the core material, is concerned with highlighting the close relations between Yemen and the Biblical world so as to present them to the northern Arabians. Firstly, Wahb's pride in his homeland and the Himyarites expressed in a different way than in the work of his compatriot Ibn Sharya. Thus, the motive for the writing of his work appears to lie less in the quest for the wonderful, which may nonetheless have had a role to play in the endeavour, than in the pride of the Himyarites of whom he was one through his mother, and also on behalf of the pious Muslim to portray the people mentioned in the Qur'an and above all to associate them with the history of the Biblical prophets and to refer to their particular place in the proximity of Allah. The Himyarites are compared with *al-sirādj al-mudī` fī l-laylati l-zalmā`* ("shining lamp in the dark nights"); God defends them against and elevates them above man.[25]

Overall, the Qur'an plays a key role for Wahb because it represented an ultimate objective with a unique value. Although both wanted to be a *Muhaddith*, of the two, in his reports and commentaries in the sense of the traditional Islamic *Hadīth*, Ibn Sharya was less religious in nature; thus, F. Krenkow was unable to find his name among the *Hadīth* transmitters.[26] In terms of the knowledge required of him at Mu'āwiya's court, 'Ubayd did not need any profound knowledge of the Islamic tradition and the Qur'an quotes peppered throughout his *Akhbār* had more to do with added zest than real substance. This explains the enormous difference between the beginnings of the two texts: Wahb's text starts with holy writs which are associated with individual Biblical personalities, from Adam to the Prophet of Islam. As opposed to this, Ibn Sharya's *Akhbār* are introduced with the history of the summoning of the story-teller by the caliph on the suggestion of 'Amr Ibn al-'As (died 43/663, or 42/662),[27] with a unique description of the powers of the ruler, his habits and the nocturnal stories taking place, about which more will be said below. Of course, both authors remain very Yemeni in their love of their homeland and the pride they take in it, but in completely different ways. These differences are historically and culturally informative; the start of Ibn Sharya's text provides astonishing information about the education and erudition of these early times, thus I will now discuss it briefly.

After the introductory *Basmala* and *Hamdala*, the narrator, who is called al-Barqī, takes over the *Hadīth*, which he quotes based on 'Ubayd Ibn Sharya. We

---

25 Ibn Hishām (1978) "*Kitāb al-Tīdjān,*" p. 64.
26 Krenkow, F. (1928) "The Two Oldest Books on Arabic Folklore." In: Islamic Culture 2, p. 55 ff., 204 ff.
27 On this, see Khoury, R.G. (1986) "'Abd Allāh Ibn Lahī'a," p. 91-93.

shall see that the word *Hadīth* has no religious meaning here in the sense of the Islamic tradition, but that of the traditional, old-Arabian and early Islamic (and later) narration, the *Qissa*, which emerged later, in particular in association with the Biblical story or *Qisas al-anbiyā`*. It is evidenced for the first time in the title of the book *Kitāb Bad` al-khalq wa-qisas al-anbiyā`* by 'Umāra Ibn Wathīma Ibn Mūsā Ibn al-Furāt al-Fārisī (died 289/902) which this son transmitted after his father Wathīma (died 237/851).[28] The use of the word *Hadīth* in 'Ubayd's book should be noted here. It could be assumed that this is a normal experience of *Hadīth* transmission; it undoubtedly involves *Akhbār*, i.e. reports, which are not religious in nature, but more secular, pagan and simply old-Arabian, thus the word *Hadīth* should be understood here in the sense of *Qissa*. Another, older – actually the oldest known example – of the same word in the sense of *Qissa* is the heading of the story of David, the oldest known one in Islam which is found in the Heidelberg papyrus of Wahb Ibn Munabbih and literally states: *Bismi (A)llāhi l-Rahmāni l-Rahīmi. Hadīthu Dāwūda* ("In the name of the Compassionate and Good God. The Story of David").[29]

I believe that I have demonstrated clearly enough that this version of the papyrus is based on a much older original papyrus, which definitely originated in the $2^{nd}/8^{th}$ century (the second half of this century at the latest) in association with the version of the above-mentioned father Wathīma al-Fārisī.[30] Concretely, this means that the two texts were recorded in written form in an epoch when the word *Hadīth* was used to refer to all kinds of narratives and also in the sense of the secular *Khabar*, i.e. report, or profane *Qissa*, i.e. story. This is no longer the case with the oldest collection of Biblical stories by Wathīma and his 'Umāra after him: the reason for this is simple, as with the second half of the $2^{nd}/8^{th}$ century material that was previously handed down orally was increasingly recorded in written form as highlighted by al-Dhahabī[31] and some Islamic historians after

---

28 S. Khoury, R.G. (1978) "Les légendes prophétiques dans l'Islam depuis le Ier jusqu'au IIIe siècle de l'Hégrie…"
29 Khoury, R.G. (1972) "Wahb B. Munabbih, Geschichte Davids," p. 34, line 2.
30 Khoury, R.G. (1978) "Les légendes prophétiques dans l'Islam," p. 158 ff., in particular p. 163-165; ibid. (1986) "'Abd Allāh Ibn Lahī'a (97-174/715-790). Juge et grand maître de l'Ecole Egyptienne," p. 27 ff.
31 Khoury, R.G. (1986) "'Abd Allāh Ibn Lahī'a," p. 26 ff., 31 f., where this passage of the Dhahabī is analysed; idem, (1994) "L'apport de la papyrologie dans la transmission et codification des premières versions des Mille et Une Nuits," p. 21-33; idem (1993) "Kalif, Geschichte und Dichtung: Der jemenitische Erzähler 'Abīd Ibn Šarya am Hofe Mu'āwiyas," p. 204-218; idem (1997) "Les grands centres de conservation et de transmission des manuscrits arabes aux premier et deuxième siècles de l'Hégire," p. 215-226; idem (1998) "Geschichte oder Fiktion. Zur erzählerischen Gattung der ältesten Bücher über Arabien," p. 370-387; idem (2000) "Die Erzähltradition im Islam, Islam – eine andere Welt?" p. 23-40; idem (2004) "L'apport spécialement important de la papyrologie dans la transmission et la codification des plus anciennes versions des *Mille et Une Nuits* et d'autres livres des deux premiers

him. Thus, taking the new situation described by al-Dhahabī and others into account, these authors no longer use the term *Hadīth* as the title of their joint work: a systematic transition and above all codification of an increasingly wider science automatically required a more specific terminology for many genres, whose names had become too general and undifferentiated in an empire which had grown in size and in which writing had become a necessary instrument of societal intercourse, which al-Qalqashandī aptly and succinctly characterizes as follows: *Al-kitābatau ussu l-mulki wa-'imādu l-mamlakati*[32] ("Writing is the foundation stone of government and the mainstay of the empire").

Hence the need for specialization and structure based on areas and genres, to which al-Dhahabī's texts refers. Therefore everything which is still titled and formulated like the aforementioned papyruses is older than the version of the book by 'Umāra and his father Wathīma and must originate from the time of the Heidelberg papyruses, which more or less originate from the collection of the Egyptian judge 'Abd Allāh Ibn Lahī'a (97-174/715-790). It must not be forgotten that the latter collected many originals and copies of originals in his unique private library and used to make them available to Egyptian students and guests and to all of the transmitters of the Heidelberg papyruses and, of course, to the aforementioned Wathīma, whose text transmitters, to whom his son refers, were Egyptians and students of the same Egyptian judge, Ibn Lahī'a. This Wathīma adopted from the direct students of the judge in Fustāt (old Cairo) the material for his histories of the prophets but had to take into account the new scientific development, the systematic reception and written recording of the scientific texts.[33]

Let us now return to the text by 'Ubayd Ibn Sharya. In accordance with the above-quoted formula, the report opens with precise information on the years of government of Caliph Mu'āwiya: ten years as "emir" under each of the three last orthodox Caliphs 'Umar and 'Uthmān – 'Alī is not mentioned by name – and then twenty further years as *Amīr al-mu`minīn* ("Prince of the Faithful"). What is interesting is that his authority and some of his habits and innovations are described in this way:

His authority was significant as *wa-dānat lahu l-mashāriqu wa-l-maghāribu* ("the east and the west were under his rule "). For this, he had "reached the high

---

siècles islamiques," p. 70 ff. Also Al-Djābirī, M. (1984) "*Takwīn al-'aql al-'arabī*," p. 61 ff., this book was not available to me at the time; I was only familiar with the opinion of al-Djābirī through the criticism made of him by Tarābīshī, Georges (1998) "*Ishkāliyyāt al-aql al-'arabī*," 11 ff.

32 On this, see al-Qalqashandī "*Subh al-a'shā*," I, 37, 11; see also this entire page on which the author presents everything that was said about the importance of writing.

33 On this, see Khoury, R.G. (1997) "L'importance des plus vieux manuscrits arabes historiques sur papyrus, conservés à Heidelberg, pour l'histoire de la langue arabe et de la culture des premiers siècles islamiques," p. 11-18.

honour of kingship ... was the first to become king (in Islam), claimed a ruler's lodge and leaned on his head when he prostrated himself in prayer and collected the monies."[34] This is a noteworthy passage which earns attention in the reference works on the period of government of the caliph due to the age of the text, as reference is often made to al-Dhahabī, who quotes Muʿāwiya's famous comment: *Anā awwalu malikin (fī- l-Islāmi)* ("I am the first King of Islam").[35]

Only after this does the narrator lead us to one of the greatest joys of the aged ruler which revives a typical old-Arabian tradition, lends it a unique dimension and is represented as follows:

Wa-kānat afdala ladhdhātihi fī ākhiri ʿumrihi al-musāmaratu wa-ahādīthu man madā ("His preferred delight at the end of his life was the nocturnal conversations and tales of early people ").[36] This clearly demonstrates the personal interest of the Umayyads – starting with their founder – for history, tradition and, of course, for the hence indispensable poetry, as can be observed below.[37]

It is relatively easy to establish the period in the life of Muʿāwiya, in which these nights, which in their general scope function as forerunners of the Tales from 1001 Nights, occurred with ʿUbayd as court story-teller: the reference to Muʿāwiya's ally, ʿAmr Ibn al-ʿĀs, which always occurs when a caliph to be paid tribute to is mentioned,[38] is helpful here, as this conqueror of Egypt remained loyal to Muʿāwiya to the end. And, thus, he speaks in Ibn Sharya's book after all the aforementioned information about Muʿāwiya had already been stated, to give the latter advice to select this Yemeni for this task at the court in Damascus. The narrator is referred to as follows here: *Min baqāya man madā fa-innahu adraka mulūka l-Djāhiliyyati wa-huwa aʿlamu man baqiya l-yauma fī ahādīthi l-ʿArabi wa-ansābihā, wa-ausāfuhu li-mā marra ʿalayhi min tasārīfi l-dahri*[39] ("[He is] of the people left over from before, as he experienced the kings of the old Arabian era and is the most experienced of those who remain in the stories of the Arabs and their genealogies, the most capable in representing the ups and downs of fate that befell him").

This description was suitable to satisfy the wish of the caliph, particularly as it originated from his particularly close emir. ʿAmr was not only the conqueror of

---

34 ʿUbayd Ibn Sharya (1347/928, n. Ed. 1978) "*Akhbār*," p. 312, 4 ff.
35 See, for example, EI², VII, p. 263 , 2 ff., and other authors who often quote a statement by al-Dhahabī (1986) "*Siyar aʿlām al-nubalāʾ*," III, p. 119 ff., 131 and, above all, 157 where he says: "*anā awwalu l-mulūki*" etc.
36 ʿUbayd Ibn Sharya (1978) "*Akhbār*," 312, 7-8.
37 See also, what Abbott, Nabia (1957) periovulsy highlighted on these characteristics, "Studies in Arabic Literary Papyri, I, Historical Texts," p. 14 ff.
38 See, for example, Abbott, Nabia (1972) "Studies Studies in Arabic Literary Papyri, III. Language and Literature." Document 3: "A Speech of ʿAmr Ibn al-ʿĀs and Description of the Ideal Maiden," p. 43-78, the Arabic text is eleven lines long.
39 ʿUbayd Ibn Sharya (1347/1928, n. Ed. 1978) "*Akhbār*," p. 312, 8-10.

Egypt, but also its first governor; he was deposed by 'Uthmān[40] because he wanted to rule all of Egypt against the will of this caliph, but was then reconfirmed in this role for his lifetime by Mu'āwiya. However, he died in 63/663 or a year earlier.[41] However, if 'Amr turned to Mu'āwiya in connection with the advice about the story-teller, it must have been between 660, the date of the seizure of power by the ruler, and 663, the year of the death of Ibn al-'Āṣ; in the text, the caliph speaks with 'Ubayd in the presence of the 'Amr, thus, this account must be taken seriously.[42] The text does not report of any kind of hesitancy on the part of the caliph as he sent for the Yemeni story-teller immediately and expressed "a great longing" (*shiddat shauq*), to meet him at his house having had him brought to him "in a sedan" (*fī mahmalin*) and "after (a journey) of many days" (*ba'da ayyāmin kathīratin*); these references are intended to convey the sense of a particular honour and the length of the journey involved.[43] The external framework comes with the description of the person of the guest at the end: *Fa-dakhala 'alayhi shaykhun kabīru l-sinni sahīhu l-badani thābitu l-'aqli muntabihun dharibu l-lisāni ka-annahu l-djada'u*[44] ("A venerable old man came to him with a healthy body and confident mind, observant and with a sharp tongue as though he were a younger man").

In summary, what we have here is a very old man who is counted among the long-lived (*al-mu'ammarūn*) by al-Sidjistānī (died 250/864) and about whose longevity fabulous information is provided.[45] To the question of Mu'āwiya regarding the advanced age which the narrator puts at 150 years, the Caliph replies: *Fa-qāla la-hu Mu'āwiya wa-mā adrakta qāla adraktu yauman fī athari yaumin wa-laylatan fī athari laylatin* ("What have you experienced; and he answered: I have lived day by day and night by night"). A series of wise observations and sayings follow further questions which he linked with a few verses about a burial which he described as a strange experience. Yāqūt ends his study on 'Ubayd here with the information of the index of books (*Fihrist*) by Ibn al-Nadīm, who provided more or less the same account of this encounter with the caliph, although we also learn from him that the author of the *Akhbār* lived up to the days of the Umayyads – Caliph 'Abd al-Malik Ibn Marwān (685-705) – and

---

40 On Caliph 'Uthmān, see my article in: EI² (2000: pp. 946-949), which takes all of the circumstances of his period of rule into account in the light of Ibn Lahī'a's Heidelberg papyrus.
41 On this point, see Khoury, R.G. (1986) "'Abd Allāh Ibn Lahī'a," p. 91-93.
42 'Ubayd Ibn Sharya (1978) "*Akhbār*," p. 313, 11.
43 Loc. cit., p. 313, 11-12.
44 Loc. cit., p. 312-313.
45 al-Sidjistānī, Sahl Ibn Muhammad Ibn 'Uthmān Abū Hātim "*Kitāb al-Mu'ammarīn*," p. 40-43.

left two books behind: *Kitāb al-Amthāl* ("Book of Proverbs") and *Kitāb al-Mulūk wa-akhbār al-mādīn* ("Book about the Kings and Reports of the Early Ones").[46]

Of course, 'Ubayd's account of the text is more detailed, the later information however acts as another guarantee of the age of such information.

What the caliph expected from his guest in terms of a programme is simple and clearly formulated in one sentence: *Innī aradtu ttikhādhaka mu`addiban lī wa-samīran wa-muqawwiman. Wa-anā bā'ithun ilā ahlika wa-anquluhum ilā djiwārī wa-kun lī samīran fī laylī wa-wazīran fī amrī.*[47] ("I wanted you as a story-teller for me, as a nocturnal story-teller and advisor. And I will send for your family and bring them to me. Be an evening story-teller for me in my nights and a vizier in my affairs").

Together with the other sources quoted, this reference demonstrates the extent of Mu'āwiya's interest in education, the word *Mu`addib* is used in the text, which he associates with pleasant conversation; we can see here how old the aforementioned concept of *Adab* is, which entered common usage with Ibn al-Muqaffa' in the Islamic culture of the $2^{nd}/8^{th}$ century.[48] The caliph makes no secret of the fact that the presence of the story-teller in his surroundings gives him great joy which is expressed not least by the warm reception the guest receives at his court:

Fa-anzalahu fī qurbihi wa-akhdamahū ... wa-wassa'u 'alayhi wa altafahu fa-idhā kāna dhālika fī waqti l-samari fahwa samīruhu fī khāssatihi min ahli baytihi.[49]
("And he had him accommodated and looked after near to him ... and he was generous and friendly to him – as soon as the time for nocturnal conversation came, ['Ubayd] was his nocturnal conversation partner in his private circle among the people of his house").

From then on the caliph's relationship with the story-teller assumed different dimensions which are no longer purely historical in nature, but also cultural as the nocturnal conversations and the poetry closely associated with them predominated. Thus it is appropriate to analyse the other events in this book from this perspective. The same applies for the *Kitāb al-Tīdjān*, whose content is far more religious and biblical in nature. Thus, all of these questions regarding the content will now be examined from the perspective of wisdom and spirituality.

---

46 Yāqūt, (1928) *Irshād*, V, p. 12 (the report on the story-teller is on pages 10 to 13 with some small additions); the author follows here the information provided in Ibn al-Nadīm's *Fihrist*, ed. by Fluegel, p. 89-90.
47 'Ubayd Ibn Sharya (1978) "*Akhbār,*" 313, 1-3.
48 On this point, see above on *Adab* and the author referred to there.
49 'Ubayd Ibn Sharya (1978) "*Akhbār,*" p. 313, 5-7.

II. The wisdom and spirituality of abiblical and prophetic yemeni tales in Early Islam

Such books represent a summary of the experience of earlier peoples who should all be considered in the context of the Semitic tradition of wisdom, a tradition which reached its apotheosis in the biblical world in particular in such religious stories of the pious, virtuous and heroes of their nations. Thus the stories about the Prophet belong to the above-described stories which were widely disseminated in Islam from an early stage and provided Qur'an commentaries on the varied figures, as stories and explanations. Some typically Arabian figures which enjoyed great adulation in Arabia prior to Mohammed, were assimilated into the Judaeo-Christian repertoire; one example of this can be found in the above-mentioned Heidelberg Arabian papyrus on the Story of David while another represents the life of the founder of the religion which for reasons of adulation was not dealt with in these actual collections but separately under *Sīra* (path through life, life story) or *Maghāzī* (campaigns) (which more or less represents the same thing).[50] All of the book collections referred to want ultimately to report on the past which was a shared biblical asset and which there was a desire to closely correlate with the Arabian past. We can see how important an author was who dealt with all of these text types and correlated the old Arabian, i.e. Yemeni, biblical and Islamic past, initially in orally transmitted versions which were transferred to written form gradually, but at an early stage. The case of the library of the above-mentioned Egyptian judge and what remains to be said about Ibn Sharya's book confirms all of these views.

To re-enact this step by step, I shall start with Ibn Hishām's book, *Kitāb al-Tīdjān*, whose content is primarily traced back to Wahb Ibn Munabbih.[51] Wahb opens die speech by specifying the number of books he had read and which he distributed among eleven prophets, starting with Adam and ending with the Prophet of Islam. In the meantime, it may be assumed that an Arabic bible was known in early Islam – even if its parts were not equally disseminated or only some of them which quote Islamic authors – as was also the Thora and some passages from the gospels. This availability cannot be disputed after detailed consideration of the information which goes back to the transmitters of the first hour. These transmitters are the main authorities, to whom Ibn Munabbih refers and whose material was recorded in writing in the circle of this family and in Egypt:

---

50 On the publication of both texts, see Khoury, R.G. (1972) "Wahb Ibn Munabbih,"I, p. 33 ff., 117 ff.; on all other figures, see, for example, Khoury, R.G. (1978) "Les légendes prophétiques dans l'Islam" (in Arabic).

51 At the beginning of the text, this author is almost the only authority, to whom Ibn Hishām refers, sometimes several times on individual pages; the frequency of these references decreases after the first third of the book; on this point, see. loc. cit., p. 2 ff.

Ka'b al-Aḥbār (died 32/632 or 34/654) and 'Abd Allāh Ibn Salām (died 43/663).[52] Wahb, who unlike the other two was not a convert from Judaism to Islam (he was born a Muslim), but was mistakenly viewed as such by Ibn al-Nadīm and also by Ibn Khaldūn after him, used their experience and tradition and expanded them to become the main source of biblical stories in Islam for subsequent generations up to Ibn Qutayba (828-889).[53] One of my doctoral students presented a detailed doctoral thesis on this author and the bible which corroborates the extreme significance of the Old and New Testaments for the Islamic generations.[54] Thus, it is not surprising to find in this classical author's work priority being given to Ibn Munabbih, who is credited with having most experience with biblical material in the numerous quotes and not only in his prophetic and Israeli stories,[55] but also because he is also credited with the translation of part of the bible: *Kitāb Zabūr Dāwūd* (the Psalms of David) which confirms his reputation as a guarantee of the biblical wisdom and spirituality. This must finally be taken into account so that this early Islamic material, which was later considered as purely Islamic without any mention of sources and – even worse – contested, is taken seriously not only in the East but also here in the West.

It should not come as a shock to establish on closer examination of this material that the treatment of these biblical sources did not (always) correspond to the norms of systematic transmission as more or less literal quotes were replaced by quotes that were looser and more Islamic in form.[56] Thus, Wahb became the model for the subsequent generations, but also *persona non grata* for many historians, including Ibn Khaldūn (1332-1406), who viewed him as *djuhhāl al-mu'arrikhīn* ("one of the ignorant historians"): this Islamic historian speaks of the Muslims of the Israelites (*Muslimat Banī Isrā'īl*) and cites the two aforementioned and Wahb by name in connection with the Qur'an commentaries; in these commentaries he highlights the fact that *there are things which were transmitted after then*, of which some elements should be retained and others discarded. He explains this with reference to the ignorance of the Arabians on these parts of old biblical history, on the one hand, and the presence – among the early Islamic scholars – of Jews (and Christians), on the other, who knew more about it and were therefore repeatedly called on. His openness in this regard is startling be-

---

52 On Ka'b, see F. Sezgin (1967) "Geschichte des arabischen Schrifttums,"I, p. 304 f.; EI², IV, p. 316 f.; on Ibn Salām, see F. Sezgin, loc. cit., p. 304; EI², I, p. 52.
53 On this author, see EI², III, p. 844-847 (Gérard Lecomte), idem (1965) "Ibn Qutayba. L'homme et l'œuvre."
54 Karoui, Said (1998) "Die Rezeption der Bibel im Werke des Ibn Qutayba," Heidelberg/Tunis.
55 On this point, see Khoury, R.G. (1972) "Wahb B. Munabbih," pp. 222-240, 246, 257.
56 On this point, see Khoury, R.G. (1989) "Quelques réflexions sur la première ou les premières Bibles arabes," p. 549-561. And Karoui, Said (1998) (see bibliography) with further bibliographical references.

cause he explains this circumstance as follows: *the Arabians had no books and no science, the character of the nomad and illiterate dominated among them;*[57] for this reason people turned to the people of the writings (Jews and Christians) on all questions regarding Creation and the secrets of existence. However, these scholars who were well-versed in the bible were also residents of the desert: all they knew about these questions was what was widely known in their milieu which was far removed from the major scholarly centres of their faiths. When they converted to Islam, most of these scholars who originated from Yemen did not give up their religious and cultural tradition and continued to explain it to the Islamic scholars, however in their own way. Thus numerous accounts of Creation and the stories or histories of the Prophets were adopted and can now be found not only in purely historical works, but also in the early Qur'anic commentaries; al-Tabarī's Qu'ran commentary is full of them and, to the delight of interested researchers, often accompanied by *Isnād*. These unique collections of reports from the first centuries of Islam are so valuable that they should be classified and analysed in greater detail.[58] Thus the true motives for the availability of this Judaeo-Christian literature in this form were ignorance, on the one hand, and more knowledge and respect, on the other. These are surely also the reasons why certain parts of the bible and biblical stories were more widely disseminated in the desert (Thora, Psalms, Gospel of St Matthew etc.), while others were hardly known or completely unknown.

It should not be forgotten here that, in such an environment, change did not always only originate from the desire to please the rulers under the religious and political imperatives of apologism; to this was also added simple uncertainty because people had blind trust in scholars in these early intellectually underdeveloped environments. The role of the scholars was almost equivalent to that of the poets and oracle men of old Arabia who had to provide answers for everything, irrespective of whether they had understood it (correctly) or not. This mentality can still be observed today in certain areas. Based on this, it is possible to imagine just how much was ascribed to such a scholar who, in the person of Wahb, represented a major cosmopolitan personality for his epoch and the first generations of Islam. Not only did this Yemeni-Islamic dimension, which was very closely associated with the biblical tradition, live on in him, but also something of his Persian past, as his grandfather had come to Yemen in 570 AD with the conquering Persian army. Thus, he belonged to the *Abnā`*, a name given to the

---

57 On Ibn Khaldūn's views of this *Muslimat Banī Isrā`īl* (the Islamic scholars of the sons of Israel), see Khoury, R.G. (1987) "Ibn Khaldūn et quelques savants des deux premiers siècles islamiques," p. 192-204.

58 Al-Tabarī took them very seriously, just like Ibn Qutayba who was one of his most important sources in this area. See Khoury, R.G. (1972) "Wahb B. Munabbih;" on al-Tabarī and his commentary, see Gilliot, Claude (1990) "Exégèse, langue et théologie en Islam. L'exégèse coranique de Tabarî ."

Persians and their descendants, who settled in Yemen after its conquest by the Sassanid rulers.[59] As a result his work is all the more interesting as it betrays a Persian character which includes the experience of this ancient people who are repeatedly referred to in connection with the work of Ibn Munabbih. Thus, it is possible to establish that concepts like education and wisdom permeate the two above-analysed works on Yemen: in Ibn Sharya's book, the desire for political education is clearly perceptible and in the case of Wahb, in Ibn Hishām's book, the focus is on the area of wisdom and its proverbs which cannot always be dissociated from the general biblical tradition.

Seen in this light, Ibn Munabbih emerges as a scholar to whom early Islamic history has much to thank for key stimuli which lend it its world-history dimensions:

First, the old-Arabian history, that of the Yemenis, from the beginning of their existence to the end of the Himyarite dynasty, which *Kitāb al-Tīdjān* preserved on several occasions. To reinforce this in religious terms, the history of the Prophets was added, and this is clearly demonstrated not only the Story of David on papyrus but also the most important elements of the collection of Wathīma and his son 'Umāra in *Bad` al-khalq wa-qisas al-anbiyā`*.

To this old pre-Islamic and biblical-Islamic past is added a purely Islamic one, i.e. the focus on the life of the Islamic prophet Mohammed to whom Ibn Munabbih devoted the oldest surviving *Maghāzī*, a title which was interchangeable with the *Sīra*. Whereas in *Kitāb al-Mulūk al-mutawwadja* ... , which provided the basis for Ibn Hishām's book and aimed to provide indisputable proof of the link between the old-Arabian and Yemeni history and biblical history, the *Maghāzī* crown these efforts with an Islamic high, i.e. the seal of the biblical tradition. However, this is not all that we know about Wahb as there is even mention of a book of his about the first caliph *Tārīkh al-khulafā`* or *Futūh*, whose traces are not as clear, however, as clear as the previously mentioned works. It is surprising, that it was he and not Ibn Ishāq, his student and teacher of Ibn Hishām, who was responsible for the extension of the historical dimensions by converting the purely Arabian and Islamic perspectives into a worldly one.

Thus his services were immense in terms linking Islamic history, with respect to its spirituality, with the oriental and, above all, biblical past, a tradition which became even stronger after him and gained ground in the ascetic and mystical spirituality in Islam. Several books ascribed to him and numerous statements and paragraphs which are closely associated with them can be cited here. The titles are:

Hikmat Wahb (The Wisdom of Wahb)
Hikmat Luqmān (The Wisdom of Luqmān)
Mau'iza l-Wahb (A Sermon by Wahb)[60]

---

59 On the *Abnā`*, see EI[2], I, 102; Khoury, R.G. (1972) "Wahb B. Munabbih," p. 9, 189 ff.
60 On the titles of these works, see Khoury, R.G., op. cit, p. 206 f., 263-272.

In addition, the aforementioned titles *Kitāb Zabūr Dāwūd*[61] (Psalms of David), one *Tafsīr Wahb* (Wahb's Qu'ran commentary) and *Kitāb al-Qadar* (Book on Freedom of Will) should not be forgotten here.

He is reputed to have written or transmitted this last work, from which he retrospectively distanced himself, but which probably cost him his life.[62] We know that the Umayyad power ideology was increasingly involved in combating the enemies of its usurpation of power and had to stand up for the associated freedom-based discussions which received particular input from those surrounding freedom of will; for this reason, not only Ghaylān al-Dimashqī (died after 724)[63] but also Wahb had to die in 728 or 732, thus approximately at the same time, the first as Christ on the Cross and the second by corporal punishment in San'ā'. The traditions which were added to these and can be traced back to Ibn Munabbih are fully enveloped in a biblical atmosphere and promote such liberal opinions. These and other moral characteristics of Ibn Munabbih increasingly irritated the tyrannical governor of Yemen, Yūsuf Ibn 'Umar al-Thaqafī (died 745 AD),[64] who was enslaved to the Umayyads, thus he welcomed the death of the scholar.[65]

In this context, it must be stressed that of the early Islamic scholars, Wahb became a particularly important source on wisdom, wise proverbs and spirituality, thus many later authors repeatedly quoted him; thus, it is possible to find sentences like the following: *Fī ba'di l-hikmati* (in a wisdom) and *qara'tu fī l-hikmati* (I read in the wisdom) etc. which can be traced back to one of the abovementioned titles, in particular that on David and on Luqmān. It is not possible to differentiate between *Hikma* and *Mau'iza* in the assembled literature referring to him: the style and content of such statements are largely reminiscent of the genre of publications by Cheikho and Krarup,[66] that is of a common heritage of devotional messages relating to way of life. It appears to be clear that Wahb used all available oral and written sources and disseminated them in an adapted form. In relation to Luqmān, whose legend assumes an honorary position in the oldest surviving collection of historical terms, the book of the above mentioned Wathīma and 'Umāra al-Fārisī,[67] Wahb was one of the most important authorities on all matters concerning spirituality and the Psalms. Based on some statements, it would appear that a *Madjallat Luqmān* (which more or less means *Sahīfa*/leaf)

---

61 Khoury, R.G., op. cit, 258-263.
62 Op. cit., 270-272.
63 On Ghaylān, see van Ess, Josef (1970) "Les Qadarites et la 'ahlāniyya de Yazīd," p. 269-286.
64 He was one of the relatives of the famous Governor of Iraq and Hedja, al-Hadjdjādj Ibn Yūsuf (died 714) who belonged to the same tribe.
65 On the death of Wahb, see Khoury, R.G. (1972) "Wahb B. Munabbih," p. 197-198.
66 On this point, see Cheikho, Louis (1910) "Quelques légendes islamiques apocryphes," p. 33-56; Khoury, R.G. (1972) "Wahb B. Munabbih," p. 266 ff.
67 On this, see Khoury, R.G. (1978) "Les légendes prophétiques dans l'Islam" (in Arabic), p. 180-222.

was circulating at the time of the Prophet Mohammed: Suwayd Ibn Sāmit from the al-Aus tribe, who was viewed as *Kāmil* (a perfect person) and like Wahb was known for the knowledge of the books, is reputed to have said to the Prophet, who had offered him conversion to the new religion, that he had *Madjallat Luqmān*, and read it to him on his request whereupon Mohammed recommended the Qu'ran to him as better.[68] Ibn Qutayba provides further witness in referring to Ibn Munabbih and informing us that this *Madjalla* was in circulation in the 1st/7th century:

Qara`tu fī Hikmatihi nahwan min `asharati ālāfi bābin, lam yasma`i l-nāsu kalāman ahsana minhu thumma nazartu fa-ra`aytu l-nāsa qad adkhalūhu fī kalāmihim wasta`ānū bihi fī khutabihim wa-rasā`ilihim wa-wasalū bihi balāghatahum[69]
("I read in his wisdom around 10,000 chapters, whereby people had never before heard a more beautiful speech; then looked and found that people had introduced them into their speech, had used them to assist them in their addresses and included them in their letters").

This testimony is clear, even without *Isnād*; for al-Tabarī also tells the story of the aforementioned Suwayd, this time with a full *Isnād*. What is interesting about this report is the fact that the *Madjalla* is expressly held as identical with the

Hikma: Fa-qāla lahu Suwayd fa-la`alla lladhī ma`aka mithlu lladhī ma`ī fa-qāla lahu Rasūlu llāhi [...] wa-mā lladhī ma`aka qāla Madjallatu Luqmān ya`nī Hikmata Luqmān[70]
("Suwayd then said to him [the Prophet]: Is what you have like that which I have? God's envoy replied to him: And what have you? He said: the sheet by Luqmān, i.e. The Wisdom of Luqmān").

Wahb' declaration appears to carry weight and highlights the significance of the material which has been put into circulation and is traced back to Luqmān. As southern Arabian, he belongs to the `ād tribe and was honoured as a hero and sage thus the Qur'an dedicated surah 31 to him[71]: without closer description of the person, reference is made in verse 12 of a *Hikma* by him which enabled Allah 'to come to him' and some good advice is mentioned which Luqmān had given to his own son.[72] Based on what has been presented up to now on Wahb in connection with the material ascribed to Luqmān, it is obvious that this *Hikma* is probably the piece introduced into circulation by Wahb which D. Gutas men-

---

68 Abbott, Nabia (1967) "Studies in Arabic Literary Papyri, II, Qur`ānic Commentary and Tradition," p. 5, 12 ff.
69 Ibn Qutayba (1960) *"al-Ma`ārif"* , p. 55, 8 ff.
70 Al-Tabarī, (1879) "Annales = *Tārīkh al-rusul wa-l-mulūk,"* ed. by de Goeje, I, p. 1207, 2 ff.
71 On him, see Enzyklopädie des Islam (1913-38), here EI, III, 39.
72 Qur'an, 31, 12 ff.

tioned in "Classical Arabic Wisdom Literature," in which my book about Wahb Ibn Munabbih is quoted extensively without, however, referring to the numerous pages on Luqmān in the book by Wathīma and his son, which represents the oldest known collection of material.[73]

During and after his time, Wahb Ibn Munabbih was viewed, particularly in Yemeni history, as the "scholar of the world" who is supposed to have read all disclosed and undisclosed writings by his predecessors. He undoubtedly made a far from small contribution to the formation of several wisdoms from the biblical and old-Arabian periods, because the majority of the reports on Prophets and sages of this world go back to him, including, of course, about Luqmān Ibn 'Ād, who succeeded his brother Shaddād Ibn 'Ād on the throne of the Himyarites, in particular the story of the seven vultures with the events that accompanied his age and his death.[74] It was also Ibn Munabbih, who according to the famous Ibn 'Abbās made Luqmān into a Prophet, however not without adding *ghayr mursal* ('not dispatched'): "Islamic history loves to sanctify the pious and wise of the past as prophets," particularly as the Qur'an 'had sanctified Luqmān as the wise proverb poet, thus everything that was held as pious and reasonable could be imputed to him ."[75] Based on this, it may be understood that Wahb did not even hesitate to describe the prayer of his Yemeni prophet in the following way:

Qāla Wahb wa-kāna Luqmān Ibn 'ād yad'ū qabla kulli salātin wa-yaqūlu
Allāhumma yā rabba l-bihāri l-khudr
Wa-l-ardi dhāti l-nabti ba'da l-qatr
As'aluka 'umran fauqa kulli 'umr[76]
("Wahb said: And Luqmān Ibn 'ād used to call God before each prayer and say:
O God, O Lord of the green seas,
And of the earth which has plants after the rain,
I ask you for an age above every age").

Thus – according to Ibn Hishām and Ibn Qutayba – Ibn Munabbih was probably familiar with Luqmān's transmission of the legend. Wahb had already earned the reputation of *Hakīm* (wise man) during his time; thus, why should he not have adopted proverbs and warnings from the *Hukamā'*, who had lived before him – and without indicating his sources as was common in his time. What Wahb did not do, was completed by his successors and subsequent transmitters. However,

---

73 Gutas, D. (1981) "Arabic wisdom literature: nature and scope" p. 50-54, 57-58 (the entire article: p. 50-86); see Khoury, R.G. (1978) "Les légendes prophétiques dans l'Islam" (in Arabic), p. 180-222. My book was published in 1978 thus it could not be used on time.
74 Ibn Hishām, (1978) *Kitāb al-Tīdjān*, p. 69 ff.
75 B. Heller, Luqmān, EI , III, p. 39.
76 Ibn Hishām, (1978) *Kitāb al-Tīdjān*, p. 70, 5 ff.

the quotes that bear Wahb's name always remained within the Qur'anic concept of Luqmān's legend; Ibn Munabbih, the Yemeni, had done everything to completely integrate the pre-Islamic history of his homeland with the biblical tradition: his entire oeuvre prophesies these efforts at every turn and this became very clear, particularly in connection with *Kitāb al-Tīdjān*. His preoccupation with the biblical stories to which the aforementioned story of David belongs, gave him a solid basis on which to establish such cross-connections in a convincing way. The two figures, i.e. the biblical figure of David and the old-Arabian figure of Luqmān, gave him *inter alia* the possibility of discovering a leitmotif in the oriental wisdom and spirituality and to present it to the Islamic and non-Islamic public. Thus, this applies not only for David, but also for Luqmān; in this way he could follow the path taken by the Qur'an, and in this way the ice was broken: "Once Muhammad had sanctified Luqmān as wise proverb poet, everything that was held as pious and reasonable could be imputed to him."[77]

When we examine some places which Ibn Munabbih introduces with Luqmān's name, we gain the impression that they belong to the same literary genre as the quotes supposedly ascribed to David which are usually introduced with the formula *yā Dāwūd* or *fī Hikmati Dāwūd*, in Luqmān with *qāla Luqmān*, or *fī Mau'iāati/fī Hikmati Luqmān*, to make the generally quoted more or less authentic material appear more plausible.

III. Narrative tradition and poetic wisdom in Islam

Unlike the work of Ibn Hishām, we have precise information on the coming into being of the book of 'Ubayd, as it can be traced back to the wish of Caliph Mu'āwiya. The beginning of the book presents us with all of the circumstances that gave rise to Ibn Sharya coming to Damascus as presented above. What is important here is that the habits of the caliph and what gave him particular joy are presented. It is described as follows in the text: *Wa-kānat afdala ladhdhātihi fī ākhiri 'umrihi al-musāmaratu wa-ahādīthu man madā*[78] ("His preferred joy at the end of his life were the conversations and tales of earlier people").

Here we have a very old confirmation of Mu'āwiya's interest in the poetry, genealogy and history (*Ash'ār, Ansāb* and *Akhbār*) of the Arabians which numerous works would later confirm (such as those of al-Djāhiā). 'Amr Ibn al-'ās[79] is supposed to have proposed this very elderly and highly respected story teller who is introduced as follows by the conqueror of Egypt and best ally of the ca-

---

77 B. Heller, Luqmān, EI, III, p. 39.
78 *Ahbār 'Ubayd*, (1347/1928, n. Ed. 1978) , p. 312, 7-8.
79 On 'Amr Ibn al-'Ās, his importance for Islam and Egypt, see Khoury, R.G. (1986) "'Abd Allāh Ibn Lahī'a," p. 91-93.

liph: he is "one of those left over from the early people as he experienced the kings of the old Arabian time and is the most experienced of those left behind today in the tales of the Arabians and their genealogies, the most skilled in the presentation of the ups and downs of fate that have befallen him."[80] No description could have been more suited to satisfying the expectations of the caliph and his joy in the quest for knowledge, particularly as the recommendation came from ʾAmr. From the beginning, the story and joy in listening, which would have been impossible to satisfy through dry reports alone, are intertwined: thus, the imaginary was something that was taken for granted in these times and we therefore rediscover the same traits of the enchantment of the world, without which the religious-cultural dimension would be unimaginable.

Further on we read:

Wa-kāna yuqassiru ʾalayhi laylahu wa-yudhhibu ʾanhu humūmahu wa-ansāhu ʾalā kulli samīrin kāna qablahu wa-lam yakhtur ʾalā bālihi shayʾun qattu illā wadjada ʾindahu fīhi shayʾan wa-farahan wa-marahan[81]
("It was ʿUbayd who shortened the nights for Muʿāwiya, drove away his worries and made him forget (them) more than any other nocturnal entertainer who had been there before; nothing ever came into his mind for which ʿUbayd did not manage to find something and also joy and mirth").

The text contains informative pages which document the caliph's great interest in the material and the history of its written recording. It continues as follows: *Kāna yuhaddithuhu waqāʾiʿa l-ʿarabi wa-ashʿārahā wa-akhbārahā* ("ʿUbayd used to tell the caliph of the events of the Arabians, their poetry and news"). This ends, however, with the order to undertake the written documentation: *Amara ahla dīwānihi wa-kuttābahu an yuwaqqiʿūhu wa-yudawwinūhu*[82] ("Muʿāwiya ordered his Diwān officials to record it and write it down in books"), whereby Ibn al-Nadīm adds: *Wa-yansubūhu ilā ʾUbayd Ibn Sharya*[83] ("and that it should be ascribed to the ʾU. Ibn Sh").

Thus, here we have the entire framework which not only introduces this text but clarifies its historical and cultural dimensions, irrespective of whether this information corresponds to the historical reality fully or only in part. We are also dealing with material here which, like the biblical stories, was under the spell of the past of the higher powers: a historically-based folk literature, without which such a past is unimaginable and which should be carefully considered as a literary memorial.[84] In

---

80 Idem op. cit., p. 312, 8-10.
81 Idem op. cit., p. 313, 7-9.
82 Idem op. cit., p. 313, 9-10.
83 Ibn al-Nadīm (1871) "Fihrist," 90.
84 On the significance of this literature for the research and reconstruction not only of early Islamic but also of Jewish and Christian circumstances, see the extremely im-

each case, in such books by Wahb Ibn Munabbih, Ibn Hishām and Ibn Sharya we have the oldest accounts of old Arabia which came into circulation from the beginning of the Umayyad period, initially orally and were recorded in writing at an early stage, at least in part. Somehow, with his strictly biblically-oriented structure *Kitāb al-Tīdjān* represents a bridge to the content of ʿUbayd's *Akhbār* which is more narrative and substantiates and illustrates vividly the genre of the *Adab* and conversation sessions at the court of the Arabian-Islamic rulers and in addition to this the early interest of the Umayyads, at this point already Muʿāwiya, in education and entertainment. All of this was intended to express the pride of the Himyarites, above all Wahb, who was Himyarite through his mother and wanted to connect the Himyarites with the biblical past.[85] The quest for the wonderful was also a shared objective although the atmosphere of the reporting in Ibn Sharya's work is more Arabian because he constantly draws on the main element of old-Arabian culture, i.e. the poetry. This is almost the main sustaining motif,[86] as it includes almost half of the text and also has a completely different dimension in the narration and representational value of the events: for both the teller and the caliph it is above all proof of the veracity of the statements. Muʿāwiya expresses this constantly by asking ʿUbayd for proof from the poetry as, for example, in the following passages:

Qāla Muʿāwiya: Saʾaltuka a-lā shaddadta hadīthaka bi-baʿdi mā qālū mina l-shiʿri wa-lau thalāthati abyātin[87] ("Muʿāwiya said: I ask you can you not strengthen your story from that which they expressed in poetry, and if only in three verses"). And he asked about other events: *Fa-hal qīla fīhā shʿirun* ("Was something said about poetry"). However, as soon as verses were there, the caliph expressed his satisfaction to him and as a showed this by making such affirmative statements as: *Qulta l-sawāba ... wa-inna kalāmaka tayyibun wa-shifāʾun li-mā fī l-sadri*[88] ("You said the right thing ... your speech is soothing and salvation for what is in the breast"). And elsewhere the caliph says: *sadaqta yā ʿUbayd wa-djiʾta bi-l-burhāni l-wādihi* ("You told the truth, ʿUbayd, and presented clear proof"); *La-qad djiʾta bi-l-burhāni fī hadīthika* ("You have brought the proof for your speech"), *Li-llāhi darruka fa-qad djiʾta bi-l-burhāni*[89] ("How excellent you are, you have brought the proof").

Many other passages demonstrate the caliph's hunger for confirmation of the events described, in particular through poetry. The book contains an often forgotten and misunderstood statement on the role of poetry in the historical representation of the old Arabians; it is put in Muʿāwiya's mouth who says:

---

portant book by Schwarzbaum, Haim (1982) "Biblical and Extra-Biblical Legends in Islamic Folkliterature," Walldorf/Hessen.
85 On this point, see Khoury, R.G. (1972) "Wahb B. Munabbih," p. 287 ff.
86 Khoury, R.G. (1993) "Kalif, Geschichte und Dichtung," p. 217 ff.
87 Ibn Sharya (s. Ibn Hishām) (1978) "*Ahbār ʿUbayd,*" p. 318, 6.
88 Idem op. cit., p. 323, 3-7.
89 Idem op. cit., p. 327, 8; 330, 12; 349, 4.

Wa-qad 'alimtu anna l-shi'ra dīwānu l-'arabi wa-l-dalīlu 'alā ahādithā wa-af'ālihā wa-l-hākimu baynahum fī l-Djāhiliyyati wa-qad sami'tu Rasūla llāhi sallā llāhu 'alayhi wa-ālihi wa-sallama yaqūlu (inna mina l-shi'ri la-hikaman)[90]
("I already knew that the poetry of the Arabians' Dīwān was the proof of their reports and their deeds and the umpire between them in the *Djāhiliyya*; I also heard God's envoy – God bless him and his house and grant him salvation – say: 'Truly, (a lot of) wisdom comes from poetry'").

It is not possible to state this any clearer: the extreme importance of poetry for old Arabia is highlighted here for all areas; at the same time, however, poetry in Islam was to be completely rehabilitated – following the turbulent statements of the Qur'an against it and the poets, and the statement which is normally ascribed to Abū 'Amr Ibn al-'Alā' (689-770 AD) goes back to the highest authority in Islam. The particularly positive nature of the statement is highlighted first through the affirmative tone and then also by *lām al-ta'kīd* the last word (*la-hikaman*), which is even used in the plural to lend it greater strength. In my view, this precludes any restrictive interpretation, instead it is a very positive statement in support of the value of poetry which – from a religious perspective – cannot be an inferior societal product, in particular as it means so much for the old Arabians and contains their wisdom. Such a strong tradition is not allowed to disappear or be disparaged – in any case not if you are called Mu'wiya. The following generations, irrespective of the ruling family from which they originated, were supposed to observe this and give the poetic element a powerful place in their culture so that poetry became the best intrinsic product of this culture and presented all areas of its achievement in a masterful way.

IV. Old vivid narrative traditions in Early Islam before the 1001 Nights

Such verifiable accounts of the early Arabian-Islamic history and culture constitute a lively tradition for the subsequent generations of Islam: poetry became for them an indispensable element of their history and culture, thus one should always speak of "Poetry and Truth." Poetry was supposed to infuse reality with a certain zest. All of the story tellers recognised this at an early stage thus they spread an Arabian-Islamic literature which was intended to catch on; for this reason they sought not only to educate – like the dry methods of the legal scholars – but to associate edification with amusement. These narrators were also story tellers; at that time it was impossible not to be. They delighted the spirit of high-ranking authors such as al-Djāhiā in particular through their "*facilité d'élocution*

---

90 Idem op. cit., p. 352, 12-15.

et le charme de leur langage"[91] (i.e. "facility of delivery and the charm of their language") as Pellat puts it so succinctly. This last circumstance played an extremely important role in the spread of such stories about the past of Arabia, the bible etc. and the poetry helped them enormously. Thus, the story-tellers of these pre-Islamic and early Islamic periods were real champions of religious zeal and local patriotism which would guarantee their region, tribe etc. an influential place within the Islamic community in the context of the conflicts between northern and southern Arabia. This was also visible in the variety of the tribes, which everyone declares to have been the first of the Arabian tribes to have accepted Islam, in the different *Sīra* versions which survived in separate form or in large general historical works.[92]

These story tellers in particular were successful transmitters of a literature which was highly valued as it embodied the literary spirit of the early generations, which in its popular erudition combined "the aims of entertainment" with those of "edification" Tory Andréa aptly describes the work of the best of them as follows: "A particular class of professional story-tellers, the *Qussās*, entertained its audience alternatively with secular fairy tales, biblical legends and glorious stories of the Prophets of Islam."[93] Thus, it is most regrettable that this kind of literature finds little respect to the present day – particularly in the West – as it is omnipresent in most typically Arabian and Semitic genres and its transmitters were highly respected and particularly eloquent personalities. There are various reasons why with time this designation came to be associated with an increasing lack of respect which Pellat highlights: the main reason undoubtedly lies in the desire of the Islamic leadership not to lend any official approbation to foreign material which could be found in the speeches and reports of the story-tellers and originated from both the Judaeo-Christian and Iranian repertoires. However, every expert knows that the measures against such *Qussās* remained more or less unsuccessful as these story tellers who, were driven out of the mosques, continued to enjoy much adulation among the masses, more than the drier *Fuqahā'* (legal scholars), in particular as they were confident speakers and included some highly educated individuals who could even fascinate al-Djāhiz who was not easily satisfied.

This, in particular, must have played a very important role in the spreading of more or less historical reports on the Arabian past, in particular when these reports could be combined with suitable poems which lent the narration a particular stamp of authority. The early Islamic story-tellers "were firstly champions of re-

---

91 Pellat, Charles (1953) "Le milieu Basrien et la formation de Gahiz," p. 110 ; EI², IV, 733/763 ff.
92 On this point, see Khoury, R.G. (1983) "Les sources islamiques de la 'Sîra' avant Ibn Hishâm (mort 213/834) et leur valeur historique," p. 7-29.
93 Andrae, Tor (1918) "Die Person Mohammeds in Lehre und Glauben seiner Gemeinde," p. 26, 7 ff.

ligious fervour before the Islamic armies, like poets in the old days [...] Thus, they naturally became popular exegetes of the Qor'ān and public homilists who became story-tellers for religious purposes."[94] That this profession was compared with that of the poet in the old days would come as no surprise to connoisseurs of the old-Arabian scene as the poet was the primary reference for all that concerned this past and poetry was seen "from time immemorial as the high point" of the culture of the Arabians and represented "for a long time virtually the only form of expression of artistic creation among the Arabians.[95] It is impossible to understand the writing of poetry and telling of stories in Islam without bearing in mind their roots in old Arabia, however with the special religious emphasis that Islam introduced – in particular if one considers old Arabic literature in general which displays little or no religious content.

All of the official measures adopted to replace the story-tellers remained, therefore, unsuccessful as the latter, who had been banished from the mosques out of fear that they would undermine the religious contribution of Islam, continued their work outside of the mosques and, above all, continued to enthuse the masses. With them survived the authority of all kinds of stories of a fashionable nature, in particular collections such as that of the 1001 Nights, whose original material can be connected with the story-telling evenings of the Arabs, i.e. long before the adoption of Persian material in this area. In conclusion, I will now briefly summarize some contributions I have made in recent years on the significance of Arabic papyrology, i.e. of the Heidelberg texts and their specialized language, in the clarification, transmission and codification of this work:[96]

1. The nocturnal art of story telling among the Arabs is confirmed early on. We have already seen its specialized language in the texts of Ibn Sharya, documented at least since Mu'āwiya although the genre is much older. Mu'āwiya literally said to his guest:

Innī aradtu ittikhādhaka mu'addiban lī wa-samīran wa-muqawwiman ... Wa-kun lī samīran fī laylī wa-wazīran fī amrī
("I wanted you as a story-teller for me, as a nocturnal story-teller and advisor ... Be a nocturnal story-teller in my nights and a vizier in my affairs").

This is the framework of what became the beginning and end of entertainment and education at the time of the subsequent caliphs.

2. A precedent was also set in other collections for entertainment and edifica-

---

94 Macdonald, D.B., EI, II, p. 1120.
95 On this point, see Wagner, E. (1987) "Grundzüge der klassischen arabischen Dichtung, I, Die altarabische Dichtung," p. 1 ff.
96 Khoury, R.G. (1994) "L'apport de la papyrologie dans la transmission et codification des premières versions des Mille et Une Nuits," p. 21-33 ; ibid. (2004) "L'apport spécialement important de la papyrologie ...," p. 81 ff.

tion, like the 1001 Nights, whose parts also betray early-Arabian characteristics and undoubtedly bear the Umayyad hallmark: as the oldest version of the book, which assumed its final form much later, we have, of course, the fragment on paper published by Nabia Abbott in 1949,[97] which must surely date to earlier than 266/879. The fragment is on two sheets, which contain pages 3 and 4 of the short text of 1001 Nights. Everything else is completely linked with a legal witness statement; Abbott notes that the witness Ahmad Ibn Mahfūz scribbles the date of the statements several times and writes: "Fifteen separate entries of the legal formula exclusive of the several scattered phrases of the same. Seven of these entries provided a complete date, four of which are still preserved in full."[98] Lucid words which clearly prove that this is the date of the statements but never that of a literary text: the documents on papyrus and paper in the framework of papyrology show it clearly. The date 266 H is, therefore, "*a terminus ante quem* for the earlier date of the *Alf Lailah*."

3. Another papyrus fragment published by Nabia Abbott in 1972 is of key importance due to its unknown connection to 1001 Nights and confirms just one early-Arabian characteristic of this work: what is involved here is the fragment on the portrait of the "ideal maiden" (*Al-djāriya l-mithāliyya*).[99] It is unimportant here whether or not it is possible to establish on closer examination a link between these few lines here and some passages of the great portrait of *Tawaddud* or other figures in the 1001 Nights, the genre and type of description of an "ideal maiden" was already highly Arabian in nature there too. In the papyrus we have two small parts, each of which consists of a few lines: ʿAmr Ibn al-ʿĀs opens the speech in the first part to draw the attention of the *Umma* to the fundamental role of the caliph in their lives (this can only have been Muʿāwiya, particularly as we know how important an ally of the conqueror of Egypt ʿAmr was for his caliph). The aforementioned portrait can be found in the second part, from line 7 on. The linking of the papyrus with the name of ʿAmr Ibn al-ʿĀs is a guarantee of its age, in particular as we could establish above in Ibn Sharya's text the role of the governor in the coming into being of the tales at the court of Muʿāwiya. However, the papyrus does not originate from the time of the caliph, as it was transmitted by Yaʿqūb Ibn ʿAtāʾ Ibn Abī Rabāh (died 155/771), whom Abbott was unable to identify and hence chronologically locate with accuracy. For this reason, she wrote: "Yaʿqūb may or may not have long survived his aged scholarly father, ʿAtāʾ b. Abī Rabāh who died in 114/732." Due to the uncertainty regarding the dating of this papyrus she added: "Nevertheless, the papyrus could as well be

---

97 Abbott, Nabia (1949) "A ninth-century fragment of the 'Thousand Nights.' New light on the early history of the Arabian Nights," pp. 129-164.
98 Idem op. cit. p. 141b, 143a.
99 Idem (1972) "Studies in Arabic Literary Papyri III. Language and Literature, Dokument 3: A Speech of ʿAmr Ibn al-ʿĀs and Description of the Ideal Maiden," p. 43-78.

from Ya'qūb's hand as from that of a younger second – century transmitter."[100] However, Ya'qūb died in 155 H. – i.e. in the beginning of the Abbasid period and his material goes back to the period of the conqueror of Egypt where the origin of the – at least orally circulating – material should be sought and betrays an old, early-Islamic tradition in terms of the type of narration.

4. This fragment on the "ideal maiden" dates, therefore, from the middle or beginning of the second half of the $2^{nd}/8^{th}$ century and not from the last quarter of this century; at most from the last years of Ya'qūb and its roots go back much further. The first aforementioned fragment on the 1001 Nights must also be dated earlier as 266 should be viewed not as its date but as that of the witness statements. Thus, both fragments can only be considered in connection with the terminology which occurs in the title of the Heidelberg story of David on papyrus and reads: *Hadīth Dāwūd*, dating from the year 229/844. It was, however, the version of an older original as I have proven on several occasions. Also the version of the *Akhbār* by 'Ubayd Ibn Sharya. All of them used the word *Hadīth* for the fashionable story in the title or title area, whose use in the title of such story books disappeared with the first half of the $III/9^{th}$ century and were reserved for the purely Islamic tradition.[101] The *Kitāb Bad` al-khalq wa-qisas al-anbiyā`* transmitted by 'Umāra Ibn Wathīma al-Fārisī (died 289/902) after his father Wathīma Ibn Mūsā Ibn al-Furāt al-Fārisī, the actual author of the work, provides us with the best proof of this: Wathīma died in the year 237/851, i.e. seven to eight years after the date of the Heidelberg Story of David from which he copied word for word. His work could no longer bear the title *Hadīth*, because a more specific terminology was required for many genres in the course of the systematic transition and, above all, codification of a science that had become vast; an ever increasing realism in which the written form had become a necessary instrument of traffic automatically required a specialization as already stressed in detail above. Hence the emergence of this order based on areas, genres. As a result, everything that is titled and formulated like the papyruses is older than the version of Wathīma al-Fārisī's book and must date back to the period of the Heidelberg papyruses which more or less originate from the collection of the Egyptian judge 'Abd Allāh Ibn Lahī'a (97-174/715-790) who collected originals and copies of originals in his unique private library and used to make them available to Egyptian students and guests, who included all transmitters of the Heidelberg papyruses and Wathīma himself. The latter received the material at least from the immediate students of the judge in Fustāt (old Cairo) and had to take into account the development, systematic reception and written recording of the sciences.

---

100 Idem op. cit. p. 78, 13-15; on this point, see Khoury, R.G. (1994) "L'apport de la papyrologie," p. 29 ff.
101 Khoury, R.G., op. cit. 30-33.

References

Abbott, Nabia (1972) *Studies in Arabic Literary Papyri, III. Language and Literature* (OIP 77), Chicago.

Abbott, Nabia (1972a) *Studies in Arabic Literary Papyri III. Language and Literature* (OIP 43-78), Chicago.

Abbott, Nabia (1967) *Studies in Arabic Literary Papyri, II. Qur`ānic Commentary and Tradition* (OIP 76), Chicago.

Abbott, Nabia (1957) *Arabic Literary Papyri, I, Historical Texts* (OIP 75), Chicago.

Abbott, Nabia (1949) "A ninth-century fragment of the 'Thousand Nights.' New light on the early history of the Arabian Nights." *JNES*, VIII , pp. 129-164.

Andrae,Tor (1918) *Die Person Mohammeds in Lehre und Glauben seiner Gemeinde*, Stockholm.

Arkoun, Mohamed (1982) *L'Humanisme arabe au IXe/Xe siècle. Miskawayh, philosophe et historien*, Paris.

Atallah, Wahib (2004) *Ibn Hichâm. La biographie du prophète Mahomet. Texte traduit et annoté par Wahib Atalla*, Paris: Fayard.

Blachère, Régis (1952) *Histoire de la littérature arabe des origines à la fin du XV² siècle de J. – C.*, Vol. I, Paris.

Al -Djabırı, Muhammad (1984) *Takwīn ul-'aql ul-'arabī*, Beyrouth.

Chelhod, Joseph et al. (1984-1985) *L'Arabie du Sud, histoire et civilisation*, 3 Vols., Paris: Maisonneuve & Larose [Vol. 1: Le peuple yéménite et ses racines; Vol. 2: La société yéménite de l'Hégire aux idéologies modernes; Vol. 3: Cultures et institutions du Yémen].

Gauchet, Marcel (1985) *Le désenchantement du monde*, Paris: Gallimard.

Gilliot, Claude (1990) *Exégèse, langue et théologie en Islam. L'exégèse coranique de Tabarî*, Paris.

Gutas, D. (1981) "Arabic wisdom literature: nature and scope." *JAOS*, CI, pp. 50-86.

Heller, B. (1913-1938) "Luqmān." In: *Enzyklopädie des Islām*, III, p. 39 Leiden/Leipzig: Brill.

Husayn, Tāhā (1968) *Fī l-adab al-djāhilī*, Kairo.

Ibn al-Nadīm (1871), *Fihrist*, (ed. by Fluegel), Leipzig.

Ibn Hishām (1978 [1347/1928]) *Kitāb al-Tīdjān fī mulūk Himyar* (edited together with Akhbār 'Abayd Ibn Sharya , *al-Djurhumī fī akhbār al-Yaman wa-ash'ārihā wa-ansābihā)*, with a foreword and notes by 'Abd al-'Azīz al-Maqālih. San'ā` [Haidarabad].

Ibn Sharya (1978 [1347/1928]) *al-Djurhumī fī akhbār al-Yaman wa-ash'ārihā wa-ansābihā* (edited together with Ibn Hishām, *Kitāb al-Tīdjān fī mulūk Himyar)*, with a preface and remarks by 'Abd al-'Azīz al-Maqālih. San'ā` [Haidarabad].

Ibn Qutayba (1960) *al-Ma'ārif* (ed. by Tharwat 'Ukāsha), Kairo.

Karoui, Said (1998) *Die Rezeption der Bibel im Werke des Ibn Qutayba.* Heidelberg/Tunis.

Khoury, Raif Georges (2004) "L'apport spécialement important de la papyrologie dans la transmission et la codification des plus anciennes versions des *Mille et Une Nuits* et d'autres livres des deux premiers siècles islamiques." In: Petra M. Sijpestein/Lennart Sundelin (eds.) *Papyrologie and the History of Early Islamic Egypt,* Leiden: Brill, pp. 63-95.

Khoury, Raif Georges (2000) "Die Erzähltradition im Islam, Islam – eine andere Welt?" Rektorat Heidelberg vom Jahre 1999 (ed.) *Studium Generale Universität Heidelberg,* pp. 23-40.

Khoury, Raif Georges (1998) "Geschichte oder Fiktion. Zur erzählerischen Gattung der ältesten Bücher über Arabien." In: Stefan Leder (ed.) *Story – telling in the framework of non-fictional Arabic Literature,* Wiesbaden: Harrassowitz, pp. 370-387.

Khoury, Raif Georges (1997) "Les grands centres de conservation et de transmission des manuscrits arabes aux premier et deuxième siècles de l'Hégire" In: H.M. Cotton/J.J. Price, D./J. Wasserstein (eds.) *Scripta Classica Israelica,* XVI (Studies in Memory of A. Wasserstein), pp. 215-226.

Khoury, Raif Georges (1997) "L'importance des plus vieux manuscrits arabes historiques sur papyrus, conservés à Heidelberg, pour l'histoire de la langue arabe et de la culture des premiers siècles islamiques." *Quaderni di Studi Arabi,* 15, pp. 11-18.

Khoury, Raif Georges (1994) L'apport de la papyrologie dans la transmission et codification des premières versions des Mille et Une Nuits (Les Mille et Une Nuits contes sans frontière), Toulouse: (AMAM), pp. 21-33.

Khoury, Raif Georges (1993) "Kalif, Geschichte und Dichtung: Der jemenitische Erzähler ʿAbīd Ibn Šarya am Hofe Muʿāwiyas" In: Zeitschrift für Arabische-Linguistik/Journal of Arabic Linguistics, 25, pp. 204-218 (Wiesbaden: Harrassowitz).

Khoury, Raif Georges (1989) "Quelques réflexions sur la première ou les premières Bibles arabes. In: L'Arabie préislamique et son environnement historique et culturel – *Actes du Colloque de Strasbourg 1987.* Leiden, pp. 549-561.

Khoury, Raif Georges (1987) "Ibn Khaldūn et quelques savants des deux premiers siècles islamiques." In: Festschrift M.J. Kister, Jerusalem Studies in Arabic and Islam, 10, pp. 192-204.

Khoury, Raif George (1986) *ʿAbd Allāh Ibn Lahīʿa (97-174/715-790). Juge et grand maître de l'Ecole E-gyptienne. Avec édition critique de l'unique rouleau de papyrus conservé à Heidelberg,* Wiesbaden : Harrassowitz (Codices Arabici Antiqui IV).

Khoury, Raif Georges (1983) "Les sources islamiques de la 'Sîra' avant Ibn Hishâm (mort 213/834) et leur valeur historique." In: T. Fahd (ed.) *La vie du Prophète Mahomet* (Colloque de Strasbourg, octobre 1980) Paris : Presses Universitaires de France 1983, pp. 7-29.

Khoury, Raif Georges (1978) *Les légendes prophétiques dans l'Islam depuis le Ier jusqu'au IIIe siècle de l'Hégrie. D'après le manuscrit d'Abū Rifā'a 'Umāra b. Wathīma al-Fārisī: Kitāb Bad` al-khalq wa-qisas al-anbiyā`. Avec édition critique du texte.* Wiesbaden: Harrassowitz (Codices arabici antiqui III).

Khoury, Raif Georges (1976), *Asad B. Mūsā, Kitāb az-Zuhd. Nouvelle édition revue, corrigée et augmentée de tous les certificats de lecture d'après les deux copies de Berlin et de Damas. Avec une étude sur l'auteur,* Wiesbaden: Harrassowitz (Codices Arabici Antiqui II).

Khoury, Raif Georges (1972) *Wahb B. Munabbih (34 H./654-55 – 110 o. 114 H./728 o. 732)* [Vol. I: Der Heidelberger Papyrus PSR Heid Arab 23. Leben und Werk des Dichters; Vol. II: Faksimiletafeln], Wiesbaden: Otto Harrassowitz (Codices Arabici Antiqui I).

Krenkow, F. (1928) "The Two Oldest Books on Arabic Folklore." In: *Islamic Culture 2,* p. 55 ff., p. 204 ff.

Kurd 'Alī, Muhammad (1946[1913]) *Ibn al-Muqaffa', Risāla fī l-sahāba,* ed. by Ibn al-Muqaffa', Damaskus [also in *Gesamtwerk des Ibn al-Muqaffa',* ed. by 'Umar Abū l-Nasr, 1966; French translation with commentary and extensive glossary by Charles Pellat, Paris 1976].

Lecomte, Gérard (1965) *Ibn Qutayba. L'homme et l'œuvre,* Damaskus (PIFD).

Leder, Stefan (Hg.) (1998) *Story-telling in the framework of non-fictional Arabic literature,* Wiesbaden: Harrassowitz.

Pellat, Charles (1953) Le milieu Basrien et la formation de Gahiz, Paris: Maisonneuve.

al-Qalqashandī (1331/1913) *Subh al-a'shā,* I, Kairo.

Sahl Ibn Muhammad Ibn 'Uthmān Abū Hātim al-Sidjistānī (1899) *Kitāb al-Mu'ammarīn,* transl. and ed. by I. Goldziher, "Das Kitāb al-Mu'ammarīn des Abû Hâtim al-Sidjistānī." In: *Abhandlungen zur arabischen Philologie,* part 2, Leiden. Verlag.

Schwarzbaum, Haim (1982) "Biblical and Extra-Biblical Legends in Islamic Folkliterature," In: Beiträge *zur Sprach – und Kulturgeschichte des Orients,* Vol. 30. Walldorf/Hessen.

Sezgin, Fuat (1967 ff.) Geschichte des arabischen Schrifttums, I, Leiden: Brill.

Al-Tabarī, (1879 ff.) Annales = *Tārīkh al-rusul wa-l-mulūk,* ed. by de Goeje, Leiden.

Tarābīshī, Georges (1998) *Ishkāliyyāt al-aql al-'arabī,* Beyrouth/London.

Van Ess, Josef (1970) "Les Qadarites et la Gahlāniyya de Yazīd," SI, 31, pp. 269-286.

Wagner, Ewald (1987) *Grundzüge der klassischen arabischen Dichtung,* Vol. I. Die altarabische Dichtung, Darmstadt.

Yāqūt (1957) *Mu'djam al-buldān,* V, Beirut.

Yāqūt (1928) *Irshād,* ed. by Margoliouth, V, Kairo.

Chapter 8

Islam and the Axial Age

JOSEF VAN ESS

Karl Jaspers and his theory

Historiography is the attempt of the human mind to put order into contingency. We discover causalities in the flow of time and elevate certain events to symbolic value. If we are audacious enough we elaborate general – or, to use the new expression: global – theories. They seem to thrive especially well in societies or periods which have lost their inherited orientation. In Germany, the 1920s were full of them and again the years after 1945. Now we get them cheaper from the United States: Huntington, Fukuyama. My experience with them goes back to the late fourties of the last century. But I went to school then, and I was not particularly impressed. I belonged to what was called shortly afterwards the "sceptical generation."

These theories – and I shall specify them in due course – have, as it seems, one thing in common: they read history backwards. They are teleological, "Heilsgeschichte" in disguise. Sure, they also differ a lot, the reason being that they are always children of their time, reflecting the mood of their period. Sometimes they are pessimistic, especially after a war which was lost; their authors then tend to ruminate about some sort of "Untergang," and the public gladly absorbs this. In such a case, the prevailing mood is one of remorse, and the main question asked is: "How could we do this to ourselves?" In Germany this was called "Kulturkritik." At other moments, the same theories are brimmingly optimistic: "How come we are so wonderful? Why is it that the 'modern subject' is so singular?" This attitude is, of course, as naïve as is the former one. But to be just: it is not so much encountered with those who invent the theories but rather with those who elaborate on them later on, during the process of reception. It is a secondary phenomenon. For it may happen that theories come back after one or two generations and find themselves surrounded by a completely new mental environment. Marxism in Western Germany during the late sixties was a good example, strangely out of focus and void of any contact with the feelings of the social class it had originally been intended for. "Weberism" is perhaps another one: the phenomenon of an author who never managed to get a book out and fell from one nervous crisis into the other[1], but then, after his death, was monopolized by a steadily growing "school" who developed his ideas into a "system" and his notes into a Scripture. Jaspers's "Axial Age" may be a third one: conceived in 1949, but short-lived and then out of sight for at least one generation until it came back in form of conferences and specialized articles in the recent past.

In this case, however, I am not so sure. I never looked at the "Axial Age" very closely, and the Suhrkamp publication of 1987-1992 which revivified its memory by-passed me completely[2]. Younger events of the same kind, the workshop held at Jerusalem which dealt with Islam (2002)[3] and a volume of assorted articles published in the periodical "Medieval Encounters" (2004)[4], seem to keep aloof from the magic word itself as much as possible[5]. At the Essen conference (2005) Shmuel Eisenstadt told me that "Axial Age" is no longer considered to be of prime importance and has been replaced by "axial syndromes." This terminological shift would not sadden me; any stepping down from capital letters to normal down-to-earth language makes me feel more comfortable.

This has, of course, something to do with the fact that I am an Islamicist. Islam does not fit into most of these general theories. They are all Europocentred, and even where one of their authors thinks that the Occident is about to perish ("Der Untergang des Abendlandes") he reserves for the Orient nothing else but Aladin's wonder-lamp ("the magic civilization")[6]. Frequently, Islam is not taken into consideration at all, in Eric Voegelin's *Order and History*, for instance (a book which, in Germany, is just being rediscovered)[7], in Alexander Rüstow's

---

1   This formulation is, I admit, somewhat flippant and, what is worse, not entirely true. According to the German academic system, Weber had had to submit two studies ("books") in order to get his professorship: his PhD thesis and a "Habilitationsschrift."
2   Eisenstadt, Shmuel N. (ed.) *Kulturen der Achsenzeit*, 1 (1987) and 2, part 1-3 (1992), Frankfurt: Suhrkamp, with articles on Islam by Lapidus, Gellner, Lazarus-Yafeh, and Levtzion. The preceding volume in English: Eisenstadt (1986) *The origins and diversity of axial age civilizations*, Albany: State University of New York Press, has different contents and contains only one contribution on Islam, a short essay written by M.A. Cook (pp. 476-483) which was not taken over into the German publication. However, Cook still appears among the authors of Schluchter 1987 (below n. 16).
3   Hoexter, Miriam/Eisenstadt, Shmuel N./Levtzion, Nehemia (eds.), *The Public Sphere in Muslim Societies*. Albany: State University of New York Press.
4   Arnason, Johann P./Wittrock, Björn (eds.) *Eurasian Transformations, Tenth to Thirteenth Century*. Medieval Encounter 10 (Special Issue), Leiden: Brill.
5   I had not yet the chance of looking at the last publication by Arnason, Johann/Eisenstadt, Shmuel N./Wittrock/Björn, *Axial Civilizations and World History*, Leiden, Brill 2005.
6   For Oswald Spengler cf. now. Radtke, Bernd (forthcoming), "Spengler und der Islam. Nachdenkliches und Persönliches." In: Der Islam.
7   Voegelin (2000 ff. [1956 ff.]) *The Collected Works,* Baton Rouge/London: Louisiana State University Press, Vol. 14-18.

Ortsbestimmung der Gegenwart (which, interestingly, is mainly a fruit of Rüstow's Turkish exile after 1933)[8], or in Alfred Weber's *Abschied von der bisherigen Geschichte* which, written at Heidelberg[9], both locally and temporally comes closest to Jaspers's *Vom Ursprung und Ziel der Geschichte*[10]. If consciously intended such abstention is nothing objectionable at all, for history is always contemporary history, to quote Benedetto Croce[11], and historiography therefore nothing else but position-finding concerning the present age ("Ortsbestimmung der Gegenwart"). We use to understand ourselves as the product of a rectilinear development in which the "before" counts a lot whereas the "besides" is bound to be neglected. Alfred Weber therefore started with a chapter on the "Sonderheit des Abendlandes," the singularity of the Occident. Even when the topic is actually pursued beyond the borders of Western civilization we rather expect to hear something about Ancient Egypt and Mesopotamia (the "forerunners" of the Greeks) than about historical phenomena of the East which were simultaneous with the West, whether Islamic or Indian, Chinese etc. Encounters were "crusades" more frequently than "dialogues."

I have to admit that the Islamic world is complicated. Max Weber was still not able to find his way through it; what he read in some hurry was not of sufficient quality, and the original sources were not accessible to him[12]. When, later on, Leon Festinger took a similar initiative and started with the first volume of what was destined to become a universal history[13] he convoked a few medievalists and islamicists to a conference at Toledo in order to get a clearer concept of how to go on[14], but then he died prematurely before he could pursue his project. Only rarely did Islamic scholars pay attention to such enterprises. Carl Heinrich Becker, who had been Max Weber's colleague at Heidelberg until 1909, briefly

---

8   Rüstow, Alexander (1950 ff.) *Ortsbestimmung der Gegenwart, eine universalgeschichtliche Kulturkritik*, 1-3, Erlenbach-Zurich: Rentsch. The only hint at an Oriental experience seems to crop up in chapter 17 of volume II: "Untergang der Antike: Barbarisierung des Westens, Byzantinisierung des Ostens." Rüstow's son Dankwart became a Turkologist who taught in the United States.
9   Weber, Alfred (1946) *Abschied von der bisherigen Geschichte. Überwindung des Nihilismus?*, Hamburg: Claaßen und Goverts. The (first) preface was signed February 1945, at a moment when the war was more or less over at Heidelberg, but when Dresden was still about to be bombed.
10 Jaspers (1949), Munich: Piper.
11 *History as the Story of Liberty* (1941), p. 19.
12 Cf. now the remarks bei Radtke, Bernd (2005) *Neue kritische Gänge. Zu Stand und Aufgaben der Sufikforschung*, Utrecht: M. Th. Houtsma Stichting, pp. 251 ff.
13 Festinger, Leon (1983) *The Human Legacy*, New York: Columbia University Press. The book is subdivided into the chapters "The Narrow Path of Evolution" and "The March to 'Civilization'."
14 In 1987, if I remember correctly; on the Islamic side, Ira Lapidus and myself had been invited. Festinger did not seem to care so much about Greek Antiquity.

commented upon Oswald Spengler[15], and Bertold Spuler jotted down a few remarks about Arnold Toynbee[16]. But there was not much to come afterwards, at least not in Germany. Jörg Kraemer, in his inaugural lecture for his professorship at Erlangen, spoke about the "problem of Islamic cultural history" (1959), but left out Jaspers as well as Max Weber completely[17]. When Wolfgang Schluchter wanted to reopen the discussion about Weber's ideas concerning the world of Islam[18] the majority of the contributors to his volume (the most notable exception being Maxime Rodinson) had to be taken from the English-speaking world where, at that moment, Weber was studied with great enthusiasm[19]. German "orientalism" had then long since passed on to the agenda.

In certain respects, however, Jaspers's *Vom Ursprung und Sinn der Geschichte* was a different case. The reception was less complex. Right from the beginning, the book presented itself in its final and accomplished form; a complete English translation appeared in 1968[20], and in 1984 (?) even a Persian one was produced[21]. As in the case of Max Weber (and later on in the ill-fated human rights debate), the Iranians showed a greater affinity to this universalist Western way of thinking than the Arabs[22]. Moreover, the book was of modest size, which is always an advantage when the reception has to cross a language barrier. It had been written by a philosopher who was neither a historian nor a sociologist and

---

15 Less negatively, by the way, as we might expect today, Becker, Carl Heinrich (1923) "Spenglers Magische Kultur. Ein Vortrag." ZDMG 77, pp. 255-271. Weber was already dead by then.
16 Spuler, Bertold (1952) "Einige Gedankensplitter zu Toynbees Bild der orientalischen Geschichte." Der Islam 30, pp. 214-221, in reality a review of Toynbee's *Der Gang der Weltgeschichte* (Stuttgart 1950) which was, in German translation, a shorter version of his original work.
17 Kraemer (1959) *Das Problem der islamischen Kulturgeschichte,* Tübingen: Max Niemeyer. Max Weber's brother Alfred is mentioned, but only in a few footnotes.
18 Schluchter, Wolfgang (1987) *Max Webers Sicht des Islams,* Frankfurt: Suhrkamp.
19 Though, as it turned out, not always with sufficient expertise; cf. Schluchter's long introduction entitled "Überlegungen zu Max Webers Sicht des frühen Islams" (pp. 11-124) where, at the end, he criticizes the approaches of Rodinson, Turner, Cook, and Crone (pp. 85 ff.). Weber's ideas had been popularized in the English-speaking world through translations which were fragmentary and not always sufficiently precise. Some of the contributors duly quote, however, *Wirtschaft und Gesellschaft* according to the German original.
20 Jaspers (1968) *The origin and goal of history*, New Haven/London: Yale University Press.
21 *Agház ve andjám-i tárikh,* Teheran : Intishárát-i Khwárazmi, by Muh. Hasan Lutfi who had already translated other works by Jaspers. The publication bears no date. For 1363 h. š. = 1984 AD I rely on the catalogue of Tübingen University Library. The translation itself seems to have been made before the Islamic revolution.
22 In the Arab world, the only hint at the "axial age" I know of is found with the Moroccan historian Abdesselam Cheddadi (2004 *Les Arabes et l'appropriation de l'histoire,* Paris: Sindbad, p. 15). Characteristically, Cheddadi has translated Marshall Hodgson's *Venture of Islam* into French (Paris 1998).

who looked at world-history as something which "makes sense" and can be grasped in a kind of "morphology," to use Spengler's expression. Jaspers shared this outlook with Alfred Weber, his colleague at Heidelberg who understood his "Farewell to history as it used to be" (*Abschied von der bisherigen Geschichte*) as an attempt at overcoming nihilism. What stuck to the reader's mind was, however, not this optimistic approach as such but the claim that the entire development could be focussed into one particular historical moment, as a "breakthrough" which happened during an Axial Age some centuries before Christ[23]. To be precise: What was new here was merely the chronological horizon and the term whereas the idea itself, namely the concept that the history of mankind could be – and had in fact been – changed by one singular event at one particular moment, had always been in existence; it was the crucial point of Christian *Heilsgeschichte*. The specific difference added by Jaspers was that now, according to his chronology, which was the chronology of modernity as it were, the breakthrough was not achieved thanks to the birth of Christ but by Greek tragedy and Old Testament prophecy. Occidental theology had been replaced by German humanism, the kind of humanism offered in the Prussian "humanistische Gymnasium" of the nineteenth century. This is why Islam could not fit. The "Axial Age" could be smoothened so far as to accommodate the Buddha and, with some good will, Zoroaster, even Echnaton and Moses, but never Muhammad. Islam seemed to remain the "heresy" it had always been.

Nobody cared. Jaspers was not particularly religious and consciously avoided religious language; when he talked about the homeland of the Prophets he did not say "the Holy Land" or "Israel" but said "Palestine" instead. As to those who read his book in Germany we may assume that they had had enough of Heilsgeschichte, at least in the form favored by the previous political regime; after the enormous loss of cultural heritage, ideally as well as materially, due to the last war, they did not mind seeing the pivot of history being shifted away from where it had been before. The only people who did not feel at ease were the Islamicists. They were not able to join the discussion unless their colleagues decided to change the outlook and the terminology, from "Axial Age" to "axial syndromes" or from "Achsenzeit" in the singular to "Sattelzeiten" in the plural[24].

---

23 "Breakthrough" is a term of this period; Alfred Weber used it a lot. I assume that in anglophone sociology it was originally borrowed from German "Durchbruch." It is true that in both languages the word is older, but only with regard to military jargon; there it dates back to the First World War (first attested usage in English according to *The Oxford English Dictionary,* sec. ed. 1989, II 517: Daily Express 5. Nov. 1918). The metaphorical usage in the sense of a scientific breakthrough seems not to have appeared, in English, before 1958, and then with regard to the production of H-bombs (ib.).

24 The term "Sattelzeit" is sometimes used by German historians, but I do not know whether there is any discussion going on between them and the "Achsenzeit"-

These are not mere verbal differences. More than ever, the terms are loaded with value judgements. Emotionalization was almost inevitable once the Axial Age was supposed to mark the birth of the modern subject. It is true that this "modern subject" is a rather mysterious being which seems to defy any definition, but what matters is that it is identical with ourselves. Liberty was chosen as its main characteristic; Jaspers conceived the human type who emerged during the Axial Age as the individual who emancipated itself from the tyrannies of the past and developed a hitherto unknown sense of singularity, lonely as yet and therefore tragic in his confrontation with the old structures but nevertheless able to serve as the nucleus of a new elite which became the standard-bearer of a better way of dealing with social and political reality. This was a rather optimistic view of things, but we should not overlook the fact that Jaspers, writing as he was in the aftermath of the Second World War, presented it in a somewhat broken form. His book is full of critical observations about the modern world, a world of machines and guns, of "Technik" as one used to say in Germany at that time, an expression used by Heidegger as well and in the same negative sense. "Technik" did not sound as vague as it does nowadays; what everybody understood by it was not the computer but the atomic bomb and, in connection with it, the impersonality of modern warfare, a gruesome and brutal impersonality which reached its peak at Hiroshima and Nagasaki. Jaspers therefore explicitly denied that his own present time could be considered a second axial age or the fulfillment of the former one[25]; his own world, he thought, was devoid of humanity ("arm an Menschlichkeit"). Strikingly enough, he did not elaborate on democracy as one of the phenomena of the axial age; we may assume that he knew his classical sources too well in order to believe that the democratic experiment at Athens could serve as a paradigm apt for imitation. And he had, of course, been witness to the Weimar democracy ending up, with the consent of almost the entire population, in a dictatorship. Alfred Weber, too, though saying fare-well to "history as it used to be" put a question-mark behind his message of overcoming Nietzsche's nihilism. Jaspers does not have much to say about Islam, but it is obvious that when remaining silent about it he does *not* do so because he thinks that the "West" is superior or less dangerous.

When our own generation is confronted with something like the "Axial Age" the reaction is different. Value discussions have had a fulminatory revival in inter-civilizational dispute, and we are even willing to wage war because of values – or, to put it more cautiously, the Western values are left over when all other reasons for going to war have faded away or are no longer fashionable. If, in our days, we exclude Islam from the breakthrough which happened during the Axial

---

school. Cf. Brunner, O./Conze, W./Koselleck, R. (1972-1997) *Geschichtliche Grundbegriffe*, 1-8, Stuttgart: Klett, Vol. I xv and III 885, n. 427.

25 Jaspers (1949), p. 127.

Age deep in the past we produce a political statement; the Muslims, as it seems then, have missed the evolution to the "modern subject." If the Western mind emerged from Greek philosophy and Israelite prophecy this sounds as if it had stopped at the banks of the Jordan river. Such a conclusion would, of course, be mere ideology and a misunderstanding for which Jaspers and those who follow his ideas in contemporary scholarship are not responsible. The problem is one of reception as I said. Jaspers himself was quite aware of the polarizing effect which his concept, if applied without caution, could possibly produce. In his view, however, the danger still came from a different angle, for at his time people were not afraid of Islam but of Asia. "Asia" was the term favored in the political discussion of his days; it had been introduced by Ernst Troeltsch who considered the Islamic world as a part of the "vorderasiatische Kulturkreis," an entity which, according to his philosophy, had nothing in common with Europe and did not allow for any cultural synthesis[26]. Jaspers therefore warns his reader not to turn Asia into a "metaphysical principle." Nevertheless he admits that there may be something like the "eternal Asiatic" ("das ewig Asiatische"): despotism, fatalism, and absence of any feeling for history ("Geschichtslosigkeit")[27] – a somewhat careless statement which when applied to the Islamic civilization or to China comes close to sheer nonsense.

Breakthroughs and ruptures. The case of Islam

What can be done in such a situation? Potential misunderstandings are no reason for giving up a theory. But they may instigate us to differentiate. What do we mean when we say that Islam is late? One millenium is certainly not a mere trifle. However, Islam is "late" only as long as we think of it as a religion; if we take "Islam" as a civilization the question is not so easy to decide. Islamic religion has a clear beginning; conversely, Islamic civilization, we may be sure, did not start from a point zero. No civilization does. The new religion brought a rupture whereas the civilization may have derived its strength from its continuity with the past. Jaspers was cautious enough not to think in terms of religion alone, but rather of human self-awareness. However, he focussed on Europe; he assumed a continuity between the axial age and modernity. In doing so he omitted the Middle Ages; in agreement with German Protestant tradition he jumped right away from Jesus to Luther. Therefore he forgot to ask the question whether the Christian Middle Ages represented a rupture; in his view the modern subject simply seemed to have disappeared for a while. A "breakthrough," however, craves for continuity; the word would be out of place if the phenomenon which "breaks

---

26 Kraemer (1959; cf. above n. 15), pp. 15 f.
27 Jaspers (1949), p. 96.

through" sinks into the ground again. Could it be then that there was less rupture in the Islamic world than in Medieval Europe?

There was a lot of continuity between Hellenism and Islam, in Umayyad Syria as well as in Abbasid Iraq. Generally speaking, the Islamic world remained close to Antiquity insofar as it was a civilization of lay people whereas the Occident, for some centuries, became a primarily clerical culture. It is true that in Damascus or Baghdad, too, there was always a number of scholars who dealt with religious questions, especially the divine law. But even they continued to live "in this world" whereas in Europe the scholars lived in monasteries – at least until the universities were founded, universities which, in a certain way, had existed in Islam long before[28]. The Arabs created the only universal empire of Late Antiquity after Alexander and Rome whereas the Germanic onslaught trickled away and merely resulted in the foundation of unstable and usually short-lived governments. It is true that Islam as a religion brought a rupture, but there was enough continuity alongside with it. Even if we define "civilization" in the narrow sense as we tend to do nowadays, as technical comfort, the relationship with Antiquity is evident. One of the symbols of the Islamic town was the public bath, like in ancient Rome; there were dozens of them in medieval Baghdad[29] whereas in Europe, up to fairly recent times, they remained an exception. Rupture and continuity are not mutually exclusive. Seen under this aspect Islamic civilization looks like the elder brother of the "West." Only when the younger brother had overcome his seclusion did he find the strength to engender the "modern subject."

It is not difficult to find further indications of this continuity. There is, of course, philosophy. European scholarship has always dwelt upon this item; even people who did not care much for Islam did not mind admitting that we owe the knowledge of Aristotle to the Arabs. But in the meantime the perspective has changed. For a long time, Western scholars were primarily interested in reconstructing texts which had been lost in Greek. That means: In a way, they always thought in terms of continuity, but this continuity was, in their view, nothing particularly positive. The question they asked was: Where was it that the human mind opened up, and who had a certain idea first? German classicists wrote fa-

---

28 Cf. especially the research done by George Makdisi: (1981) *The Rise of Colleges. Institutions of Learning in Islam and the West* and (1990) *The Rise of Humanism in Classical Islam and the Christian West, with special reference to scholasticism*, both Edinburgh University Press, books which remain valuable because of the material collected in them even if their overall thesis (the dependence of the West on Islam in these matters) remains controversial or is simply ignored.

29 Grotzfeld, Heinz (1970) *Das Bad im islamischen Mittelalter. Eine kulturgeschichtliche Studie*, Wiesbaden: Harrassowitz. In general cf. *Encyclopaedia of Islam* III 139 ff. s. v. "Hammam" (J. Sourdel-Thomine).

mous books entitled "Vom Mythos zum Logos"[30] or "Die Entdeckung des Geistes"[31]. The idea of the "axial age" owed its existence to this same question. Only now do we recognize that, in Arabic philosophy, we are not simply dealing with the transmission of a heritage and a mere "translation movement" but with an overall and original adaptation of scholarly material which, one way or the other, had always been available and then was changed or improved in the process. The "Theology of Aristotle" is a case in point, or the text which, later on, in Latin, was called "Liber de Causis." The best examples, however, stem from outside philosophy proper: from astrology, from medicine, from alchemy, i.e. from those sciences where people were expected to make predictions or diagnoses and where, for mere practical reasons, the ancient errors had to be rectified. This was a kind of knowledge which was of immediate use, and the errors which were detected were best corrected right away in the process of copying, i.e. in the manuscript where the information was found: certain calculations in Ptolemy, for instance, or medical recipes, horoscopes etc. Gerhard Endreß and Remke Kruk, in the title of a recent publication (1997), therefore speak of "the ancient tradition in Islamic Hellenism," and what they mean by "Islamic Hellenism" is Abbasid Iraq in the second and third century Hijra[32].

We should, however, not forget that, as a consequence of the expansion of the Islamic empire, the transmission did not only go via Syria or Ptolemaic and Christian Egypt but also via ancient Iran, taking up the heritage of the Sasanids. Philosophy and the sciences could emerge from the East as well – like the watermelons or the citrus trees which migrated all the way from India to Spain in the Umayyad period[33]. The most famous astrologer of the time, Abu Ma'shar, the Albumasar of the Latin tradition, had come to Baghdad from Balkh, i.e. ancient Bactria. Already one century before Islam, during the reign of Khosrau Anoshirwan, a few Greek philosophers, among them Simplikios, the famous pagan commentator of Aristotle, had sought refuge at the Sasanid court which, at that time, was situated in Iraq, at Ctesiphon. Justinian, the Christian Byzantine emperor, had made their life unpleasant in Athens. Up to the time of Biruni and Avicenna the most remarkable achievements in science and philosophy were made in the Eastern part of the Islamic world.

During Late Antiquity, Upper Mesopotamia (the area around Nisibis, Edessa etc.) had been the border-line – and, for a considerable time, the no man's land –

---

30 Nestle, Wilhelm (1940) *Vom Mythos zum Logos. Die Selbstentfaltung des griechischen Denkens von Homer bis auf die Sophistik und Sokrates*; Stuttgart: Kröner.
31 Snell, Bruno (1946) *Die Entdeckung des Geistes. Studien zur Entstehung des europäischen Denkens bei den Griechen*; Hamburg: Claaßen und Goverts.
32 *The ancient tradition in Christian and Islamic Hellenism.* Leiden: Research School CNWS.
33 Andrew M. Watson (1983) *Agricultural innovation in the early Islamic world*, Cambridge University Press, p. 8 ff. and 42 ff.

between the two superpowers Rome and Iran. This was now a matter of the past; Iran had become the bridge to India. Evidence for this may be found not only in the Indian origin of our "Arabic" numeral system but also in astrology and in medicine. David Pingree was perhaps the scholar whose work was most influential in this respect. But we find examples for the phenomenon even in a field where we would expect them least: in literature. The Greek novel "Metiochos and Parthenope" the original of which is lost reappears in 'Unsuri's Persian epic *Wāmiq u 'Adhrā'* which is partially preserved. All the names in the Persian version are still Greek, with exception of *'Adhrā'* which is Arabic but at the same time a "calque" of *Parthenope* since both words are derived from the same meaning: virginity[34]. The plot, if looked at with sympathy, seems to give us a presentiment of the "modern subject," for the heroes of these ancient Persian love stories behave like those we know from Hollywood films. Jaspers would perhaps not have been pleased, but we are less fastidious in this respect, I bet.

One might object that, in contrast to the Persians, the Arabs were less openly receptive of Antiquity in the sphere of belles lettres; as is well-known they never developed any interest in Greek theatre or in Homer's Iliad. But on the other hand their way of producing books, especially in the academic sphere, strongly resembled Hellenistic practice, at least in the beginning. Gregor Schoeler has shown[35] that in early Islam we have to differentiate between two sorts of writings: literary texts on the one hand which were destined for a larger public and had a definite and polished, unalterable form, and less elaborate products on the other which resulted from lecture courses, i.e. through direct contact between teacher and disciple, as a kind of aide-mémoire. The terms used by the Greeks in this respect were συγγραμμα and υπομνημα respectively. Plato's dialogues are συγγραμματα, Aristotle's treatises were only υπομνηματα since they were not put together into a final corpus until much later, "Literatur der Schule für die Schule" as Werner Jaeger once called it. The same still applies, by the way, to Hegel's philosophical works; they are merely "Nachschriften," notes taken by the students. Right from the beginning, book-production was a very conservative cultural phenomenon which could easily be handed on from one civilization to the other.

So much for continuity. The items I mentioned support a working-hypothesis current among Ancient historians in the English-speaking world, at least for the moment: the assumption of a so-called "long" Late Antiquity which includes the Umayyad period, as opposite to decline theories of the Gibbon type. This is, of

---

34 Richard Davis (2002), *Greek and Persian Romances*, in Encyclopaedia Iranica XI 339 ff. s. v. "Greece" where this is only one of several examples.
35 First in German (in several articles which were published in the periodical "Der Islam" between 1985 and 1992), but now also in French, in book form: Schoeler (2002) *Ecrire et transmettre dans les débuts de l'islam*; Paris: Presses Universitaires de France.

course, mainly a matter of periodization. But periodization is usually not as innocent as it looks. Andrew Watson's book about "Agricultural Innovation in the Early Islamic World" stirred up a discussion about whether the Umayyads could really have been able of such an achievement, for provided they had been mere uncultivated bedouins they would not have contributed to "innovations" with regard to the ancient world, and least so in a field as quintessentially "cultural" as agriculture where the Latin term *cultura* had been derived from. I am not yet sure whether protests of this kind may be regarded nowadays as mere rearguard actions. But at least the term "Late Antiquity" as such is old; it was brought up by the Austrian art historian Alois Riegl (1858-1905)[36] and then taken over by the French scholar Henri-Irénée Marrou and others. Today Garth Fowden, Irfan Shahid, Oleg Grabar and others pursue this approach[37]. Could it be then that the Islamic "rupture" in which we tend to believe more than ever in these days loses some of its obviousness if looked at more closely? Is religion alone a category sufficient for a historiographical model? We have to admit that, in the case of Islam, religion, because of its triumphant emergence, was soon associated with a second factor which symbolized rupture in a very tangible way: Arabic language. Islam had succeeded in creating an empire, and the language of the new revelation, the *lisan 'arabi mubin* of the Quran (sura 16: 103), quickly served as a tool for Arab administration. We should, however, not exaggerate. In the Orient, language was for a long time – up to the twentieth century, as a matter of fact – not a criterion as dominant as it had become for modern European nation-building, and religion, even when presenting itself as a product of strikingly new prophecy, could not live without exegesis and theology. Theology, however, was again a field where rupture quickly mixed with continuity. The result could amount to an astonishing originality.

I choose merely one example: atomism, something which, as "modern subjects," we would not expect in theology at all but which, in early Islamic thought, turned out to be the prevailing model, and not only in theology at that. We are still not entirely sure whether Islam had learnt about atomism from Greece or from India (mainly because there is nobody in today's scholarly world who is equally competent in the three languages and civilizations concerned). But for the moment the balance is tipped in favour of Greece. The influence was not exerted through books but through a subterranean intellectual tradition, a "transmission diffuse" as Paul Thillet would call it. Therefore the point of departure was not

---

36 Riegl, Alois (1901) *Die spätrömische Kunstindustrie nach den Funden in Österreich-Ungarn*: Vienna: Österreichische Staatsdruckerei, but also already in Riegl (1889) *Die ägyptischen Textilfunde im K. K. Österreichischen Museum*; Vienna: KK. Österreichisches Museum für Kunst und Industrie.
37 Cf. generally Clover, F.M./Humphreys, R.S. (1989) "Toward a Definition of Late Antiquity." In Clover/Humphreys (eds.) *Tradition and Innovation in Late Antiquity*: Madison: The University of Wisconsin Press, pp. 3-19.

Democritus who, chronologically speaking, was much too far away, but Epicurus with his theory of *elákhista* (or *minima,* to use Lucretius's term). What happened to Epicurean philosophy in the Orient during the centuries after his death is shrouded in darkness. The Christian Churchfathers did not particularly like him, and when his ideas came up again in Islam they looked rather rudimentary and disjointed; not even his name was any longer connected with them. What remained of the original system was a theory of movement, i.e. locomotion in an atomic, discrete space, and, in addition to that, perhaps the explanation of speech as a chain of isolated, "atomic" sounds which are represented by the letters of the alphabet. Islamic theology, however, when adopting these elements, mixed them with something which had never been associated with them before, namely the idea of a God who, as the creator of everything, keeps nature in his hands. Not that God uses the atoms as pre-existing parts which are available to Him like a *materia prima,* for then He would depend on them. He rather creates the things by His Word, the imperative "Be" as was said in the Quran. But when they have thus come into existence they consist of atoms so that He is free to dissolve them again, simply by taking out the link between the atoms; we call this "death," annihilation etc. And He can add this link again, in order to re-create the same entities a second time; we call this "resurrection." Atomism had become a means of explaining God's omnipotence. Epicurus would not have dreamt of that, and no Christian Churchfather had ever had such an idea. The Islamic theologians had managed to put Epicurus from his feet on his head, as it were.

What I have said so far about the cultural transfer concerned is certainly not the last word in this affair; too much work has still to be done with regard to the "dark centuries" which separate Islam from the heyday of Hellenistic thought[38]. But it shows at least that religious speculation did not necessarily pursue a completely different track by the mere fact of new prophecy; only people who think in terms of true and false can believe this. What Islam offered to its community was a new "constitution," a Law which regulated the life of the believers and thus furnished "right guidance." Even in this respect, though, i.e. on the social level, there was more continuity than we tend to assume. Let me take, as a final example, the so-called *millet*-system which we know from the Ottoman Empire, i.e. the restricted juridical independence of the Christian and the Jewish communities which harks back to the first centuries of Islam. We are normally told that it is in the Quran, but as a matter of fact it was worked out by the *fuqaha,'* the jurists. They were obviously confronted with a social reality which they had not

---

38 For a preliminary summary cf. the chapter on atomism in van Ess, Josef (1997) *Theologie und Gesellschaft im 2. und 3. Jahrhundert Hidschra,* Berlin/New York: Walter de Gruyter, Vol. IV, pp. 459-477; also van Ess (2002) *60 Years After. Shlomo Pines's* Beiträge *and Half a Century of Research on Atomism in Islamic Theology,* Jerusalem. The Israeli Academy of Sciences and Humanities, Proceedings VIII/2.

created themselves but were simply asked to codify. This reality preceded the Quran; it seems to have originated in Sasanid Iran, during the last two centuries before Islam, the period when the Jews collected the so-called "Babylonian" Talmud and when the Nestorian Church built up its ecclesiastical law, a kind of law, as a matter of fact, which in spite of being "ecclesiastical" exceeded the affairs of the clergy and included everyday life in the community. What we notice here really deserves being called an "innovation;" there is no trace of it in the Hellenistic heritage. On the contrary: The Nestorians were forerunners, not followers, and forerunners insofar as they had to find their own way to "Daseinsbewältigung," separated as they were from the Byzantine, Greek-speaking High Church. To use Michael Morony's words, we are dealing with "the part of a general social transformation taking place in southwestern Asia from the fourth to the ninth century (CE)" which, as such, became "the single most important distinction between Muslim and Hellenistic society" (1984: 277 ff.)[39].

The Axial Age and other explanatory models – a free market

Would inclusion into an Antiquity of *longue durée* elevate Islam then onto the civilizational highway which led from the Axial Age to modernity? Possibly, though only *con amore*. But if we ask the other way round: Is it necessary for a positive understanding of Islam to assume something like an Axial Age? I am less sure of how to answer. Not so much because I have my doubts about the "modern subject." Jaspers had them already, and Alfred Weber even more so. When reading the introduction to Weber's (Alfred, not Max!) "Farewell to History" we get the impression of being confronted with a forecast of globalization. Alfred Weber saw the freedom of the modern subject threatened by the power of anonymous institutions, and what we feel ourselves nowadays seems to differ from this only insofar as, from the late forties onward, German intellectuals were afraid of the "masses." Ortega y Gasset had set the key (1930), and Elias Canetti was to elaborate on the topic later on (1960) in "Masse und Macht." It is true that Alfred Weber rather focussed on Nietzsche and the desastrous influence of his *Übermensch*; he does not quote Ortega, and he may have realized that it is difficult to speak of the masses in an age of democracy. But the new spirit has not guarded us from barbarity, neither in the century which has just passed nor in the one which is now in its first years; we can watch war again, and not only that, but also torture and impersonal brutality of all sorts. This may simply be the ongoing reality of history "as it used to be." Nevertheless: If we indulge in speaking of

---

39 Morony, Michel G. (1984) *Iraq after the Muslim Conquest*, Princeton: University Press.

"breakthroughs," should we not speak of relapses as well? To make things clear: Of relapses which occur in our own civilization, not in those of the others for which we are responsible only in a somewhat derivative sense. And if we admit that U-turns are possible on the royal road to civilization, should we not persuade then ourselves to weigh the pros and cons of differing historiographical models which claim the same universality as does the Axial Age?

There are not many of them nowadays, and I am not in the position to pass a sentence anyway. Goitein once called Islam the "Intermediate Civilization," a civilization which had a value of its own because "for the first time in history (it) formed a strong cultural link between all parts of the ancient world"[40]. That is to say: Islam engendered a civilization of its own by taking up the heritage of the ancient world. But Goitein pronounced his statement only for the period of "classical" Islam which ended at a certain moment, just as the Christian civilization found its definite shape in the European and Byzantine Middle Ages and "ended" with enlightenment. In both cases the specific moment of the end would be difficult to fix, but we would have to assume that what we see happening in the Islamic world nowadays has its roots in modernity rather than in the "Middle Ages." Such a periodization would perhaps spare us some problematic value-judgments. Unfortunately, it would also burden us with new chronological problems. But this is our lot as historians.

Or, just in order to continue in this vein: Hans Küng recently published his volume on Islam[41], the last one of a trilogy[42] which explains the growth of the three Near-Eastern prophetic religions as a sequence of parallel steps following the "paradigm"-concept of Thomas Kuhn[43]. Küng's model is unabashedly theological, and its parallelisms are invitations to dialogue. Dialogue was not foreseen in Jaspers's book; his concept still had a slightly authoritarian ring, and be it only by taking the Occident as the exemplary model. Afterwards the intellectual climate changed, at least for a certain period; there was not only a dialogue of religions, but even of civilizations. Islam took part in it, especially with Iran under Mohammad Khatami's presidentship. Franco Cardini showed in his "Europe and Islam. The History of a Misunderstanding" to what extent Western historiography was affected by this approach[44]. Küng for his part has no place for the Axial Age. Nevertheless he, too, starts with a symbol far back in the past, a figure

---

40 Goitein, Shlomo Dov (1963) "Between Hellenism and Renaissance. Islam, the Intermediate Civilization." Islamic Studies (Karachi) 2, pp. 217-233, see p. 218 f. and 222. Reprinted in Goitein (1966) *Studies in Islamic History and Institutions*, Leiden: Brill, pp. 54-70.
41 Küng, Hans (2004) *Der Islam. Geschichte, Gegenwart, Zukunft,* München: Piper.
42 Cf. Küng (1991) *Das Judentum* and Küng (1994) *Das Christentum. Wesen und Geschichte,* both München: Piper.
43 Kuhn, Thomas S. (1962) *The Structure of Scientific Revolutions*, Chicago: University Press.
44 Cardini, Franco (1999) *Europa e Islam. Storia di un Malinteso.* Rome-Bari: Laterza.

which preceded the Axial Age by centuries: Abraham. We are thus confronted with a different foundation myth. Abraham had nothing to do with the "modern subject;" on the other hand he could be regarded as the "father" of the three monotheistic religions. He could, of course, play this symbolic role all the more easily since we know even less about him than about the Axial Age. But this is not the point. "Father" means here: the person whom all three religions equally venerate, the point of orientation where they would meet when they were to retrace their footprints into the past. Küng became acquainted with this idea when he attended the second Vatican Council; the concept had been developed by an Orientalist, Louis Massignon, and Father Georges Anawati, another Orientalist and an Egyptian at that, took care of its being inserted into the Declaration about the Muslims. When Massignon, a French Catholic, chose Abraham as a key symbol he had the Quran in mind rather than the Old Testament, and Islam was integrated into an extended vision of salvation history where it ceased to be the outsider who was one millenium late. Certainly, Küng's work has not met with unanimous assent, and Thomas S. Kuhn's "change of paradigm" is, as far as I can see, no longer received with a heartily welcome either, at least not in the field it was originally intended for, i.e. history of science. But for a fruitful discussion, and as a contrast to Jaspers's crypto-Protestant model, Küng's approach is worth some reflection.

And let us not forget, for a change, the Muslims themselves. What would they say if they were allowed (and ready) to have a word in these deliberations? They would, of course, have as many different views as we have. But let us try to think in the vein of the traditional Islamic "Geschichtsbild" and then imagine what would happen if they were to universalize it the way we are used to. They would probably interpret Muhammad's historical appearance as a "breakthrough," a radical change of perception accompanied by a strong "pathos of negation," to use Nietzsche's expression. Seen against the background of Eastern Christianity Islam would then be a kind of reformation, the first reformation which hit Christianity. For according to the image which Muhammad had of himself, he had not brought something entirely new but rather come with an old message in order to purge Christianity and Judaism from their aberrations. He believed that whoever had preceded him as a prophet had established his own covenant with God and that these covenants had successively been broken by those to whom they had been addressed. "Covenant" is a concept taken from the Old Testament; the Christians had made it malleable by assuming an Old and a New Covenant, and now the Quran claimed the same concept for a third Prophet's message[45]. This idea, which was not without some inherent logic,

---

45 Cf. sura 57:8 and the parallels mentioned in Paret, Rudi (1971) *Der Koran. Kommentar und Konkordanz*, Stuttgart: Kohlhammer, p. 470; C.E. Bosworth in *Encyclopaedia of Islam*, sec. ed. VII 187 f. s. v. *Mithak*; G. Böwering in: Encyclopedia of the Qur'an I 464 ff. s. v. *Covenant*. For the connection with hebr. *berit* cf. Wansbrough, John (1977) *Quranic Studies*, Oxford University Press, pp. 8 ff.

would even survive a change of terminology, for even when Christian theologians of our days prefer talking about a "First" and a "Second" Covenant instead of an Old and a New one (or a First and a Second Testament) it would be still possible to ask: If God really made two wills, why not three? Under this premiss and in the context of salvation history, the almost total disappearance of Christianity in the areas occupied by Islam could then be interpreted as a providential act. As a matter of fact it would not be far-fetched to assume that Christianity had lost a great deal of its spiritual vigour in the Orient when Islam set on its triumphant advance. The bitter struggle about coining the correct formula for incarnation and trinity had visibly split the community, and many a convert to Islam may have left his old religion because he had ceased experiencing Christianity as anything else but a conglomerate of at least three different churches. Christian theology had ended up in a deadlock and in constant strife; the Quran was quite aware of this danger[46]. This may have also been the erason why in Islam the speculative theologians never played the role they had played in Byzantium during the centuries after Constantine.

This is only a thought experiment. But we cannot deny that Christianity, apart from the rather reduced Byzantine territory where it survived until 1453, became a phenomenon of the Roman West. In Europe Islam never presented itself as a reform movement but simply as a heresy. Yet when Western Christians had to define their historical locus they were in a rather awkward position. Squeezed in between Judaism and Islam they had to pretend, against Judaism, that they represented a more developed stage of religion, as people of a new "covenant," whereas against Islam they were forced to claim that whatever was new in the sphere of religion was wrong. Theologically speaking they had to put much emphasis on faith as such, for when asked for their ultimate criterion of truth they could not but point to a miracle: resurrection. Compared to this, a prophetical message was a simpler thing; prophecy could always be justified by its mere contents, as a rational necessity, whereas resurrection could not. Resurrection had originally been the expedient of the "Urgemeinde" to get away from the sad fact that Jesus had died on the cross, but when their belief survived just for this reason they had to stick to it for ever. In order to further explain it they had to insist, in one way or the other, on the divine nature of Christ, and the concept of incarnation then led them to the dogma of trinity. This sequence of ideas was as inevitable as it was irrational. Islam laid bare the axiomatic character of the procedure and could therefore claim having brought clarity again, "knowledge" (*'ilm*) according to the vocabulary of the Quran, as opposite to mere "opinion" (*zann*) which had characterized the period of ignorance (*al-jahiliyya*). As a matter of fact, Muslims never speculated about the tension between knowledge and belief;

---

46 Sura 11:118 f. or 42:8; cf. Y. Friedmann in: EQur I 538 f. s. v. *Dissension* (also S.H. Griffith, ib. I 312 ff. s. v. *Christians*).

this topic remained a priviledge of medieval Christian thought. Admittedly miracles were in the long run accepted in Islam, too, but they did not become as indispensable as in Christianity. Thus Christianity, though suffering badly in the East, could survive in the West, in Europe, where the new religion spread among a young and rather unexperienced population for whom miracles were not a metaphysical problem. The Muslims, on the contrary, stood in a long and uninterrupted tradition of sophistication, at least in the urban areas of their empire which already during Late Antiquity had been the intellectually prominent part of the Roman world.

Would this tell us anything about the "modern subject"? The modern subject emerged when, due to the onslaught of enlightenment, the European Christians gave up their belief in miracles. But this "breakthrough" equally affected the foundations of Christian dogmatics. In order to make up for this defeat the "West" turned towards ethics, a move which the Christians shared, in the nineteenth century, with European Judaism. Ethics lent itself to be presented on a rational basis; in our days human rights are the best example. When reacting against this change of paradigm the Muslims never lost the impression that the so-called enlightenment they were now supposed to learn from the West was already found in the Quran. The discussions which ensued from this were, and are, full of misunderstandings and therefore not void of tension and aggression. And ethics can, of course, never be the same as religion.

Are "Gedankenexperimente" of this kind[47] legitimate or even useful? Perhaps insofar as they help us to discover that historical models, wherever they come from, are based on "Vor-Urteile," pre-judices in the Heideggerian sense. We should not take them too seriously; they may turn out to be mere chimeras. Nor should we, however, demonize them. All models are primarily a game of our intellect, axiomatic, but not dangerous unless they ossify into an ideology. They widen our horizon and tend to engender valuable detailed studies, but it may happen that the more we know about them the less we trust them. What is important is that they are indispensable for any research, they are the pattern according to which we select or interpret what we consider to be the "facts." We are then not necessarily simply giving a meaning to something meaningless ("Sinngebung des Sinnlosen") as Theodor Lessing put it shortly after the First World War when people like Troeltsch (1865-1923) or Spengler (1880-1936) were still alive[48]. Talking about the sense of history, its "origin and aim," rather contributes to the discovery of our civilizational identity. We should only retain a critical distance:

---

47 Like "breakthrough," the term "thought experiment" seems to be of German origin. In an English context it was still used in its German form in 1958 (cf. *The Oxford English Dictionary* ²VI 417 s. v.). There is, though, a first attested usage of the English parallel ("thought experiment") already in 1945 (ib. XVII 985).

48 Lessing, Theodor (1919) *Geschichte als Sinngebung des Sinnlosen oder Die Geburt der Geschichte aus dem Mythos.* Revised edition ⁴1927 Leipzig: Reinicke.

Any civilizational identity is neither static nor universal, and the freedom of the "modern subject" should not be used to impose own axioms on others but rather stimulate us, in a self-referential way, to continuously check what, in all sincerity, we still have to offer to the world. "Historical significance is one of the most difficult concepts to treat or to measure"[49], and breakthroughs are perhaps not for ever. Axial syndromes are probably easier to verify than the Axial Age.

---

49 Morony, Michael G. (1989) "Teleology and the Significance of Change." In F.M. Clover/R.S. Humphreys (eds.) *Tradition and Innovation in Late Antiquity*, Madison: The University of Wisconsin Press, pp. 21-26; cf. p. 25.

Cultural and Institutional Dynamics

Chapter 9

Islam and the Path to Modernity: Institutions of Higher Learning and Secular and Political Culture

SAÏD AMIR ARJOMAND

In a companion essay (Arjomand forthcoming) I have examined the role of the cities, guilds and *futuwwa* associations of men and youths in the developmental path of Islamicate civilization. In this paper, I wish to do the same with the institutions of higher learning and the culture they produced. As in the earlier case, I will pay special attention to the legal framework of civic agency as it affected the constitution of the *madrasas*. I will, however, go beyond the earlier analytical scheme by also focusing on intercivilizational encounters and their institutional frames as an important feature of what might be called late axiality, and show their decisive importance in determining the directionality of social and civilizational transformation.

The recent move from Karl Jaspers' idea of a specific Axial Age in world history to a typological conception of Axial Civilizations (Arnason/Eisenstadt/Wittrock 2005) is an important theoretical advance. Its focus on the dynamics rather than origins of the institutionalization of transcendence brings out several urgent analytical needs. Of these I will concentrate on the significance of common or interconnected cross-regional patterns and the role of intercivilizational encounters (Nelson 1981). As Arnason, Eisenstadt and Wittrock (2005: 12) point out, the typological thesis forces us to move from the model of (ahistorically conceived) insulated civilizational complexes with distinctive dynamics to world-historical transformations and intercivilizational processes. This requires a historicization of Axial constellations, especially in later formative periods, often involving intercivilizational dialogue. I consider the reception of Aristotle in medieval Christianity and Islam as a common encounter with the Greek civilization with, needless to say, different outcomes. I will attempt to explain different consequences of this encounter in terms of differences in law and institutional structures between the universities and the *madrasa*s, and finally comment on the effect of this differential reception on the divergent paths to modernity in the Western and Islamicate civilizations.

In contrast to Toby Huff's (1993) focus on the unique modern science in the West, my contrast centers on the rise of universities and their decisive contribution to secular culture, especially the political culture. My focus is thus on the development of modern political thought in the West and the contingent and structural factors that hindered a similar development in the Islamicate civilization. This should in turn throw some light on the differentiation of religious and political cultures that have been singled out in this volume as the problematic feature of Islamicate axiality.

Madrasas, universities and the law

The absence of the concept of corporation and juristic personality in Islamic law was highlighted in Joseph Schacht's (1935: 225) early essay, and has more recently been singled out as the key factor hindering the development of modern science in Islam (Huff 1993: 79, 127-29). It is equally true that the possibility of municipal self-government was also adversely affected by this lack, and it is certainly true that no elected city officials emerged in the Islamicate world. The influential Oxford symposium on the Islamic City (1970) proposed a different legal explanation for the lack of urban political autonomy – indeed for the failure of Islam to develop modernity: the individualism of Islamic law, which can conceive no intermediate legal personality between the individual and the *umma* (universal community of believers). The *Shari'a* is accordingly said to withhold recognition to the most crucial such intermediary, the city (Hourani 1970; Stern 1970). According to this theory, the individual freedom of action, contractual obligations, notably commercial partnerships and transactions in private property are legally protected by the *Shari'a*, but free and autonomous civic and public action is severely restricted because no intermediaries between the individual and the universal *umma* is recognized in the Islamic law.

The assertion of the absence of intermediaries between the individual and the *umma* has been vigorously refuted with reference to the Ottoman guilds by Haim Gerber (1994: 119), who states that "the guild system enjoyed a wide measure of autonomy and [...] its legal basis was customary law." Gerber is absolutely right that guilds were covered by customary law, which was in turn recognized by the *Shari'a*. The agency of guilds was made licit as custom and thus granted autonomy by the legal order in principle. The legal position of the city is, however, more complicated. I have similarly argued against this view elsewhere (1999), maintaining instead that a sphere of autonomy and universality along the lines of Hegel's conceptual definition of civil society was in fact constituted and protected by the *Shari'a*, in particular by the law of endowments (*waqf*). The (civil) law of *waqf* served as the basis for the creation of a vast sphere of educational and charitable activity; and the same civil law granted the ruler, the royal family and the highest office-holders an instrument of public policy which they could activate as individual agents[1] The strength of that civil society should be seen as historically variable, whereby protection by the law is one factor among many, and in fact was overwhelmed by a contrary development in nomadic state formation after the 11th century.

In his magisterial studies on the Islamic educational system, George Makdisi (1961; 1981; 1990) traces three stages in the development of the *madrasa* into colleges for the study of the Koran, the Traditions of the Prophet and jurisprudence. The three stages are the following: 1) the development of teaching circles (halqas) for various subjects in mosques from the earliest times to the 10th century, 2) the emergence of the "mosque-inn colleges" toward the end of the 10th century, and finally, 3) the development of the "*madrasa* colleges of law," in which the functions of the mosque and the hostel were combined in an institution based on a single deed of endowment. Makdisi includes the official establishment of the *madrasa*s by the great Seljuq vizier, Nizam al-Mulk, in the second half of the 11th century in this stage. Makdisi offers an incisive analysis of the impact of the Islamic law of endowment (*waqf*) on the development of Islamic education as the instrument of foundation of the *madrasa*s.

This account needs to be modified in some important respect. Roy Mottahedeh (1997) has shown the alleged second stage, which Makdisi further considered the prototype of European colleges, to be based entirely on the misreading of a single text. It has also been pointed out that the *madrasa*s were not just colleges of law but also taught other subjects, except for philosophy, and that the development of the *madrasa* in northeastern Iran predates Nizam al-Mulk's policy by a good century and a half (Mottahedeh 1997; Arjomand 1999). Yet Makdisi's (1981) argument that the *madrasa* professors enjoyed exclusive "teaching authority" to issue the *ijazat al-tadris/licentia docenti* to their graduating doctors in jurisprudence and the science of Traditions holds firmly. The fact that there was no "episcopal authority" in Islam from which it could be disengaged, however, leaves it both more undifferentiated and not extendable to other fields of knowledge that actually were, or could potentially be, taught in colleges.

Furthermore, Makdisi's account of the development of colleges does not go far enough in history. What he does not consider is a further stage of the development of the institutions of learning which begins in the latter part of the 13th century, and is marked by the emergence of what I call the educational-charitable complex (Arjomand 1999). The consequences of this omission are not merely chronological but substantive. On the one hand, this development invalidates Makdisi's assertion that philosophy and medicine were not taught in the *madrasa*s. On the other, it brings out certain deleterious effect of the organizational

---

1   A crucial implication of this Islamic legal system is that the private/public distinction of Roman Law applies very imperfectly, as the line between the two sphere was drawn very differently.

form for the autonomy of the *madrasa*s and the development of secular culture that Makdisi leaves out.

The law of *waqf* served as the instrument of agency in a civic, public sphere of charitable and educational institutions. Furthermore,

> the possibility of affecting the constitution of the public sphere [...] was open to a private person and a public official alike. The civil law of *waqf* therefore served as an instrument of agency available both to the individuals in the civic community and the rulers and officials of the patrimonial state.

The law of *waqf* was, however, quite rigid, in large part due to the fact that Islamic law had no concept of corporation (*universitas*). To be more precise, it

> enabled the founder of an endowment to create public space and specify the sociocultural activity for which it was to be used. With the combination of the mosque and the college in the institution of the *madrasa* by a single deed of *waqf*, the founder of a *madrasa* could determine the subjects to be taught and the credal and denominational affiliation of the beneficiaries.
> [...] the personal nature of delegated authority under patrimonial monarchy meant that the significant acts of the vizier always had a public character, and, more importantly, that there was no real distinction between the private property of a vizier and the public funds at his disposal. Amassing enormous property holdings was inseparable from their extensive procurement of the means of administration, and a part of that property could be expected to be used in pursuit of state policy. This was done in the sphere of education and welfare through the instrumentality of the (civil) law of *waqf* (Arjomand 1999).

In other words, the dead hand (mortmain) of the founder lay upon the college instituted through the law of wafq and deprived it of the built-in mutability and active agency of a corporation.

Makdisi (1984; 1989; 1994) has also claimed corporate status for the schools of Islamic law, arguing that they were, by the 11th century, indeed corporations and "guilds of law"[2] (Makdisi 1984: 239). His argument, however, is based on a loose and flawed analogy between the hierarchical status terms in guilds and schools of law. It is invalidated by the fact that the schools of law, though consisting of individual jurists authorized to issue an *ijâza*, which he sees as the literal origin of the European *licentia docenti*, were translocal and transgenera-

---

2 Makdisi is correct in asserting that the transformation of "the followers" of prominent individual jurists into the (eventually) four Sunni Schools of Law (*madhhab*s) was of crucial importance. However, there is some exaggeration in his statement that "the new professional system, *autonomous* in its guild, *exclusive* in its colleges, and *monopolistic* in its doctorate, was a veritable revolution in higher learning in Islam" (Makdisi 1994: 25). In any event, the *ulema* were not a guild and had no governing body.

tional. Probably the correct sociological concept for what Makdisi has in mind is what Weber called a *Rechtsgenossenschaft* ("legally recognized sodality") and not a corporation.

Immediately after the period studied by Makdisi, changing fashions produced varying blueprints for charitable foundations, which included *madrasa*s. The complex, on the basis of the Islamic law of *waqf*, typically came to consist of a mosque, a *madrasa*, a public bath, a soup kitchen and the tomb of the founder. This is worth noting as the major institutional innovation of 13th-century Iran that might have contributed to a breakthrough in the Islamicate civilization. It was certainly adopted by the Delhi and Mamluk sultans, and by the Ottomans at the beginning of their empire. Orkhan Ghazi (1326-1359) modified the use of the *waqf* complex into an instrument of urban development, and built a bedestan at the center of the Ottoman capital, Bursa. In the bedestans or more generally the 'imaret complex the Ottomans set up as *waqf*s in the commercial centers in their cities and they made increasing use of new urban property, mostly shops, in addition to rural estates that had constituted the bulk of the Il-Khânid endowments in Iran. *Waqf* was similarly used throughout the next century of Ottoman conquests as an instrument of state policy for the development of the cities of Edirne and Istanbul (Inalcik 1973: 142-44). Creation of *'imârets* around their tombs as public *waqf*s by the great Sultans, notably Mehmed the Conqueror and Suleyman the Lawgiver, was imitated by Ottoman officials, who also acted as endowment administrators, and became an important means for urban development in Istanbul.

Having traced the development of colleges as a component of the charitable-educational complex created, however, I found this procedure of lumping together various components on terms rigidly fixed in the deed of endowment very detrimental to the autonomy of the colleges. Other activities of the complex could take precedence over the needs of the college and stifle its growth. Maya Shatzmiller (2001) points to the rigidity and economic inefficiency of the charitable foundations caused by the restrictions of the law of wafq, considering them more deleterious in the Mâliki Andalusia and the Maghreb than the Hanafi and Shâfi'i East.

The collegium as a component of European universities had the greatest affinity with the *madrasa* in that it often included a hostel for students. For this reason, Makdisi aptly calls the latter 'college.' However, beginning with the establishment of the Sorbonne in 1257, the residential connection became looser, and many scholars at Oxford, Cambridge or Cracow rented lodgings in town (Leedham-Green 1996: 20-21; Podlecki/Waltoœ 1999). Other differences between the *madrasa*s and universities were more consequential.

The *madrasa* had two major disadvantages as compared to the newly established European universities of the 13th century: corporate legal personality, and legal jurisdiction. Although major centers of learning called *studia generales* had been and continued to be established by the bulls of popes, emperors or kings, which laid certain conditions for their constitution and operations as did the deeds of *waqf*, they became by law capable of autonomous agency as *universitas* in the 13th century. Bologna was established in 1193 as a university or corporation of students, and Paris was make into a university or corporation of masters in early 13th century. They provided the alternative archetypes or blueprints for European universities. By the 15th century, the distinction between the two terms was lost and they became synonymous (Rashdall 1936, 1: 4-17). The union of *studium generale* and *universitas* was responsible for the elevation, during the 13th century, of studium alongside the two long established forms of authority, *sacerdotium* and *imperium* as the three powers "by whose harmonious cooperation the life and health of Christiandom are sustained" (Rashdall 1936, 1: 2).

The University of Paris had already been a renowned *studium generale*, and had thus emerged, around 1200, as a new order alongside temporal and spiritual authority. In the next two centuries, "teaching authority" became differentiated from "episcopal authority" and was variously appropriated by university professors as experts in knowledge, as in the writings of William Ockham, or more exclusively by the masters of theology at the university (Thijssen 1998: 93-117). As a corporation and a new order of authority, the University of Paris played a major role in the politics of France in the 14th and early 15th centuries (Rashdall 1936, 1: 540-84). This had no parallel in the 14th-century urban politics of Iran (Arjomand forthcoming). In the latter case the ulema could play a role as individuals but not as representatives of a corporate entity. The corporate legal status of the universities contributed to the institutionalization of European politics, a possibility precluded by the legal status of the *madrasa*s.

Secondly, the rectors or chancellors of universities were freed from subjection to episcopal confirmation by the end of the 14th century while enhancing their internal disciplinary and penal jurisdiction over the community of scholars and with regard to the immunities of university. Their courts and courts of the masters became firmly institutionalized (Leedham-Green 1996: 8-15). At the same time, the deliberations of academic assemblies were formalized and written down as early as 1250 in Cambridge in a form which may be taken as an official code of statutes (Leedham-Green 1996: 6-7). Furthermore, the universities developed extensive institutional interlinkages to both temporal and religious structures of authority. They had special privileges in the ecclesiastical court system, and developed their court and consistory and their "magisterium to suppress false teaching" in the course of the 13th century. In short, the university capitalized on its legal status as a corporation in order to establish its autonomy and self-government (Thijssen 1998: 5-6, 96). The *madrasa*s did not develop a similar jurisdiction and institutional interlinkages, and did not benefit from a similar legal status.

The conception of corporation (*universitas*) in Roman law was as a matter of course the critical legal foundation for the autonomy of European universities and development of their jurisdiction. The absence of a parallel concept in Islamic law hampered the autonomous agency of the *madrasa* as a civic organization. The absence of the legal concept of corporation is thus the fundamental factor differentiating the Christian and Islamic paths of development of higher education in the Middle Ages. The historical evidence we have clearly shows that the colleges could neither free themselves from the weight of the other components of the educational-charitable complex, nor from the control and public authority of the patrimonial state, because of the absence of the idea of corporation in Islamic law in general, and in the law of *waqf* in particular. Without this legal prerequisite, the *madrasa*s could not become autonomous universities. I think this emerges clearly from a book on the ethics of the *madrasa* and the mosque written in 1710, toward the end of the last period of unusual flourishing of the *madrasa* culture in Isfahan. The fact that the author was commissioned by a civic benefactor to write on the appropriate ethical rules for mosques and colleges lumped together is in itself revealing of a lack of differentiation harmful to the institutional autonomy of the latter. But it is above all the rambling and formally incoherent content of the tract (Tabrizi 1995) that is worlds apart from the statutes of the governing bodies of the self-governing European universities.

Intercivilizational influences on the Islamicate and Western transformation

Wittrock's (2001) provocative suggestion of a "Eurasian ecumenical renaissance" focuses our attention on common patterns of development across Eurasian civilizations, and the search for such patterns highlights inter-civilizational encounters as an easy way of explaining commonalities. The two critical factors making for the great transformation of the 13th century are the Mongol ecumenical empire, with branches in China and Iran as well as Russia, and the "dialogue between the living and the dead involving Greeks, Arabs [read Muslims] and Europeans" (Huff 1993: 13). Where the former facilitated the most significant encounter between the Islamicate and the Chinese civilizations, the latter marked the divergent path of late axial development of the Christian and Islamicate civilizations set in motion by their respective encounters with the same Greek civilization of antiquity.

The Chinese-Islamicate encounter requires a separate treatment, but I will mention one significant scientific encounter concerning astronomy as it concerns the protagonist of the next section of this paper. Huff (1993: 50) notes the transmission of trigonometry to Chinese astronomy through the employment of "Arab" astronomers in the Astronomical Bureau in Beijing from the 13th century onwards, but he does not seem aware of the fact that, on the Iranian side, Nasir al-Din Tusi employed Chinese mathematicians and astronomers in his famous observatory in Marâgheh (see below), translated the date of the year of the Pig (1203) to various other calendars and "made extensive use of Chinese technical jargon […] and the Chinese names for the ten celestial stems and twelve earthly branches of the sexagenary cycle" (Lane 2003: 218). Whatever the impact of such specific cultural exchanges, there can be no doubt about the flourishing of Persianate culture and the revival of the very idea of Iran, with the pictorial assimilation of the ancient Persian kings to the new Mongol rulers in the illustrations of Ferdausi's Shâhnâma (Soudavar 1996), in the Il-Khanid period. George Lane (2003) aptly subtitles his comprehensive study of the reign of Hülegü (1256-65) and his successor as "a Persian renaissance" and reminds us that the troops of the Atabeg of Fars, the great patron of learning and culture and of the great Persian poet, Sa῾di of Shiraz (d. 1291), who wrote the most moving elegy on the demise of the last ῾Abbasid Caliph, in fact accompanied the Mongol conqueror in the fateful siege of Baghdad in 1258 (Lane 2003: 30).

The encounter with the Greek civilization was, however, of much greater axial significance for Christianity and Islam. The transmission of Greek scientific and philosophical texts through Arabic and of the Muslim medical treatises to Europe in the Middle Ages is indisputable. The importation of institutions has not been proven, however. There is little evidence for the influence of the fully developed *madrasa*s on the nascent European universities in the 13th century. Makdisi's argument for the influence of the mosque-khân model on the Inns of Court as the first English law colleges set up in London in the 12th century by the Knights Templar returning from the Holy Land rests on a misreading of the textual source and is therefore unacceptable. Inspired by Makdisi, Monica Gaudiosi (1988) claims the law of *waqf* as a source of the English law of trust or use, and argues that the 1264 statutes of the House of Scholars of Merton, the deed of trust that set up the first Oxford College, can "be analyzed as a *waqf* instrument" (Gaudiosi 1988: 1250). But she can only show generic similarities between the deeds of trust and *waqf* rather than giving any direct proof of borrowing. It is true that the influence of the trust's founder was as great as that of a *waqf* endowment. Walter de Merton names members of his own family as the primary beneficiaries. Hugh of Balsham, the Bishop of Ely, founded the first Cambridge College, Peterhouse, in 1284 "for the sake of public utility" *(pro utilitate rei publicae)*. It was, however, explicitly modeled on Merton and reserved the appointment of the master and confirmation of fellows for the bishop (Leedham-Green 1996: 21-22). Merton College was soon incorporated by a subsequent deed of 1274, however, and it was not the unincorporated Inns of Court or Peterhouse but, as we have seen, the corporations of masters and/or scholars of Paris or Bologna that provided the blueprint for European universities[3] and assured their autonomous civic agency.

Makdisi's (1981) argument from the literal correspondence of *ijâzat al-tadris*

---

3 The first university at Cracow, established in 1364, was modeled on Bologna, and students elected the Rector. When it was reestablished in 1400, like Heidelberg (1386) and other more recently established universities, it used the Parisian model for its constitution, with the masters electing the Rector (Podlecki, J./Waltoœ 1999).

and *licentia docendi* is somewhat stronger, but he goes too far in claiming that "Islamic seeds were planted for what was soon to become a second magisterium in Christianity, that of the professors of theology" (Makdisi 1990: 128). Again, this probable original influence cannot explain the enormous growth of the university trained doctors of theology who outnumbered the priests and bishops at the Council of Basel in 1439 by 300 to 20 (Makdisi 1990: 129).

One of the least appreciated features of the Islamicate civilizational synthesis perfected in the 13th century is the composite medieval Muslim conception of state and society. I have argued that certain features of pristine Islam invited the political thought of other civilizations, in particular the Indian science of government and the Greek political science. With the cultural integration of Iran into the Muslim Caliphate, especially after the 'Abbasid revolution in the mid-8th century, the Indian borrowing via the Middle Persian translations emerged as an integral part of the Arabic and Persian literature on statecraft. The reception of the Greek political science was integral to the translation of Greek philosophy and medicine into Arabic a century later, and was developed into the discipline of practical philosophy or political science. Through the mutual accommodation of the *Shari'a* and a political culture derived from Greek and Perso-Indian sources, the civilizational encounters under consideration introduced an unmistakable element of pluralism – or at any rate, dualism -- in the normative order of medieval Islam (Arjomand 2001). The consummate presentation of this medieval synthesis, which remained definitive for the early modern Muslim "gunpowder empires" as well, is found in the Akhlâq-e Naseri, whose author is no other than Nasir al-Din Tusi. Works on ethics and statecraft by Tusi's epigones as well as his own treatise dominated the political thought of the Ottoman, Safavid and Mughal empires, and other than the immediate Islamic rejectionist reaction of the Hanbalite Ibn Taymiyya, to be discovered and cherished by the contemporary Islamic fundamentalists, there was no Islamic reaction before the reassertion of the *Shari'a* in the late-17th century Ottoman empire and the reign of Auranzeb and Shah Wali Allâh of Delhi in the 18th century.[4] Down to that century, a university educated European and a *madrasa* graduate, if they could communicate in a common language, would have shared the Aristotelian division of the human sciences into ethics, economics and politics as pertaining to the management of the individual self, the household and the polity. This similarity, however, is somewhat deceptive as the development of political thought in the two civilizations follows a sharply divergent path.

---

4 The fact that the Islamic reaction was so late in coming should cast doubt on Huff's (1993) attribution of the failure to develop modern science to medieval Islamic ethos, which was in fact less hostile to science than the medieval Christian ethos.

Nasir al-Din Tusi the vizier and Thomas Aquinas the professor

Two great intellects of the 13th century died three months apart in the same year of 1274: the professor friar Thomas Aquinas at Fossanova on his way to the Council of Lyon in March, and the vizier Khwâja Nasir al-Din Tusi in Baghdad, while inspecting the accounts of colleges and other endowments, in June. Nasir al-Din Tusi was prominent among the elite of the radical heterodox *Ismâ'ili* sect until his mid-50s, and joined the more moderate heterodox Twelver *Shi'a* when entering the service of the non-Muslim Mongol ruler of Iran. Both were, however, deeply involved in the institutions of higher learning and key figures in the reception of Aristotle into the secular and political cultures of their respective civilizations. Aquinas was the champion of Christian orthodoxy and a member of the Dominican Order set up in its defense, at the service of the pope.

The Dominican Order had been established in the year of Thomas's birth to preach orthodoxy against the Cathars and to defend the Christian faith by fortifying it with Aristotelian logic. The year he arrived in Paris to begin his studies at the university, 1252, the Cathars assassinated the Italian inquisitor, Peter of Verona. Nasir al-Din Tusi was at that time at the service of the last ruler of the *Ismâ'ili* fortresses in the northern Iranian mountains, and was to arrange his surrender to the Mongols in 1256, whereupon he entered the service of Ghengis Khan's grandson, Hülegü, and accompanied him in the sack of Baghdad and the overthrow of the `Abbasid Caliphate in 1258. The *Ismâ'ilis*, Hodgson's "order of Assassins," were the most radical of the heterodox Shi'ite sects, and are generally considered the transmitters of Dualism to the Cathars through the Bogomils of Bulgaria. After jumping the rocky *Ismâ'ili* boat into the solid Mongol ship, Nasir al-Din declared his belonging to the non-radical Shi'ite sect, the Twelvers. Tusi made an important contribution to Twelver Shi'ite rational theology as the leading intellectual and political figure in the sect, as he had done earlier for the Ismâ'ili doctrine. Tusi's heterodoxy entailed, as his autobiography shows (Tusi 1998: 3-5, 19), his love of secular culture and the dislike of all religious doctrines, which he considered distortions of the same ultimate truth. His philosophical, ethical and political writings were accordingly completely non-sectarian. According to the contemporary Jacobite monk, Bar Hebraeus, "he held fast to the opinions of the early philosophers, and he combated vigorously in his writings those who contradicted them" (Cited in Lane 2003: 214)

Aquinas was a product of the great University of Paris and a professor par excellence. A decade before Aquinas's birth, a "university of masters" had been established in Paris, already an illustrious center of learning, and quickly developed in his lifetime, and with his participation, into the first "university of masters and scholars" or the first autonomous corporation with the right of self-government identical to that granted to a guild or a communia (Ferruolo 1985: 3-5). His teaching career in Paris is closely tied to two epochal institutional developments. The first is the struggle over the combination of two new institutions: the mendicant orders and the universities. Thomas was imposed upon a combative party of secular masters who were demanding the exclusion of the mendicant masters from the university as a corporation during the 1252-1257 anti-mendicant controversy, which was accompanied by violence in the streets of Paris. His first appointment to one of the two chairs of theology reserved for the Dominicans was in 1256, when Thomas was only thirty-one – four years younger than the minimum age for masters. He held the chair until 1259, and returned to Paris to occupy the chair of theology unusually for a second time from 1269 to 1272 in order to defend the right of the Dominican and Franciscan Orders to hold chairs of theology (Weisheipl 1974: 80-103, 263-72; Inglis 2002: 11). His task was to consolidate the fusion of the college and the convent which was facing the determined opposition of the secular masters at the University of Paris for a second time – a remarkable parallel to the fusion of the *madrasa* and the Sufi convent attempted by Caliph al-Nâsir half a century earlier, and equally unsuccessful in the long run. In the subsequent century, however, the Faculty of Arts became predominant at the University of Paris. The predominance of the Faculty of Arts in 14th century Oxford was even more conspicuous (Rashdall 1936, 1: 439-71; 3: 60). European universities primarily became centers of secular learning.

The second development was the reception of Aristotle. In March 1255, the year before the inception of Thomas in the Dominican chair for foreigners, the Faculty of Arts had passed new statutes that put most of the books of Aristotle on the curriculum (van Steenberghen 1955: 164-65, 191-92). Aquinas' second mission when sent back to Paris in 1269 was indeed to justify the use of Aristotle in rational theology in defense of revelation as advocated by the Dominicans. Here, he found himself in complete sympathy with the secular masters of the Faculty of Arts and was later considered their accomplice by the conservative clerics.

Nasir al-Din Tusi had a higher supervisory authority over all the *madrasa*s of the Il-Khânid empire as the vizier in charge of the *waqf* revenues of the empire which supported them. He translated his love of philosophy and dislike of the religious sciences of Traditions (hadith) and jurisprudence into educational policy. According to the historian Ibn Kathir,

Khwâja Nasir set the stipend of the students of philosophy at three drachmas a day, that of the medical students at two, that of the students of Islamic law at one, and the Traditionists' at one half of a drachma. For this reason people crowded the colleges of philosophy and medicine over those of law and Traditions, whereas earlier those sciences were taught in secret (cited in Arjomand 1998: 120).

A generation later, however, the great Mongol Vizier, Rashid al-Din Fazl Allah (d. 1318), though a late convert from Judaism, put the Islamic law above other subjects and did not favor philosophy. Being a physician by training, he also set up chairs and assistantships for the study and teaching of medicine in the numerous colleges he founded with the enormous revenues and resources he appropriated as vizier. From the comparative point of view, there was no mechanism available to the *madrasa*s, which were not self-governing corporations, for bringing about either of the above changes in the curriculum or any other themselves, as the Faculty of Arts of the University of Paris had done in 1255. Nevertheless, despite the handicap of the law of *waqf*, the reception of Aristotle did result in the multiplication of disciplines or branches of learning. The growth of secular sciences was not as spectacular as in Europe, where the proportion of theologians dropped from some 40 per cent to some 15 per cent between the 13th and early 15th centuries (Leedham-Green 1996: 19), but it was substantial. It is interesting to note that a century later, Ibn Khaldun, who affirmed that "sciences multiply with the increase of civilization and the growth of cities" (Muqaddima, 465 [Bk 6, title of ch. 3; tr. Section 8 [2: 434] modified)^5 enumerated a large number of secular sciences^6 and went so far as to state that, because heretics and innovators have been destroyed, "the science of theology is not something that is necessary to the contemporary student."^{7} (Muqaddima, 499; tr. 3: 54 modified)

In 1259, Hülegü put him in charge of building an observatory in his capital, Marâgheh, and appointed him the head of the *waqf* bureau of the empire, a position he held for fifteen years. Nasir al-Din Tusi used *waqf* not only for the foundation of the observatory but also as a general instrument of public cultural policy. He appointed officials in each district responsible for remitting one tenth of the revenues of the endowments (the usual administration fee) to the treasury, mainly for expenditure on the observatory. The building of the observatory was completed under Hülegü's successor, Âbâqâ (1265-81). Nasir al-Din also

---

5   This assertion, and the fact that over a third of the *Muqaddima* is devoted to sciences as the culmination of the superior type of civilization, namely urban civilization, confirms Arnason and Stauth's (2004: 37) doubts "about the universality and invariance of cyclical models" attributed to him.
6   These include practical sciences based on experience (*tajriba*) as they cover man's life in society (Muqaddima, 501-2). This chapter is for some reason not included in Rosenthal's translation.
7   Having explained the decline of sciences with the collapse of strong dynasties and languishing of city life in the Maghreb (Muqaddima, Bk 6, ch. 2), Ibn Khaldun turns to explaining the flourishing of sciences in the last two centuries in Egypt, where he had taken up residence, in institutional terms in a way that brings out the personal motives of the Mamluk elite in using the law of *waqf*:
    The Turkish amirs under the Turkish dynasty were afraid that their ruler might proceed against their descendants, in as much as they were his slaves and clients, and because the chicanery and confiscation were to be feared from royal authority. Therefore they built a great many colleges and Sufi convents, and endowed them with income-producing waqfs [...]. Students and teachers increased in number, because a large number of stipends became available from the endowments [...]. Thus the markets for sciences flourished and seas of science swelled to the brim." (Muqaddima, 465-66, tr. 2:435, modified)

brought the books captured in Khorasan (from the Ismâ'ili fortresses), Mosul and Baghdad, and housed them in the library of the observatory which is said to have contained four hundred thousand volumes. Tusi personally directed the research at the Marâgheh observatory. "And there were gathered together about him in Marâgheh [...] a numerous company of wise men from various countries" (Bar Hebraeus as cited in Lane 2003: 214). Tusi spent the last dozen years of his life on astronomy in the Marâgheh observatory, developing the planetary and lunar models as well as "the Tusi couple" that were all later drawn upon by Copernicus, making the latter "the most notable follower of the Marâgheh School" (Swerdlow & Neugebauer as cited in Huff 1993: 57). Khwâja Nasir al-Din traveled to Iraq to collect more books in 1264, and "since the councils of all the mosques and the houses of instruction (i.e., colleges) of Baghdad and Assyria were under his direction, he used to allot stipends to teachers and to the pupils who were with him" (Bar Hebraeus as cited in Lane 2003: 214).

Tusi died in Baghdad while inspecting the accounts of its *waqf* department in June 1274. His son, Sadr al-Din 'Ali, succeeded him as the director of the observatory and administrator of its endowment. Except for a brief interruption in the late 1280s, the administration of the endowment for the observatory remained in the hands of Nasir al-Din's sons well into the 14th century. Öljeitü (1305-1317) visited the observatory and appointed Tusi's second son, Asil al-Din, to the position of court astronomer (Arjomand 1998: 120). By that time, the Mongol rulers of Iran had converted to Islam and created extensive endowments of their own, while their grand viziers resumed the traditional role of being the benefactors of civic institutions through equally extensive *waqf*s.

Differential reception of Aristotle and political modernity

In this final section, I want to argue that the greatest disadvantage of the Islamicate world for a medieval breakthrough was due to a gap in the reception of Aristotle. Thomas Aquinas and his teacher, Albert the Great, were the key figures in the reception of Aristotle in Western Christendom. Aquinas was completely familiar with the translations of the Philosopher from the Arabic that came from Toledo and from Sicily distributed among the Italian universities by Emperor Frederick II in the 1230s, and studied Ethics with Albert in Cologne, compiling the surviving notes for his course (van Steenbeghen 1955: 90-91, 167). Aristotle's Politics was not yet available, as it had to be translated from the Greek. But once its translation by William of Moerbeke was published, both Albert (ca. 1265) and Thomas (1269-72) wrote commentaries on it that undoubtedly contributed to the revolutionary impact of that work in Western political thought and constitutional law (Canning 1988: 260). Not only did Aquinas transmit the key Aristotelian political ideas in his introduction of politics as an independent science and the most important of practical sciences (Aquinas 1965: 198-99), but he put forward a remarkably Aristotelian definition of law as "nothing else than a rational ordering of things which concerns the common good, promulgated by whoever is charged with care of the communit" (Aquinas 1965: 112-113). This paved the way for making the integration of Aristotle's natural law into divine law as "participation in the eternal law by rational creatures" (Aquinas: 114-15) the cornerstone of Thomism. Human laws proceed from natural law to more particular dispositions, and are "directed to the common good of the city" (Aquinas: 130-31). Therefore,

Human law has the quality of law only in so far as it proceeds according to right reason; and in this respect it is clear that it derives from the eternal law. In so far as it deviates from reason it is an unjust law, and has the quality not of law but of violence (Aquinas: 120-21).

Furthermore, Aquinas elaborated his "constitutionalism" (Sigmund 1993: 219-22), using both Aristotle's ideas of the commonwealth (*res publica*), in which the whole body of citizens rule for the attainment of the common good, and of a mixed constitution as the judicious combination of monarchy, aristocracy and democracy, defined by the participation in some respect of all the members of a city or nation in government (Aquinas: 148-49; Pennington 1988: 448), together with a corporatist differentiation of community following Aristotle's division of the city (Quillet 1988: 526-30). Aristotelian political ideas could be readily combined with other legal notions. In combination with the canonistic corporate theory, they produced the constitutional conception of the structure of the church (Pennington 1988: 448). And in combination with Roman corporate theory and public law, they gave birth to the modern idea of the state (Canning 1988: 361).

The reception of Aristotle in the Muslim world had taken place some three centuries earlier, and the Mu'tazilites had used him as the First Teacher to defend the faith by creating rational theology *(kalâm)*. There was, however, one startling Muslim omission in the Arabic Aristotelian corpus. Unlike Aquinas, Nasir al-Din Tusi and the Muslim philosophers were unfortunate in that the one and only one work of Aristotle which was not translated into Arabic was his Politics. They therefore tended to mistake Plato's Republic as the natural extension of Aristotle's Ethics, as Averroes did explicitly. To make good the lacuna, Nasir al-Din Tusi had written Akhlâq-e Nâseri, a much expanded translation of the commentary on Aristotle's Ethics by Ibn Moshkuya (d. 1037; Miskawayh in Arabized form), which was to remain the main work on political ethics and statecraft taught in the colleges of the early modern Muslim empires. Partly for this reason, with Tusi and after him, Persian norms constituted much of the substance of the new political theory, while Greek practical philosophy provided its form. To give one crucial example, Tusi's treatment of justice begins with an interesting general philosophical discussion, but when he turns to the topic in the chapter on statecraft and kingship, which is immediately followed by the need for spies in statecraft, the Greek spirit is subordinated to the ethos of the Persian social hierarchy (Arjomand 2003a).

Tusi's groping toward the missing concepts of the Philosopher is evident. In Akhlâq-e Nâseri, he develops (207-12, 307-8) the Aristotelian notion of "the common good" (Tusi: 207-12, as "*maslahat-e 'omum*," 307-308 as "*khayrât-e moshtarak*"). In a short tract he wrote much later for the Mongol emperor Hülegü, the idea of common good is applied systematically to distinguish between the king's personal (khâssah) revenue and expenditure and those pertaining to "public royal goods" (mâl-e masâleh-e pâdshâhi). Gifts, benefices and jewelry should be paid for from the private purse, while the public revenue of the kings should be spent on the army and the bureaucracy, the poor and orphans, couriers and ambassadors, and a postal service throughout the empire (Arjomand 2003a). Nevertheless, it is clear that Tusi could not go far enough on his own, and his synthesis contains only a remote echo of Aristotelian political thought as compared to that of Aquinas. The unavailability of Politics meant continued unawareness of many key Aristotelian political concepts that became available to Aquinas and others in the 13th century and shaped Western political thought, such as the commonwealth *(res publica)* and the rule of law (government by laws and not men), with the citizen being the ruler and the ruled at the same time (Aquinas: 138-39). These ideas penetrated the Islamicate world as the implicit conceptual substratum of modern constitutionalism in the 19th and 20th centuries. Only much later did modern translations of Politics appear, and then as something of an antiquarian text in the history of philosophy.

My final counterfactual question is who would have been the social bearers of Aristotle's Politics for it to have made a difference in the Islamicate developmental path? The simple answer is: the very graduates of the post-Mongol *madrasa*s, just as did the graduates of Western universities, especially those of the law faculties. But that would also have required finding an alternative to the civil law of *waqf* as a means for institutionalizing politics.

References

Aquinas, Thomas (1965) *Aquinas Selected Political Writings*, A.P.D'Entreves, ed. and tr. by J.G. Dawson, Oxford: Basil Blackwell.
Arjomand, S.A. (1999) "The Law, Agency and Policy in Medieval Islamic Society: Development of the Institutions of Learning from the Tenth to the Fifteenth Century," *Comparative Studies in Society and History*, 41.2: 263-93.
Arjomand, S.A. (2001) "Perso-Indian Statecraft, Greek Political Science and the Muslim Idea of Government," *International Sociology*, 16.3: 461-80.
Arjomand, S.A (2003) "Medieval Persianate Political Thought," *Studies on Persianate societies*, 1: 5-34.

Arjomand, S.A (2007) "Transformation of the Islamicate Civilization in the Thirteenth and Fourteenth Century," In: J.P. Arnason/B. Wittrock (eds.), Special Issue of Medieval Studies on Eurasian Transformations.

Arnason, J.P. & Stauth, G. (2004) "Civilization and State Formation in the Islamic Context: Re-reading Ibn Khaldun," *Thesis Eleven*, 79: 29-48.

Arnason, J.P., Eisenstadt, S.N. & Wittrock, B.(eds). (2005) *Axial Age Civilisations and World History*. Leiden, Boston: Brill.

Canning, J.P. (1988) "Introduction: politics, institutions and ideas [c. 1150- c. 1450]." In: J.H. Burns (ed.) *The Cambridge Medieval political Thought*, Cambridge University Press.

Ferruolo, S.C. (1985) *The Origins of the University. The Schools of Paris and their Critics, 1100-1215*, Stanford University Press.

Gaudiosi, M.M. (1988) "The Influence of the Islamic Law of Waqf on the Development of Trust in England: The Case of Merton College," *University of Pennsylvania Law Review*, 136: 1231-61.

Gerber, H. (1994) *State, Society and Law in Islam. Ottoman Law in Comparative Perspective*, Albany: State University of New York Press.

Hourani, A.H. (1970) "Introduction: The Islamic City in the Light of Recent Research." In A.H. Hourani/S.M. Stern (eds.) *The Islamic City*, University of Pennsylvania Press.

Huff, T.E. (1993) *The Rise of Early Modern Science. Islam, China and the West*, Cambridge University Press.

Inglis, J. (2002) *On Aquinas*, Wadsworth.

Ibn Khaldun, 'Abd al-Rahman (1992) *Muqaddima, Vol. 1: Târikh (Kitâb al-'Ibar)* Beirut: Dâr al-kutub `Ilmiyya.

Ibn Khaldun (1958) *The Muqaddimah*, 3 Vols., transl. by F. Rosenthal, Princeton University Press.

Lane, G. (2003) *Early Mongol Rule in Thirteenth Century Iran. A Persian renaissance*, London: Routledge Curzon.

Leedham-Green, E. (1996) *A Concise History of the University of Cambridge*, Cambridge: Cambridge University Press.

Makdisi, G. (1981) *The Rise of Colleges. Institutions of Learning in Islam and the West*. Edinburgh: Edinburgh University Press.

Makdisi, G. (1984) "The Guilds of Law in Medieval Legal History. An Inquiry into the Origins of the Inns of Court," *Zeitschrift für Geschichte der Arabisch-Islamischen Wissenschaften*, 1: 233-52.

Makdisi, G. (1989) "La Corporation à l'époque classique de l'Islam," In: C.E. Bosworth et al., *The Islamic World. Essays in Honor of Bernard Lewis*, Princeton, NJ: Darwin Press.

Makdisi, G. (1990) "Magisterium and Academic Freedom in Classical Islam and Medieval Christianity," In: N. Heer (ed.) *Islamic Law and Jurisprudence*, Seattle: Washington University Press.

Makdisi, G. (1994) "Tabaqât-Biography: Law and Orthodoxy in Classical Islam," *Islamic Studies, Occasional Papers*: 8, Islamabad: Islamic Research Institute.
Mottahedeh, R.P. (1997) "The Transmission of Learning: The Role of the Islamic Northeast," In: N. Grandin/M. Gaborieau (eds.) *MADRASA. La Transmission du savoir dans le monde musulman*, Paris: Arguments, pp. 65-72.
Nelson, B. (1981) On the Road to Modernity, Totowa, NJ: Rowman & Littlefield.
Pennington, K. (1988) "Law, legislative authority and theories of government, 1150-1300," In: J.H. Burns (ed.), *The Cambridge Medieval Political Thought*, Cambridge University Press.
Quillet, J. (1988) "Community, council and representation," In: J.H. Burns (ed.), *The Cambridge Medieval Political Thought*, Cambridge University Press.
Rashdall, H. (1936) *The Universities of Europe in the Middle Ages*, 3 Vols., ed. by F.M. Powicke & A.B. Emden, Oxford University Press.
Sigmund, P. (1993) "Law and Politics," In: N. Kretzman/E. Stump (eds.) *The Cambridge Companion to Aquinas*, Cambridge University Press.
Shatzmiller, M. (2001) "Islamic Institutions and Property Rights: The Case of the 'Public Good' Waqf," *Journal of the Economic and Social History of the Orient*, 44.1: 44-74.
Stern, S.M. (1970) "The Constitution of the Islamic City," In: A.H. Hourani/S.M. Stern (eds.) *The Islamic City*, University of Pennsylvania Press.
Soudavar, A. (1996) "The Saga of Abu-Sa`id Bahador Khan. The Abu-Sa`idname," *Oxford Studies in Islamic Art*, 12: 95-218.
Tabrizi, Mohammad Zaman b. Kalb-'Ali (1995)[1710]/1375[1122] *Farâ'ed al-Favâ'ed dar Ahvâl-e Madâres va Masâjed*, R. Ja`fariyan, ed., Tehran: Ehya-e Ketab.
Tusi, Nasir al-Din (1990/1369) *Akhlâq-e Nâseri*, ed. by M. Minovi/`A.-R. Haydari, Tehran: Khwârazmi.
Tusi. Nasir al-Din (1998) *Contemplation and Action. The Spiritual autobiography of a Muslim Scholar (Sayr wa Sulûk)*, ed. by S.J. Badakhchani, London: I.B. Tauris.
van Steenberghen, F. (1955) *Aristotle in the West. The Origins of Latin Aristotelianism*, Louvain: E. Nauwelaerts, Publisher.
Weisheipl, J.A. (1974) *Friar Thomas d'Aquino*, New York: Doubleday.
Wittrock, B. (2001) "Social Theory and Global History. The Periods of Cultural Crystallization," *Thesis Eleven*, 65: 27-50.

Chapter 10

Global Ages, Ecumenic Empires and Prophetic Religions

ARPAD SZAKOLCZAI

Introduction: naming 'modernity'

Since the moment sociology came into being, one of the favourite – and arguably most pointless – predilections of social theorists was to find a name that best captures the new, epochal reality. Is this new type of society 'modern' or 'industrial'? Should it be called as 'capitalism,' or rather as 'modern capitalism'? Or are we living inside a new period within modernity, a 'late' or 'post'-modern age; which then, with an 'inventive' use of the suffix 'post,' can be also characterised as 'post'-industrial, 'post'-materialistic, 'post'-Fordist, and so on?

At least some of the reasons for the attractiveness of such verbal games are quite evident. It is part of an infatuation with concepts and a mistaken identification of language with the act of naming; a development that more or less destroyed medieval philosophy and that again gained ascendancy with German idealism, especially with neo-Kantianism. It is a part and parcel of ideological thinking, another main characteristic of modern thought, a way to describe 'us' (part of the theoretical or political sect) from 'them,' who use a different, ideologically/politically 'incorrect' terminology. It is part of the hubristic identity of our age, the belief of us 'moderns' that we are living in a not just different but new and better age, in opposition to all those other cultures and civilisations who were all 'traditional' (Latour 1991). Finally, it is part of a theoretical hubris, the smug satisfaction of the thinker who fancies to come up with a new and better definition of the age that so far everybody attempted in vain; or, even more, to identify the signs of the times and recognise, as a herald, a brand new epoch.

The new label 'globalisation,' which pushed literally out the term 'postmodern' from the top of the hit-parade of such expressions, is mostly just another fancy of the intellectual fashion. The general quality of the literature hailing the new intellectual idol is certainly not above the level of the discussion of postmodernism. There is some sense, however, in which this new expression, maybe against itself, carries new potentials. First of all, the term is effectively value free – even though such a claim may seem paradoxical, even untenable, given the current, highly politicised debate on globalisation and the activity of various type of 'anti-global' movements. But the term 'global' is purely formal term describing extension and not development, not even in the sense of growth. Second, and most importantly, it does not define the epoch in terms of an absolute novelty, and in this way it allows to bring out parallels between this age of 'globalisation' and other historical periods that could be characterised with similar kind of increasing interconnectedness. Most importantly, from this perspective it becomes possible to revisit the problem of the links between the 'ancients' and the 'moderns;' especially the striking parallels between the world-conquering empires of long bygone times and our own age.

Taken seriously, this perspective leads to a fundamental reversal of perspective on the thought of the last two centuries; probably even going back to the times of the Renaissance and the Reformation. The dividing lines between the main modern theories and ideologies become small, each of them losing much of its inflated importance and studied seriousness. The first thinker who reached the height of such a perspective was Nietzsche, in his diagnosis of modern nihilism and the idea of the 'eternal recurrence of the same,' even if – as it often happens– his truly pioneering ideas were muddled together with gross errors and huge exaggerations. The central analytical tool which Karl Jaspers developed, in the footsteps of Nietzsche and especially Max Weber, was the by now well-known thesis about 'axis time' or 'axial age.'

Revisiting the 'Axial Age' thesis

There are two aspects of the axial age thesis that I'd like to revisit here: the question of whether it is possible to give some kind of explanation for the startling coincidences; and whether this period of 6-5th century BC was indeed the turning point of history. The standard answer, I believe, is no to the first question and yes to the second. I suggest that the two questions closely belong together, can be thus answered at the same time, but in a manner that is opposed to the classical account.

The sudden outburst of spiritual movements in various parts of the globe can be explained through the concept of liminality, as applied to the outbreak of a global empire building process that took increasingly shape from the 8th century BC onwards. It started with the neo-Assyrian empire, spreading first towards the West (Lydian and Phrygian empires), then towards the East (Median and Persian empires). The aim of these empires was – arguably – completely new: to conquer the entire planet. The results were also unprecedented, in terms of the size of the armies suddenly mobilised, the wealth amassed (one only has to think about still widely used expressions as the 'Midas touch' or 'rich as Croisus'), and the bloodshed and mass suffering created. The first empire to gain an – almost – global status was the Persian, after its victory over Croisus in 546 BC and the conquest of Asia Minor, the victory over Babylonia in 538 BC, and finally the conquest of Egypt in 525 BC.

The connection between the axial age and empire building was already noted by Jaspers and emphasised by Voegelin, who proposed to replace the concept 'axial age' with that of 'ecumenic age.' Through the concept of liminality, however, it is possible to give both a precise conceptual definition and a respective timing of these periods. According to this theoretical framework, the 'axial age' is a typical liminal phenomenon, emerging at the temporal and spatial limit, or 'limes,' of the emerging global empire.

Concerning space, the key developments of the axial age took place in Palestine, a coastline on the margins of Assyria, and Ionia (the birth-place of all major early Pre-Socratics), another coastline on the margins of the Lydian and Phrygian empires; while Northern India, where Jainism and Buddhism arose, was also at the limits of Persian expansion. China was not directly touched by imperial conquest; however, it had contacts with both Persia and India, and it would be difficult to argue that it was completely unaware and sheltered from the impact of such developments.

Moving to temporal liminality, I will only call attention to a singular point. It has been pointed out by Jaspers, and emphasised ever since, that the most striking coincidence in the axial age was the almost identical life span of three among its most important and characteristic figures: Heraclitus, Confucius and the Buddha, each being born around 550-540 BC and dying around 480 BC. This coincidence, and thus the height of the axial age, can possibly be explained by the fact that the crucial period in the rise of the Persian Empire, the decades lasting from 546 to 525 BC was at the same time the formative period in the life of each of these epochal figures.

I would like to stress that the explanation offered here is of a very specific, formal kind, with strict limits. Liminality refers to a certain type of situation, and certainly cannot explain in any way the content of the ideas, religious, spiritual or philosophical, that emerge in a liminal time or place. Even further, as Victor Turner emphasised it, the aim of rituals that staged liminality was by no means to stimulate creativity or innovation (though this also can happen in liminal moments), rather to evoke and render manifest the 'sacred' that was at the heart of the value system of the community. It is, however, exactly such intensive evocation of the most important values and traditions of the community that can be noticed among the most important figures of the axial age, especially in its early period. The great prophets of the 8th and 7th centuries BC did not create a new religion, rather re-stated, in the context of threats of Assyrian and then Babylonian conquests, and in a particularly concise and effective way, the central tenets of the religion of the fathers, including a call for a return to the traditional ways. The same traditionalist perspective animated the ideas of Lao-Tzu, the great figure of Taoism, or Mahavira, the founder of Jainism. Thus, first of all, and especially in its early period, the 'axial age' was not an unprecedented and simultaneous eruption of the transcendent into the world, rather an intensification of the various classical traditions as a response to the rising global empire.[1]

It is true that with the three great figures mentioned above, and their various contemporaries, a new tone is being introduced into the picture. Buddha is different from Mahavira, and also more 'modern,' moving further away from the classical ways, and the same contrast can be established between Confucius and Lao-Tzu, or Deutero Isaiah and Jeremiah. This new note, however, is not simply a novel transcendence, and not even an effective, resounding response to the troubles of the age, rather a novelty that can be best characterised as an increasing *resignation* to the inevitable, a tone of hopelessness only coloured by excessive and unrealistic expectations. It is this resignation which can be identified as the common mentality behind the Nirvana of Buddha, the propagation of the ritualised learning of the Confucian courtly gentleman, or the pre-Socratic sage epitomised by Heraclitus, while the ecstatic but unrealistic hope can be captured in the vision of the new Messiah, whose first great prophet was Deutero Isaiah.

If the axial age, especially in its early moments, was the expression of trauma (Alexander 2003; Giesen 2004), the threat produced by the liminal moment of the rising empires, then the classical thinkers of the axial age rather reflected the reality of the emerging age of empires. This would suggest a quite gloomy outlook: the solution to the 'time of troubles' was not provided by the great thinkers of spiritual reformers, rather by the grim reality of empire-building.

There was only one exception to the rule; a temporary exception, it is true, but extremely significant, and this was Athens. As it is well-known from history, in the Persian Wars the Greek city-states under the leadership of Athens managed to defeat the Persians, against all the odds, and thus not only delayed the emergence of the first 'truly global' empire by a century and half, but also produced an astonishing flourishing of culture, having at its centre the city where both democracy and philosophy were born. Three aspects of this development will be singled out for attention here. First, this period of Athens has been repeatedly characterised by the expression 'grace.'[2] Second, after only a few decades, Athens itself succumbed to the pursuit of an imperial politics. Third, there is the question of the paradoxical role played by the sophists in Athenian history, especially the contrast between the sophists and Socrates; a contrast that seems to have been fundamental for Socrates, Plato and Aristotle, and thus to classical philosophy; but also a difference that time and again seems to have been lost – not the least, in our own age, which tends to treat Socrates as just another sophist.

---

1   This was argued by Béla Hamvas (cf. Szakolczai 2005).
2   See Meier (1987) and MacLachlan (1993). Foucault's concern with parrhesia, which could be defined as charismatic or graceful speech, also belongs here (see Foucault 1996; and Szakolczai 1998, 2003).

After this Athenian 'interlude,' however, with the rise of the Macedonian Empire and the conquests of Alexander the Great, it was a clear victory for the age of global empires. It was this recognition that made Eric Voegelin to suggest the idea that instead of an 'axial age,' one should rather talk about the 'ecumenic age.' The ecumenic age, however, if we take it to include the Persian, Macedonia and Roman Empires, is an extremely huge time period, covering about a thousand years, and the original idea of Jaspers about an 'axis time' in history becomes lost. It seems to me much more rewarding to return first to the original definition of the axial age by Jaspers as the period between 800-200 BC, but revisiting its various sub-periods instead of considering it as a whole. There, after the interlude of Athens, the axial age according to Jaspers ends with the various Hellenistic religious and philosophical movements. These movements, however, are indeed developing under the shadow of the age of empires, magnifying and exaggerating exactly those elements of resignation and hopelessness on one hand, and of exaggerated, unrealistic hopes on the other, that we have already seen with the great figures of the late 6th and early 5th centuries BC. Thus, in the field of religion, the Hellenistic age is increasingly characterised by the various apocalyptic, dualistic, Gnostic and Messianistic sects, or the 'religious rejections of the world' (Weber); while at the philosophical level by the proliferation of the various sophist, cynic, stoic, epicurean and sceptic schools; and even the utopianism characteristic of Plato and Platonism can be situated here. Of particular importance is the rise of Cynicism, that can be traced directly to the disciples of Socrates, and was identified by Foucault as lying both at the limit and heart of Ancient philosophy for about 8th centuries,[3] and whose central characteristic was to turn, in a true trickster fashion, the 'natural' functions of human beings (like eating, defecating and copulating) into the essence of mankind that must be constantly revealed and performed in public, thus allegedly demonstrating the 'deeply secret' truth that human beings are simply animals.

This argument will be concluded by two comments. First, even this short enumeration alludes to a series of striking parallels with modernity, or the 'new' or 'second age' of globalisation, and especially its current phase in which we are living. It would be an interesting and instructive game trying to identify our popular and influential philosophical, spiritual or ideological movements by the various sects and schools of the Hellenistic period. Second, in this way the thesis of Jaspers can clearly be refuted, at least in one important sense. Jaspers attempted to shift the centre of world history, in a polemics again Hegel, from the birth of Christ (allegedly of relevance only in one tradition) to a period in which fundamental spiritual and religion movements started all around the globe. However, as we have seen, the axial age did not produce *new solutions*; and the em-

---

3 In the as yet unpublished 1984 Collège de France lectures, available at the Foucault Archives; see Szakolczai (2003: 202-9) for details.

phasis is placed separately on both the words *new* and *solutions*. The ideas of the axial age were not that new; and in so far as they were genuinely new, they did not really produce solutions; at any rate, by the end of the period identified by Jaspers, they were overtaken by (or degenerated into) the various religious and philosophical rejections of the world.

The axial age did not produce solution. The genuine, lasting and effective solutions were produced by the great prophetic, monotheistic or salvation religions.

Revisiting the 'prophetic religion' thesis

Seemingly, this leads us back from the axial age thesis to the old thesis of Max Weber, and many others, concerning the unique significance of prophecy in world history, especially the prophecies that gave rise to the three great monotheistic religions. However, I would like to argue that the axial age discussion was by no means a mere digression, as this discussion can shed new light on the understanding of the specific characteristics of prophetic religions.

First of all, just to restate the obvious, the main prophetic world religions, Judaism, Christianity and Islam, even Zoroastrism, emerged outside the axial age, no matter how broadly we draw its boundaries. This fact led Eisenstadt to coin the concept 'secondary breakthroughs,' which is somewhat problematic, as – given their effective impact – it is difficult to consider Christianity and Islam as 'secondary' compared to the spiritual movements of the axial age.

Second, the axial age hypothesis was reinterpreted, following Voegelin's ideas, in the context of the rising age of global empires. This also helps to shed a somewhat new light on the rise of the three great prophetic religions, as each of them emerged in the very specific context of major empires. Judaism emerged – and the crucial element here is the tradition, not the impossible question of whether Abraham or Moses were 'historical' figures of not – in between and in the context of the two great empires of the early times, Mesopotamia and Egypt. Christianity came into being together with the rise of the Roman Empire; and in this context it is of special symbolic value that Jesus was reputedly born exactly the moment in which, as a particularly striking act of hubris, the first self-acknowledged Roman emperor wanted to count the number of his subjects. Islam, finally, as it has been powerfully argued by Henri Pirenne, emerged out of the context of the collapse of the Roman Empire, indeed bringing the protracted last moments of this empire to an end.

The third point, however, seems the most important of the three, especially because of its deeply paradoxical character. It is simply taken for granted that the great monotheistic religions came up with a solution that was not only different from the logic of empires, but radically opposed to it as well. Yet, and most paradoxically, each of them developed, almost since the beginnings, a peculiar – one is tempted to say: almost 'perverted' – affinity with such imperial logic. For the founders of ancient Judaism the great cities and empires embodied hell on Earth; and yet, the great promise of Yahweh to Abraham was a rule of his heirs over the world. For the early Christians the Roman Empire was the embodiment of the Antichrist; and yet, a few centuries later, it became first the official religion of the Empire, and then of the so-called 'Holy Roman Empire;' not to mention the various adventures of the papal state, a main model for the modern state. Finally, and probably in the least controversial manner, less then a century after its emergence Islam created an empire on its own.

The question is whether it is possible to explain, in a coherent framework, both the radical innovations and promises, and the problems, of the prophetic world religions in a single and coherent theoretical framework.

Elements of a theoretical framework

In a very sketchy and preliminary manner, three elements of such a theoretical framework will be presented in the following. The first is related to the distinction between good and bad in the form of the benevolent and the evil, central for the world religions; the second attempts to capture the dynamics of the change characteristic of the ecumenic age; while the third revisits a fundamental theme of social and political theory, the question of order.

The setting up of a new and definite measure for values, a distinction between good and bad, in the specific form of opposing good and evil was perhaps the single most important characteristic of prophetic and salvation religions. This was also the aspect singled out for target in Nietzsche's attack against the alleged 'revaluation of values' brought about by such prophetic religions. It seems thus an almost inevitable starting point for our analysis. However, instead of starting with a critique, this paper suggests an effort of contextualisation, relying on the combined tools of comparative anthropology and mythology, offering the contrast between charisma (or the charismatic hero) and the Trickster as the context in which the opposition between the divine and the diabolical can be situated.

The concept 'charisma' is well-known from the works of Max Weber, so only a few comments will be offered. First of all, Weber took the term from the Christian theology of *grace* – a term that will be revisited soon in greater detail. Second, in elaborating his term, especially in discussing the military hero or the charismatic magician, Weber made ample use of anthropology and mythology. Finally, partly preparing the later discussion of grace, I would like to emphasise that the theological concept of grace, just as the Weberian concept charisma, has a fundamental link to the idea of gift.

The term 'trickster' is much less known in sociology, though quite familiar in anthropology. It is one of the most archaic, and most ambivalent, figures in folktales and myths. Its classic exposition can be found in the works of Paul Radin (cf. also Baumann 1978), a main protagonists of the founding period of modern anthropology. The Trickster is a prankster and joker, always ready for a laugh, and is thus often a very pleasant company, his cunning and funny stories much loved by children; but his tricks often involve deceptions, the laughs can easily turn sour, and the nice fellow can be suddenly transformed into merciless impostor, even a cruel murderer. The Trickster is always a thief, while a recurrent theme of the various trickster stories is his fascination with human bodily functions. It has an insatiable appetite, and the same applies to his sexual organs and activities, often being depicted with an enormous phallus. Finally, one of his preferred theme for jokes concerns defecating, an activity which he also loves to perform in public.

Let me call attention to a few aspects of the trickster that are specifically relevant for this paper. First, trickster figures often play a mediating role between humans and divinities; they are sometimes even explicitly defined as the messengers of gods. This is true particularly for the Greek Hermes, an archetypal trickster (Kerényi 1958, 1984), but it is just as significant that Satana, out of whose figure the devil emerged, already in Hellenistic Judaism, was also originally one of the angels, or messengers of Yahweh (Pagels 1995). Second, a key personality characteristic of the trickster is a basic human defect: a lack of ability to be grateful, especially to give or to return gifts. This feature is again brought out in several important works of art about the figure of the devil,[4] but is analysed with particular clarity in an amazing work written in the early Renaissance, the *Momus* by Leon Battista Alberti.[5] Momus was a marginal figure of Greek mythology, given some prominence by Lucian: another figure in between gods and men, mostly involved in the spinning of intrigues, trying to convince the gods to destroy humans, and trying to convince the humans that the gods don't exist.

Finally, a most perplexing feature of the trickster is his role is a second creator of the world; in particular, as a creator of culture. In fact, Radin sometimes speaks of the trickster as being not even separate from the culture hero. This is especially striking given the contrast between the Trickster and the charismatic hero. In spite of all the importance of the latter, its potential impact is limited to *restoring* order, while the deeply ambiguous and often repulsive Trickster is outright credited with the *foundation* of culture. This is certainly a puzzle that needs to be solved.

The second point is related to the problem of social change. My central point is that the most widely used theoretical models, like the idea of a gradual, natural, organic growth, or the dialectics of opposites and their struggle, are simply irrelevant for capturing the particular dynamics characteristic of the ecumenic age. The movement instead has the character of turbulence, avalanche, maelstrom, whirlwind, hurricane or tornado, starting from small, almost imperceptible movements, then gradually gaining momentum and developing into an irresisti-

---

4   See for e.g. the classic epic poems by Milton, Goethe, or Madách.
5   I owe this point to Agnes Horváth.

ble storm. This type of movement is captured by chaos theory, but in the world of human beings the animating force of the movement is *imitation*. This indicates that the paradigm of the rationality of human beings must be bracketed in favour of a study of the imitative nature of humans, an approach pioneered by Le Bon and Tarde, and which had an major impact on such classics as Durkheim, Pareto and Freud, while in contemporary social theory it was developed further by Norbert Elias or René Girard. The spiralling movement of imitative behaviour can take off with especial force under volatile, malleable 'liminal' conditions.[6]

One of the fundamental implications of such a model concerns the much-debated question of resistance. The term has become the key word for any approach that does not accept and take for granted the contemporary world of modernity, modern capitalism or globalisation. However, it is clear that a hectic, frenetic movement spinning out of control cannot be resisted. One can only wait and hope for the storm to pass; anybody trying to resist it will be either simply carried away life a leaf or, even worse, contribute to animate the same spiralling movement. This is best visible in the fact that all those political and social movements who put resistance into the banner simply became just another players in the same game, often changing sides, individually or collectively in the process. Opposites within a spiral have no stable, distinct substance, as it is really of not much interest who and from where is spinning further the turbulence.

Apart from remaining stable, in a Stoic manner, there is only one option: this is conversion,[7] or the radical transformation of the movement into a completely opposite type of dynamics. The completion of such a reversal involves the question of grace; and this opposite type of spiral is illustrated in an at once simple and striking manner by the figure of the Three Graces.

The third point concerns another of the central issues of social and political theory, the question of social order. My observations will take off from Alessandro Pizzorno's seminal article (Pizzorno 1991), which revisited the Hobbesian problem and questioned the very foundations of an individualistic approach to the problem of social order.

One of the central issues concerning social order is inequality. It seems to me that practically all the different contemporary approaches share the premise that full equality is a desirable model for the relationships between human beings; and that the problem is how to reconcile this unquestionable ideal with the realities of existing inequalities. This idea, however, is based on certain assumptions which are not only mistaken and untenable, but positively harmful and dangerous.

---

6   Two representative poets of the twentieth century use a stunningly similar spiralling metaphor in two key poems; see 'The Second Coming' (1919) by William Butler Yeats, and 'I Live in Expanding Rings' (1905) by Rainer Maria Rilke.
7   This has been discussed in contemporary thought by Pierre Hadot, Michel Foucault, Franz Borkenau or Károly Kerényi, much influenced by another famous line of Rilke, the call for 'change your life.'

First of all, I suggest to situate the discussion of equality or inequality on the broader plain of the question of the symmetry or asymmetry of relationships. The usefulness of this distinction becomes visible in the second step, concerning the possible modalities of establishing a new relationship between human beings. The central point here is that such an introduction, initiation or initiative must of necessity be asymmetrical. Somebody must *start* to act and speak; and if by accident both sides start doing something at the same time, the result will be unintelligible or threatening – which more or less amounts to the same thing, as lack of intelligibility is always threatening.

There seems to be two, and in this case *only* two, possibilities for the establishment of a link between two persons. One is the application of force, constraint or violence – to impose one's own will or desire, or simply one's self, on the other. The other is the exact opposite: to withdraw or subordinate one's self, and instead of asking or forcing something; to present a gift, or to give a present.

Within the limits of this paper only a few preliminary comments will be offered. First of all, it seems quite peculiar that while the problem of force and violence took up a major place in classical political thought, the question of gifts and gift-giving was hardly discussed, its importance being only pointed out in modern anthropology by Malinowski or Polányi, but especially by Marcel Mauss (1990). In political thought, the classical presentation of the first point was given in Plato's *Gorgias*. As the argument is well-known, I only single out one point: that in this highly programmatic piece of Plato the argument that unavoidable violence is the foundation of social order is presented by the Sophists; indeed, this is one of the main point identifying the sophist position. Second, the problem of the necessary asymmetry of an initiating contact between two human beings can be solved by the introduction of a third person, who indeed 'introduces' the side. This resembles to the logic of the legal system – but is not a solution of the problem at all, and for at least two different reasons: either because this third person knows both, thus it is not really the establishment of a brand new link; or because this third person possesses power or authority, thus the asymmetry is solved only through another asymmetry.[8]

Third, it should be pointed out that such introductions are accompanied by words and expressions like 'thanking,' 'greeting,' 'gratitude,' or the like; and that each such expression in most languages is etymologically linked to words depicting the giving or receiving of gifts. Finally, and perhaps most importantly, behind these two possibilities, force or gift-giving, there is a definite state of mind that can be described as *benevolence* or *malevolence*. I want to emphasise that this refers to a character trait, not simply a matter of a single intention behind a single

---

8   The term 'asymmetry,' as used in this paper, stands in between the usual meanings of inequality and difference: it is less than the huge and abusive contrasts of wealth and power implied by the word 'inequality,' but more than mere 'difference.'

act; thus, to an entire mode of being and not only a feature of a concrete and well-defined action.⁹

From here, one could move to the easy generalisation that there are therefore two types of durable social relationships: one based on force, violence, oppression, repression, exploitation and the like, and the other based on generosity, magnanimity and benevolence. This, however, would overlook the problem that one cannot start *ex nihilio*: there is always already a social relationship, or an entire social order; and the question is on what principles it is based. Bypassing, among other things, the mystery of the origin of language, I only refer to one concept, or rather one fundamental, original experience: the experience of home, or of being at home in the world, an experience that is the foundation for every single human life, from the earliest days of childhood, yet has been very little theorised in social thought.¹⁰

Again, only two short comments will be made. First, the basic mode of being associated with the experience of home, and of living in a family, can again be best characterised by the word benevolence. A home, and a family, only exists in so far as it is based on principles of gift-giving and magnanimity, and not mutuality of interests. Second, relationships at the level of the home or the family, are again profoundly asymmetrical, though this by no means can be reduced to force or even inequality. This is partly because asymmetries related to age are fleeting and reversible – the helpless baby (whose powers are in many respects extraordinary) becomes a child, then an adolescent, then perhaps a head of family, finally again helpless and powerless in old age; while the asymmetries related to gender – again except very specific times and places – are also labile and reversible; the thesis about the universal rule of patriarchy being just as untenable, even nonsensical, as the Marxist claim about the universality of class struggle – of which it was directly derived.

Asymmetrical relations are therefore pervasive in the life on any human community – and it is on this basis that we can understand the various manners in which *symmetrical* social relationships develop. The first point to notice is that all such relations are profoundly *artificial*; and even further, that they are originally looked upon by deep suspicion, even horror, that can be observed in the almost universal horror the birth of twins creates in simple human communities. Symmetry undermines the distinctions that are the basis of healthy, mutual, benevolent relations in a community; the possibility of a trust that is the basis of stable, durable relations: that a gift given will be eventually returned, and abun-

---

9   In line with the etymological meaning of 'bene-' or 'male-'volence, it has to do with good or bad will. In this sense, it qualifies Nietzsche's 'will to power' in the sense of Weber's charisma. What matters, *pace* Nietzsche, is not simply the quantity of will, but its quality or direction.
10 This line of argument is explicitly opposed to Heidegger, and represents a slight change of emphasis compared to the classical sociology of family.

dantly. It also helps to identify the fundamental principle underlining the drive for symmetry: a growing suspicion and mistrust, that such gifts will not be returned; that the fountain of benevolence feeding a community is being exhausted, and that therefore everybody should be concerned not about the magnanimous *giving* of gifts and favours to the others, but rather to assure the *reception* of a fair share of the pie.

Having defined these three modalities of social relationship: asymmetry based on force, asymmetry based on benevolence and assured by gift-giving, and symmetry animated by a growing suspicion 'foul play,' we can return to the analysis of the ecumenic age.

The dynamics of the ecumenic age

At the phenomenological level, the age of growing imperial conquests can be described – and has indeed been described by the very first historical and philosophical analysts – as a tempest, a whirlwind, an epidemic, a spiralling movement of violence that is increasingly spinning out of control. The origins of this movement are lost in the mythical past; though the scenes evoked by Herodotus, the series of rapes (of Europa, Io and Helen) do possess a crucial explanatory power, linking violence and sex, the two most powerful human emotions, and also the most imitative aspects of human behaviour, at the source of the frenetic movement.

Warfare and conquest on an unprecedented scale create similarly unprecedented sufferings, but also the accumulation of huge fortunes, thus the growth of inequalities, or of asymmetries of the abusive kind. But such 'simple facts' of political 'realism' are also accompanied by an intellectual, reflexive interpretation, a growing conviction that not only such developments are inexorable, but that *this* is really life; this is the rule of existence; and furthermore, that the only way to 'resist' such developments is to assert, as an ideal, a world of complete equality; or a world of fully symmetrical relations. I think it is here that we can trace the phenomenon that Nietzsche first identified as the great 'revaluation of values,' the source of nihilism, and which he mistakenly assigned to the Judeo-Christian morality. Nietzsche's diagnosis was modified by two great thinkers of the past century: by Weber, who called it the 'religious rejections of the world;'[11] and by Voegelin, who identified this, in various stages of his work, with inner-worldly eschatology, with Gnosticism, and with the Sophists.

It is at this point that I will return the third of the major theoretical tools introduced in the previous section, the conceptual pair 'Grace vs. Trickster.' The

---

11 It should be noted that for Weber Ancient Judaism, early Christianity and Islam emphatically were *not* world-rejecting religions.

first point is the draw close parallels between the Sophists and the Trickster, and also with some key features of modern, secular, Enlightenment humanism. The second is to indicate how the theology of grace, as central to each of the three main monotheistic religions, suggests a solution exactly to the problem of the ecumenic age as exposed above.

As it is well-known from the law of entropy, symmetry is the death of movement; it is the elimination of the tension that enables something to happen. The ideal of full symmetry, one could thus say, is deeply nihilistic; and it is by no means accidental that in folktales, in art, in architecture, or in the number of flowers one is supposed to give to the loved one, human beings were always keen to avoid even the appearance of symmetry.

However, the problem, and the danger of the Sophist Trickster, is even more complex. This is because human beings are not simply particles that attract or push back each other. They always have their internal moving forces. The consequence of symmetry is therefore not the absence of movement, rather the stimulation, excitement or incitement of an ever increasing, eventually frenetic, spiralling movement, because of the absence of limiting and regulating, 'educating' asymmetries. The best metaphor from the physical world is therefore not stasis, rather short-circuiting.

The nature of the activity of the Sophist Trickster can be captured through Girard' analysis of the scapegoating mechanism. The trickster is the human being with a singular psychiatric defect, close to the sense of Radin: he cannot give gifts, lacking any benevolence or magnanimity himself, thus lacking any trust or confidence in the others. He is the par excellence anti-social outcast and outsider; but who therefore, short of hating himself, must elevate rigid and rigorous, immediate and generalised symmetry and equality to the centre of social life; who, therefore, feels much at home in the special type of crisis situation when the internal order of a society breaks down in a mimetic crisis.

Let me single out here again the fundamental symmetry between the positions of the charismatic hero and the trickster. Both of them are figures of the out of ordinary, not at ease, or not in place, in normal, ordinary social life. Their time comes in crisis and emergency; but in a completely different way. A charismatic hero is called upon when the community is threatened from the outside. He manages to defeat the enemy, to unify the community, to generate consensus and support against the threats. A charismatic person, however, is helpless in a situation of an internal collapse of order, when the distinctions and dividing lines break down, the community is segmented into hostile and warring factions, and by necessity he would immediately be classified as being just a member of one of the factions. The problem of an internal collapse of order as a problem of symmetry, or equality – and this is when the time of the trickster comes, the homeless outcast who is at home exactly in a time of trouble where both the community at large and any potential charismatic heroes are at a loss.

The trickster is not afraid of symmetry and equality, as it is his ideal; the situation in which his deep deficiencies are cancelled. Because he speculated so much about equality – had the time to speculate, being impotent and useless for the normal business of life, and thus escaping into a fantasy world, sulking on his resentment, as Nietzsche analysed it so well -, he understood its greatest secret: that the solution of the problem of equality lies through terror, through the sacrifice of an innocent victim on whom the violence and hatred spinning out of control can be focalised. In this way, through the founder murder, out of the outcast the Trickster becomes the culture-hero.

A detailed study of the history of political thought would be required to show how the logic of the Sophist Trickster became, from the late Renaissance and the Enlightenment, through the English and French Revolutions, and then especially the various left and right-wing revolutions of the 20th century, a basic principle of modern political life.

The solution to the problem of the spiralling logic of the ecumenic age, and its ideologisation by the Sophists Trickster and its fellow travellers, is a return to the logic of gift giving. This is what – among others, but with particular force – the three monotheistic religions attempted, in spite of all the other, by no means negligible, differences. In this section, I offer a very preliminary analysis of the related ideas.

In the Old Testament, grace is expressed through two different family of words. The first, belonging to the root 'hnn,' refer to a 'gifted initiation of relationship' (Campbell 1993: 259-61; Weiser 1998: 351-2). In this sense Yahweh is the one who gives, who distributes favours, being the source of hope, and the role of human beings is to imitate him and behave accordingly to their fellows. The second root is 'hsd,' which also means favour but in the sense of compassion or mercy, and shifts the focus on the side of the human recipients. The mercy of god reaches the needy, the poor, those who are desperately in need of saving acts; but also those who committed sins, who erred, and who therefore are in need of a saving grace, for a turning back of god's favour towards them.

Grace is thus fundamental for the relationship established between the deity and human beings, between Yahweh and his people; and it is also a fundamental asymmetrical relationship. The deity initiates and gives, while humans – who desperately need this saving act – receive, or are given. However, since the very first moments of contact, a different type of link is also present, inscribed in the interaction between the deity and Abraham: a contract, covenant or alliance; a legal, thus strictly symmetrical relationship, where both sides make certain promises and are therefore bound to behave according to this pre-established and mutual agreement. There are two comments I want to make here concerning this quite perplexing insertion of symmetrical legal ties at the heart of a fundamentally asymmetrical relationship. First, it is exactly here that the problem identified above can be located: the 'promised land' offered to the 'chosen people,' and the ensuing repetition of the exact imperial ambitions against which the tradition of ancient Judaism emerged. Second, the legal perspective, and the related rationalisation of the world-view, occasionally resulted in quite striking formulations, like the following statement from Wajikra Rabba: "An agreement was stipulated between them [i.e. God and Israel] that [God] would not repudiate them and they would not repudiate him" (Weiser 1998: 352); a formulation which seems to replace a saving act of divine grace with a mutual clause of refraining from harmful acts, or a positive deed with a double negation.

Grace in the New Testament closely follows the Old Testament meaning (Campbell 1993: 259-61; Weiser 1998: 352-4). The two Greek words used, *charis* (Latin *gratia*, or grace), present especially in the Pauline corpus, and *eleos* (Latin *misericordia*, or mercy), closely correspond to the two basic Hebrew roots, denoting respectively the pure, undeserved divine gift on the one hand, and his compassion on the other. The fundamental difference lies in the way for Christians the grace of god has become incarnated in Christ, the very embodiment of divine love and a gift for mankind, who has thus become the mediator of human salvation.

This implied first of all not simply a 'new covenant,' but a paradoxical, radical reassertion of asymmetry in the links between God and Man. Grace is a free, gratuitous act of God, done without any act or even invocation of human beings, and therefore the divine-human relationship cannot be in any way ascribed in a legal terminology. This novel emphasis on inequality, on the other hand, is paradoxical, as it is a consequence of the human incarnation of God, in the figure of Christ. This paradox will occupy a fundamental place in theology, perhaps most importantly (and certainly most controversially) as related to the figure of the Mother of Jesus, Mary.

Given this fundamental asymmetry, in so far as human beings are concerned the emphasis shifts even more on the part of imitation. Grace is a gratuitous act of god, but human beings also have a task in preserving and remembering such acts of grace, developing them into an entire mode of life, a *habitus*. In the language of Aquinas, the freely given grace (*gratia gratis data*) must turn the recipient into a 'graceful' person, in the sense of a person filled with grace (*gratia gratum faciens*) (Lonergan 1970). The word *habitus* was used both by Weber and Elias, later becoming a central term in the sociology of Bourdieu, and not without a profound reason, as it implies a constant concern with the reflexive improvement of conduct, itself relying on the idea of the care of the self or the soul (Foucault 1984b; Patocka 2002; Szakolczai 1994), that lies at the heart of the European civilising process.

The acknowledgement of the radical asymmetry between the divine and human sides rendered any 'contract' or 'covenant' impossible. Yet, it was exactly at the heart of the Christian theology of grace, in the writings of Paul, that in the specification of the human response two closely related and highly problematic elements came to be introduced: the doctrine of justification and the emphasis on individual salvation. The first re-introduced a legal terminology, that will have specially fateful effects with the Reformation; while the second contributed to the assimilation of Christianity with the 'salvation religions' and the 'religious rejections of the world,' shifting the emphasis from the re-instatement of the logic of gift-giving (or the 'Kingdom of God,' Mk 1: 15) into the heart of human relations to the escapist and egoistic implications of individual salvation.

Both in terms of form and substance, the concept of grace in Islam is just as closely tied to the Christian interpretation as the New Testament was to the Old Testament (Weiser 1998: 354-5). First of all, as a form of greeting the word '*Rahim*' (usually translated as 'merciful,' close to the meaning of the second Hebrew root for grace 'hsd') introduced all but one of the Suras of the Koran, just as it was used abundantly in the opening sentences of Paul's letters, and most importantly by Gabriel when meeting Mary in the scene of the Annunciation (Cook 1986: 307). '*Rahim*' is also the Arabic term for the womb, evoking the idea of a 'gratis' protection through the womb.[12] Together with the crucial importance played by the angel Gabriel in the revelations given to Mohammed, this establishes extremely close contact between the formal aspects of grace in Christianity and Islam.

Concerning the theological substance, even in Islam grace is an unmotivated act of god, conceding favours and pardons to its undeserving recipients. The divinity who acts in this way is characterised as the Indulgent, the Pitiful, the Benevolent, the Magnanimous and the Dispenser of love. The role of human beings is to recognise this grace and to be grateful for it, and then to imitate this mode of being in their own lives. Given their own nature, human beings cannot act rightly without this divine grace, which is their only hope in overcoming the difficulties of their lives.

The revelations of divine grace were granted to Mohammed through the angel Gabriel. Mohammed, on his turn, became then the mediator of human beings for the restitution of their sins and the help for their salvation. This aspect of individual salvation, and the promise of Paradise, already problematic in Christianity, became particularly strongly accentuated in Islam, turning into the driving force of quick and spectacular military conquests.

In spite of significant differences, there is a definite and unique pattern shared by all three great world religions. According to this, grace is the eruption of the divine into the world, an unrequited, gratuitous gift of the deity who in this way reveals himself. It established, or reveals, a fundamentally asymmetric relationship between God and Man, with the initiative fully on the side of the divine. This gift does not have the character of an object, and cannot even be reduced to a specific, concrete favour granted to a concrete individual; it is rather the demonstration of a fundamental predisposition of benevolence, of loving care, and the consequent message of hope that human beings are not alone in the world.

Though the asymmetry is total, and the original grace granted can in no way

---

12 I would like to thank Armando Salvatore for his clarifying comments concerning this issue.

be merited by the person(s) touched by it, human beings also have their task, and this is to preserve the original gift, to imitate it not simply by giving or returning gifts, but to turn benevolence and charity into the guiding principle of their life conduct, to transform the sudden and surprising eruption of grace into a permanent and effective force. It is this transformation that the word conversion captures: in limit cases, the sudden and radical change of the entire personality touched by the divine. But there is something more in it, and it is exactly here that the fundamental connection with the line of argument presented in this paper lies. Beyond the change of individual life and salvation, and beyond even singular sects or entire religions, arguably the crucial message, shared *by* all three world religions and thus uniting them, is the promise, and the heroic attempt to restore, in a world threateningly and hopelessly dominated by abusive asymmetric relationships, graceful asymmetry in the heart of human relationships; the only type of social relationship that has the power to reverse the spiral of violence and desire fuelling abusive asymmetry, and to remain untouched by the sirens luring the careless towards the legal-economic dream of symmetry and equality.

As a last note, let me point out that the monotheistic religions are not alone in posing grace into the heart of their world-view. The same has been attempted, with remarkable success, in the line of development that connect the ancient Minoan civilisation of Crete, through the Mycenean world, to classical Greece, especially the 'miracle' of Athens (Hall 1998; Meier 1987, 1996).

One could object that Greek grace was a purely aesthetic concept, with no relationship to the divine grace of monotheists, the similarity being only superficial. This, however, is not true; and the profound connections go way beyond the use of the same word (*charis*) in both cases. The Greek concern with aesthetics, as Foucault argued recently, was inseparable from ethics; while the Czech philosopher Jan Patocka pointed out the close connections between Greek epistemology and aesthetics in the emphasis placed on the manifestation of truth (Patocka 2002). Even further, it was a principle central for Athenian democracy, animating the conduct of the democratic citizens, as Christian Meier argued it. It is also central for the conflict between Socrates/Plato and the Sophists.

But gracefulness, together with beauty, and beyond, was also central to Greek religion, going back to its roots in Crete. Let me mention only two examples. One is the tradition of seals and signet rings in Cretan art, one of the most graceful manifestation of Minoan culture, and the stunning scenes of epiphanies some of its best pieces evoke. The other is the figure of the Three Graces, central especially to Hellenistic art and religion, and resurrected with particular emphasis in some of the most important books and paintings of the Renaissance: a group that manifests, in its very composition, the spiral of giving, receiving and returning of gifts.[13]

---

13 Such considerations were by no means restricted to Western Christianity; see Evdokimov (1990).

Conclusion: Hope beyond modernity

Let me formulate my concluding remarks in a provocative way. The current intellectual mood is to assign the cause of troubles in the current world to the prejudices of the past, especially the survival or religion; while the hope, supposedly, lies in the enlightened attitudes of secularised intellectuals who overcame these errors and who can lead a rational discourse towards the establishment of a just an equal world. The historical overview presented in this paper, and the conceptual framework that has been worked out to understand its implications, however, comes to the exactly opposite conclusion. According to this, it is the Enlightenment model that is chimerical, a modern resurrection of ancient Trickster-Sophist-Cynic attitudes and worldviews; while the solution can only come through a concern with grace, shared by all the three great world religions, and also by classical Greek culture, acknowledging and accepting benevolent, loving asymmetry.

References

Alberti, Leon Battista (2003) *Momus*, Cambridge: Harvard University Press.
Alexander, Jeffrey C. (2003) "Cultural Trauma and Collective Identity." In *The Meanings of Social Life: A Cultural Sociology*, Oxford: Oxford University Press, pp. 85-107.
Assmann, Jan (1997) *Moses the Egyptian: The Memory of Egypt in Western Monotheism*, Cambridge, MA: Harvard University Press.
Bauman, Zygmunt (1978) "Paul Radin, or an aetiology of the intellectuals." In *Legislators and Interpreters: On Modernity, Postmodernity, and Intellectuals*, Cambridge: Polity, pp. 8-20.
Campbell, Edward F. (1993) "Grace." In B.M. Metzger/M.D. Coogan (eds.) *The Oxford Companion to the Bible*, Oxford: Oxford University Press.
Cohn, N. (1970) *The Pursuit of the Millennium*, London: Paladin. [1957]
___ (1993) *Cosmos, Chaos and the World to Come: The Ancient Roots of Apocalyptic Faith*, New Haven: Yale University Press.
Cook, Michael (1986) "Muhammad." In Keith Thomas (ed.) *Founders of Faith*. Oxford: Oxford University Press.
Eisenstadt, S.N. (1982) "The Emergence of Transcendental Visions and the Rise of Clerics." *Archives Européennes de Sociologie* 23/2, pp. 294-314.
___ (ed.) (1986) *The Origins and Diversity of Axial Age Civilisations*, New York: SUNY Press.
___ (1995) *Power, Trust and Meaning*, Chicago: University of Chicago Press.
___ (1999) *Fundamentalism, Sectarianism, and Revolution: The Jacobin Dimension of Modernity*, Cambridge: Cambridge University Press.

Eisenstadt, S.N./Giesen, Bernd (1995) "The Construction of Collective Identity." *Archives Européennes de Sociologie* 36/1, pp. 72-102.

Elias, Norbert (1987) *Involvement and Detachment*, Oxford: Blackwell.

___ (2000) *The Civilising Process*, Oxford: Blackwell. [1938-9]

Evdokimov, Pavel N. (1990[1972]) *Teologia della bellezza: l'arte dell'icona*, San Paolo: Cinisello Balsamo.

Foucault, Michel (1984a) *L'usage des plaisirs*, Paris: Gallimard.

___ (1984b) *Le souci de soi*, Paris: Gallimard.

___ (1994), *Dits et écrits*, 4 Vols., Daniel Defert/François Ewald (eds.), Paris: Gallimard.

___ (1996) *Discorso e veritá nella Grecia antica*, Firenze: Donzelli.

___ (2001) *L'herméneutique du sujet: Cours au Collège de France (1981-1982)*, Paris: Gallimard/Seuil.

Giesen, Bernhard (1998) *Intellectuals and the Nation: Collective Identity in a German Axial Age*, Cambridge: Cambridge University Press.

___ (2004) *Triumph and Trauma*, Boulder, CO: Paradigm.

Girard, René (1972) *Violence et le sacré,* Paris: Grasset.

___ (1978) *Des choses cachés depuis la fondation du monde,* Paris: Grasset.

___ (1982) *Le bouc émissaire*, Paris: Grasset.

___ (1994) *Quand ces choses commençeront*, Paris: Arlea.

___ (1999) *Je vois Satan tomber comme l'éclair*, Paris: Grasset.

Guenther, Mathias (1999) *Tricksters and Trancers: Bushman Religion and Society*, Bloomington: Indiana University Press.

Hadot, Pierre (1993) *Exercices spirituels et philosophie antique*, Paris: Institut d'études Augustiniennes.

Hall, Peter (1998) *Cities in Civilization*, London: Weidenfeld & Nicolson.

Horváth, Agnes (1998) "Tricking into the position of the outcast." *Political Psychology* 19/3, pp. 331-47.

Jaspers, Karl (1953[1949]) *The Origin and Goal of History*, New Haven: Yale University Press.

Kerényi, Carl (1958) *The Gods of the Greeks*, Harmondsworth: Penguin.

___ (1976) *Dionysos: Archetypal Image of Indestructible Life*, Princeton: Princeton University Press.

___ (1984) *Hermész, a lélekvezetö: Az élet férfi eredetének mitologémája* (Hermes, the guide of the souls: The mythologem of the male origins of life), Budapest: Európa.

Latour, Bruno (1991) *Nous n'avons jamais été modernes: essai d'anthropologie symmétrique*, Paris: Découverte.

Lonergan, Bernard J.F. (1970) *Grace and Freedom: Operative Grace in the Thought of St. Thomas Aquinas*, London: Darton, Longman & Todd.

MacLachlan, Bonnie (1993) *The Age of Grace*, Princeton: Princeton University Press.

Mauss, Marcel (1990[1924]) *The Gift: The Form and Reason for Exchange in Archaic Societies*, London: Routledge.

Meier, Christian (1987) *La politique et la grâce*, Paris: Seuil.

___ (1996) *Atene: La città che inventò la democrazia e diede un nuovo inizio alla storia*, Roma: Garzanti.

Nietzsche, Friedrich (1967) *On the Genealogy of Morals*, New York: Vintage.

Pagels, Elaine (1995) *The Origin of Satan*, New York: Random House.

Patocka, Jan (2002) *Plato and Europe*. Stanford: Stanford University Press.

Pizzorno, Alessandro (1987) "Politics Unbound." In: Charles S. Maier, (ed.) *Changing Boundaries of the Political*, Cambridge: Cambridge University Press.

___ (1991) "On the Individualistic Theory of Social Order." In Pierre Bourdieu/Pierre/James S. Coleman (eds.) *Social Theory for a Changing Society*, Boulder: Westview Press.

Radin, Paul (1972) *The Trickster: A Study in American Indian Mythology*, with commentary by Karl Kerényi and Carl G. Jung, New York: Schocken.

Szakolczai, Arpad (1994) "Thinking Beyond the East West Divide: Foucault, Patocka, and the Care of the Self." *Social Research* 61/2, pp. 297-323.

___ (1998) *Max Weber and Michel Foucault: Parallel Life-Works,* London: Routledge.

___ (2003) *The Genesis of Modernity*, London: Routledge.

___ (2005) "In between Tradition and Christianity: The Axial Age in the Perspective of Béla Hamvas." In Johann P. Arnason/S.N. Eisenstadt, S.N./Björn Wittrock (eds.) *Axial Civilisations and World History*, Leiden: Brill.

Turner, Victor W. (1967) "Betwixt and Between: The Liminal Period in *Rites de Passage*." In Idem, *The Forest of Symbols*, New York: Cornell University Press.

___ (1969) *The Ritual Process*, Chicago: Aldine.

___ (1982) *From Ritual to Theatre: The Human Seriousness of Play*, New York: PAJ Publications.

___ (1985) "Experience and Performance: Towards a New Processual Anthropology." In Edith Turner (ed.) *On the Edge of the Bush*, Tucson, Arizona: The University of Arizona Press.

Voegelin, Eric (1952) *The New Science of Politics*, Chicago: Chicago University Press.

___ (1956-87) *Order and History*, 5 Vols., Baton Rouge: Louisiana State University Press.

___ (1997-99) *The History of Political Ideas*, 8 Vols., Columbia: University of Missouri Press.

Weber, Max (1948a[1915]) "The Social Psychology of the World Religions." In

___ (1948b[1915]) "Religions Rejections of the World and Their Directions." In Hans Gerth/C. Wright Mills (eds.) *From Max Weber*, London: Routledge.

___ (1952[1921]) *Ancient Judaism*, New York: The Free Press.

___ (1976[1904-5]) *The Protestant Ethic and the Spirit of Capitalism*, London: Allen and Unwin.

___ (1978[1921-22]) *Economy and Society*, Berkeley: University of California Press.

Weiser, A. (1998) "Grazia." In: Adel Th. Khoury (ed.) *Dizionario comparato delle religioni monoteistiche: Ebraismo – Cristianesimo – Islam*. Casale Monferrato: Piemme.

Wind, Edgar (1968) *Pagan Mysteries in the Renaissance*, London: Faber and Faber.

Chapter 11

Reflexivity, Praxis, and "Spirituality": Western Islam and Beyond

ARMANDO SALVATORE

Introduction: reflexivity, praxis, and "spirituality"

Axial Age theory is a research program for locating and explaining, in comparative-historical, sociological terms, the crucial breakthrough that allowed, through the shaping of notions of transcendence, for the emergence of institutionalized forms of human reflexivity through a transition conventionally identified as the passage from mythos to logos, or – sociologically speaking – from a compactness of visions of order to a differentiation of the religious and political spheres, and in particular towards critical reflexivity (Jaspers 1953 [1949]; Eisenstadt 1986; Stauth 1998). However, as suggested by Johann Arnason, this theory possesses a wider heuristic and methodological significance, since "the interpretation of the Axial breakthrough serves to concretize a critique of functionalism – and especially of functionalist conceptions of culture – that had been in the making at least since the early 1960s" (Arnason 2005: 37). Indeed, Axial age theory has been used as a compass in the long march of reckoning with modernization theory and represents a novel port of entry into the sociology of modernity.

If it is true that the Axial rupture implied the emergence of agential forms of reflexivity, transcendence itself should not primarily to be interpreted in theological terms, but as the capacity to imagine an order that transcends the particularism of rituals more immediately tied to the reproduction of life and generational cycles within a given community order based on cultic forms of representations of godly power and bestowal of prosperity. Thus the main novelty of axiality seems to reside in "the capacity of human beings to reflect upon and to give expression to an image of the world as having the potential of being different from what it was perceived to be here and now" (Wittrock 2005: 62). On the other hand, this key axial dimension cannot be rigidly equated with the demise of a certain type of cosmology (a cosmology of the mythos) and its replacement with an outright new cosmology (a cosmology of the logos). Transcendence gains a new profile within Axial breakthroughs or "syndromes" if we disjoin it from a cosmological typology and consider it the engine of a specific type of experience-rooted discourse proclaiming the problematic if not unsustainable character of any mundane order left on itself and the necessity to transcend it: by making the power holders accountable to a transcendent power or divinity. God (or equivalents thereof) takes over the traits of unitary and supreme majesty over the cosmos, over human society, and over the individual soul. Reflexivity is therefore a function within the tension determined by transcendence.

A crucial node related to the issues of reflexivity is therefore the question of prophecy. Eric Voegelin, a virtual early participant in this theoretical field particularly concerned with the dimension of transformation (cf. Arnason/Eisenstadt/Wittrock 2005: 9), has evidenced a chain of momentous shifts of the discourse of the Hebrew prophets that targeted the shortcomings of the sociopolitical order. This is a good example of a path of reflexivity tied to transcendent within an unfolding Axial order. He called this discourse "metastatic," because characterized by subsequent waves of instructing-exhortative speech that reassemble and metamorphose symbols of mundane and transcendent orders. The metastatic effect is to continually push forward the boundary between those orders, up to trespassing the critical threshold when the Hebrew prophecy was no longer concerned with the restoration of the Covenant that Moses did with Yahvé in the name of the "chosen people." In this way, successive prophetic voices altered the meaning of Exodus, the Covenant, and the attainment of the "promised land," by reflecting on their insufficiencies in containing the tension between mundane and transcendent orders. The metastasis results in nothing less than a full-fledged notion of "salvation," which thus becomes one possible outcome of Axial reflexivity (Voegelin 1956: 428-513). Transcendence is rehabilitated as a propeller of reflexivity and so of Axial transformation. Moreover, Voegelin's metastatic model of prophecy has the advantage of bringing to relief a cumulative change and not a "breakthrough." Consequently the metamorphosis activated by prophecy, marked by increases and consolidations of reflexivity, was to last till Muhammad.

Yet there are key thresholds in the metastatic change, and the climax of the Axial drama among the Jews is reached when the prophets Jeremiah and Isaiah acknowledge that there is no one-for-all covenantal solution to the problem of order. This problem can only be managed via an ongoing "Exodus of Israel from itself"(zitat von wem?) that exemplifies in the most extreme fashion the rupturing potential of Axial transformations: that transcendence has less immediately to do with specific doctrines of the thereafter and dramas of salvation, than with the articulation of a discourse facing "the experience of the gulf between true order and the order realized concretely by any society." The consequence is that "the terminus ad quem of the movement is not a concrete society with a recognizable order" (ibid.: 491). Transcendence is synonymous with movement, as the source of order but also as the perpetual questioning of any existing order.

Building on Voegelin, Jan Assmann (2005) has maintained that the Axial impetus is basically a revolution in the model of authority, which is solemnly declared independent from political domination, above of it. The notion of "salvation," accordingly, is not a purely "religious" concept, but is – sociologically speaking – a vector of the crystallization of a radical, metastatic contestation of political domination and of the foundation (subject to subsequent alterations and contestations) of a new, much more plastic notion of authority. Heil can only be understood as the antidote to absolute Herrschaft.

Due to the metastatic character of Axial transformations, the patterns of dependence of the derivative (mundanely socio-political) from the ultimate (transcendent) level of order cannot be a plain homework for orthodox virtuosi. Their emergence, the idea itself of orthodoxy, is the result of the need to tame the metastasis. Prophetic warnings, excoriating, and exhortations are first and by necessity couched in a poetic-imaginative language. The post-prophetic era of theological systematization intervenes after the proclamation of the end of the metastatic chain of prophecy. This is specific to each religious tradition. With Christianity, it was inaugurated by the coming of the Christ, while with Islam, were messianism is put at the margins or outside its orthodoxy and the Christ is consciously rejected, this era started right after the Qur'anic revelation, which was given to Muhammad, whom scripture proclaims the seal of all prophets. It is also symptomatic that both in Christianity and Islam, during the post-prophetic era the role of thematizing and reclaiming the implications of the imperatives of the salvational path for the socio-political order is most typically performed by heterodox movements, many of which not surprisingly reclaim a renewal or restoration of prophetic charisma. These movements are sometimes reabsorbed within institutional orthodoxy as "reform" movements.

Through such dynamics social conflicts became more complex and irreducible to contests for power and riches, since inherently clothed in a discourse that did not refer to localized and circumscribed issues, but to the wider realm of symbolic evocations of moral and transcendent order. At the same time when protest and reform movements tried to restore the balance, they also acted as forces of destabilization (Szakolczai 2001: 359). Orthodoxies and their virtuosi controlled the metastasis but could not neutralize it, in spite of frequent calls to the annihilation of heterodox movements, often pushed up to justifying the physical suppression of all its adherents (like with the Catholic extermination of the Cathars in the 12th century, or with the followers of the radical Christian movements led by Thomas Münzer and Jan van der Leyden in the 16th centuries).

We should acknowledge therefore that reflexivity denotes at the same time too much and too little of the specific format of prophetic discourse. As stressed by Voegelin (1997: 69-85), the "parabolic" nature of prophetic discourse requires to build a symbolically dense nexus between the perception of wrongness in ordinary interactions among people and a sense of disintegration of the cosmological order. The latter is the consequence of the erosion of the integrative force of the "pre-Axial" empires of the Nilotic and Mesopotamian areas. It has been observed that this type of rupture and corresponding reconstruction of order occurs in periods and situations of acute "liminality" (Eisenstadt 1985; Szakolczai 2003). This concept, launched by Victor Turner, was redefined, in the context of

Axial age theory but also of the sociology of modernity, as denoting the destructuring of social relationship and the rebuilding of order from its borders or limits. The prototypical example of this liminal situation can so be identified with the metastatic climax of prophetic voices proclaiming the collapse of the order and reclaiming a new order through salvation (ibid.).

At this point, however, in order not to remain trapped in the plot of the Axial prophetic narrative, the focus should be shifted from metastatic dramas of salvation to the concrete social patterns that facilitated prophetic intervention into everyday situations, which legitimized the deep metamorphosis of concepts of order: on the shaping of a praxic, interactional compassion for the other as the "poor." The specific focus of this chapter is in a distinctive Islamic trajectory, with specific developments centered in the Western part of the Islamic world, indeed in Europe, which particularly exalts the praxic dimension of Axial reflexivity. This development also constitutes an immunization of Islamic traditions from the post-eschatological separation of the spirit from praxis that influenced the totalistic and immanentistic syndrome of what Voegelin called modern European "political religions" (Voegelin 1993 [1938]). Nested within certain intellectual and juridical cultures within specific schools of Sunni Islam, this praxic orientation emerged in spite of their sharing some "reformist" and "gnostic" motives with the European Latin Christianity that provided the background to modern political religion. The issue of reflexivity as it emerges from the analysis of these developments might assist us in the work of reassessing and reformulating basic Axial categories in their relations to the theory of modernity/modernities. In particular reflexivity is related to practical rationality and communication, which are key concepts in modern theories of the "public sphere." The implication of this move is that some dimensions and trajectories within Islamic traditions not only prove their Axial affiliation and post-Axial development, but contribute key elements to distinctive patterns of modernity within the history of Western Europe or the "West" at large. Moreover, these emerging patterns, which have been quite influential in the elaboration of Muslim reformers worldwide from the 18th century to the present, are particularly interesting for their distance from the modern syndromes and tragedies that political religions, which, as truly Axial heterodoxies which both affirmed and denied key Axial tenets, have inflicted on the shaping of Western European modernity: from the liquidation of the Jewish and Muslim presence in the Iberian peninsula and the massacres of those who resisted the English Puritan Revolution, to the destruction of the two world wars and the genocidal crimes of 20th century totalitarianism.

But let us start over again from those ends of prophetic chains that Axial Age theory for a while improperly identified as "secondary" and even "tertiary" breakthroughs (Arnason/Eisenstadt/Wittrock 2005: 4), more than as large scale processes of governance of the metastasis and of its symbolic apparatus. The final prophetic voices, who happened to be founders of new religious traditions – like Jesus, Mani, and Muhammad – made use of a discursive approach that linked the parabolic form of prophesy to more continuous and effective mechanisms of inculcation and dissemination of their messages. These transformations made preaching particularly important as a discursive genre. This perfecting of the effectiveness of the exhortative instruments of the Axial traditions went along with momentous reformulation of the attending forms of reasoning, based on the act of making the logos itself available to the faithful: through the Christ in Christianity, and through the Qur'an in Islam. Axial traditions became intrinsically discursive tradition (cf. for this definition Asad 1986).

In particular, the work of the emerging Axial virtuosi of the word was concentrated on justifying the supreme good with regard to a more mundane notion of the "common good," which ended up occupying a strategic position within the hierarchy of goods of excellence. The culmination of this work on the common good was reached in the 13th and 14th centuries, at the end of an era which, both in Latin Christian Europe and within the area dominated by Sunni Islam, can be defined as the "Axial renaissance": an epoch of intensive elaboration on the traditional fundaments of Axial thought and practice in order to make them match a social reality in upheaval and fit with the emergence of new social actors within the thriving town economies (cf. Salvatore 2006). As evident in the work of Aquinas, who engaged directly with Ibn Rushd (Averroes) at a time when the new Dominican monks started to build the intellectual leadership and cadres to the Spanish *reconquista*, Catholicism and Islam are not only competitors, but interactant in the process. At stake were not only purely theoretical concepts (philosophical and theological), but the modalities to implement them not only within social worlds that were growing increasingly complex, but also through a more assertive universal projection of the message.

A model of praxic Axiality?

By the 7th century AD, Christianity found a valid Axial emulator and a powerful challenger in Islam. The centrality of preaching is a strong element of commonality between Christianity and Islam in spite of all their institutional and dogmatic differences, which also reside in the different status of "scripture" as logos and speech, within the textual and discursive economy of the tradition. There are several reasons why focusing on Islam can substantially enrich and complexify the view of the post-Axial potential of elaboration on praxis, communication and reflexivity. Islam is the latest comer in the family of Abrahamic prophetic religions. Its scriptural bases and the ensuing traditions are quite coherently reflected in the awareness by the prophet Muhammad and his successors among the leaders of the Islamic community that they were grounding – via revelation, its recording, canonization, and authoritative interpretation – a religious civilization setting upright and remolding key elements of the other main "religions of the book," i.e. Judaism and Christianity. Additionally, the Greek philosophical heritage had a substantial influence on key tenets of Muslim traditions. Even Roman law had an impact on some aspects of Islamic law and jurisprudence, though the measurement of this influence remains controversial (cf. Crone 1987; Masud 1995 [1977]). As a result, it is fair to say that Islam has attempted to bring to perfection a crucial feature of Axial civilizations in the reconstruction of the social bond, through the final overcoming of archaic ties of authority and domination lacking a transcendent source of legitimacy. Its goal was the reconstruction of an uncontaminated nexus of "connective justice" inscribed in the triad between ego, alter, and God. As aptly formulated by Shmuel N. Eisenstadt,

the emphasis on the construction of a political-religious collectivity was connected in Islam with the development of a principled ideological negation of any primordial element or component within this sacred political-religious identity. Indeed, of all the Axial Age civilizations in general, and the monotheistic ones in particular, Islam was, on the ideological level, the most extreme in its denial of the legitimacy of such primordial dimensions in the structure of the Islamic community [...] In this it stood in opposition to Judaism, with which it shared such characteristics as an emphasis on the direct, unmediated access of all members of the community to the sacred (Eisenstadt 2002: 148-149).

The rise of Islam is therefore the last and most consciously managed manifestation of the Axial transformations in the "West," in spite of the fact that Islam later spread in Central and Eastern Asia as well. The Qur'an gives prominence to the earlier chains of Judaic prophets, from Abraham to Jesus, and stresses the opposition they met in their call to submission to God's will, which is condensed in the meaning of the Arabic word islam. In this sense, Muhammad's message was neither new nor intended to be new, but was conceived as the full restoration of the true Abrahamic faith through a completion of its prophetic chain and, though it, a final and unequivocal revelation of God's word and will to humankind.

However, not only the content of the Qur'an but the communicative and authoritative infrastructure itself of prophetic discourse and its means of inculcation were made particularly effective by Muhammad and by the generations of Islamic scholars and "friends of God" (the Sufi spiritual leaders) who came after him. God's message revealed through the earlier prophets had been received and incorporated in Judaism and Christianity in imperfect ways – so Muhammad's message – due to sectarianism. Islam, the new-old call to submission to God, was to overcome sectarianism and embrace mankind in a truly universal *umma*, i.e. community of all believers.

However, the model of constructing the ego-alter-God triadic link was a quite pristinely Abrahamic one, based on faith, compassion, and obedience. And it was the sweeping success, after initial resistance and difficulties, of Muhammad's career in the specific Semitic tradition of the armed prophet that made the turn from parabolic exhortation to an activist reconstruction of the social fabric a crucial part of his preaching and leadership during the last part of his own life. Muhammad's practice and judgment in shaping and regulating human relationships acquired paradigmatic value beyond the Qur'an itself, which, centered on the call to conversion and on the retelling and reshaping of several Biblical and other mythical narratives, only dealt – unlike the encompassing Deuteronomic Torah – with a limited number of issues immediately related to the ordinance of social life. Law emerges therefore less from a covenantal process than through the building of a tradition of modes of interaction and judgement that could be referred back to the life of Muhammad and his companions. To dare a synthetic formula, Islam is built on a re-energized, but also secularized kernel of Western prophetic axiality, reflected in a just mundane order regulated by the obedient and active commitment of man to God that makes him his trustee and "viceregent" (the meaning of "caliph") on earth. If each Axial pattern is a set of selective radicalizing shifts compared with earlier patterns (Arnason 2005: 41), the rise of Islam consciously selects out the Christ and radicalizes the focus on the moral glue of the community to be reached through reaching out to the other as a brother in faith. The gap between mundane and transcendent orders neither produces a metastasis of the orders nor its encapsulation into a mystery of incarnation, but a relatively open-ended balance with mild messianic undertones.

The nexus between salvation and human action in the Qur'an appears from a Christian viewpoint, but also from the perspective of the salvational drama of metastatic prophesy depicted by Voegelin, as not the primary concern of Islam. Islam's founding document is a teaching chiefly concerned with producing the correct approach to human action, understood as *'ibada* or "the service due to God," in order to produce and maintain the open-ended balance between *al-'alamayn*, the two worlds. The Qur'an, therefore, emphasizes all those psychological tensions that, rooted in that unstable balance, generate the correct moral frame for action and interaction. A crucial warning in the core Islamic scripture is directed against positing human agency as proudly self-sufficient, while on the other hand the Qur'an also scorns passivity and hopelessness. A key exhortation to man is to be one's own guard via fear of God *(taqwa)*, while the faithful is also reassured about God's mercy toward his creatures, based on the assumption that man has been created good in essence (Rahman 1979 [1966]: 241).

Even more since distant more than a millennium from the original Axial "breakthrough," the type of Axial transformation reflected by Islam's irruption into world history is a unique case of traditionalization and canonization of prophetic discourse, and of its amalgamation with other sources and forms of post-Axial and post-prophetic conceptions of legal and political order. It is also a case of strong and early social objectivation of the normative import of prophetic discourse. The Qur'an itself consecrates the Prophet's *sunna* as authoritative, and Muhammad adjudicated and pronounced authoritatively on a number of problems or disputes, so the prophet's voice, claiming to convey God's speech, was immediately effective in its own time. However, the social objectivation of the normativity of prophetic discourse went one step forward, based on the fact that most social transactions in the pristine Muslim community were settled without the intervention of the Prophet or his close companions, yet in terms that were largely understood as reflecting the new faith and its normativity (ibid.: 51). We see here a specific sociological strength of Islam and its immunization from an uncontrollable eschatological metastasis, in spite of the fact that many aspects of Muhammad's preaching, especially in its earlier face, did have a strong eschatological connotation, in line with earlier prophetic speech. Now however instead of opening up new breaches in the conceptualization of order, prophetic discourse (indeed not only Muhammad's but, retroactively, the interpretation of the entire prophetic chain included in the Qur'an) acquires a paradigmatic value through its extension and "application" to actual social practice: not however based on a listing of rules like in the Torah, but mostly through the delineation of key principles of correct behavior to be submitted to human, and so consciously imperfect interpretation and application. Islam so closes the normative gaps of earlier Abrahamic manifestations of prophetic voices that had metastatically anticipated – yet in reality indefinitely deferred – a just world of reconciliation with God. While a messianic projection is not erased by Islam, for which the Day of Judgement is as central an article of faith as is belief in God's oneness and in Muhammad's prophecy, Islam tames symbolism, myth and messianism through a normative approach whose solidity yet also flexibility is unprecedented – not surprisingly, due to the historical distance from the original breakthrough – compared with other Western Axial traditions.

A concomitant factor of differentiation of Islamic orthodoxy was that the process of canonization of sources and traditionalization of methods and schools was not centralized. As we will see, disagreement emerged and crystallized first of all on the issue itself of what tradition is and how it has to be constructed. "Orthodox," Sunni Islam was based on a principled acceptance of a regulated disagreement and on the rejection of any charismatic source of authority in adjudicating the "dogma" (in fact, the *sunna*). The orthodox Islamic community emerged as a basically lay ecumene engaged in a competitive search for knowledge *('ilm)*. AYN Its inherent risk of fragmentation created a counter-impulse to establish non-scriptural ordering principles. These were found in the principle of *ijma'* AYN (consensus) and in the notion of *maslaha*, covering a semantic terrain close to common good, public weal, *res publica*.

Essential to both the idea of consensus and the search for implementing the common good was the method of *ijtihad*, intended as an original effort of jurisprudential reasoning necessary to supplement the insufficiency of the other main sources of the law. However, *ijtihad* was gradually hijacked by a more basic and less creative method of analogical reasoning *(qiyas)* that in particular the *Shafi'i* school of law succeeded in consecrating as a canonical method of jurisprudence formally on a par with *ijma,'* and factually with a much larger practical influence in everyday jurisprudential work. *Qiyas* was a quite strict method of deduction of rulings by analogy from other rulings anchored in the text (Qur'an or certified *hadith*). Therefore, it imposed strict limits on *ijtihad*. This latter method was inherently bent to a more inductive, less text-oriented, and therefore more creative kind of reasoning, which found much less application in routine jurisprudence (Rahman 1979 [1966]: 71-77). On the other hand, neither *ijtihad* nor *ijma'* were ever fully institutionalized. While the former depended on the commitment of the individual scholar to pushing forward the jurisprudential reasoning wherever no solutions were readily available on the basis of the study of the main sources, *ijma'* was more of a pragmatic approximation of the ideal, and never accomplished situation where all those who possess knowledge by necessity agree on truth.

The emergence and consolidation of four schools within the Sunni orthodox mainstream (the Shafi'i, the Maliki, the Hanafi, and the Hanbali schools, all named by their founders) out of several hundreds restricted this potential of ordered disagreement, up to the point that the myth of a "closure of the gates of *ijtihad*" emerged by the 10th century AD. The conditions for exercising *ijtihad* were then formulated in such a restrictive way as to make this method unfeasible for normally talented practitioners. *Ijma,'* now facing a truncated *ijtihad*, ended up being absolutized at an ideological level, though its impact on actual jurisprudence was limited. A doctrine of the infallibility of *ijma'* emerged, which severely restricted its original scope of consecrating the authority of the living tradition through pragmatic accommodation. This authoritarian dogmatization of consensus did not rest on concilia like in Catholicism, presiding over the fixation and revision of dogma. Therefore, the infallibility of *ijma,'* and its authoritarian potential, remained largely fictitious and scarcely effective. It simulated the existence of an impossible consensus and reduced the stimuli for creativity, while factual spaces of autonomy were preserved as essential to the daily work of Sunni jurisprudence.

We can now better appreciate the degree of complexity, ambivalence, but also sophistication of tradition-making in Sunni Islam, which makes it a unique case for conceptual and theoretical reflection on the post-Axial development of patterns of practical rationality, reflexivity and communication. It is also a good case for showing how restrictive the obsession with consensus can work when authority is structurally fragmented. But this limitation was matched by the ongoing, never suppressed strength of Sunni Islam in streamlining theological nodes of Abrahamic Axiality and prophetic discourse and combining them with the aspiration to a greater and more realistic adherence of doctrine to practice. The grand scheme of classification of action within Islamic legal-moral traditions – under the five categories of *wajib* (mandatory), *mandub* (recommended), *mubah* (permissible or indifferent), *makruh* (reprehensible), and *haram* (illicit, forbidden) – offers a particularly ingenious grid of categories to all practitioners, including the commoners. It also encourages a diffuse effort to categorize types of action and determine the degree of creative interpretation permitted vs. undue innovations (or "heterodox" practices). The consequence is an ongoing work of reformulating and reconceptualizing the spaces of freedom and the responsibility of the agent and of persuading a Muslim audience that any such solution is acceptable (Asad 1993: 211-212).

Being based on a grid and not on a strictly binary code of good and bad, the actions that are covered by all categories and on particular by the three mediane ones have to fit into a general rule of "resoluteness and relaxation." This approach exalts the link between the agent's practical judgment in the application of a given rule to a specific situation, and the modulation of his will that is therefore no subjective *voluntas*, but an interaction-oriented channeling of "intention" *(niyya)*. The frequent verbalization of the agent's will through the formula "I intend" clarify the voluntary character of the action, yet through its subsumption under a given rule the action is also pragmatically linked to the given interactive situation. This operation does not entail a philosophically or theologically cogent substantiation of human will as e.g. related to the avoidance of sin. Thus Sunni Islam inoculates against an hyperinflation of subjectivity, a risk luring behind the Augustinian, and, to a minor extent, the Thomist elaboration of the will underlying action within Latin Christianity.

This channeling of intention by the agent clarifies reflexivity as first of all a reflective understanding of the situation. Therefore, while the Qur'an's goal is to create a just society by shaping righteous men and women submitting to a God enjoining good and prohibiting evil, the emphasis is on faith guiding action via a praxis-oriented reflection (Rahman 1979 [1966]: 85). While '*ilm* was intended as knowledge in the sense of learning, the activity of *fiqh* denoted the capacity to understand a situation on the basis of '*ilm*. *Fiqh* means therefore praxis-oriented interpretative activity, finally coinciding with (juris) prudential work, which is the way it is usually translated (ibid.: 101; Crone 1987: 103). However, *fiqh* still retains a shade of the meaning of judgement based on Aristotelian phronesis, which is exactly the capacity to act based on a telos and given all factors at stake and in particular he legitimate interests of all interactants. This reflective competence cannot be completely incorporated into a body of knowledge.

Knowledge, spirituality and praxis within the Sunni consensus

A non-speculative, quite anti-metaphysical philosophy of law reached its peak in 14th century al-Andalus (the Islamic name of the Iberian peninsula) and laid the basis for the reconstruction of reflective public reasoning in Islam well into the modern era. It would be however a gross mistake to think of speculative philosophy or philosophy proper *(falsafa)* as being erased from any influence on the Islamic consensus and thus on this trajectory of public reasoning. Islamic philosophy contributed key elements to a theory of prophetic discourse that affected, though indirectly, the most penetrating reflection of the Islamic philosophy of law. The same Islamic philosophy was also to enter reflections on the common good and the res *publica* within European modernity in particular through the work of Spinoza, a thinker of Jewish-Sephardi origin heir to the rich theoretical heritage of al-Andalus, from which his family fled due to the Christian persecutions. In particular the leading Islamic philosopher, Ibn Sina (980-1037), known in Europe as Avicenna, formulated the path-breaking hypothesis that prophetic discourse was wrapped in mythical imagery in order to match the imagination of the commoners and induce them to perform good. This does not mean – so his argument – that prophetic discourse is untrue (Rahman 1958). The use of imaginative symbols is necessary for effectively communicating the truth of religion. Ibn Sina was the prime formulator of a theory of religion as an equivalent of philosophy of and for the masses that found eager reinterpreters among leading modern European thinkers such as Spinoza, Vico, Leo Strauss and even Gramsci. According to this theory the prophets translated the philosophical maxim "if you pursue moral good, your mind shall attain the real spiritual freedom which is bliss" into the command "if you are virtuous and perform these specific acts, you shall enter Paradise and will be saved from the flames of Hell" (Rahman 1979 [1966]: 119-120).

Not unlike his European followers, however, Ibn Sina's theory had an intellectualist bent and elitist overtones. It was mainly for this reason, and not for any heretical character towards Sunni dogma – since it acknowledged that specific discursive forms of prophetic speech were carriers of truth – that this approach and *falsafa* in general raised the suspicion and often the overt opposition of the orthodox legists. In other words, *falsafa* had a different constituency from *fiqh*. While it was the most ingenious systematization of the relationship between revelation-based and speculation-driven strands of Axial thought, between "Jerusalem and Athens," Islamic philosophy was in itself of limited practical use in reconstructing the Sunni consensus. In spite of these limitations, *falsafa*'s later influence on the modern European coping with prophetic discourse as "religion" shows how this theory was a unique contribution to the long term post-Axial debate on the fundaments and modalities of reflective public reasoning. The relation of philosophy to Islamic jurisprudential traditions will leave nonetheless significant traces, however indirectly. Many among those scholars who were overtly using the rational methods of *falsafa*, like Fakhr al-Din Razi (d. 1209), or writing against philosophy, like Abu Hamid al-Ghazali (1058-1111), or taking a distance from philosophical methods, like Abu Ishaq al-Shatibi (d. 1388), contributed to introduce philosophical rigor into theology, Sufism, and, finally, into the theory or philosophy of law.

With philosophy on the sidelines of the socio-political confrontation, Sufism represented the biggest challenge to the hegemony of the legists. The precarious balance that resulted from the challenge favored the crystallization of weakly institutionalized models of governance of the social bond. The advantage of the

Sufi approach, compared to the theologians and the philosophers, was in its capacity to anchor its spiritual goals within collective practices. This focus helped Sufism avoiding the dogmatist impasse of the theologians and the elitist trap of the philosophers. The roots of Sufism are as old as the translation of Muhammad's message into practice by his companions and other contemporaries. From a first nucleus of Medinese piety and asceticism based on the Qur'anic notion of faithful trust in God *(tawakkul)* and of love for God, the Sufi path took a first shape during the first two centuries of Islam. It was however not before the 11th and 12th centuries that Sufism was included into the mainstream Islamic consensus and took up a clear organizational form (Hoexter and Levtzion 2002: 12).

At that stage, the Sufi path appeared as highly innovative in that it formulated a solution to the problem of the relationship between rational speculation on the one hand, and the prophetic discourse's impact on the categories of practitioners on the other. This inherently tense relationship seemed to have reached a grave stalemate in the Sunni Islamic world with the work of the Andalusi philosopher Ibn Rushd (d. 1198), known in Europe as Averroes. His rationalist philosophy was the object of vehement attacks by the *fuqaha,'* in spite of the fact that he was also a leading jurist. Sufism exploited this tension to its advantage in order to show its commitment to orthodoxy via a focus on the exemplary value of the *sunna* of the Prophet. Sufism demanded to the single Muslim the appropriation of the *sunna* through a disciplined training placed under the guide of a master, and finalized to access the essential truth, the haqiqa. This inner truth could only be achieved through establishing a close relationship to the human being who is particularly close to God, the prophet Muhammad, and to the other "friends" of God, the new Sufi saints.

However, Sufism was in many ways the flip side of the legists' authority in Sunni Islam, and took upon itself the task of shaping that form of faithful trust among brothers in faith that the *fuqaha'* discourse was not able to capture on its own. This is why several interpreters (among whom the already mentioned, authoritative 20th century Muslim scholar and reformer Fazlur Rahman) tend to see the relationship between Sufism and jurisprudence more as a concerted, though tense division of labor than as a conflict between mutually exclusive approaches to Islam. Noteworthy is that the emerging orthodox shape of Sunni Islam prevented Sufism from establishing a form of monasticism, which was not unknown to the spiritual ferments in Arabia that provided the immediate antecedent to Muhammad's preaching. Similarly, however, to the new monastic movements in 13th century Latin Christian Europe, the simultaneous consolidation of Sufism took from the beginning the form of a socio-religious movement of the commoner. The main differences with Latin Europe concerned the institutional environment, the organizational forms of Sufism, and its understandings of the basic disciplines demanded to its practitioners.

While liminality was a key element of Axial transformations and in particular of prophetic discourse, it acquires in the 13th century a distinctive sociological anchorage. At this historical stage marginal forces occupying a low institutional level within hierarchies of Axial authority start to play a central role both in Latin Christian Europe and in the Islamic world, and initiate a lengthy and continuous – though in no way smooth – march into social institutions. While the connecting and in-between role of these forces is not a novelty, what is new in this period is that they developed their strengths and penetrative capacities starting from the margins or interstices of the socio-political order (Szakolczai 2001: 361-362).

In the case of the European *saeculum* these forces – whether they were ecclesiastical or lay, and Franciscans did at the beginning understand themselves as lay – manifested an acutely liminal character by showing an initial resistance to follow a clear path of institutionalization. While they spurned social and cultural creativity, they also engendered a spiraling confusion on the categorization of the ongoing process of the fragmentation of the Latin Christian ecumene. Partly in analogy and partly by contrast to them, the most interesting aspect of the wave of institutionalization of Sufism in the 12th and 13th centuries was that while the new monastic movements in Europe colonized civic life, the Sufi movement entered into a symbiotic relationship with urban associations. Sufism provided them a permanent infrastructure of ties of trust, underpinned by the authority of the shaykhs of the brotherhoods. The associations that overlapped with the brotherhoods were the craftsmen guilds and other groups, including military or paramilitary organizations, like, among the Ottomans who were advancing in the Anatolian peninsula, the Turkish Janissaries and groups of frontiers warriors, as well as the urban *futuwwa*, a sort of youth gangs based on a chivalry code and committed to the protection of shared values.

Sufi leaders played a role of conciliation and arbitration in civic disputes, up to the point that their houses were considered sanctuaries, also in the sense of extraterritorial sites for peace and arbitration meetings, and therefore safe havens from factional violence (Levtzion 2002: 110). Sufi orders reached out to a variety of constituencies, like traders, townspeople, peasants, and people of diverse social classes, regions, and economic condition. Sufi leaders used not only scholastic Arabic but also the vernacular languages of their regions. Ruling authorities were often suspicious of the orders because of their autonomy and capacity for independent action, linking the local with much wider spheres of influence. For the same reasons, rulers often sought links and advice from Sufi shaykhs.

It is important to keep in mind the praxic orientation of Sufism and its material foundations, in order not to misunderstand its "spiritual" orientation as an "Eastern" illuminationist doctrine with dubious relationships to the core, orthodox Islamic teachings. This is also what set it apart from the socio-religious movements of 13th century Europe, in which Voegelin saw seeds of the immanentist, subjectivist, and spiritualist twist of modern political religions (Voegelin 1994). Nasab al-khirqa, one of the last writings of the "great master" of Sufism, Ibn al-'Arabi (1165-1240) from Murcia, al-Andalus, and in many ways the testament of his praxic spirituality, delineates the relationship between the inner and the outer dimensions of the truth. It provides an almost prototypical catalogue of Axial praxic compassion, calling to observance of pious behavior to Other (Elmore 1999). The *khirqa,* i.e. the mantel of Sufi initiation, is *malabis ahl al-taqwa,* i.e. the vestiture of the God-fearing, which is the core Islamic virtue to operate wisely and interactively in a social and practical life of orientation to Other. The spiritual realm is not constructed as a separate domain of the Geist, but is solidly anchored in praxis. "What stands out in Sufi esoterism is that it relates to the domain of Islam's faith and works, and it is contrasted with an exoterism that relates to the same domain" (Chittick 1992: 9). Ibn al-'Arabi grew in al-Andalus, in the far West of the Islamic world, not only influenced by Sufi masters but also through matching his own mystical experience against the background of the great philosophical teachers, among which, prominent in his age, Ibn Rushd, whom he knew personally. At the age of 35 he started disseminating, in a continual development, his teachings into the East, through North Africa, towards Mecca and Damascus.

It is not surprising, therefore, that partly in analogy and partly in contrast with the new, mendicant, monastic movements that mushroomed in Latin Christian Europe in the 13th century, the Sufi orders provided moral leadership, a discourse of justice, and a permanent channel of communication that facilitated the link between commoners and authorities (Levtzion 2002: 117). The monastic movements in Europe were able to take over the issue of local sainthood so as to mediate between popular drives and the church's suspicion towards a bottom-up approach that challenged the centralized procedures of saints' canonization. They thus made local saints the symbols of civic allegiances. The Sufi brotherhoods, instead, followed a straighter path: they instituted on their own a notion of saintliness that was in principle excluded by the Sunni dogma. This was and still is a contentious issue. The Sunni incorporation of prophetic charisma into a highly fragmented notion of authority does not recognize, in principle, authoritative sources external to the Qur'an and the *sunna*. Therefore, the making of saintliness through movements and groups distinct from the colleges of teachers and the corporations of lawyers, yet laying a claim to the preservation and transmission of Qur'anic piety, constituted a new, parallel form of authority that also claimed orthodox status and inclusion in the consensus.

In organizational terms, the Sufi movements impacted on the socio-political configuration of forces in both urban and rural contexts. The making of saintliness became strictly associated with autonomous civic powers, mostly linked to professional organizations, not unlike in Europe. In the Islamic case there was a weaker religious legitimacy of political power in increasingly fragmented Muslim potentates after the 11th century, and towards which the Sufi organizations acted as a bulwark and as a permanent source of popular unrest. Yet the main difference with Europe was that the organizational unit of Sufism, the *tariqa*, was kept much more malleable than the monastic form prevalent in Europe, which ended up imprinting on even those radical monastic movements which were initially conceived as alternative to it. The *tariqa* did not necessarily coincide with a brotherhood and not even to a lay confraternity like those promoted in urban contexts by the new monastic movements in Europe. A *tariqa*, which literally means a "way," remained basically a network of variably organized levels of master-disciple relations, kept together by strong congregational moments epitomized by the collective séances of the adepts. It might appear as a puzzle – at least from a Weberian perspective – that the lower formalization and institutionalization of Sufi authority made it less "liminal" and more institutionally "absorptive," to use Voegelinian categories (cf. Szakolczai 2001).

We can therefore summarize the picture by identifying in the urban centers a variable geography of legal schools (several hundreds in the early centuries, then consolidating into a dozen, and with four emerging as "canonical schools"), guilds, brotherhoods and ethnic communities. This organizational map found a transversal institutional glue in how public services were funded: not by non-existing municipalities, but by pious endowments, originating from the institution of *waqf* (Mardin 1995: 286-287). More than a prevalence of outright informal ties in the relationships among scholars and between scholars, commoners, and rulers, we see here an approach to organization of a more "scalable" kind than in European counterparts, in terms of degree (and reversibility) of formalization. At stake here is the type of reflexivity incorporated into institutions. This is nicely illustrated by the institution that best incorporates the inclusion of the commoners in the practices and discourses of doing good: the waqf. While *shari'a*-based jurisprudence provided the normative ideal to Muslim society, and Sufi orders provided it moral leadership, the *waqf* represented the social and even fiscal infrastructure that secured the public weal. Though being a clearly formalized type of institution, based on a specific law, unlike the legists' schools and the Sufi orders, the *waqf* retains and optimizes the scalability of formalization and flexibility of use of resources for the pursuit of its institutional ends, based on local demands but also structures of power based on networks and clans. For sure, this flexibility did not protect it from abuses and diversions of resources from their institutionalized objectives. The imperative of "doing good" and the principle of "common good" were nonetheless well served by a continuous renegotiation and interpretation of all legitimate interests at stake. Therefore it is through the practice of *waqf* and not only through jurisprudential reflection that an "ongoing discourse" on common good and associated methods of public reasoning emerged. This process facilitated the emergence of a rich jurisprudential knowledge, but also one that eschewed rigid codification. To the theoretical fundaments of this ongoing, practical and juridical, yet also reflective, discourse on the common good I will now turn.

The philosophy of law of praxic Axiality

The fundaments of jurisprudence, the usul al-fiqh, required a method of reasoning different from that of theology and philosophy. They demanded a focus on the simultaneously intentional and interactional dimension of human action, in order for man to be held not just morally but also legally responsible for his acts. It has been stated that the main issue of the philosophy of law was that, "since obedience to Divine Commands [...] depends on human volition, the Command must be shown to be motivated by the consideration of human interest" (Masud 1995 [1977]: 119). It is therefore unsurprising that especially from the 11th century onwards various thinkers started to concentrate their reflections on *maslaha* (common good/public weal) as the universal general principle which permeated all commands with legal value (ibid.: 122). *Maslaha* provided the conceptual proof stone for underpinning theoretically informed but practice-oriented views of the common good liable to become platforms for concrete articulations of the pursuit of the public interest.

The notion of *maslaha* is based on the root s-l-h that denotes being and becoming good, in a sense that conveys the full scale of positive values from uncorrupted to right, honest, virtuous, and further up to just (ibid.: 135). By the 11th century, *maslaha* and the related notion of *istislah* – stemming from the same root, and indicating the actual method of reasoning for seeking *maslaha* – emerged as the principal key-words in the discussion. The emerging method of reasoning stood out against other approaches that sought an exclusive basis on scriptural sources. But it is also interesting to note that in the method of the Maliki school, one of the four canonical Sunni legal schools – the one among them that worked to uphold the centrality of *maslaha* most consistently – the approach to *maslaha* was also employed to discard the earlier mentioned limitations of the notion of *ijma,'* i.e. consensus.

The orientation to *maslaha*, which still stands out as the most progressive and open method of Islamic legal reasoning, appears, symptomatically, not only a less text-bound and more context-friendly approach, compared to other methods. It also promotes a processual view of the common good not enslaved to a fictitious, fragile, and largely arbitrary view of consensus existing at any given point in time. The related methodology *(istislah)* was from its inception quite suitable to shift the boundaries of any existing consensus, on the basis of modes of public reasoning applied to any given actual situation (ibid.: 137). Concomitantly, any reduction of *istislah* to a form of *qiyas*, i.e. to an analogic reasoning strictly adhering to textual sources, was rigorously opposed. The attempt to dilute the approach to *maslaha* in terms of *qiyas* was upheld especially by Shafi'i jurists and, most strongly, by al-Ghazali, who confined *istislah*, i.e. the seeking of *maslaha*, to the discretionary realm of the *mujtahid,* and therefore subjected it to the strict limitations and exceptional character of *ijtihad* (ibid.: 140-142).

Using in particular the method of induction and generalization shaped by the

Hanafi school, and merging it with the Maliki notion of the common good as intrinsic to *shari'a*, the Andalusi jurist al-Shatibi asserted that the principle underlying all *shari'a* rulings is and cannot be other than *maslaha*. It is the intent of the Lawgiver, and therefore the objectives of the law *(maqasid al-shari'a)*, that make *maslaha* central to legislation (ibid.: 118). In other words – so his claim – legal reasoning could not focus on a single doctrine or case while looking at the legal sources, but had to simultaneously relate to the telos of the law. The theological premise was as simple as it had been controversial in the earlier philosophy of Islamic law: "the premise is that God instituted the [...] laws [...] for the [...] good of the people, both immediate and future" (ibid.: 119). According to this approach a reliance on *qiyas* (analogic reasoning) was not acceptable, because it limited legal reasoning to deducting rulings from a particular text, thereby inhibiting any inductive reasoning based on aggregated textual evidence and not on a single text (ibid.: 128).

Furthermore, *istislah* as the method of inductive search for *maslaha* differed from the *istihsan* preferred by the Hanafi school. While the latter promoted the discretion of the individual jurist in searching for the most useful solution to a given case whenever the reasoning by analogy would yield a solution harmful to such utility (and has been therefore compared to the notion of equity in common law), *istislah* relied on a more integrated method for identifying and promoting the public interest (ibid.: 129). In this sense, *istislah* departs form any merely utilitarian logic, which is not completely extraneous to Islamic thought. The result is that, based on *maslaha* and on *istislah*, a ruling should not be simply useful in itself, i.e. by reference to a notion of utility seen as inherent in a given empirical situation, but with regard to a wider concept of common good, comparable to the *res publica* of the Roman law tradition and that provides the root concept to all European notions of the public sphere (Salvatore 2006). The common logic is the application of existing rules within the background and with the backup of a wider collective interest that corresponds to the basic finality of the law itself (Masud 1995 [1977]: 130-131). This is a remarkable achievement in the long Axial genealogy of ideas of connective justice rooted in prophetic discourse (cf. Assmann 2005).

Maslaha is different from sheer utility and has a clear Axial prophetic affiliation also because it is not limited to this world but links the good in this world to the hereafter. Sociologically, it does not limit the common good to material utility, and especially not to the sum of the utility of various agents (Masud 1995 [1977]: 132). Moreover *maslaha* does not show the limitations of the *utilitas publica* of Roman law (Crone 1987: 11), whereby the faculty to reinterpret a law in the name of the public weal became in the imperial epoch subordinated to the prerogative of edictal legislation that undermined the traditional law and reconstructed ad hoc rulings based on specific situations, thereby torpedoing the ratio of *res publica* at its fundaments (ibid.: 104-105). In those cases, *utilitas publica* hijacked *res publica*, while *maslaha*, as a theoretical construct, approximates an interpretation of *res publica* uncontaminated by power considerations, also thanks to its Axial prophetic origin. In more recent epochs and also in the popular perception, however, *maslaha* also became associated with power abuse for pure expediency.

One can detect a sense of caritas incorporated in *maslaha*, which crosscuts the service function of the *waqf* institution, as the pivotal establishment for seeking and implementing *maslaha*. However, this cannot be equated with the incorporation of caritas that was the achievement of European Latin Christianity, via the elaboration on the notion of *respublica christiana* developed during the Middle Ages. The latter was the product of the combination of at least two different traditions (the Christian tradition of caritas and the legal tradition of Roman law centered on *res publica*), while *maslaha*, although it incorporated several legacies ranging from Greek philosophy, to the influence of Judaism and Christianity, and to Roman law itself, was developed in a more linear way from within the assets of the ongoing and precarious search for an Islamic consensus.

At the same time, the notion of *maslaha* can be easily articulated in a plural way, in the form of the *masalih* (plural of *maslaha*), i.e. the goods to be sought in different situations and legal cases. In this sense, it structurally crosscut the realm of private and public law. Nonetheless, *maslaha* is never a particularistic good even when it is identified with a discrete good. Various species of *maslaha* refer to *maslaha* as a genus. It is interesting that in a fatwa (legal opinion) on a case concerning a *waqf* controversy issued by al-Shatibi, the principle of *maslaha* was applied in order to safeguard the nature of *waqf* as a type of endowment that creates a good that is collective yet specific (a particular mosque, or school etc.). Al-Shatibi's ruling was intended to fight the practice, which was widespread at his time, of using *waqf* revenues for the undifferentiated funding of a general category of collective service (i.e. all mosques in a town) and therefore as a supplement to the sultanic treasure (bayt al-mal) (Masud 1995 [1977]: 93). The protection of *maslaha* – al-Shatibi judged – requires to stick to the particular will of the endower, provided it is finalized to *qurba* (coming closer to God) and conform to the related notion of actively performing the good that is required by this search for closeness to God.

The solution pursued by al-Shatibi highlights the relation between phronesis and telos from a practical and legal angle that helps evidencing some of the nodes encountered in the process of upgrading practical reasoning into reflective public reasoning. Moreover, it shows a conception that makes transparent how phronesis, in such a developed post-Axial prophetic context, is still linked to command, while on the other hand it cannot be defined by authority alone and has to rest on reasoning and reflection. God's command – according to most theologians, including al-Ghazali – has to coincide with the *maslaha* of man, but "in order to decide that something is *maslaha*, even to say that God's commands are based on *maslaha*, some criterion outside of these commands has inevitably to be accepted" (ibid.: 145). *Istislah* represents therefore nothing less than the specific phronetic criterion to ascertain and seek in concrete situations the *maslaha* on which God's commands are based. Al-Shatibi inherited from some of the theorists spanning the period from the 11th century to the 14th century the view that the objectives *(maqasid)* of God's will, and therefore of the *shari'a*, are derived from the *maslaha* of the people. He was particularly straightforward in considering the finality of the *shari'a* being one with *maslaha*. We find therefore a view of *maslaha* that is at the same time strongly objectified and quite concrete, not unlike the pristine Roman view of *res publica*, with the difference that as a theoretical notion denoting good or interest, *maslaha* was also immediately applicable to the modalities of legal reasoning. It is symptomatic that in his work on the philosophy of law, al-Shatibi manifested his outright distaste for any purely intellectual or theological discussion of *shari'a*.

Wherever unrelated to questions immediately relevant for action and judgement, such an abstract discussion was, in his view, hostile to the scope itself of *shari'a*. It is remarkable that it was precisely on the basis of such a radically anti-intellectualist platform that al-Shatibi delivered the probably most compelling theoretical formulation of Islamic notions of "common good" and "public interest." The emergence of his concern for *maslaha* was also stirred up by the serious socio-economic changes that Andalusian society was experiencing in the 14th century. These transformations made a reliance on analogy and precedent insufficient to solve legal cases, and raised the necessity to reflexively reconstruct broader principles of Islamic law from which to derive rulings (ibid.: 55).

Al-Shatibi was quite outspoken in asserting that within legal reasoning one must give priority to the results of action in order to check whether any given action serves the purpose of law (ibid.: 123). He also introduced a welcome element of complexification when he insisted on distinguishing between the *masalih* as defined in the discourse *(khitab)* of the Lawgiver, and as found in the world of human life and relations. He thus considered the discursive tradition and the world of practice and "common sense" as two distinct, though interrelated layers of human action and reflexivity. And he admitted that human relations are complex enough, so that they cannot configure pure *masalih*, i.e. goods to pursue for the human benefit, but are mingled with hardship and discomfort.

For Al-Shatibi it is habit and practice *('ada)* that customarily defines certain things as *masalih* and other as *mafasid* (nuisances, discomforts). This specification indicates that practical common sense is not purely receptive towards needs, but has also a definitional and, as it were, discursive and reflexive capacity (ibid.: 155). It is therefore social practice in the first instance that deploys phronesis in seeking *maslaha*. This faculty is not part of a specialized enterprise led by expert knowledge, but is in the hands of the commoner, so it is – we would say – common sense driven. On the other hand, one cannot deny that the discourse of *shari'a* also defines the *masalih* in a more direct way. As an extension of the function of prophetic discourse, this definitional effort by the experts of the law inculcates a telic sense of right and wrong in human agency and practical rationality, without which action would degenerate into a pure utilitarian hunt for discrete and separate goods.

It is precisely in this permanent tension between the complexity of the social world were goods and ills are not found in a pure form, and the moral command of *shari'a*, that the agential capacity of phronesis grows on the bedrock of the faculties of man as a free agent *(mukhtar)* who is responsible for his acts, not only morally, but, through his inclusion in an ordered community, also legally (ibid.: 156). In those cases where neither habit or custom, nor the *shari'a* provide a clear definition of what is right or wrong, *ijtihad* (the effort to find creative solutions through reasoning) has to be exerted. Laying emphasis on *ijtihad* is for al-Shatibi essential to explain deliberation and satisfying the underlying need for certainty in the legal process. After all hypothetical answers to the question whether a certain act is right or wrong (like e.g. whether eating carrion is allowed when it is indispensable to survival) have being weighed off, the decision of the mujtahid has to be considered binding (ibid.: 157).

The complexity of the social worlds and the related intricacies of the process of defining and adjudicating *maslaha* are incontestable, yet this recognition cannot be equated with a relativistic conception. Al-Shatibi firmly distinguishes *maslaha*, which carries – since it is plunged into an intrinsically plural dimension of human action – the connotation of "interest" in the general sense of what is good to man, from the pursuit of purely particularistic interests, personal preferences and passionate desires. Al-Shatibi clearly reaffirms that *maslaha*, in as far as it is the motor of the human pursuit of the objectives of the *shari'a*, is finalized to free the human actor from the dictates of passion and make him the servant of God and his Law (ibid.: 158). He insists in clarifying that *maslaha* is the engine itself of the law in that it serves human welfare and the removal of hardship in general, and is therefore present as a genus in all rules. It is retrieved by the phronetic approach of jurisprudence via the application of the method of *istislah* and cognates. In contrast with the hierarchic-dualistic model of the subject prevalent in Latin Christian Europe and that liberal modernity will not dissolve but aggravate (see Santoro 2003 [1999]), in the Islamic case epitomized by al-Shatibi's post-Axial, legal and social thought the superior interest is not rooted in a pure volition of the virtuous subject, but emerges through interaction and is therefore intrinsically intersubjective.

It is revealing that one synonym of *istislah* used by al-Shatibi is istidlal, which does not mean "finding good" in a given situation but "finding the right sign" (Masud 1995 [1977]: 161-162). This is not surprising, because al-Shatibi's theory of law reposes on a theory of language that compares the *shari'a* issued of prophetic discourse to an "ordinary language." The Islamic scholar maintained quite straightforwardly that "the judgement *(hukm)* is not derived on the basis of what meanings are posited (wad') for the words but on some other basis, that is the aspect of following the action *(iqtida' bi-l af'al)*" (ibid.: 175). Al-Shatibi explains the enigmas of the regulating impetus of the "logic of practice" via the *ummi* ("common" or "ordinary") character of prophetic discourse, i.e. its being addressed to the "common man." One cannot understand *shari'a* and its objectives without referring to the common sense of the addressees of the Qur'an, who are commoners. Clearly – and this sets the prophet Muhammad apart from his predecessors – the *ummi* disposition of the receptor of the Qur'anic message matches the character of the speech of al-nabi al-*ummi*, as Muhammad is designated in the Qur'an, i.e. "the common prophet," or "the prophet of the commoners." Here the Axial sense of connective justice culminates into the Islamic invention of the pious commoner.

The ordinary character of prophetic speech might seem to clash with the concomitant notion of the sacral, miraculous features of Qur'anic discourse. However, the latter was understood as rooted in the immediacy or unmediated power of the word. The words of the Qur'an weren't even mediated by "scripture," since the prophet Muhammad was considered illiterate, and the written recording of the Qur'an is a later process determined by obvious practical and institutional reasons, on whose necessity, significantly, Muhammad was completely silent. Clearly the Qur'an, which means recitation or precisely speech, intended to abrogate the previous scripture – collected in the Bible – exactly because they were scripture, and so they had been – according to Qur'an – manipulated by impious and unscrupulous men for their own particularistic interests. This time God speaks to Muhammad through Jibril (Gabriel), and the prophet in turn transmits the revealed word to his followers who retain it by heart. The Qur'an is thus held to have been recited and transmitted in "pure Arabic."

Al-Shatibi clarifies that the first level of intelligibility of *shari'a* resides precisely in the fact that its primary source, the Qur'an, was cast in ordinary Arabic, which makes the rules, on a first level, context-bound. The ideal speech situation configured by the Qur'an and the circumstances of its initial transmission build, nonetheless, a second level of intelligibility that is universal since translatable in all existing languages. This level operates via a mechanism of retrieval through the type of reasoning promoted by al-Shatibi, consisting in an induction of collective meaning from the text on the basis of the presumption of *maslaha* inherent in the situation addressed. It is this type of induction that helps instituting universal intelligibility. In other words, it is through this method of *istislah* telically oriented to the objectives of *shari'a* that the pure ordinary language of prophetic discourse is translated into a universal language upholding and regulating social practice. Its phronetic dimension is brought to a level of sophistication that helps transcending the close boundaries of a given primordial community, and therefore constitutes a high point in the Axial pursuit of universality on a practical level. The analogic method of *qiyas*, in its double constraint of being text-bounded and based on a binary, scarcely dialectical Aristotelian logic, is insufficient for responding to this Axial promise of universality (ibid.: 178-179).

Al-Shatibi goes one step further and clarifies that the attribute *ummi* as used by the Arabs for designating themselves and their language was also intended to differentiate them from the Greeks and all civilizations of antiquity that rested on literacy and on the massive use of the written world, while they, the Arabs, preferred oral transmission and tradition. This orientation was due to change quite rapidly in the first two centuries of Islam, mainly as an effect of Islam's rise and rapid spread. This process also encompassed the recording first of the Qur'an and then of *hadith* collections, and encouraged the flourishing of the written sciences of the law, theology, philosophy, not to speak of medicine and other sciences in which the Arabs attained excellence, not least in the rich social and cultural worlds of al-Andalus. In spite of the acquisition and development of these post-Hellenistic cultural assets that were quite consolidated by the time of al-Shatibi, his insistence on the *ummi* character of the Islamic *shari'a* as well as of the prophetic discourse from which it originated is a clear rebuttal of the specific trajectories of the civilizations of the written world which culminated in philosophy, but were deprived of prophetic voices, like the Greek civilization.

Al-Shatibi's theory puts in evidence how in the shaping of what he – and indeed many Muslim reformers inspired by him up to our times – saw as the superior Axial universality of Islam's notions of connective justice based on a praxic reflexivity the civilization of the written world played the role of a sufficient condition for the spread and consolidation of the civilization, while prophetic discourse in its pure *ummi* form was the necessary one. This observation can be linked to what some scholars have evidenced as a likely concurrent meaning of *ummi* as referred to Muhammad, his language, and the Arabs in general. It is a meaning derived from Hebrew and denoting "the people of the world in general," therefore with a meaning close to "gentile." Muhammad as the "gentile prophet" would then highlight an additional dimension of post-Axial maturity of his message, i.e. its capacity to transcend its first level of being *ummi*, i.e. native and confined to a given community of ordinary language seeing itself as the chosen people. This second meaning of *ummi* could be linked to the asserted character of Muhammad's prophecy as completing and sealing the whole chain of Semitic prophecy, by projecting it towards embracing the people of the world in general, i.e., "man" (ibid.: 179).

Even if the reference to Ibn Sina is not explicit, it is apparent how al-Shatibi's argument owes something to the above mentioned theoretical approach to prophetic discourse by the leading Islamic philosopher, in spite of al-Shatibi's ostentatious disregard for philosophical, and in particular Aristotelian discourse, and his more general conviction of the superiority of the prophetic way. The Andalusi scholar, who not unlike Ibn Sina considered not only Muhammad but all his prophetic predecessors and their laws (shara'i,' plural of *shari'a*) as admonishing and exhorting their people to the right path in ordinary language, has the merit, however, of putting on its head the elitist approach of Ibn Sina. Instead of assuming a superior truth made understandable and palatable to the commoner who cannot command the sophisticated rational discourse of the philosopher, al-Shatibi takes entirely the perspective of the common social and legal actor and asserts that legal obligation can only be legitimate if a rule can be understood by the commoner. For him there is no responsibility of the legal actor without comprehension of the law.

This is also the part of al-Shatibi's argument where it appears that one cannot rely on a self-enclosed view of ordinary language matching a Bordieuian "logic of practice." Any self-sustaining practice needs efficient communication, and it is the understanding and active seeking of *maslaha* that makes communication among human actors possible via agreements on shared goods and methods to attain them. Here it also appears that the phronetic, reflective and communicative task of the jurist only is only feasible as an extension of the phronetic activity residing in the practice of ordinary people. This basic layer of practice, however, already incorporates a knowledge of *maslaha* through the intelligibility of *shari'a*. In this sense, *maslaha* has not to be taught and inculcated ex nihilo by a class of 'ulama, neither does it ground obligations for the elite of knowledge alone. Obligation in the *shari'a* is rational and therefore universally comprehensible. The task of the jurists is to keep open and functioning the circles of communication, seeking in *maslaha* the methodological guidance necessary for helping to solve those problems of the commoners that they cannot solve on their own. The condition for performing this job is to cast into a *ummi*, comprehensible, ordinary language the solutions sought under the umbrella of the universalistic method of induction provided by *istislah* (ibid.: 181).

Faced with the problem of how to deal with what by his time was a quite powerful and established spiritual elite, i.e. the Sufis, who had recruited wide masses of commoners and had penetrated many civic institutions, al-Shatibi drew a distinction between the ordinary people who act on the basis of self-interest (and therefore need the guidance of *maslaha*), and the Sufis, whose approach to *shari'a* obligations he considered extraordinary and therefore transcending the rule applicable to common man. He called the Sufis "the people who disregard their self-interest," and therefore saw them as consciously transcending the common sense of right and wrong of the ordinary people. Though it is known that al-Shatibi did not sympathize with the Sufis, he justified their approach as indirectly beneficial to how *maslaha* orients the legal actors toward the just middle between the opposite extremes of too much hardship and too much laxity in performing obligations, thus echoing a well-known Aristotelian motive concerning the virtues (ibid.: 192-193). He saw that the great stress laid on piety and asceticism by the Sufis was ultimately useful, on a social level, to counter the looming risk of a fall into laxity of commoners. Sufism therefore contributed to Islamic normativity through their permanent, exemplary correction of the latent laxity of the commoner, in spite of a lack of regulative strength, in strictly legal terms, of their way, or *tariqa*.

It remains that al-Shatibi's view of the legal actor, of his obligations and of the notion of *maslaha* underlying them was based – in an indeed quite anti-Aristotelian and in general un-Greek fashion – on a view of the actor not as a "subject" of virtuous or vicious conduct, but as a genuinely relational agent, who discharges duties incumbent on him, whose origin and justification are inscribed in the triangular relationship between ego, alter, and God, and therefore on the proto-Axial view of "connective justice." God matters here as the initiator of a Law that provides goals and guidelines, and activates an engine (*maslaha*) that gives orientation, activates discernment and induces reflexivity into human agents. Whereas Sufism reflects the closest approach in Islam to a subjectivity of virtue and excellence through an ethic of renunciation – the nearest therefore to the monastic path, whose legitimacy was explicitly denied in a famous *hadith* by the prophet Muhammad – al-Shatibi was coherent in considering the Sufi path as subsidiary and not central to the Islamic view and practices of the common good.

Conclusion. Which reflexivity: interactive vs. subjectivity based?

In spite of the evident differences with the synthesis achieved in Latin Christian Europe by Aquinas, al-Shatibi's challenge of Sufi asceticism's claim that only the negation of selfish interest is a basis for true obedience to God echoes Aquinas' response to the challenge of the new monastic orders. The common answer was that self-interest is not denied by the notion of obedience to God, since conformity with the will of the lawgiver (based on *maslaha*) is what constitutes obedience to the law of nature (ibid.: 196). If fitting into *maslaha*, the pursuit of self-interest is not only legitimate, but necessary for common welfare. This apparently simple answer pushed al-Shatibi – similarly to Aquinas – towards clarifying and complexifying the view of the legal agent and the category of intention in a way that, while it added sophistication to his theory, put in evidence its points of vulnerability. Practice, custom and the pursuit of legitimate self-interest therein are embedded in a sort of natural law whose relationship with *shari'a* has been scarcely problematized in Islamic legal philosophy. Al-Shatibi's distaste for Aristotelian approaches and more generally for the speculative theology that had largely relied on Aristotle – in spite of his partial and unacknowledged indebtedness to *falsafa* – was doubtless a limiting factor in his theorizing. However, the terrain on which al-Shatibi's theory sought to vindicate its coherence is where he established a nexus between act and intention, with a strategy quite different from the Christian Thomist theory of voluntas, which was still dependent on the Augustinian construction of the sinful subject.

Al-Shatibi maintained that intention *(niyya)* is necessary for an action to be valid. The social actor as a *mukhtar*, i.e. as an agent of choice endowed with freedom of the will, manifests, through acting, his intention to obey to the commands of the Lawgiver via orientation to *maslaha*, or to disobey. Seeking *maslaha* is therefore a requirement for a correctly directed intention, which is in turn indispensable to act (ibid.: 206-207). This definition of intention is called to attenuate the ambiguities of al-Shatibi's dealing with passions, self-interest, and common good. Ultimately the commitment to *maslaha* and the orientation of self-interest to it become a matter of responsibility and reflexivity of the free agent. He adds a welcome sophistication to this view by admitting that in his seeking to do good, ego may happen to do harm to alter. The agent therefore should concur to the definition of *maslaha* in every specific case through undergirding his pious intention with a reflection upon the consequences of action. This operation requires going beyond the appearance or the simple assumption of good and bad, and the development of an analysis of the complex ways in which benefit and discomfort are intermingled in social life (ibid.: 209).

Therefore, the agent's responsibility does include reflexivity, and reflecting about one's action's consequences is considered the highest form of phronesis, in spite of the fact that it is no antidote against macro-sociologically unintended consequences of action. This is a type of practical reflexivity that can be only ascertained after the fact, based on its effects, and cannot therefore be preemptively subsumed within a higher, collective dimension that *maslaha* is supposed to institute. This form of reflective phronesis is ultimately applied through *ijtihad*, as expounded above, intended as "a process in which one exhausts one's efforts to one's full capacity in order to acquire exact or probable knowledge to reach judgement in a given case" (ibid.: 230). We know that modern social theory is also concerned with the social technologies that are deputed to "anticipate" and neutralize such unintended consequences. Modern normative views of the public sphere do encompass – and often aspire to tame – such social technologies (cf. Eickelman and Salvatore 2004 [2002]). What I have analyzed here is that prior to the grounding of these social techniques, the modalities of intersubjective engagement instituted and nurtured by the praxic Axiality of the Western Islam from al-Andalus were based on a view of scientific probability that makes any dualism between traditional phronesis and modern techné extraneous to the development of this particular tradition.

As Aquinas, al-Shatibi clearly bypassed the type of Axial dichotomic polarization between *civitas terrena* and *civitas* Dei as constructed by Augustine in late antiquity, i.e. towards the end of what we might still call the primary Axial cycle of transformations. It is fair to say that the Dominican monk and the Andalusi jurist represent the culmination of a renaissance that reconstructed Axial formulas in an almost proto-sociological fashion, and can be therefore tentatively termed "Axial renaissance" (Salvatore 2006). But it is also possible to observe that as a representative – though not an uncontested one – of the Islamic philosophy of law, and more general as an Islamic theorist of the social and legal agent and, concomitantly, of the common good and public interest, al-Shatibi has the merit of posing limits to the unsociological oversubjectivation of the agent that has affected the Christian Europe's genealogy of the hierarchic-dualistic subject and finally produced the Voegelinian syndrome of the "free spirit." Al-Shatibi has the merit of sticking to a relational view of the agent as ego relationally involved with alter on all nodal issues attending the construction and maintenance of the social bond. Therein the agent's responsibility is upheld without falling into the trap of oversubjectifying its volition by insulating reflexivity from its practical effects. Probably weaker in purely theoretical and theological terms if compared to the masterful architecture of its Thomist counterpart, al-Shatibi's approach holds a stronger potential for a socio-anthropological reconstruction of the social agent under modern constraints.

References

Arnason, Johan P. (2005) "The Axial Age and its Interpreters: Reopening a Debate." In: Johann P. Arnason/Shmuel N. Eisenstadt/Björn Wittrock (eds.) *Axial Civilizations and World History*, Leiden: Brill, pp. 19-49.
Arnason, Johan P., Shmuel N. Eisenstadt, and Björn Wittrock (2005) "General Introduction." In: Johann P. Arnason/Shmuel N. Eisenstadt/Björn Wittrock (eds.) *Axial Civilizations and World History*, Leiden: Brill, pp. 3-18.
Asad, Talal (1986) *The Idea of an Anthropology of Islam*, Washington, DC: Georgetown University (Center for Contemporary Arab Studies).
Asad, Talal (1993) *Genealogies of Religion: Discipline and Reasons of Power in Christianity and Islam*. Baltimore and London: Johns Hopkins University Press.
Assmann, Jan (2005) "Axial 'Breakthroughs' and Semantic 'Relocations' in Ancient Egypt and Israel." In: Johann P. Arnason/Shmuel N. Eisenstadt/Björn Wittrock (eds.) *Axial Civilizations and World History*, Leiden: Brill, pp. 133-156.
Chittick, William C. (1992) *Faith and Practice of Islam. Three 13th Century Sufi Texts*, Albany, NY: SUNY Press.
Crone, Patricia (1987) *Roman, Provincial and Islamic Law. The Origins of the Islamic Patronate*, Cambridge: Cambridge University Press.
Eisenstadt, Shmuel N. (1985) "Comparative Liminality: Liminality and Dynamics of Civilization." *Religion* 15, pp. 315-338.
Eisenstadt, Shmuel N. (1986) "Introduction: The Axial Age Breakthroughs: Their Characteristics and Origins," In: Idem (ed.), *The Origins and the Diversity of Axial Age Civilizations*, New York: SUNY Press, pp. 1-25.
Eisenstadt, Shmuel N. (2002) "Concluding Remarks: Public Sphere, Civil Society, and Political Dynamics in Islamic Societies." In: Miriam Hoexter/Shmuel N. Eisenstadt/Nehemia Levtzion (eds.) *The Public Sphere in Muslim Societies*, Albany, NY: SUNY Press, pp. 139-161.
Elmore, Gerald (1999) "Ibn al-'Arabi's Testament on the Mantel of Initiation (al-khirqa)," *Journal of the Muhyiddin Ibn 'Arabi Society* 26, pp. 1-33.

Hoexter, Miriam and Nehemia Levtzion (2002) "Introduction." In: Miriam Hoexter/Shmuel N. Eisenstadt/Nehemia Levtzion (eds.) *The Public Sphere in Muslim Societies*, Albany, NY: SUNY Press, pp. 9-16.

Jaspers, Karl (1953 [1949]) *The Origin and Goal of History*, New Haven, NJ and London: Yale University Press.

Levtzion, Nehemia, 2002, "The Dynamics of Sufi Brotherhoods." In: Miriam Hoexter/Shmuel N. Eisenstadt/Nehemia Levtzion (eds.) *The Public Sphere in Muslim Societies*, Albany, NY: SUNY Press, pp. 109-118.

Mardin, Sherif (1995) "Civil Society and Islam." In: John Hall (ed.) *Civil Society: Theory, History, Comparison*, Boston: Polity Press, pp. 278-300.

Masud, M. Khalid (1995 [1977]) *Shatibi's Philosophy of Islamic Law*, Kuala Lumpur: Islamic Book Trust.

Rahman, Fazlur (1958) *Prophecy in Islam. Philosophy and Orthodoxy*, London: George Allen & Unwin.

Rahman, Fazlur (1979 [1966]) *Islam*, Chicago and London: University of Chicago Press.

Salvatore, Armando (2006) *The Public Sphere: Genealogies and Traditions*, New York: Palgrave Macmillan.

Santoro, Emilio (2003 [1999]) *Autonomy, Freedom and Rights. A Critique of Liberal Subjectivity*, Dordrecht: Kluwer.

Stauth, Georg (1998) "Nachwort: Geschichte, Modernität, Fundamentalismus Eisenstadts zivilisationstheoretischer Ansatz zum vergleichenden Studium moderner fundamentalisticher Bewegungen." In: Shmuel N. Eisenstadt *Die Antinomien der Moderne. Die jakobinischen Grundzüge der Moderne und des Fundamentalismus. Heterodoxien, Utopismus und Jakobinismus in der Konstitution fundamentalistischer Bewegungen*, Frankfurt: Suhrkamp.

Szakolczai, Arpad (2001) "Eric Voegelin's History of Political Ideas." *European Journal of Social Theory* 4/3: pp. 351-368.

Szakolczai, Arpad (2003) *The Genesis of Modernity*, London and New York: Routledge.

Voegelin, Eric (1956) *Order and History, Vol. I: Israel and Revelation*, Baton Rouge: Louisiana State University Press.

Voegelin, Eric (1993 [1938]) *Die politischen Religionen*, München: Wilhelm Fink.

Voegelin Eric (1994) *Das Volk Gottes*, München: Wilhelm Fink.

Voegelin, Eric (1997) *The History of Political Ideas, Vol. 1: Hellenism, Rome, and Early Christianity*, Columbia, MO: University of Missouri Press.

Wittrock, Björn (2005) "The Meaning of the Axial Age." In Johann P. Arnason/Shmuel N. Eisenstadt/Björn Wittrock (eds.) *Axial Civilizations and World History*, Leiden: Brill, pp. 53-85.

Chapter 12

Public Spheres and Political Dynamics in Historical and Modern Muslim Societies

SHMUEL N. EISENSTADT

Introduction

In this paper I would like to analyze briefly from a comparative civilizational point of view some of the characteristics of public sphere in Muslim societies as they developed in 'traditional' Muslim societies and to point out to some important tendencies of their transformation in modern ones.

For a very long time there has been prevalent in scholarly literature as well as in – especially Western – public discourse the view that in Muslim societies, in contrast especially to the Western societies, there did not develop a strong, autonomous public sphere or civil society. This view was closely related to the – Orientalist – conception of the political regimes that developed within them as epitomes of Oriental despotism – of Muslim (as well as Chinese and even Indian kingdoms) societies ruled by Oriental despots, in which all the power was seen as concentrated in the hands of the rulers and the various sectors of society were not granted any autonomy beyond purely local affairs, with even these affairs being often tightly regulated by the Great Despots. One of the best-known illustrations of this conception was Karl Wittfogel's book Oriental Despotism, in which he applied this term to the Chinese imperial system (Wittfogel 1957).

This line of argument was continued in the more recent discussion in which the absence or weakness of the public sphere and civil society in various Asian, including Muslim societies served often as an "explanation" for the difficulties of establishing democratic regimes within them. In this discourse two very strong assumptions emerged: first, that the development of a public sphere and civil society constitutes a critical condition for the formation and development of constitutional and democratic regimes; second that the concepts of public sphere and civil society are often coupled, overlapped, almost conflated, without clear distinction between them (Cohen 1999; Galston 1999; Mardsen 1999; Barber 1999). However a look at the available historical and contemporary evidence shows these assumptions to be very problematic. First, the relations between civil society, public sphere and the political arena are much more variable than is implied in these assumptions. Second, and closely related, the public sphere and civil society should not be conflated. The public sphere must be regarded as a sphere situated between the official and the private, which expands and shrinks according to the constitution and strength of those sectors of society that do not share in the rulership. Civil society entails a public sphere, but not every public sphere entails a civil society – whether of the economic or political variety – as defined in the contemporary discourse or as it developed in early modern Europe through direct participation of corporate bodies or a more or less restricted body of citizens in the political process in which private interests played a very important role (Eisenstadt, Schluchter and Wittrock 2001). Whatever the differences with respect to the relations between the public sphere, civil society, and the political arena, in all societies these relations have entailed continual contestation about power and authority, as well as about their legitimation and accountability. The concrete ways in which such negotiations or contestations develop differ greatly among diverse civilizations – attesting to the different ways in which power and culture are interwoven – and shape their distinct dynamics.

The public sphere in Muslim societies: the role of the *ulama*

A closer critical look at Muslim societies does indeed indicate that there developed within them a very vibrant and autonomous public sphere that was of crucial importance in shaping the dynamics of these societies (Hoexter, Levtzion and Eisenstadt 2001). As stated by Hoexter and Levtzion:

The picture is that of a vibrant public sphere, accommodating a large variety of autonomous groups and characterized by its relatively stable but very dynamic nature. The community of believers was the center of gravity around which activity in the public sphere revolved. Its participation in the formation of the public sphere was a matter of course; its well-being, its customs and consensus were both the motives and the main justifications for the introduction of changes in social and religious practices, in the law and policies governing the public sphere. The independence of the *shari'a a*nd the distribution of duties towards the community between the ruler and the *'ulama,'* established very clearly in Islamic history, were crucial factors in securing the autonomy of the public sphere and in putting limits on the absolute power of the ruler (Hoexter and Levtzion 2002).

These public spheres were arenas in which different sectors of the society could voice their demands in the name of the basic premises of Islamic vision. Indeed the dynamics of these public spheres cannot be understood without taking into account the crucial importance in them of the place of the community, rooted also in the basic premise of Islam – the equality of all believers and their access to the sacred. These conceptions have necessarily given members of the community a right to participate, if not directly in the central political arena, certainly in the communal and religious ones, in the promulgation and voicing of norms of public order. It was indeed the *ulama*, however weak their organization, who were the guardians of the pristine Islamic vision, upholders of the normative dimensions of the umma, and keepers and interpreters of the *shari'a*. They were the religious leaders, the custodians of the divine law, and through it of the boundaries of the Islamic community. They performed important juridical functions but mostly acted in concert with other social actors, with the representatives of families and members of community or communities as well as, of course, with the rulers. As Hodgson has indicated, it was the *ulama* who, through their activities in schools of law, the *waqf* (charitable endowment), and the Sufi orders, constituted the public spheres in Islamic societies and provided arenas of life not entirely controlled by the rulers (Hodgson 1974).

From among the many organizations that developed in Muslim societies, it was mainly the schools of law, the *waqf*, and the different Sufi orders that constituted the most important components of the public sphere. While the relative importance and scope of these institutions did change in different historical settings and periods, some combination of them seems to have existed in all cases. Many aspects of the institutional arenas constituting the public sphere varied in different societies and periods; though regulated by the ruler, they were yet autonomous and could exert far-reaching influence on the ruler: an influence that went far beyond simple subservience to official rule or attempts to evade it.

It was indeed the central place of the *ulama* – its relatively high symbolic standing despite minimal organizational autonomy – that distinguished Muslim regimes from other traditional patrimonial regimes in South or Southeast Asia or in the early Near East. Truly enough, this highly autonomous religious elite did not develop into a broad, independent, and cohesive ecclesiastic organization. The religious groups and functionaries were not organized as a distinct, separate entity; nor did they constitute a tightly organized body – except, and even then only partially, in the Ottoman Empire (Gibb 1968; Inalcik 1973; Gerber 2002), where large sectors of the *ulama* were organized by the state, or in different modes in *Shi'a* Islam (Arjomand 1988). Yet even in the Ottoman Empire the *ulama* were largely autonomous, in that they were constituted according to distinctive – even if highly informal – criteria of recruitment and were, at least in principle, independent of the rulers. It was these religious leaders who created major networks that brought together, under one religious – and often also social-civilizational – umbrella, varied ethnic and geopolitical groups, tribes, settled peasants, and urban groups, creating mutual impingement and interaction among them that otherwise would probably not have developed. And it was the *ulama*, acting through different, often trans-state networks, who were the crucial element forming the distinctive characteristics of public spheres in Islamic societies.

The *umma* and the political community

Most important among the factors bearing on the constitution of public spheres in Islam were the ideal of the *umma* – the community of all believers – as the major arena for the implementation of the moral and transcendental vision of Islam, the strong universalistic component in the definition of this Islamic community, the closely connected emphasis on the principled political equality of all believers, and the continual confrontation of this ideal with the political realities of the expansion of Islam.

This pristine vision of the *umma*, probably implicit only in the very formative period of Islam, entailed a complete fusion of political and religious collectivities, the complete convergence or conflation of the sociopolitical and religious communities (Cook 1983; Hodgson 1974; Lapidus 1997; Schluchter 1987: 11-124; Gibb 1968). Indeed, the very conceptual distinction between these two dimensions, rooted as it is in the Western historical experience, is probably not entirely applicable to the concept of the *umma*.

In this vision strong tensions developed from the very beginning of Islam's history between the particularistic primordial Arab components, seemingly embodied in the initial carriers of the Islamic vision, and the universalistic orientation. Such tensions became more important with the continual expansion of Islamic conquest and incorporation into its frameworks of new territorial entities and ethnic groups (Lapidus 1997).

The final crystallization of this universalistic ideology took place with the so-called Abbasid revolution of the 8th century AD. Paradoxically, also in this period – indeed, in close relation to the institutionalization of this universalistic vision – there developed, especially within Sunni Islam, a de facto separation between the religious community and the rulers. This separation, partially legitimized by the religious leadership, was continually reinforced, above all by the ongoing military and missionary expansion of Islam: expansion far beyond the ability of any single regime to sustain it (Shaban 1970; Sharon 1983; Lapidus 1975; Lapidus 1996).

In the various Muslim regimes that developed under the impact of the continual expansion of Islam, a separation took place between the *khalifa* and the actual ruler, the sultan, heralding de facto separation between the rulers and the religious establishment mainly represented by the *ulama*. This process culminated in the 11th century and became further reinforced under the impact of the Mongol invasions. The *khalifa* often became de facto powerless yet continued to serve as an ideal figure – the presumed embodiment of the pristine Islamic vision of the *umma* and the major source of legitimation of the sultan – even if de facto he and the *ulama* legitimized any person or group that was able to seize power. Such separation between the *khalifa* and the sultan was reinforced by the crystallization (in close relation to the mode of expansion of Islam, especially Sunni Islam) of a unique type of ruling group – namely, the military-religious rulers, who emerged from tribal and sectarian elements. It also generated the system of military slavery, which created special channels of mobility – such as the ghulam system in general and the Mamluk systems and Ottoman devshisme in particular, through which the ruling groups could be recruited from alien elements (Ayalon 1951; Ayalon 1996; Pipes 1981; Crone 1980). Even when some imperial components developed – as was the case in Iran, which became a stronghold of *Shi'a* Islam in which relatively continuous, strong patrimonial regimes developed – a complete fusion between the political ruler and the religious elites and establishment did not ensue (Rosenthal 1958; Arjomand 1999).

The decoupling of the public sphere from the political arena

It was in this framework of continual tension between the ideal of the *umma* and the sociopolitical realities that there developed a continuous yet variable vitality of the public spheres in Muslim – especially but not only *Shi'a* – societies characterized by the autonomy of the *ulama* and the hegemony of the *shari'a*. But the vibrancy of these spheres did not however imply a direct autonomous access to the political arena, i.e. to the domain of rulership, as they did in European parliaments and corporate urban institutions. Needless to say some – often very strong – attempts to exert such influence did develop in many Muslim societies. But in concrete matters, especially foreign or military policy, as well as in such internal affairs as taxation and the keeping of public order and supervision of their own officials, the rulers were quite independent from the various actors in the public sphere.

Indeed the separation between *khalifa* and sultan was in a way taken as given in the mainstream of Islamic (Sunni) religious thought which tended accordingly to legitimize any ruler who ensured the existence of the Muslim community and the upholding of the *shari'a*. At the same time this mode legitimated – indeed assumed – the possible coercive nature of such rulers and their distance from the pristine Muslim ideal regarding the moral order of the community. But while rulers, even oppressive ones, were legitimized in the seemingly minimalistic tone necessary for the maintenance of public order and of the community, they were not seen as the promulgators, guardians, or regulators of the basic norms of the Islamic community. Whatever the extent of the acceptance of their legitimation, it usually entailed the rulers' duty to uphold the social order and to implement *shari'a* justice – and hence also the possibility of close scrutiny of their behavior by the *ulama* – even if such scrutiny did not usually have clear institutional effects. Paradoxically enough, the fact that political problems constituted a central focus of Muslim theology was to no small extent rooted in this disjunction between the ideal of the Islamic ruler as the upholder of the pristine transcendental vision of Islam and the reality of his rulership (Rosenthal 1958).

Thus in Muslim, especially Sunni, societies there developed a very interesting decoupling between the make-up of the public sphere and access to the political arena proper and the decision making of the rulers. This decoupling was manifested in the combination, on the one hand, of large sectors of the society, the major actors in the public sphere having rather limited autonomous access to concrete policymaking, and on the other hand, the fact that the upholding of the moral order of the community was vested in the *ulama* and in the members of the community, with the rulers playing a secondary role.

It was this decoupling between the make-up of the public sphere and access to the decision making of the rulers that gave rise to the wrong perception of the rulers of Muslim societies as Oriental despots. This image is wrong because in fact the scope of the decision making of these rulers was relatively limited. Even if the rulers could behave in despotic ways in their relations with the officials most close to them, or even towards any single subject, in internal affairs beyond taxation and the keeping of public order their process was limited, and not only because of the limits of technology. Their power was limited also because, unlike the European experience, rulership ("politics") especially in Sunni dominated societies did not constitute – contrary to the pristine image of the Muslim ruler as the embodiment of transcendental vision of Islam – a central ideological component in the upholding of the moral order. Moreover the "political" weakness of many of the major organizations in the public sphere, as Arjomand has shown, is to be attributed not to the despotic tendencies of the ruler but to the absence of legal concepts and of corporations (Arjomand 1999).

This decoupling of an autonomous and vibrant public sphere from the political arena – or to be more precise from the realm of rulership – which differed greatly from its counterparts in Europe, especially Western and Central Europe, constituted one of the distinctive characteristics of Muslim civilization. It was distinct, too, from the relations between the public sphere and the arena of political rulership that developed in other, non-Muslim Asian civilizations. It differed from India, where the political order did not constitute a major arena for the implementation of the predominant transcendental and moral vision, sovereignty was highly fragmented, and rulership was to a large extent embedded in the very flexible caste order, giving rise to a public sphere with relatively strong access to the rulers. And it differed from China, where the political order constituted the major arena for the implementation of the transcendental vision but where it was the rulers who, together with the Confucian literati, constituted the sole custodianship of this order, leaving very limited scope for an autonomous public sphere (Eisenstadt 2002).

Characteristics of Islamic public spheres

The constitution of the public spheres in Muslim societies and the mode of interaction between different actors within these spheres were very much influenced both by some of the basic premises of Islam as well as by the relative distance from direct involvement in political decision making. This mode of interaction was characterized by close physical interaction between different actors, by the development of some common modes of dress and food and of many strong informal, labile ties, often cutting across more formal institutions, which even when porous were yet very forceful. These ties were of crucial importance in the continual constitution and activities of public spheres in which many people and social sectors could interact.

Concomitantly, there developed within this public sphere a very strong potential for what may be seen as crowd-like outbursts. It was often the oscillation between the continual informal ties and membership, and outbursts that characterized many of the public spheres in Muslim societies. Such outbursts could also serve as important signals of political discontent – and in more extreme cases they could serve also as components or bases of sectarian activities which presented themselves as the bearers of the pristine Islamic vision and which constituted a very continuous component of the socio-political dynamics Muslim societies.

It is in the framework of these developments that the specific combination of a vibrant public sphere with highly limited autonomous access of the major social actors to the rulers' decision making gave rise in Muslim societies to a quite paradoxical situation with respect to the impact of these actors on changes in the political arena. The most important fact here – one that seemingly strengthens the view of these regimes as despotic – is that despite the potential autonomous standing of members of the *ulama* no fully institutionalized effective checks on the decision making of the rulers ever developed in these societies. Therefore there was no machinery other than rebellion through which to enforce any far-reaching "radical" political demands.

And yet in contrast to other – for instance South-East-Asian or Mesoamerican – patrimonial regimes, the potential not just for rebellion but also for principled revolt and possible regime changes was endemic in Muslim societies. True, as Bernard Lewis has shown (1973: 263-93), a concept of revolution never developed within Islam. Yet at the same time, as Ernest Gellner indicated in his interpretation of Ibn Khaldun's work (Gellner 1981), a less direct yet very forceful pattern of indirect ruler accountability and the possibility of regime changes did arise. This pattern was closely connected with a second type of ruler legitimation and accountability in Muslim societies that was embodied in the ruler's perception as the upholder of the pristine, transcendental Islamist vision. This conception was promulgated above all by the different sectarian activities that constituted a continual component of the Islamic scene. These sectarian activities were connected with the enduring utopian vision of the original Islamic era, and with the fact that this vision was neither fully implemented nor ever fully given up. Such sectarian-like tendencies have indeed existed in the recurring social movements in Muslim societies; and one of their distinctive characteristics has been the importance within them of the political dimensions, frequently oriented toward the restoration of that pristine vision of Islam, which has never been given up.

While the possibility of implementing the pristine vision of Islam, of achieving that ideal fusion between the political and the religious community, of constructing the *umma*, was given up relatively early in the formation and expansion of Islam, yet although never fully attained, it was continually promulgated, as Aziz Al Azmeh has shown, with very strong utopian orientations, by various scholars and religious leaders, in the later periods. Given the ongoing perception of the age of the Prophet as an ideal, even utopian model, the idea of restoration constituted a perennial component of Islamic civilization, promoted above all by some of the most radical; reformist movements. Muhammad's community in Medina became, in the apt phrase of Henry Munson Jr., the Islamic "primordial utopia" (Munson Jr. 1998). Many of the later rulers (the Abbasids, the Fatimids, and others) came to power on the crest of religious movements that upheld this ideal and legitimized themselves in such religious-political terms.

By virtue of the combination of this mode of Islamic expansion with such sectarian, reformist orientations, Islam was probably the only Axial civilization in which sectarian-like movements – together with tribal leadership and groups – often led not only to the overthrow or downfall of existing regimes but also to the establishment of new political regimes oriented, at least initially, to the implementation of the original pristine, primordial Islamic utopia. But significantly enough once these regimes became institutionalized they gave rise to patrimonial or imperial systems within which the "old" Ibn Khaldun cycle tended to develop anew.

Such orientations were embodied in the different versions of the tradition of reform, the mujaddid tradition (Lamdau Tasseron 1989), focused on the person of a *mahdi* and/or promulgated by a Sufi order in a tribal group such as the Wahhabites, or developed within a school of law. Such political, often reformist orientations could be directed toward active participation in the political center, its destruction or transformation, or toward a conscious withdrawal from it. But even such withdrawal, which developed both within the *Shi'a* and in Sufism, often harbored tendencies to pristine renovation, leading potentially to political action.

The fullest development of the political potential of such tendencies took place when they became connected with a tribal reassertion against "corrupt" or weak regimes, rooted in the mode of Islamic expansion. This tendency became closely related to the famous cycle depicted by Ibn Khaldun – namely, the cycle of tribal conquest, based on tribal solidarity and religious devotion, giving rise to the conquest of cities and settlement in them, followed by the degeneration of the ruling (often the former tribal) elite and then by its subsequent regeneration out of new tribal elements from the vast – old or new – tribal reservoirs. Such new "converts"– along with the seeemingly dormant tribes of the Arabian peninsula, of which the Wahhabites constituted probably the latest and most forceful illustration – became a central dynamic political force in Islamic civilization. Naturally the concrete thought of these reform tendencies varied greatly in different

Muslim societies and in different periods of their history, but they constituted a continual component in the constitution of public spheres in Muslim societies (Voll 1991).

In so far as such movements did not create, in the Ibn-Khaldunian mode, new regimes, their impact on Muslim societies, as that of many other groups, was through the continual reconstruction of autonomous and vibrant public spheres, especially of the schools of law, the *waqf* and Sufi orders. As we have seen, these public spheres were largely autonomous in the sense that they were constructed according to autonomous criteria of recruitment and action. They constituted also arenas in which different sectors of the society could voice their demands in the name of the basic premises of Islamic vision. Although these public spheres were, of course, de facto often highly dependent on the rulers, yet their development was to a very large extent autonomous, creating also wide, trans-state networks, and there could develop confrontational stances between them and the rulers.

It was indeed in these contexts that the construction of such autonomous public spheres gave rise in the historical experience of Muslim societies to specific patterns of pluralism that are characteristic of these societies. Such pluralism was characterized, even in imperial Islamic societies, by very strongly patrimonial features such as the existence of segregated – regional, ethnic and religious – sectors; and by a relatively weak permeation of the center into the periphery and impingement of the periphery on the center; as well as the prevalence of multiple patterns or bases of legitimation. But in contrast with those patrimonial regimes which developed in such non-Axial civilizations as Mesoamerica, the ancient Near East, or (Hinduized) South Asia, the Muslim patrimonial regimes were in constant tension with the more sectarian tendencies and they could be undermined by the more extreme proto-fundamentalists, who could attempt like, for instance, the Wahhabis to establish new "pristine" regimes.

The impact of modernity on Muslim public spheres

Not surprisingly, the constitution of public spheres, above all in relation to the political arena, has greatly changed with the onset of modernity and with the constitution of modern states (Eisenstadt, Schluchter and Wittrock 2001). Many of the characteristics of the "traditional" Muslim public sphere – its very vitality, the multiplicity of informal ties, of direct physical encounters and interaction, is the strong emphasis on patterns of dress and on public appearance and interaction, and the possibilities of eruption of "crowd"-like confrontation– have continued, but given both the basic premises of the modern state as well as of modern means of communication, have became subject to deep changes. There developed multiple new "modern" social actors and associations such as professionals, intellectuals, media experts and the like, quite often in close relation with new modes of political organization – be it social movements, or political parties. Concomitantly there developed many new religious groups or movements – be it the transformation of the older Sufi orders or modern religious movements, including the fundamentalist ones – not embedded in the traditional Islamic institutions. All these groups naturally attempted to carve out distinct new public social and even political spaces for themselves. The extent to which there developed contacts between the more "traditional" types of public action, grounded in the Islamic tradition and institutions and the modern actors varied greatly between different societies yet on the whole for a long time they tended to develop in separate niches; and it is only lately that there developed more intensive cooperative or competitive contacts between them. Yet another most important new development in the public spheres of Muslim societies in the contemporary era, both among more modern but also, significantly enough, also in the new religious groups, was the growing autonomous participation and visibility of women and women's movements.

Yet it was not only that the incorporation of the actors in the public sphere in Muslim societies has greatly changed in modern times – important as these changes have obviously been – but above all the very premises of this sphere, above all in its relation to the state, have been dramatically transformed. The single most important aspect of this change was, of course, that given the basic premises of modern polities the traditional separation, even if partial, between the public sphere and the political arena has seemingly almost disappeared. There developed a very strong tendency to a more direct engagement of the actors both in the public sphere and in the political arena. But while the tendency to the emergence of many new cultural or political actors in the public spheres attests to the potential democratization thereof, it did not necessarily always broaden the scope of autonomous political participation and of pluralism. Instead there increased also possible confrontations of the actors in the public spheres – rooted in the ideological premises of modernity with their strong emphasis on political homogeneity – with the newly constituted modern political regimes; with the state attempting to appropriate, control, and even monopolize it. Accordingly, the autonomy of the public spheres could also be greatly undermined and there developed continual tensions and contestations between the various actors in the public sphere and between them and actors in the political arenas.

Thus these modern developments have exacerbated the tensions and confrontations between pluralistic and totalistic tendencies in Muslim societies, "open" and repressive tendencies within them to a much greater extent than was the case in "traditional" Muslim societies. These problems became even more acute with the rise of contemporary fundamentalist movements that build on the older sectarian tendencies and politicize them into hitherto unknown extent. Many of these movements developed from within the public sphere and often combine the control mechanisms of the modern states with strong Jacobin tendencies, legitimized in terms of an essentialized tradition.

But the developments within the religious arena need not always develop in a totalistic direction. Indeed, some very interesting developments like among Sufi groups in Indonesia and elsewhere have led to greater pluralistic open spaces and directions, and also to the constitution of vibrant public spheres which disengaged to some extent at from the state (Howell 2001). These developments constitute part of attempts of many social sectors to develop new vibrant public spheres which in a "post-modern" way attempt to distance themselves from the state by carving autonomous spheres for themselves without direct political disengagement. Thus contemporary Muslim societies can be seen as moving between two poles: attempts to establish territorial states with some elements of pluralism that build on their earlier historical experience but are reconstituted in novel ways; and strong anti-pluralistic tendencies in the form of either extreme, secular, oppressive – often military – regimes or of Jacobin fundamentalist ones.

References

Arjomand, S.A. (1999) "The Law, Agency and Policy in Medieval Islamic Society: Development of the Institutions of Learning from the Tenth to the Fifteenth Century." *Comparative Studies in Society and History 41/2*, pp. 263-93.

Ayalon, D. (1951) *L'esclavage de Mamelouk*, Jerusalem: Israel Oriental Society.

Ayalon, D. (1996) *Le Phenomene Mamelouk dans l'orient Islamique*, Paris: Presses Universitaires de France.

Barber, B. (1999) "Civil Society: Getting Beyond the Rhetoric: A Framework for Political Understanding." In: J. Janning/C. Kupchan/D. Rumberg (eds.) *Civic Engagement in the Atlantic Community*, Gütersloh: Bertelsmann Foundation Publishers, 115-142.

Cohen, J. (1999) "Trust, Voluntary Association and Workable Democracy: The Contemporary American Discourse of Civil Society." In: M. Warren (ed.) *Democracy and Trust*, Cambridge: Cambridge University Press, 208-48.

Cook, M. (1983) *Mohammad*, Oxford: Oxford University Press.

Crone, P. (1980) *Slaves on Horses*, Cambridge: Cambridge University Press.

Eisenstadt, S.N. (2001) "Concluding Remarks – Public Spheres, Civil Society and Political Dynamics in Islamic Societies." In: M. Hoexter/N. Levtzion/S.N. Eisenstadt (eds.) *Public Sphere in Islam*, Albany, N.Y: SUNY Press, 139-162.

Eisenstadt, S.N./W. Schluchter/B. Wittrock (eds.) (2001) *Public Spheres and Collective Identities*, New Brunswick: Transaction, pp. 105-132.

Galston, W. (1999) "Social Capital in America: Civil Society and Civil Trust." In: J. Janning/C. Kupchan/D. Rumberg (eds.) *Civic Engagement in the Atlantic Community*, Gütersloh: Bertelsmann Foundation Publishers, 67-78.

Gellner, E. (1981) *Muslim Societies*, Cambridge: Cambridge University Press.

Gerber, K (2001) "The Public Sphere and Civil Society in the Ottoman Empire." In: M. Hoexter/N. Levtzion/S.N. Eisenstadt (eds.) *Public Sphere in Islam*, Albany, N.Y: SUNY Press, pp. 65-83.

Gibb, H.A.R. (1968) *Studies on the Civilization of Islam*, Princeton, NJ: Princeton University Press.

Gibb, H.A.R. (1968) *Studies on the Civilization of Islam*, Princeton, NJ: Princeton University Press.

Hefner, R. (2000) *Civil Islam*, Princeton:Princeton University Press.

Hodgson, Marshall G.S. (1974) *The Venture of Islam. Conscience and History in a World Civilization,* Vols. 1-3, Chicago: University of Chicago Press.

Hoexter, M./Levtzion, N/Eisenstadt, S.N. (eds.) (2001) *Public Sphere in Islam*, Albany, N.Y: SUNY Press.

Howell, Julian D. (2001) "Sufism and the Indonesian Islamic Revival." *Journal of Asian Studies 60/3*, pp. 701-729.

Inalcik, H. (1973) *The Ottoman Empire: The Classical Age, 1300-1600*, London: Weidenfeld & Nicholson.

Landau Tasseron, E. (1989) "The 'Cyclical Reform': A Study of the Mujadin Tradition," *Studia Islamica 70*, pp. 79-118.

Lapidus, I.M (1991) *History of Islamic Sicuetues*, Cambridge: Cambridge University Press.

Lapidus, I.M. (1975) "The Separation of State and Religion in the Development of Early Islamic Society." *International Journal of Middle Eastern Studies 6/4*, pp. 363-85.

Lapidus, I.M. (1996) "State and Religion in Islamic Societies." *Past and Present 151*, pp. 3-27.

Lapidus, I.M. (1997) *A History of Islamic Societies*, Cambridge: Cambridge University Press.

LeGoff, J. (ed.) (1968) *Heresies et Societes, Civilizations et Societes*, Paris, Mouton & Co.

Lewis, B. (1973), *Islam in History*, London: Alcove Press, pp. 253-266.

Mardsen, R. (1999) "Community, Civil Society, and Social Ecology." In: J. Janning/C. Kupchan/D. Rumberg (eds.) *Civic Engagement in the Atlantic Community*, Gütersloh: Bertelsmann Foundation Publishers, pp. 97-114.

Munson, H. (1998) *Islam and Revolution in the Middle East*, New Haven: Yale University Press.

Pipes, D. (1981) *Slave Soldiers and Islam*, New Haven: Yale University Press.

Rosenthal, E. (1958) *Political Thought in Medieval Islam*, Cambridge: Cambridge University Press.

Schluchter, W. (1987) "Einleitung. Zwischen Welteroberung und Weltanpassung: Überlegungen zu Max Webers Sicht des Frühen Islams." In: idem (ed.) *Max Webers Sicht des Islams: Interpretation und Kritik*, Frankfurt: Suhrkamp, pp. 11-124.

Shaban, M.A. (1983) *The Abbasid Revolution*, Cambridge: Cambridge University Press.
Sharon, M. (1983) *Balck Banners from the East*, Jerusalem: Magnes Press.
Voll, J.E. (1991) "Fundamentalism in the Sunni Arab World: Egypt and the Sudan" In: M. Marty/R.S. Appleby (eds.) *Fundamentalism Observed*, Chicago: University of Chicago Press, pp. 345-403.
Wittfogel, K. (1957) *Oriental Despotism*, New Haven: Yale University Press.

Abstracts

Marshall Hodgson's Civilizational Analysis of Islam: Theoretical and Comparative Perspectives
Johann P. Arnason

Marshall Hodgson was one of the very few area specialists who not only adopted a civilizational perspective, but also formulated an explicit and distinctive theoretical approach to civilizational studies. The paper reconstructs his basic assumptions and main lines of argument, and links them to current debates in the field of civilizational analysis. Hodgson's conceptual framework developed in relative isolation from sociological inquiry, but his ideas are in some ways comparable or complementary to those of the sociologists who have ventured into the field of large-scale comparative studies. That applies, in particular, to his understanding of cultural traditions and their transformations during the Axial Age. In the broader context of comparative history, these themes can also be linked to his trans-cultural concept of absolutism, which appears as an alternative to the Weberian model of patrimonialism. When it comes to the analysis of early and classical Islam, the theoretical orientations and their implications must be discussed in connection with more recent historical scholarship in the field. Hodgson's interpretation would seem to be compatible with a more revisionist historical account than the one it relies on, and it even prefigures some revisionist arguments. But it is not compatible with radical revisionism; in that regard, it anticipates some of the metacritical objections to revisionist criticism. If Hodgson's analysis of the classical phase is reconsidered in light of these questions, a somewhat different perspective emerges: a more differentiated picture of the very early stages, but also a stronger emphasis on divergent trends and problematic legacies of the classical period.

The Middle Period Islamic Axiality in the Age of Afro-Eurasian Transcultural Hybridity
Babak Rahimi

An attempt is made to develop Marshal Hodgson's notion of "interrelations of societies in history" by focusing on the Afro-Eurasian landmass from the $9^{th}/10^{th}$ to the $13^{th}/14^{th}$ centuries. This study identifies this period as the age of transcultural hybridity, defined as the inauguration of a period in the escalation of shifts in civilizational hybridization dynamics towards hemispheric integration, fusion and cross-fertilization that brought about an impressive degree of intense creativity and exceptional broadening of cultural horizons. In the first section, while briefly covering regions like China, Japan, Southeast Asia, north Africa and Europe, it is argued that the age of transcultural hybridity was formed as a result of contact between societies and the formation of new hybrid civilizational complexes with the increase of interaction between cultures that led to the proliferation of myriad forms of public spaces, social organizations, institutions and political orders. Yet the upshot of such transcultural interactive zone in the Afro-Eurasian landmass was determined by conflict, rivalry, exchange, encounter and chronic collision between competing forms of political orders that, in turn, led the way to complex processes of greater intercivilizational hybridization. The second section focuses on the appearance of the Turkish and Persianate cultures, marking an era of unprecedented political fragmentation and cultural creolization in the context of nomadic and sedentary relations. "The Middle Period" of Islamic history, which marked the formation of new Islamic civilizational complexes, was the result of cultural encounter and civilizational cross-fertilization between the Central Asiatic and the Iran-Mesopotamian societies as a result of successive waves of Turkish tribal migration from the steppe grass lands of Central Asia to the settled regions of Anatolia and the Iran-Mesopotamian plateaus. Accordingly, the proposed notion of the "Middle Period Islamic Axiality" denotes the emergence of new modes of reflexivity and communication in Islamic history, in relation with the crystallization of distinct social movements and political orders and in the context of heterdoxical and orthodoxical settings, as a result of such interciviliational encounters.

Identity Formation in World Religions:
A Comparative Analysis of Christianity and Islam
Arpad Szakolczai

The aim of the paper is to compare the manner in which the unique charisma and mission of the founders of the two most influential world religions, Jesus and Mohammed, was recognised in the early part of their mission by their immediate followers and disciples. For this purposes, apart from the Weberian concept of 'charisma,' the paper relies on Alessandro Pizzorno's theoretisation of identity formation through recognition, and also on the work of Victor Turner about liminality and René Girard ideas about the mimetics of desire and rival brothers.

The comparative analysis of the earlier period of Christianity and Islam focuses on four main themes. The first contrast the way the descent of Jesus breaks with traditional genealogical lineage on both ends with the problematic of the descent and the 'true heir' of Mohammed. The second theme moves from issues of personal identity to identity as a religious founder, and focuses on the exact sequence in which charisma was recognised, and the link between this recognition and various experiences. The next section contrasts the different kind of persons who first recognised, or failed to recognise, charisma in the two traditions, including other prophets, women, children, and disciples, focusing especially on the question of the difference between recognising human sincerity and prophetic or in general charismatic gifts; and the extent to which the pronouncements of personal acquaintances on such qualities can be taken as authoritative. Finally, the last section of the paper moves to the image of the enemy, contrasting and comparing the attacks of Jesus on the Pharisees, using Weber's brilliant but little known essay at the end of *Ancient Judaism*, with the attacks of Mohammed on the 'hypocrites' (*munafiqun*).

The Emergence of Islam as a Case of Cultural Crystallization. Historical and Comparative Reflections
Johann P. Arnason

The concept of cultural crystallization has been used to describe world-historical transformations of a particular kind: those that combine major redefinitions of cultural premises with corresponding institutional innovation and the formation of traditions that generate their own internal disputes and conflicts. This model has proved particularly relevant in the context of debates about the Axial Age and its place in world history. The emergence of Islam would seem to be an exemplary case in point, all the more so since the formation of a new monotheistic religion was – within a strikingly short span of time – combined with the construction of a new empire and the cultural unification of a large, central and diverse region. But discussion of the Islamic historical experience has been obstructed by dominant trends in civilizational analysis: both classical and contemporary approaches have tended to neglect the Islamic world and focus on issues more attuned to confrontation of the West with East or South Asia. On the other hand, attempts to redress the balance must come to terms with changing historical perspectives on the sources, beginnings and early developments of Islam as a religion and a civilizational core. Traditionalist view have been found wanting, but radical revisionism has also been criticized on convincing grounds. A tentative account of the Islamic crystallization must distinguish a pre-conquest, intra-Arabian phase from the post-conquest one. Within the latter, further distinctions are best based on the changing relationship between religious and political forms of central authority and social power.

Revolution in Early Islam. The Rise of Islam as a Constitutive Revolution
Said, A. Arjomand

Muhammad's unification of the Arabian tribes on the basis of a new monotheistic religion is analyzed as a revolution and in the light of a typology of revolutions in world history. From the viewpoint of sociology of revolution, it is found to fit closely the ideal-type of 'constitutive revolution.' Contrary to conventional wisdom, Muhammad did not constitute a centralized state or even provide clear guidelines to that end. By contrast, it did create a new supra-tribal political community, and mobilized it for revolutionary struggle in the path of the one God.

The cultural pre-conditions for the unification of Arabia and the Messianic stimulus to it are presented as the background to the constitution of the new community and its revolutionary mobilization. The essay concludes with an analysis of the succession to Muhammad's charismatic authority as the decisive factor in setting the direction of the consequences of the revolution.

'Abdallah b. Salam: Egypt, Late Antiquity and Islamic Sainthood
Georg Stauth

Ancient Egypt, with the exception of Moses and his times, was sidelined in Axial Age theory. Focussing on monotheism and revelation, Egypt was hardly made an issue of axial breakthroughs and of the emerging patterns of cultural reconstruction culminating in Early Christianity and Islam. This paper brings Egypt into the story of the formation of Islam. It attempts to show some of the antagonisms which relate to the synchronic co-existence between 'primary' civilisational heritage of Egypt and the axial impacts on the absolute monotheistic principles followed by Islam. It are these antagonisms which have shaped the vitality of a lived religion, and specifically, as viewed here, in local contexts of the eastern Nile Delta. Taking a view on the role of 'Abdallah b. Salam – the first Jewish witness of Muhammad's monotheistic revelations in the prophetic tradition, and at the same time a local Islamic venerated saint today – it becomes evident that the "negation" of 'Egypt' is as much a source of orthodox monotheist reconstruction in Islam (as it was in Christianity) as much as it bears a great part of the 'primary' symbolic, legendary and mythological civilisational heritage. In this it is important to know that 'axiality' can not merely explain new symbolic and institutional order. It are the negations of Pharaonic civilisation and its miracles and wonders which occupy – and have occupied – a great role in Islam. Paradoxically, it is the negation which also preserves and incorporates the archaism which is so important to understand mass religion and the terms of its modern continued importance.

History, Knowledge and Spirituality:
The Yemen as the Turning Place between the Persian, Arab and Biblical Traditions
Raif G. Khoury

Yemen was an important cultural centre in pre-Islamic times, it also formed a field of intensive cultural exchange which had a great impact on later Islamic traditions. Story telling in the main, wisdom literature and prophetic tales have entered this field and were passed on to the expanding Islamic world. Thus, the Yemeni share in institutional and religious settings of Early Islam was highly significant and can be traced today mainly in fields of Early Islamic narratives. In

Yemen some very well established literary figures like for example Wahb b. Munabbih, who was a wandering figure between Persian, Arabic and Jewish identities, developed and maintained the art of transmitting mythical, prophetical and literary wisdom in a region that seemed marginal to the major civilisational events of the time. However, as it more and more becomes clear to historians and literary specialists today, the Yemeni crossroads of highly intensive cultural exchange shaped much of the religious and literary tastes of later Islamic periods. Public life in Early Islam where story telling and representation of religious and historical wisdom became so important, was shaped drastically by institutional and conceptual imprints which Yemeni figures left behind. A large body of later Islamic historiography and literature can be traced back to the Yemeni meeting ground of Persian, Arabic and Biblical traditions.

Islam and the Axial Age
Joseph van Ess

The article mainly intends to express some doubts about the validity of the Achsenzeit-model. In its first part the author tries to put Jaspers's concept into its historical context, with regard to German and European thought after World War II. The second part raises a few points concerning Islam, the "belatedness" of its civilization and its connection with a Late Antiquity of longue durée. The third part compares Jaspers's Achsenzeit with other and more recent models; it also ponders over the hypothetical question whether there could be a genuine Muslim positioning of Islamic history within world history.

Islam and the Path to Modernity: Institutions of Higher Learning and Secular Political Culture
Said A. Arjomand

This essay is part of a series of studies that examine the thirteenth and fourteenth centuries as a possible turning point in Eurasian social transformation with reference to the Islamicate civilization. Following an earlier study of urban politics in this period, the present paper focuses on the colleges of higher learning (*madrasa*s), and the impact on political culture of their teaching. Comparing the legal foundations of the *madrasa* in Islamic law to that of the newly established European universities of the thirteenth century in Roman law, it finds the latter suffered from two major disadvantages: lack of corporate legal personality as *universitas*, and the consequent lack of autonomy and legal jurisdiction. Turning then to a comparison of the reception of Aristotle in the Western and Islamic institutions of higher learning in the same period, the fact that *Politics* is the one and only major work of Aristotle that was not translated into Arabic is singled out as a serious setback for the development of political modernity in the Islamicate civilization.

Global Ages, Ecumenic Empires and Prophetic Religions
Arpad Szakolczai

The aim of this paper is to revisit, jointly, the 'axial age' thesis and Weber's ideas about the importance of prophetic religions, and to draw some consequences both for social theory and concerning the rise and dynamics of modernity. It starts by arguing that the remarkable spiritual outbursts that constitute the core of the axial age, especially the co-temporaneity of Heraclitus, Confucius and the Buddha, can be explained as the outcome of the temporal and spatial liminal conditions produced by the rise of the first truly global empire, the Persian. The problem with Jaspers' idea of the 'axis time,' however, is that the three emergence of the three great world religions (Judaism, Christianity and Islam) escape this time frame, suggesting a return to Weber's thesis about prophecy, though recognising the links between the emergence of prophetic religions and the rise and fall of major empires.

On this basis, the paper develops three elements of a theoretical framework. It argues that the contrast between charisma and the Trickster present a broad, anthropologically, mythological and theologically based framework for the sociology of shifting normative evaluations; that the metaphor of the spiral can serve as a model to capture the type of changes represented by the emergence of world-conquering empires and in general of global ages; and that the model of gift-giving, developed in the footsteps of Marcel Mauss, can serve as a third model for establishing social order, beyond the duality of violence and the law. On the basis of this theoretical framework, the paper argues that the dynamics of global ages can be explained by the activity of Trickster-like figures who help to escalate the movement, while a genuine solution to such maelstrom-like, all-encompassing social changes can provided by a different type of spiralling movement, connected to the way 'grace,' in its various meanings, equally emphasising the theological and the philosophical, and within it the epistemological, ethical and aesthetic components, can be turned into a lasting guiding force of human conduct.

Reflexivity, Praxis, and "Spirituality":
Western Islam and Beyond
Armando Salvatore

The approach to axial transformations has laid a privileged emphasis on the emergence of specific patterns of reflexivity, considered as the axial contribution to later modern trends in public and political life. This study critically reconsiders the centrality of reflexivity within western axiality and situates it within the problematique of the relation between the prophetic and the philosophical modes of axial transformations. It focuses on the theoretical development of praxic and institutional forms of reflexivity within Islamic traditions.

After a synthetic portrayal of Islam as a plea for taming the sequence of prophetic eruptions and therefore as moderating their long term messianic impetus, the study probes into the specific strength of the Islamic philosophy of law in imposing a common denominator on Islamic traditions (prophetic, philosophical, juridical and "mystical," i.e. Sufi) through the elaboration on the concept of *maslaha*. This is translatable as "common good" or "public interest," and its theorizing culminated in the work of the Andalusi jurist al-Shatibi in the 14th century.

The approach to *maslaha* and the trajectory of its maturation are examined in their capacity to provide a model of praxic reflexivity, which is integral to the history of Europe before the end of the Christian *reconquista* of the Iberian peninsula, and in contrast with the sectarian and often spiritualist movements that have characterized European history since the 13th century and even stronger after the Reformation, finally ushering in what Voegelin has called "political religions."

The patterns of praxic and institutional reflexivity produced by Western Islam lived on in the work of thinkers like Spinoza, whose family was also of Andalusi origin, and provide seeds of a post-axial alternative to both the totalitarian and the liberal trends that have dominated European modernity thus far. It is not surprising that these seeds have been revived first by Muslim reformers under European colonial domination, and now even stronger in the contemporary configurations of Euro-Islam. It is the process through which *maslaha* is folded into *res publica* and revives it, also affecting the latter's conflicted and securitized nature.

Public Spheres and Political Dynamics in Historical and Modern Societies
Shmuel N. Eisenstadt

For a very long time there has been prevalent in scholarly literature as well as in – especially Western – public discourse the "orientalist" view that in Muslim societies, in contrast especially to the Western societies, there did not develop a strong, autonomous public sphere or civil society. In this paper will show in contrary that a very vibrant and autonomous public sphere was of crucial importance in shaping the dynamics of Muslim societies. Of crucial importance to understand these vibrant dynamics, in them is the place of the community, rooted also in the basic premise of Islam – the equality of all believers and their access to the sacred. These conceptions have necessarily given members of the community a right to participate, if not directly in the central political arena, certainly in the communal and religious ones. This is where a decoupling between the make-up of the public sphere and access to the political arena proper and the decision making of the rulers is to be observed. This decoupling was manifested in the combination, on the one hand, of large sectors of the society, the major actors in the public sphere having rather limited autonomous access to concrete policy-making, and on the other hand, the fact that the upholding of the moral order of the community was vested in the ulama and in the members of the community, with the rulers playing a secondary role. The constitution of public spheres, above all in relation to the political arena, has greatly changed with the onset of modernity and with the constitution of modern states. The single most important aspect of this change was, of course, that given the basic premises of modern polities the traditional separation, even if partial, between the public sphere and the political arena has seemingly almost disappeared. There developed a very strong tendency to a more direct engagement of the actors both in the public sphere and in the political arena – with the newly constituted modern political regimes, with the state attempting to appropriate, control, and even monopolize it. Accordingly, the autonomy of the public spheres could also be greatly undermined and there developed continual tensions and contestations between the various actors in the public sphere and between them and actors in the political arenas. These modern developments have exacerbated the tensions and confrontations between pluralistic and totalistic tendencies in Muslim societies. These problems became even more acute with the rise of contemporary fundamentalist movements that build on the older sectarian tendencies and politicize them into hitherto unknown extent. Many of these movements developed from within the public sphere and often combine the control mechanisms of the modern states with strong Jacobin tendencies, legitimized in terms of an essentialized tradition.

Contributors

Saïd Amir Arjomand (Ph.D, University of Chicago, 1980) is Distinguished Service Professor of Sociology at the State University of New York at Stony Brook. He was the inaugural Crane Fellow and Visiting Professor of Public Affairs at the Woodrow Wilson School of Princeton University (2004-5), and is Visiting Fellow at its Department of Near Eastern Studies (2006-8). He was Editor of *International Sociology*, from 1998 to 2003, and is the founder and President (1996-2002, 2006-10) of the Association for the Study of Persianate Societies. His books include *The Turban for the Crown. The Islamic Revolution in Iran*, Oxford University Press, 1988, and *Rethinking Civilizational Analysis*, London: Sage Publications, 2004 (edited with Edward A. Tiryakian). He is currently working on a constitutional history of the Islamic Middle East as a Carnegie Scholar (2006-8).

Johann P. Arnason is Emeritus Professor of Sociology at La trobe University, Melbourne, and was until recently editor of the journal Thesis Eleven. His research interests are in comparative historical sociology and civilizational analysis. Recent publications include *Civilizations in Dispute: Historical Questions and Theoretical Traditions* (Leiden, Brill, 2003); *Eurasian Transformations, Tenth to Thirteenth Centuries* (edited, with Bjorn Wittrock; Leiden, Brill, 2004); *Axial Civilizations and World History* (edited, with S.N. Eisenstadt and Bjorn Wittrock; Leiden, Brill, 2005).

Shmuel N. Eisenstadt, PhD. Jerusalem 1947. Professor Emeritus, The Hebrew University of Jerusalem. Senior Research Fellow at the Jerusalem Van Leer Institute. Member of many academies and recipient of honorary doctoral degrees. Areas of major interest: Comparative research of modernities and civilizations; The historical experience of Japan from a comparative perspective; Patterns of civil society and democracy in different societies and cultures; Changing movements and heterodoxy in civilizatory dynamics; Sociological and macro-sociological theory. Publications: Political Systems of Empires; Power, Trust and Meaning; Japanese Civilization – A Comparative View; Paradoxes of Democracy, Fragility, Continuity and Change; Fundamentalism, Sectarianism and Revolutions; Die Vielfalt der Moderne; Comparative Civilizations & Multiple Modernities; Explorations in Jewish Historical Experience.

Josef van Ess, born 1934, PhD Bonn 1959, "Habilitation" Frankfurt 1964, Visiting Professor UCLA 1967 and American University of Beirut 1967-8, Chair of Islamic Studies and Semitic Languages Tübingen University 1968-1999, Emeritus Professor since 1999. Honorary degree Paris (Ecole Pratique des Hautes Etudes, Sorbonne) and Washington (Georgetown University). Member/Fellow of

Heidelberger Akademie der Wissenschaften, Académie des Inscriptions et Belles Lettres (Paris), Real Academia Barcelona, Academia Europaea, Iranian Academy of Philosophy, Iraqi Academy, Tunisian Academy, Medieval Academy of America. Publications in German, French, English, Arabic and Persian. Main work: Theologie und Gesellschaft im 2. und 3. Jahrhundert Hidschra, 1-6 (Berlin 1991-1997).

Raif Georges Khoury, PhD Sorbonne/Paris 1963, Habilitation Heidelberg 1970, Visiting Professor at different universities of Paris, among them Collège de France, Sorbonne, Ecole des Hautes Etude, is Emeritus Professor of Arabistik at Heidelberg University where he managed the cooperations with universities in Europe, in particular France as well as in diverse North African, Near Eastern and Far Eastern countries. Since recent years he is Visiting Professor at the Hochschule der Jesuiten in Munich and at the University of Munich. He is the author of a huge body of books and articles on scriptures of Early Islam, Islamic literature in the Middle Ages and of the Arabic world of the 19. und 20. century and its relation to Europe. He is the editor of the series *Codices Arabici Antiqui* and of the series *Tradition und Modernität in der arabischen Welt gestern und heute.* His most recent work is the editing of *Platonismus im Orient und Okzident. Neue platonische Denkstrukturen im Judentum, Christentum und im Islam* (Heidelberg 2005).

Babak Rahimi receieved his Ph.D from the European University Institute in 2004 and is now an Assistant Professor, Department of Literature, Program for the Study of Religion, at the University of California, San Diego. His research interests include public sphere and state formation in Islamic societies. He has published articles in the Journal of Iranian Studies and Thesis Eleven. He is currently working on a book project entitled, "The Isfahani Public: the Emergence of the Early Modern Iranian Public Sphere in the Safavid Period, 1590-1666."

Armando Salvatore obtained his Ph.D. in Political and Social Sciences from the European University Institute, Florence (1994) and his German *Habilitation* in Sociology from Humboldt University, Berlin (2005). He is Senior Research Fellow at the Institute for Advanced Studies in the Humanities, Essen (KWI) and at the Institute of Social Science, Humboldt University, Berlin. His research focuses on the significance of modern concepts of religion for Social and Political Theory, with particular regard to the Euro-Mediterranean civilizational area. Among his most recent publications, *Public Islam and the Common Good*, Leiden/Boston: Brill, 2004 (ed., with Dale F. Eickelman), *Religion, Social Practice, and Contested Hegemonies*, New York: Palgrave Macmillan, 2005 (ed., with Mark LeVine), and, *The Public Sphere between Tradition and Modernity*, New York: Palgrave Macmillan, forthcoming in 2007. He is the editor of the *Yearbook of Sociology of Islam* (with Georg Stauth).

Georg Stauth teaches Sociology at the University of Bielefeld, Germany. In the period 2003-2005 he has directed an international study group on Islam and Modernity at the Institute of Advanced Studies in the Humanities (KWI-NRW), Essen, At the University of Mainz he is co-directing research on saintly places in Egypt and Ethiopia. He has widely published on Islam and theory of modernity. His most recent book is *Ägyptische heilige Orte I. Konstruktionen, Inszenierungen und Landschaften der Heiligen im Nildelta: 'Abdallah b. Salam*, Bielefeld: transcript, 2005. He is the editor of the *Yearbook of Sociology of Islam* (with Armando Salvatore).

Arpad Szakolczai studied at the University of Budapest and has a PhD from the University of Texas at Austin. His recent and major publications include *The Dissolution of Communist Power* (Routledge, 1992; with Agnes Horvath), *Max Weber and Michel Foucault: Parallel Life-Works* (Routledge, 1998), *Reflexive Historical Sociology* (Routledge, 2000), *La scoperta della società* (Rome, Carocci, 2003; with Giovanna Procacci), and *The Genesis of Modernity* (Routledge, 2003), as well as articles and essays among others in *Social Research*, the *American Journal of Sociology*, *Theory, Culture and Society*, *Theoria*, *The European Journal of Social Theory* and *The European Sociological Review*. He is Professor of Sociology at University College, Cork, Ireland. He is currently finishing a manuscript on the sociology of the Renaissance that focuses on various aspects of 'grace,' to be published by Routledge in 2006, and is working on two further book projects: one provisionally entitled 'Overcoming Nihilism,' in which he aims to contrast Nietzsche's illuminating but often erratic insights with anthropological findings; and on another, together with Agnes Horvath, about the figure of the Trickster.

List of previous volumes

Volume 1, Islam – Motor or Challenge of Modernity. Edited by Georg Stauth. Hamburg: LIT, 1998. New Brunswick (USA), London (UK): Transaction Publishers. Contributors among others: M. Arkoun (Paris), F. Colonna (Paris), Sh. N. Eisenstadt (Jerusalem), R. Schulze (Bern), S. Zubaida (London).

Volume 2,The South-South Dimension of Islam and Modernity.Edited by Helmut Buchholt and Georg Stauth. Hamburg: LIT, 2000. New Brunswick (USA), London (UK): Transaction Publishers. Contributors among others: M. Abaza (Cairo), S. F. Alatas (Singapore), H. Khondker (Singapore), R. Loimeier (Bayreuth), C. Nelson (Cairo), Lani Probojo (Bielefeld/Frankfurt a.M.).

Volume 3, Muslim Traditions and Modern Technics of Power. Edited by Armando Salvatore. Hamburg: LIT, 2001. New Brunswick (USA), London (UK): Transaction Publishers. Contributors among others: Iman Farag (Cairo), B. Dupret (Paris), A. Salvatore (Florence), P. Werbner (Manchester/Keele).

Volume 4, Islam in Africa. Edited by Thomas Bierschenk and Georg Stauth. Hamburg: LIT, 2002. New Brunswick (USA), London (UK): Transaction Publishers. Contributors among others: G. Abdoulaye (Cotonou, Benin), Q. Gausset (Kopenhagen), S. Nageeb (Bielefeld/Khartum), A. Piga (Rome), M. Singleton (Louvain), T. Tamari (Paris).

Volume 5, On Archeaeology of Sainthood and Local Spirituality in Islam. Edited by Georg Stauth. Bielefeld: transcript, 2004. New Brunswick (USA), London (UK): Transaction Publishers. Contributors among others: Ch. Ahmed (Berlin), S. Andezian (Marseille), El.-S El-Aswad (Tanta, Egypt; Bahrein), C. Mayeur-Jaouen (Paris), S. Schielke (Leiden/Amsterdam), E. Spadola (New York).

Volume 6, Islam and the New Europe. Continuities, Changes, Confrontations. Edited by Sigrid Nökel and Levent Tezcan. Bielefeld: transcript, 2005. New Brunswick (USA), London (UK): Transaction Publishers. Contributors among others: St. Allievi (Padua), G. Klinkhammer (Bremen), M. LeVine (Irvin), Sch. Amir-Moazami (Constance/Florence), S. Zubaida (London).

English Volumes
Global | Local Islam

Gerdien Jonker,
Valérie Amiraux (eds.)
Politics of Visibility
Young Muslims in European Public Spaces

Juni 2006, 226 Seiten,
kart., 27,80 €,
ISBN: 3-89942-506-5

Sigrid Nökel,
Levent Tezcan (eds.)
Islam and the New Europe
Continuities, Changes, Confrontations
(Yearbook of the Sociology of Islam 6)

Januar 2006, 326 Seiten,
kart., 29,80 €,
ISBN: 3-89942-302-X

Georg Stauth
Politics and Cultures of Islamization in Southeast Asia
Indonesia and Malaysia in the Nineteen-nineties

2002, 302 Seiten,
kart., 30,80 €,
ISBN: 3-933127-81-5

Georg Stauth (ed.)
On Archaeology of Sainthood and Local Spirituality in Islam
Past and Present Crossroads of Events and Ideas
(Yearbook of the Sociology of Islam 5)

2004, 228 Seiten,
kart., 26,80 €,
ISBN: 3-89942-141-8

**Leseproben und weitere Informationen finden Sie unter:
www.transcript-verlag.de**